THE EARLY WORKS
OF ORESTES A. BROWNSON

VOLUME I:
THE UNIVERSALIST YEARS, 1826-29

Edited by Patrick W. Carey

MARQUETTE
UNIVERSITY

PRESS
2000

MARQUETTE STUDIES IN THEOLOGY NO. 23
Andrew Tallon, Series Editor

Library of Congress Cataloguing in Publication Data

Brownson, Orestes Augustus, 1803-1876.
  [Selections. 2000]
  The early works of Orestes A. Brownson / edited by Patrick W. Carey.
    p. cm. — (Marquette studies in theology ; no. 23)
  Includes indexes.
  ISBN 0-87462-647-1 (v. 1 : pbk. : alk. paper)
  1. Philosophy. 2. Theology. I. Carey, Patrick W., 1940- II. Title.
  III. Marquette studies in theology ; #23.
B908 .B612 2000
191—dc21

                                99-050779

Member, THE ASSOCIATION OF AMERICAN UNIVERSITY PRESSES

MARQUETTE UNIVERSITY PRESS
MILWAUKEE

The Association of Jesuit University Presses

MARQUETTE UNIVERSITY PRESS
MILWAUKEE WISCONSIN USA
2000

THE EARLY WORKS OF ORESTES A. BROWNSON
VOLUME I: THE UNIVERSALIST YEARS, 1826-29

TABLE OF CONTENTS

ACKNOWLEDGMENTS

I owe a debt of gratitude to a number of persons and institutions who have contributed to the first volume of Orestes A. Brownson's early works. Off and on since the late 1970s I have been collecting and examining Brownson's early works, intending from the beginning to publish a critical edition of those works, most of which were never included in Henry Brownson's twenty-volume collection of his father's writings. During this process I have been assisted by a number of graduate research assistants, but those most helpful in bringing the first volume to completion were Anne Slakey and Jeffrey Barbeau. Anne Slakey not only typed numerous corrections on the texts, but helped me identify sources and proofread the entire text. Her hand is on every page. Jeffrey Barbeau contributed greatly to the final proofreading process. I also thank Aldemar Hagen who, using difficult-to-read originals, typed the texts into the computer.

I am also grateful to the staffs at the Archives of the University of Notre Dame, Harvard University, the American Antiquarian Society (Worcester, MA), and various other libraries in Vermont and upstate New York for their help in locating and obtaining for me a number of texts that were not available to me. I am especially thankful to Joan Sommers and the Reference and Interlibrary Loan staffs of Memorial Library at Marquette University who periodically over the last twenty years processed numerous requests for texts. The project is also indebted to Father Thaddeus Burch, S.J., Dean of Marquette's Graduate School, for a number of summer research grants to complete this project. Dr. Andrew Tallon, director of Marquette University Press, encouraged this project and graciously offered to publish the multi-volume collection. He has also been very helpful in providing technical assistance in the production of the final text.

INTRODUCTION

This volume is the first of a multi-volume set of Orestes A. Brownson's early works, covering a period from 1826, the date of his first known publication, until his conversion to Catholicism in 1844. Most of these works were never printed in Henry Brownson's edition of his father's collected works.[1] The first volume of the works assembles sermons, essays, and articles he published when he was a Universalist pastor and essayist-editor in upstate New York from 1826 to 1830.

The introduction that follows is divided into three major sections. The first section outlines briefly Brownson's early biography until his separation from the Universalist Church and ministry in December of 1829. The second places Brownson's Universalist writings in the intellectual context of his upstate New York experience. The third focuses on the editorial principles that guide this and the subsequent volumes.

BROWNSON'S EARLY LIFE

Vermont was home to Orestes A. Brownson and a number of his contemporaries who made significant contributions to American religious and intellectual life. Joseph Smith (1805-44), founder of the Mormons, was born in Sharon, Vermont; Brigham Young (1801-77), Smith's trusted advisor and president of the Mormons from 1847 until his death, in Whitingham, Vermont; William Miller (1782-1849), founder and leader of the Adventist movement in the United States, in Pittsfield, Vermont; and John Humphrey Noyes (1811-86), religious perfectionist and founder of Bible Communist and free-love communes, in Brattleboro, Vermont. Brownson—minister, journalist, and philosopher in various religious and intellectual movements—was born in Stockbridge, Vermont on September 16, 1803. Stockbridge was a small rural community located on the White River sixteen miles northeast of Rutland, Vermont. Like his contemporaries he lived in obscure rural villages in Vermont (on the outskirts of American culture), had little access to formal higher education, was devoid of much religious instruction, and, like many of them, he migrated before the 1820s with his family to upstate New York where he started his careers as a teacher, preacher and journalist.

[1] *The Works of Orestes A. Brownson,* ed. Henry F. Brownson, 20 vols. (Detroit: Thorndike Nourse, 1882-87). Hereafter referred to as *Works.*

Brownson was part of the mobile younger generation from Vermont who went west in search of a better way of life. Like many of his young contemporaries, moreover, he was troubled by the doctrinal and institutional conflicts within the various religious and theological communities (i.e., Congregationalists, New and Old Light Presbyterians, Universalists, Christians, Baptists, Methodists, deists, and those called Nothingarians) that fought for survival or dominance in Vermont and upstate New York in the early nineteenth century.[2] He was also influenced by the rationalism and even the skepticism of his deist Vermont roots, and by the general emphasis upon reason and human rights in the political culture. Things religious and political were in flux in the early nineteenth century, especially in rural Vermont and upstate New York, and Brownson was a part of that general mobility, instability, and cultural searching that made young men move from town to town in search of work and a way of life. Religious experimentation, novelty, and creativity were characteristic of the lives of many young rural persons especially during the first thirty years of the nineteenth century. Brownson was one of those young religious searchers who was generally on the outside of nineteenth century Protestant orthodoxy in its Calvinist or evangelical-revivalist forms.

What makes Brownson's early life and writings interesting is not his creative intellect but his clear articulation of the religious and intellectual conflicts that tried some young men's souls during the period. Like many of his contemporaries, he cannot be neatly put into one of the major religious categories of religious identification: he was in neither the Calvinist nor the Arminian camps, but represents a strange mixture of these camps with an affinity for deist and rationalist ideology and rhetoric.

Orestes Augustus was born to Sylvester Augustus Brownson (1773-1805) and Relief Metcalf Brownson (1776-?). Sylvester Brownson, like many other Vermonters, had migrated before 1800 to Vermont from Connecticut. The Brownson family had a long history in Connecticut prior to Sylvester's move to Vermont. John and Richard Brownson, the American founders of the family, came from England to Hartford, Connecticut in 1636. Relief Metcalf was born

---

[2] For a variety of different reasons the lack of Christian unity disturbed many young men and became a major theme for the Disciples of Christ, Christians, Mormons, Millerites, Universalists, deists, and others. On this, see, for example, David L. Rowe, *Thunder and Trumpets: Millerites and Dissenting Religion in Upstate New York, 1800-1850* (Chico, CA: Scholars Press, 1985), 29f.

in Keene, New Hampshire, but little else is known about the Metcalf history.[3]

Brownson's father, who was probably a farmer and sheepherder in Vermont, died in 1805, when Orestes was two years of age. The experience of death and fatherlessness, a not uncommon experience for many young persons according to some historians of the early nineteenth century,[4] became one of the controlling interests in Orestes Brownson's later life. Sympathetic concern for widows and orphans, moreover, was a preoccupation of his adult years and he frequently cited those biblical passages that related to widows and orphans.

In 1805, Relief Brownson was left with a family of five children: Orestes's two older brothers (Oran and Daniel), an older sister (Thorina), and a twin sister (Daphne).[5] The family was so poor that the younger children had to be sent to relatives and neighbors to be raised. Separated from his mother at the age of six, Orestes lived with James Huntington (or Hunting) and his wife who farmed in Royalton, Vermont, on the White River five miles north of Stockbridge. Orestes remained with this couple until he was fifteen.[6]

Our knowledge of the religious tradition in which young Brownson was reared comes almost exclusively from his autobiography.[7] Brownson's father had been a Presbyterian and his mother was a Universalist, but apparently there was little concern for Orestes's early religious formation. Even infant baptism, which would have been customary for Presbyterians of the time, was not given to Orestes. The Huntingtons, who raised him from the age of six to fifteen, were Congregationalists who rarely attended or took Orestes to church meetings, but they did teach him the *Shorter Catechism,* the Apostles'

[3] On the Brownson genealogy, see Theodore Maynard, *Orestes Brownson: Yankee, Radical, Catholic* (New York: Macmillan, 1943), 23-24, n. 8.

[4] See, for example, Joseph F. Kett, "Growing Up in Rural New England, 1800-1840," in *Anonymous Americans,* ed. Tamara K. Hareven (Englewood Cliffs, New York: Prentice-Hall, 1971), 2.

[5] On Brownson's siblings, see Thomas R. Ryan, *Orestes A. Brownson: A Definitive Biography* (Huntington, IN: Our Sunday Visitor Press, 1975), 302-03.

[6] On the religion and social history of Vermont during Brownson's youth, see Randolph A. Roth, *The Democratic Dilemma: Religion, Reform, and the Social Order in the Connecticut River Valley of Vermont, 1791-1850* (New York: Cambridge University Press, 1987), 41-79.

[7] I am consistently referring to *The Convert* (1857) when I speak of the autobiography and will use the reprint edition found in *Works* 5:1-200. Another helpful source on Brownson's early religious experience and upbringing is William J. Gilmour's "Orestes Brownson and New England Religious Culture, 1803-1827," Ph.D. diss., University of Virginia, 1971.

Creed, the Lord's Prayer, and a few other prayers.[8] He learned from the Huntingtons and from what he read as an early teenager the religious tradition of a modified American Calvinism. He demonstrated early on, as he admits in his autobiography, that he had an interest in things religious.[9] He learned to read when he was very young and read the Bible repeatedly, committing many passages to memory as his writings clearly reveal. Before he left the confines of his guardians' home, moreover, he had read Isaac Watts's (1674-1748) *Psalms of David* and *Divine Songs, The Franklin Primer,* Jonathan Edwards's (1703-58) A *History of the Work of Redemption,* and a few other religious works from the American Puritan tradition.[10]

Brownson also became acquainted with the American revivalist tradition at Royalton. During his early teenage years, in about 1816, when Vermont was in the midst of a new major religious revival,[11] he had something of a Methodist conversion experience.[12] Although he did not record the experience in his autobiography, he did mention it once or twice during his late twenties and early thirties.[13] The conversion experience at thirteen, however, did not lead him to join a church. That would not come for another five years.

In 1818, Brownson migrated with his mother and siblings, whom he had not seen since he was eight years of age, to Ballston Spa, New York, (a small town twenty-eight miles north of Albany, New York, and six miles south southwest of Saratoga Springs) in search of a

---

[8] *The Shorter Catechism* (1648) was established by the Westminster Assembly and played an important role in the catechesis of Presbyterian, Congregationalist and Baptist children.

[9] *Works* 5:5.

[10] Watts' *Psalms* (London, 1719) and his *Divine Songs* (London, 1715) reflected a modified form of Calvinism. *The Franklin Primer,* edited by Samuel Willard (1775-1859), was a catechism of the American Calvinist mind. Edwards's A *History* (London, 1774; Philadelphia, 1800; and other editions) became one of his most popular books in the nineteenth century; it represented a Calvinist providential view of history, but it placed revivals of religion at the center of the providential plan for human redemption.

[11] On the revival, see David M. Ludlum, *Social Ferment in Vermont, 1791-1850* (New York: Columbia University Press, 1939; AMS Press, 1966), 51; P. Jeffrey Potash, *Vermont's Burned-Over District: Patterns of Community Development and Religious Activity, 1761-1850* (New York: Carlson, 1991), 155.

[12] Historians tell us that teenage conversions were becoming common experiences during the early nineteenth century. On this, see, e.g., William Gilmour, 104-22, and Kett, "Growing Up in Rural New England," 3, 10.

[13] See the semi-fictional accounts of his early autobiography in "Patrick O'Hara, Chapter VI," *The Philanthropist* 1 (July 23, 1831): 141-43, and in *Charles Elwood* (1840) in *Works* 4:190. See also Brownson's letter to Edward Turner, July 17, 1834, in Universalist Archives, Andover-Harvard Archives.

more satisfying life. The years 1816 and 1817 had been particularly hard on Vermonters, many of whom suffered from famine and fled from Vermont to upstate New York.[14] The Brownsons were part of that massive migration.

Brownson joined his mother and siblings in Ballston Spa where he attended the Ballston Academy for a couple of years. Thereafter or during his school years he worked as an apprentice for a Universalist publisher and printer. Apparently during the Ballston Spa years his mother's sister, who was a Universalist, and a neighbor introduced him to a number of writers who had advocated the doctrine of universal salvation (e.g., Elhanan Winchester [1751-97], Charles Chauncy [1705-87], Joseph Huntington [1735-79], and especially Hosea Ballou [1771-1852]).[15] These authors made an impression on him but not one sufficient to make him join a Universalist church—that would come after a brief association with the Presbyterians.

In 1822, at the age of nineteen, he one day attended a Presbyterian Church in Malta, New York (a small village south and east of Ballston) that was having a revival meeting. He experienced a religious conviction during that meeting and told Reuben Smith (1789-1860), the pastor of the Presbyterian Church in Ballston Spa, about it.[16] Subsequently he related the experience to the local Presbyterian Session, which apparently tested the authenticity of his religious con-

---

[14] On the famine and terrible economic conditions in the hill country, see Stephen A. Marini, *Radical Sects of Revolutionary New England* (Cambridge, MA: Harvard University Press, 1982), 30.

[15] *Works* 5:21. See also Winchester's *The Process and Empire of Christ. A Course of Lectures on the Prophecies That Remain to be Fulfilled. The Universal Restoration* (Brattleboro, 1805), Huntington's *Calvinism Improved* (New London, CT, 1796), Chauncy's *The Mystery Hid from the Ages and Generations, Made Manifest by the Gospel Revelation: or The Salvation of All Men* (London, 1784), and particularly Ballou's *A Treatise on Atonement* (Randolph, VT, 1805). Russell Miller calls Ballou the greatest theologian of the Universalist Church. He made three major theological contributions to Universalism: (1) a developed Unitarian view of God and Christ; (2) an emphasis upon the finiteness of sin and punishment; (3) a new conception of the Atonement that asserted that Christ came to earth not for the release of human sin but to lead humans to divine love, a view opposed to the received tradition of vicarious suffering. By 1820, according to Miller, many if not most Universalists had moved, under the influence of Ballou, from Trinitarianism to Unitarianism. See Russell E. Miller, *The Larger Hope: The First Century of the Universalist Church in America, 1770-1870* (Boston: Unitarian Universalist Association, 1979), 98-105.

[16] For a biographical sketch of Smith, see William Gilmour, 142-66, especially 148, n.45.

version (as was the normal procedure),[17] and on a Sunday in October of 1822 he was baptized and admitted into the Presbyterian Church.

During the time he belonged to the Ballston Presbyterian Church, a period of nine months, he kept a personal diary[18] which reflects a combination of Calvinist doctrines and soul-searching accounts of the nineteen year old's religious state. The diary also records a gradual assertion of the role of reason in religion and the beginnings of his disaffection with the revivalist Presbyterian tradition of which he had become a part. On the one hand the diary is preoccupied with accounts of the transitoriness of all things human (wealth, fame, security, happiness), the fall of human empires, the meaning of death, human misery and helplessness, the deceptions and conceits of the human heart, the weakness and constant fluctuations of human reason; the lack of his own religious feeling or the coldness of his religious experience, and the lack of clear religious assurance. On the other hand, the diary reflects his sense and contemplation of God's glory, predestination, sovereignty, and mercy, and his realization of the absolute necessity of grace as the source of all religion. The diary demonstrates, moreover, his anxiety to determine whether or not he had grace, whether or not he was among the elect. Religion, he assured himself in the diary, calmed the human passions and was a source of wisdom and knowledge; it relieved sinners of their guilt; it provided a source of wisdom which the weakness of human reason could not obtain; it awakened sympathy particularly for widows, orphans, the poor and outcasts of society; and it tended to ameliorate the conditions of unfortunate suffering humanity. He argued with Pelagianism and Arminianism, meditated on the fall of human empires, reflected on the folly of heated dogmatic debates, demonstrated his interests in the origins of law and government, and perceived nature as a

---

[17] See Reuben Smith, "Orestes A. Brownson's Development of Himself," *Princeton Review* 30 (April 1858): 890-92, for an acknowledgment of the procedures followed.

[18] What I am calling Brownson's diary is actually designated "A Notebook of Reflections, 1822-1825" in the Archives of the University of Notre Dame where it is located. See also microfilm roll 10 of the Orestes Brownson Papers, and *A Guide to the Microfilm Edition of Orestes Augustus Brownson Papers*, ed. Thomas T. McAvoy, C.S.C., and Lawrence J. Bradley (Notre Dame, IN: University of Notre Dame Press, 1966). I am referring in the footnotes to "Diary 1" to indicate this "Notebook." This diary has extant entries from December 1822 to August of 1825, but there are significant ellipses, the most important one being a cessation of entries between August 19, 1823 (one month after he left the Presbyterian Church) and July 3, 1825. Some reflections from that missing period are found in what I am calling the second volume of the diary. On this see footnote 24.

Newtonian machine of immutable laws as well as a revelation of God's greatness, goodness, and majesty. In the diary he returned again and again to the theme of friendship and the need for a friend.

Brownson's autobiography claims that he gradually became disaffected with Presbyterianism because it did not own up to any legitimate authority for its positions and its own exercise of authority.[19] He reported there that his central question was "by what or whose authority am I to believe?" The diary and his former pastor, Reuben Smith, do not support this post-factum and pro-Catholic interpretation of what occurred during his retreat from Presbyterianism.[20] Other things seem to have motivated his departure. The diary shows that he was gradually disaffected about his own religious coldness. Periodically he confided to his diary that the church experience was fleeting and had no staying power with him. The dogmatic preaching he encountered in church, moreover, did not captivate his senses and consequently he forgot all that had been said before he returned from church. Gradually, too, he became disaffected with what he called the baneful effects of the current system of missionary "priestcraft" of both the Calvinists and the Arminians.

On June 6, 1823, Brownson approached his pastor, Reuben Smith, and related to him some doubts he was having about his religious convictions and by July of 1823 he stopped going to the Presbyterian Church. The diary during the months of July and August indicate some reasons for his disaffection with his Calvinist tradition. During those months, while he was employed as a teacher in Stillwater, New York (outside of Ballston), he reflected in his diary repeatedly on the culture of the mind and its hidden potential and powers. He also raised again questions about the cause of human misery (a constant theme throughout his life), asking whether the cause is either the "unavoidable lot of our nature or the effect of our own misguided choice?" By August of 1823 he could respond, against his Presbyterian view but probably in conformity with what he had read in Universalist writings prior to his conversion to Presbyterianism, that human misery and unhappiness were not the result of fate or the Providence of God, but of "our own misguided choice." "Man," he

---

[19] *Works* 5:13-14.

[20] Reuben Smith was particularly incensed by Brownson's autobiographical assertion in *The Convert* (1857) that he had renounced his private opinions when he joined the Presbyterian Church. See Reuben Smith, "Orestes A. Brownson's Development of Himself," 890-92. Brownson's autobiographical recollections of his earliest years are in some cases, as Smith points out, deficient either because of faulty memory or because of "fabrication."

wrote, "is the arbiter of his own fortune, a certain consequence will attend every act. Though God governs all things he does not infringe upon the power he has delegated to man."[21] Human wretchedness was the result of free will. Brownson's emphasis here upon free agency was consistent with the battles that were going on in the American Protestant community at the time; he was siding with the advocates of free agency. He was not, as his autobiography claims, disaffected with the lack of legitimate authority within Presbyterianism; he was seeking emancipation from positions he believed denied free will and the role of reason in religion.

Brownson was preoccupied with the cause of human suffering both before and after his Presbyterian experience. Was nature the necessary cause or was it the abuse of liberty? This question plagued him during his early years, but by the summer of 1823, as he confided to his diary, he had come to believe that those who saw human suffering as the result of nature or Providence (as he believed the Presbyterians did) had simply used necessity as an ideological excuse to avoid any human effort to relieve human suffering. To his diary in August of 1823 he confessed that human sympathy with the poor and suffering was natural, and indeed the surest proof of "our divine extraction." Human activity to relieve the wants of the needy, moreover, was an imitation of Christ who went about doing good. By August of 1823 he was saying that human beings glorified God best by displaying the divine perfections in all human conduct. We glorify God when we imitate his character, and we do this best when we attend to the wants of suffering humanity.[22]

By the beginning of 1824 Brownson had clearly moved away from Presbyterianism and joined the ranks of "liberal Christianity," becoming a Universalist. Brownson's autobiography considered this first notable change in his life a movement from supernaturalism to rationalism, and the movement to Universalism was for him the commencement of his intellectual life.[23]

Sometime during the first months of 1824 Brownson moved west, first to Camillus in western New York (eight miles west of Syracuse) where he more than likely stayed for a couple of months (March and April at least) with the John Healy (1773-1826) family and perhaps taught some of his daughters, one of whom, Sally, would even-

[21] Diary 1:86. The page numbers I am using here refer to the page numbers on the original manuscript, not to page numbers on my typescript copy that I have placed in the Archives of the University of Notre Dame.
[22] Diary 1:89.
[23] *Works* 5:19.

tually become his wife.[24]   By June or July he moved to Springwells, Michigan (on the Rouge River a few miles outside of Detroit) where he was also employed as a teacher. His son Henry reported that he contracted malaria and ague (an illness which bothered him off and on for the remainder of his life) while in the Springwells area and was confined to his bed for long periods.[25]   It is uncertain how long he stayed in the Detroit area, but we do know from the second volume of his diary that by March of 1825 he was back in Camillus, New York[26] with the Healy family, engaged in teaching again.

The second volume of Brownson's diary, which places him in western New York and the Detroit area from March of 1824 to March of 1825, is filled with a variety of topics indicating something of his intellectual and religious interests and development. In it, for example, he reflects on the nobility of education and the necessity of cultivating the mind. But, the diary records, Brownson discovered

[24] A second volume of what I am calling Brownson's diary (hereafter referred to as Diary 2) places him in Camillus in March and April of 1824; see Diary 2:4, 49, 50, 53, 83, and 84 . The second volume of his diary is what the Archives of the University of Notre Dame has designated Brownson's "Notebook of Clippings" (see the microfilm edition of the Brownson Papers for this notebook), which contained newspaper clippings of Brownson's articles primarily from the *Boston Reformer* (1836). In 1986-87, the Archives removed the clippings that were pasted into the notebook, uncovering a hand written diary of writings Brownson (and a few others, notably his future wife Sally Healy) had produced between March 2, 1824 and March 6, 1825. For this uncovered "diary" (or "Notebook"), see Orestes Brownson Papers, box 29[1/2], Archives of the University of Notre Dame. I have transcribed this diary, a copy of which is located in the Archives of the University of Notre Dame, and renumbered each original manuscript page, from 1 to 138. The page numbers cited above refer to my renumbered manuscript. The diary contains collections of poetry (some of it copied from Milton, Pope, Young, Cowper, Fenelon, Thompson, Watts, and others; some of it original pieces from Brownson, the Healy daughters, and a few others who appear to have been Brownson's students), wisdom sayings and proverbs, brief biographical sketches of important persons (e.g., George Washington), hand-written recordings of newspaper and magazine articles Brownson found interesting, periodical reflections on the state of Brownson's soul, and parts of sermons based on biblical texts. Some parts of the diary could not be restored because the removal of some newspaper clippings destroyed the hand-written texts behind them. This was particularly the case with the sermons at the end of the diary. Consequently the recovered sermons have numerous ellipses, but one can still grasp the state of Brownson's mind during this period of his life when he was apparently considering the Universalist ministry as his vocation in life. This section of the introduction is based almost exclusively upon an analysis of the second volume of the diary, the first time any biographer has taken advantage of this source.
[25] Henry F. Brownson, *The Early Life of Orestes A. Brownson, 1803-1844* (Detroit: Henry F. Brownson, 1898), 20.

that teaching had its difficulties. Education, he complained, lacked parental support and the task of teaching was "tedious and wearisome." His young students, too, could be full of "stubbornness, indocility, and natural dullness."[27] Teaching the young was not to be in his future.

The diary also records Brownson's youthful views of a variety of other topics like the science of government and the nature of good economics. One surprising position, especially in view of his later intellectual development, is his position on economics and taxation. He asserted that government should not intervene, through taxation and tariffs, in "private" matters of commerce and trade. The best governmental policy was laissez-faire; trade ought not to be limited by governmental policy.[28] Although consistent with his increasing emphasis upon individual freedom, it was clearly contrary to positions on the necessity of governmental regulation of commerce that Brownson developed later in his life.

The diary indicates, moreover, something of the state of his soul during this period. Periodically it records his soul-searching attempts to penetrate the recesses of his heart to uncover the self-awareness needed to develop his character. Part of what he discovers there is the transitoriness of all things human, the vanity of life, the alternating experiences of melancholy, grief and joy, the experience of the follies and inconsistencies of youth, and a feeling of homesickness. Although he discloses to himself his own feeling of loneliness and the need for friendship, he is also aware that friendship, too, is fleeting and open to the possibilities of self-deception. Here his own experience of being abandoned (by his father's death, his removal from his mother and siblings, and his disassociation with Presbyterianism) reveals his own sense of transitory relationships. One's happiness, he records, cannot be found in others.

> Miserable indeed must he be if he have no fund of happiness but in others. Often will they disappoint or leave him. Then he must sink into himself, and if his mind is uncultivated or tortured with guilt, melancholy surely will be his situation.[29]

[26] Henry Brownson, *Early Life*, 480-81, referred to the place where the Healy's lived as Elbridge, New York (a small town sixteen miles west of Syracuse), not Camillus. The second volume of the Diary always refers to the place where the Healys lived as Camillus. The Diary places Brownson there in March of 1825.
[27] Diary, 2:76.
[28] Ibid., 67.
[29] Ibid., 46.

Much of the second volume is devoted to his views of religion and shows evidence that Brownson was considering a vocation to the Universalist ministry. It is clear from the diary that he accepted much of the Christian tradition: its belief that the Bible was inspired, that all were conceived in sin, that Jesus Christ was God and man, that he became man to free the world from sin, and that faith in him constituted the avenue to eternal salvation. Some things in the received tradition, however, he found troublesome. He was disturbed, as were many other contemporaries, by the discordance of religious beliefs and the unremitting battles over Christian doctrine. For him faith was "an involuntary act of the mind entirely dependent on the force of evidence accompanying the [tenets] to be believed."[30] Faith was an act that demanded evidence and thus Christianity should allow the greatest degree of liberty of thought and inquiry to discover that evidence for oneself. The love of liberty and rational inquiry is a natural, God-given impulse, "being inhaled with our earliest breath." Thus Christianity should allow the greatest latitude relative to what individuals believed. Reason and freedom were God-given gifts, moreover, that were inherently at war with superstition, bigotry, fanaticism, priestcraft, and clerical machinations—all of which were evident, according to Brownson, in religious debates.

Brownson believed in the Bible because it provided humans with a map and a compass to human happiness. "I believe it because it presents a supply of all my wants, a cordial for every fear, a balm for every wound."[31] But, the Bible itself had become a bone of contention in the community and a source of discord because of differing interpretations of life after death. Since human beings, however, have freedom of thought as a natural right, individuals have the right to decide the issue for themselves. The primary biblical issue for him at this point in his life was whether or not the idea of endless punishment was justified by reason and the Bible. In the diary he marshals numerous biblical passages to support the idea that all human beings will eventually be saved. Universal salvation, moreover, is justified by rational reflection on the implications of the goodness and love of God.

By the Spring of 1825, the diary records, Brownson was clearly focused on preparing himself for a ministerial career. The sermon-like quality of the entries at the end of the diary indicate that his heart was finally set on entering the Universalist ministry, although

[30] Ibid., 47.
[31] Ibid., 56.

the diary does not directly refer to that intent. By the summer of 1825 he had decided to become a Universalist minister.

Some time during the summer of 1825 Brownson left Camillus and traveled east to Ballston Spa, where his mother lived.[32] He was on his way to Hartland, Vermont, where in the autumn he applied to the General Convention of Universalists, which met that year in Hartland, for a letter of fellowship that would allow him to preach. The first volume of his diary indicates that while in Ballston in August of 1825 and for a period thereafter Brownson constructed his own creed as a Universalist and had written out a number of sermons on specific biblical passages. The simple four-article creed asserted his belief in one God, infinite in power and goodness; in the common wants and equal rights of all human beings; in Jesus Christ as the Son of God who revealed God's true character; and in the living out of this divine character of love.[33]

Brownson spent about a year in Vermont as an apprentice preacher under the tutelage of Samuel C. Loveland (1787-1858), a Universalist pastor in Reading, Vermont (1819-42).[34] Under Loveland's supervision and instruction Brownson was introduced to a systematic study of Universalist sources. Like many other young Universalists who spent several months reading theology with a teaching pastor (rather than attending a seminary or college) in preparation for the ministry, Brownson probably read John Locke (1623-1714), Isaac Watts, William Duncan (1717-1760), Hugh Blair (1718-1800), Isaac Newton (1642-1727), George Stanley Faber (1773-1854), Hosea Ballou, Elhanan Winchester, John Brown (1722-87), and Alexander

[32] Diary, 1:98, clearly places Brownson in Ballston Spa on August 12, 1825.

[33] For his creed see Diary, 1:98. For his early sermons, see pp. 99 to 149. The sermons are commentaries on John 4:19, (99-108), 1 John 4 (109-17), Job 3:17 (118-21), Job 3:15 (122-42), Ecclesiastes 12:1 (143-49). See also, Diary 2:110-38. Creating creeds was not unprecedented for Universalists. Vermont Universalists had created a creed in 1803. On this, see Edith Fox MacDonald, *Rebellion in the Mountains: The Story of Universalism and Unitarianism in Vermont* (Concord, NH: New Hampshire Vermont District of the Unitarian Universalist Association, 1976), 4-5. Brownson constructed other creeds in 1829. See his "My Creed," *Gospel Advocate and Impartial Investigator* [hereafter *GAII*] 7 (June 27, 1829): 199-201, and "A Gospel Creed," *GAII* 7 (October 3, 1829): 310-11.

[34] On Loveland, see Edith Fox MacDonald, 154-55; Russell Miller, 659-60. Loveland was a leading Vermont Universalist who had trained and educated a number of prominent young Universalist ministers. He was also a Restorationist Universalist, believing that sinful human beings would experience a limited punishment for their sins after death, but that eventually all human beings would be restored and be saved. He opposed those Universalists, like Hosea Ballou, who believed that there was no punishment for sinners after death.

Cruden (1701-70). These were at least the persons one of Brownson's contemporaries indicated he had read in preparing for the Universalist ministry.[35] Under Loveland's guidance, moreover, Brownson was apprenticed in the practice of preparing sermons, which he delivered, he tells us in his autobiography, in the Vermont counties of Windsor (his home county), Rutland, and Rockingham.[36]

After about nine months of ministerial education and practice, Brownson was ordained to the Universalist ministry on June 15, 1826 in Jaffrey, New Hampshire. After his ordination Brownson preached in Vermont and New Hampshire for the next few months and had one of his sermons published in the *Christian Repository*, the first Universalist magazine in Vermont, a paper which Loveland had initiated and edited for a number of years (1820-25, 1828-29). In October of 1826 Brownson returned to New York to take up his ministry.

Russell Miller has created a portrait of the Universalist ministry that, with a few exceptions, characterizes Brownson's early career. A typical Universalist minister, he notes,

> would be a farmer or mechanic in background, with not much more than a "common school" education, and would be likely to serve in the ministry on a part-time basis. His origins would be rural rather than urban (sharing this background with the majority of his countrymen), and his commitment to Universalism would have come at a relatively early age—in his teens or early twenties. He would have been licensed to preach without any very exhaus-

[35] Stephen R. Smith (1788-1850), a leading Universalist minister in upstate New York indicated that he had read some of the following texts in preparation for the Universalist ministry: Locke's *Essay Concerning Human Understanding* (London, 1690), Watts' *Logic* (London, 1725), Duncan's *Elements of Logic* (London, 1748), Blair's *Essays on Rhetoric* (London, 1784), Newton's *Observations Upon the Prophecies of Daniel and the Apocalypse of St. John* (London, 1733), Faber's *A Dissertation on the Prophecies* (3rd ed., London, 1808), Ballou's *A Treatise on Atonement* (Randolph, VT, 1805), *A Candid Review of a Pamphlet Entitled a Candid Reply: The Whole Being a Doctrinal Controversy Between the Hopkintonian and the Universalist* (Portsmouth, NH, 1800) and *Notes on Parables of the New Testament* (Randolph, VT, 1804); Pattipierre on Divine Goodness [Smith's reference to this author and text could not be identified], Winchester's *The Universal Restoration, Exhibited in a Series of Dialogues Between a Minister and His Friend* (London, 1788) or *Dialogues on the Universal Restoration* (Boston, 1795), Brown's *Dictionary of the Bible* (Philadelphia, 1792), Cruden's *A Complete Concordance to the Holy Scriptures of the Old and New Testament* (London, 1737; Philadelphia, 1806; New York, 1823). On these sources, see Smith's *Historical Sketches and Incidents, Illustrative of the Establishment and Progress of Universalism in the State of New York* (Buffalo: Steele's Press, 1843), 52-53.

[36] *Works* 5:29.

tive inquiry into his background or qualifications, and he would not have expected much material compensation, if any, for his efforts. If seriously devoted to the denomination, he would be more likely at first to travel than to settle for any length of time in one community, and would be expected to meet opposition from "orthodox" clergy; his reputation might be based, in fact, on how well he could handle himself in public debate, usually arranged extemporaneously. He would depend on the generosity of both friends and strangers in his travels, as well as on a dependable horse and a sturdy pair of boots. He would be willing to countenance rebuffs as well as to welcome hospitality, and hope that when adversity struck, his family would somehow be provided for. In spite of discouragements, he would be an optimist, buoyed by his religious convictions, and would be likely to exaggerate his successes and to minimize his failures. He was not likely to be an "original thinker," but the greater his knowledge of the Bible, the better.[37]

Brownson was one of those early nineteenth century itinerant Universalist ministers. By the time he began preaching in New York State, though, the Universalist ministry was gradually moving from itineracy to stationary pastorates,[38] but their lives and ministry were anything but settled.

Brownson came back to New York at a period when American society was moving west and upstate New York was the fastest growing territory in the country.[39] The Erie Canal, Clinton's ditch, which began construction in 1817 and was completed by 1825, had become a pivotal waterway to the West and the principal commercial link between upstate New York and New York City. People from New England traveled along its route and built small towns that had the potential of developing into large cities. During the late 1820s, the western territory along the waterway was teeming with activity, growth, and constant movement. Most of the towns Brownson lived in during the 1820s, however, were small and without any developed cultural institutions.

The religious situation, too, even in small towns was in a state of flux and contention. One upstate New York Universalist reported in 1830 that in any town of 3000 there could be societies of Presbyterians, Episcopalians, Methodists, Baptists, Universalists, Mormons,

---

[37] Miller, 233-34.

[38] On this, see S. R. Smith, *Historical Sketches*, 142f.

[39] Curtis D. Johnson, *Rural Religion in Upstate New York, 1790-1860* (Ithaca: Cornell University Press, 1989), 34.

some deists and Nothingarians.[40] Presbyterians, Methodists, and Baptists appeared to have had the largest numbers in the small towns of upstate New York, but Universalists, always in contention with these dominant traditions, were growing rapidly in the early nineteenth century.

In 1805, three societies of Universalists, with three preachers to serve them, had been established in upstate New York. By 1820 there were about seventy societies (i.e., about 35% of the total population of Universalists in the United States) in New York State; by 1830 150 societies were served by fifty preachers. During the 1820s the number of Universalist societies increased by about 115%, providing something of a justification for the feeling among Universalists like Brownson that Universalism was to be the religion of the future in the United States. In fact, by the early 1830s, Universalists, according to some estimates, were the sixth largest denomination in the United States.[41] The Universalist societies in New York, as elsewhere, could have as many as several hundred congregants or as few as ten. The societies as well as the ministers were in a state of flux, moving from place to place in search of a better and more prosperous life. Many Universalist ministers, moreover, could rarely support themselves solely by their preaching; many of them had to have other work (usually teaching, farming, or conducting a small business).[42] Or, like Brownson, some were engaged in writing and journalistic work to supplement the small salaries they received from their congregations.

Universalists were still something of a religious minority in upstate New York during the 1820s. Generally they lived in communities which had large numbers of Presbyterians (New Lights as well as Old Lights), Methodists and Baptists. Revivalism, which had its ori-

[40] Miller, quoted on 686.

[41] For these statistics, see Miller, 161-62, 686. The most recent sociological study of church growth in the United States has no statistics on Universalists to either confirm or deny Miller's report. See Roger Finke and Rodney Stark, *The Churching of America, 1776-1990: Winners and Losers in Our Religious Economy* (New Brunswick, New Jersey: Rutgers University Press, 1992). Edwin S. Gaustad, *Historical Atlas of Religion in America* (New York: Harper & Row, 1962), 43, 130-31, indicated that in 1820 Universalists had about 200 churches, making them the ecclesiastical body with the nineth largest number of churches in the United States. In 1830, Universalists had 300 churches with a total membership of probably no more than 20,000 members (if each church averaged about 65 members, a number that seems consistent with Gaustad's statistics).

[42] For one example of the multiple roles Universalist ministers played in order to sustain themselves and their families, see S. R. Smith, *Historical Sketches*, 137.

gins in the area after the War of 1812, was by the 1820s exploding with activity along the entire route of the Erie Canal. Whether revivalist or not, the various Christian denominations were trying to gain a foothold in the newly expanding territory and competition was rampant among the various denominations. Universalists were by the 1820s a viable and lively alternative to the more traditional and even the new revivalist orthodox Protestant denominations.

The mobility that was characteristic of upstate New York society as it moved west was evident in Brownson's early ministerial career. During the first year of his ministry (from about June of 1826 to October of 1827), for example, Brownson moved from Vermont to eastern New York State where he preached for a month or two in the towns of Fort Anne and Whitehall (both towns in Washington County to the north of Ballston Spa). By November, he had moved west to Litchfield (in Herkimer County, to the south and east of Utica) where he ministered about a year (November of 1826 to October of 1827). After his Litchfield ministry, he spent about one year in Ithaca (October of 1827 to December of 1828), a few months in Geneva (in Ontario County, at the north end of Seneca Lake), and then at the beginning of 1829 he moved again, this time to Auburn where he took up pastoral duties and where he served as editor of the Universalist paper the *Gospel Advocate and Impartial Investigator*. After he left the Universalist ministry and the editorship of the paper in December of 1829, he remained in Auburn for a few months. By July of 1830 he had apparently moved to Leroy, New York, a small town about twenty miles west of Rochester. For about six months in Leroy he became a co-proprietor and editor of the *Genesee Republican and Herald of Reform*, a paper on behalf of the workingmen's movement and party. Some time in November of 1830, after the elections of that year, he moved back to Ithaca where he remained until the summer of 1832 when he took up a Unitarian ministry in New Hampshire.

From the time he was nineteen years of age until he was twenty-seven he had not lived in one place much longer than a year. Brownson's case may be somewhat unusual, but not terribly so because numerous young men were extremely mobile in early nineteenth century upstate New York as each searched for a career, employment, wife, and prosperity.

Brownson was trying to find himself in an upstate New York society and culture that was rootless and mobile. His geographical mobility was matched by other kinds of mobility in his life as he started his career as a minister and writer, and tried to find an intellectually satisfying position for those problems that were foremost in

his mind. During the early years of his Universalist ministry, as he
moved from place to place, moreover, he married (on 19 June 1827)
Sally Healy (1804-72), one of his former students from Camillus
who had written poems periodically for his diary while he was a teacher
there.[43] Ten months later (18 April 1828), after the Brownsons had
moved from Litchfield to Ithaca, Sally gave birth to Orestes Augustus
Brownson, Jr., the first of their eight children. A year later on April
14, 1829, after the Brownsons had moved from Ithaca to Geneva to
Auburn, Sally gave birth to their second son, John Healy Brownson
(d. 1858). Almost nothing of the personal pressures that the
Brownsons must have felt in these circumstances is reflected in the
journal articles Orestes wrote during the period, nor is there any
evidence in his later autobiography. Brownson's writings were preoccupied with ideas and with controversies over ideas.

THE INTELLECTUAL CONTEXT

Brownson's autobiography and his early diaries clearly indicate
that his primary interest in life was with ideas and the conflicting
ideas that had developed in American religious communities.
Throughout the four years of his Universalist ministry he was defining his own religious stance, which he developed in conflict and debate with old school Presbyterian Calvinism, with the emerging evangelical revivalist tradition (whether Presbyterian, Methodist, or Baptist), with unbelievers or radical socialists, and with those in his own
communion who were called ultra-Universalists (i.e., those who believed in no future punishment) or who considered him a deist or
atheist. His thought developed dialectically as he challenged and ab-
sorbed many of the contradictory intellectual and religious currents
that were running through upstate New York in the 1820s. His early
sermons and essays, republished in this volume, reflect a strange and
sometimes contradictory mixture of arguments drawn from the biblical tradition, the rationalist-deist tradition, and the popular com-
mon-sense tradition of American democracy. At times he could sound
very much like a Marxist (before Marx) in his criticism of all religion as
ideology. At other times he could sound like a supernatural rationalist
who believed in the Christian tradition. Then, again, he could sound

[43] The Healys, like the Brownsons, were old Yankee stock. The Healys, although of Irish ancestry, came from England to Roxbury, Massachusetts, be-
tween1630 and 1635. Sally's father John (1773-1826) was a prosperous farmer
who had moved to upstate New York when he was a young man. On the Brownson
and Healy genealogies, see Maynard, 23-24, n. 8.

like a traditional Calvinist who had a strong sense of the presence of God revealed in the Bible, history and creation.

The Universalism to which Brownson belonged was a rural form of liberal Christianity, existing, unlike Unitarianism, outside of the primary centers of intellectual activity in the United States. Universalism was also a kind of half-way station for many young men in the early nineteenth century, a temporary place on the way to other religious traditions or to unbelief. Universalists combined, as did Hosea Ballou, its primary theologian, the biblical tradition with something like Ethan Allen's (1738-89) *Reason the Only Oracle of Man* (1785), i.e., a combination of biblical rhetoric and deist or Enlightenment rationalism. Many of the Universalists, like nineteenth century evangelicals, had also combined the biblical tradition with the imperatives of the democratic culture in which they lived, emphasizing in particular radical change, localism, liberty, unalienable rights, and autonomy.[44] Universalists, though, like some other Christian traditions which Stephen Marini has labeled "radical sectarians,"[45] were rooted in an evangelical Calvinism (but without Predestination and the doctrinal tradition) that rejected the strict rationalism that would have characterized someone like Ethan Allen. Although they emphasized liberty, the right of free inquiry, and reasonable religion, they relied heavily, according to Marini, upon the experience of the Holy Spirit as a hermeneutical guiding principle.[46] Universalists were liberal, not evangelical, Christians, but their emphasis upon liberty, reason, individualism and institutional minimalism[47] made them kindred spirits with the evangelicals. That strange combination of the biblical tradition and the Enlightenment cultural imperatives, which constituted what Nathan Hatch has called the anti-elitist "popular theology" of the early nineteenth century,[48] had the potential of leading young Universalists in very different directions depending on which side of the combination received primary attention: some, like Abner Kneeland (1774-1844),[49] eventually renounced Christianity and became avowed rationalists; many, like Adin Ballou and the young

[44] On this see *Maine in the Early Republic: From Revolution to Statehood*, ed. Charles E. Clark et al. (Hanover, NH, 1988), 143.

[45] Marini, 137-38.

[46] There was very little evidence, however, in Brownson's early thought that he appealed to the presence of the Holy Spirit as a hermeneutical principle. He would have seen such appeals as ideological fanaticism.

[47] Marini, 107.

[48] Hatch calls the phenomenon a "Blurring of Worlds"; see his *The Democratization of American Christianity* (New Haven: Yale University Press, 1989), 34-40.

[49] On Kneeland, see Miller, 1:185-96.

Brownson, moved in the direction of Unitarianism; and a few others, like the middle-aged Brownson, moved in the direction of a more
traditional Christianity like Catholicism.

During the late 1820s Brownson hammered out his religious
ideology as a controversialist, generally defining his position in opposition to that of others. His essays opposing the "Orthodox" Calvinist, therefore, must be read in tandem with those opposing the
strict rationalist to understand how his mind was developing during
this period. He is not always very clear about precisely where he stands,
and his views are not very nuanced during this youthful period, but
the essays and sermons do show the emergence of certain key ideas
and principles like freedom and authority, reason and revelation, sin and
salvation, that are emerging as central issues in his thought even though
they are merely juxtaposed without much attempt to reconcile them.

His own religious views developed in reaction to a series of si-
multaneous debates with various branches within the Reformed tradition. Like other Universalists, he participated in the intense criticism of the reigning Calvinist orthodoxy and articulated the moral
arguments against Calvinist predestinarianism and hyper-supernatu-
ralism. In fact, the issues he discussed in rural upstate New York were
issues that had already been defined within the Reformed tradition
during the late eighteenth and early nineteenth centuries.

Brownson took issue with Presbyterian Calvinists in particular.
Although he had been a Presbyterian for only nine months, he carried with him for almost the rest of his life an animus against the
Presbyterians, and the reasons for that particular animus are not altogether clear from the sources. What is clear is his general acceptance
of the Universalist argument against the so-called "Orthodox" system of theology, whether in its Dortian form (as expressed by Jonathan
Edwards), in its Hopkinsian form (as expressed by Samuel Hopkins [1721-
1803]), or in its nineteenth century revivalist forms (as expressed by various early nineteenth century revivalists in upstate New York).[50]

[50] It is doubtful if Brownson ever heard of Charles Grandison Finney (1792-
1875) during his days in upstate New York, but he did know a number of other
revivalist Presbyterians. His own former Presbyterian pastor, Reuben Smith, was
an old school Presbyterian, but like Asahel Nettleton (1783-1844) he held numer-
ous revivals in his parish. William Wisner (1782-1871), Presbyterian pastor in Ithaca,
New York, also supported orthodoxy and revivalism, and directly challenged
Brownson's Universalist theology during the period from 1827 until Brownson left
New York in the summer of 1832. On Wisner, see *The Memoirs of Charles Grandison
Finney: The Complete Restored Text*, ed. Garth M. Russell and Richard A. G. Dupuis
(Grand Rapids, MI., 1989), 328, n. 3.

The Calvinist system, with its assertion of divine predestination and irresistible grace, was for Brownson unreasonable, unbiblical, and ultimately a denial of human freedom and moral accountability. It was clear from his early diary that Brownson had accepted the Calvinist views on these issues while he was a Presbyterian, but gradually he could not reconcile that system with his desire for and his understanding of human freedom. Nor could he accept the idea of the endless punishment of sinners in hell. Such a doctrine contradicted his understanding of the goodness and benevolence of God.

To some extent, Brownson carried with him for the remainder of his life the issues of absolute divine sovereignty and human freedom as they were defined in the Reformed community, whether from the Calvinist or the Universalist side of the ecclesiastical divide. During his Universalist ministry, he touted the doctrine of the "march of the mind" to such an extent that he at times appeared to be an out and out rationalist—and some indeed, friend and foe alike, saw him as such. The essays and sermons in this volume illustrate the Christian rationalist dimension of his mind as he struggles to define his religious position vis-à-vis the inherited Calvinist tradition.

Reason became for him the divinely created faculty that was the receptacle of all biblical revelation and ultimately its judge and interpreter. But reason had its limits. It could not penetrate all the mysteries of life; revelation provided human beings with a kind of telescope, which could enhance reason to reach beyond its limits into the mystery of divine and human life. No matter how much Brownson's youthful writings sounded like a rationalist diatribe against all organized religion, and Presbyterianism in particular, he never lost his acceptance of revelation as the divinely given doctrine of the meaning and ultimate destiny of human life. But, the battle with Calvinism was part of his youthful emancipation from a system of theology that he believed incapable of explaining divine goodness, human freedom, and the perfectibility of human beings and human culture. Calvinism had become for him what Catholicism was for many in the American Protestant and deist culture: a relic of the past, a lower stage of human development, and a religious tradition incompatible with the modern American democratic and egalitarian world. It was out of tune with reason's progressive march toward the truth.

Brownson's hostilities toward Presbyterianism (or "Orthodoxy," the wider term he used to designate traditional Christian belief) were matched by his enmity toward the evangelical revivalists and their increasing attempts to create a benevolent empire in the United States.

What he found particularly disgusting, and this language is not too strong for the feelings it represents, in the orthodox evangelicals was their constant clamor about "getting religion." Their emphasis on the new birth, their tactics to drum up a conversion experience, and their failure to attend to the moral and social needs of the poor and afflicted in society, he found particularly obnoxious. The revivalists' attempts to interpret the biblical new birth as a conversion experience, he believed, was part of an attempt by an elite clergy to retain their power and authority over the people in a society that was becoming increasingly more egalitarian, anti-elitist, and democratic. For him, the biblical new birth was a call to moral responsibility, not an other worldly soul-experience. Christianity, for him, was primarily a moral system, a tradition devoted to a morally upright life and to service to the poor and dispossessed in society. The evangelicals had turned it into a fanciful preoccupation with the supernatural.[51]

The Protestant evangelicals had not only organized seasons of revival in various rural communities in upstate New York during the mid and late 1820s but they were also becoming organized across denominational lines to have an influence upon the wider American society. The evangelical movement to create voluntary societies for a variety of religious, social, and legislative purposes worried Brownson because he saw these movements to create a benevolent empire in the United States as a control tactic on the part of religious societies who had, because of the separation of church and state in American society, lost their influence over and their dominance in the culture. The creations of Bible and tract societies, foreign missionary enterprises, Sabbath schools, the attempts to ban through federal legislation the sending of mail on Sundays, or the campaign to create a Christian party in politics (for the purposes of electing only evangelical Christians to public offices), Brownson interpreted as just a new attempt to do an old thing: namely, to support party purposes and the sectarian spirit, to convey erroneous theology, to promote and assure clerical dominance in society, and ultimately to reunite church and state under the authority of the church.[52]

---

[51]On the major revivalist campaigns in upstate New York after 1826, see Whitney R. Cross, *Burned-Over District; Social and Intellectual History of Enthusiastic Religion in Western New York, 1800-1850* (New York, 1950), 153f.

[52] For an example of these charges, see "Sabbath School," *GAII* 6 (August 30, 1828): 285-86. On the creation of the benevolent empire in upstate New York from 1825 to 1831, see Cross, 126f.

Like many Universalists, other liberal Christians, and even Catholics,[53] he opposed these attempts by the "saints" to create a Christian America. He was adamantly opposed to Ezra Stiles Ely's (1786-1861) call for a "Christian Party in Politics." On July 4, 1827, Ely, President of the Presbyterian General Assembly (National Convention) and a pastor in Philadelphia, gave an Independence Day talk that was widely distributed and commented on in the press. The speech, "The Duty of Christian Freemen to Elect Christian Rulers," called for, among other things, the election of only evangelical Christians to public office. He asserted that "every member of this Christian nation, from the highest to the lowest, ought to serve the Lord with fear, and yield his sincere homage to the Son of God. Every ruler *should* be an avowed and sincere friend of Christianity. He should know and believe the doctrines of our holy religion, and act in conformity with its precepts." He was not calling for a union of church and state. He explicitly stated: "let Church and State be for ever distinct; but, still, let the doctrines and precepts of Christ govern all men, in all their relations and employments."[54] To carry out this purpose he proposed the establishment of a "*Christian Party in Politics.*"[55] Ely's speech, repeatedly commented on by Brownson and other Universalists, revealed what Brownson considered the ultimate purpose behind the entire benevolent empire, namely the creation of a country where the rights of the minority (especially deists, Unitarians and Universalists whose election to public office Ely's campaign was indirectly trying to prevent) would be trampled upon and where the church would eventually control not only the culture but the federal and state legislatures. For Brownson the issue was clear: religion must be kept out of government. But he was significantly aware that the battle he and other Universalists were fighting was going against a major, if not the dominant, stream of current religious opinion in the United States.

Brownson's relationship to unbelievers and radical social reformers also helped him define his religious and ideological position and helped others to perceive a revolutionary direction to his thought. He was favorably impressed, for example, with the writings and work

---

[53] For a Catholic assault on the benevolent empire, see John England's "The Republic in Danger," in *The Works of the Right Rev. John England, First Bishop of Charleston,* ed. Ignatius Aloysius Reynolds, 5 vols. (Baltimore: John Murphy & Co., 1849), 4:13-68.

[54] Ely's speech reprinted in *American Philosophical Addresses, 1700-1900,* ed. Joseph Blau (New York: Columbia University Press, 1946), 553-54.

[55] Ibid., 556-57.

of Frances (Fanny) Wright (1795-1852) and her *Free Enquirer* paper. Wright's and Robert Owen's (1771-1858) promotion of social utopian communities at Nashoba, Tennessee and New Harmony in Indiana had failed to materialize, but both Wright and Robert Dale Owen (1801-77), Robert's son, continued in the 1820s to support radical ideas on the education of children, on marriage, and on the rights of workingmen, believing that the ills of society were caused by the institutions of property, marriage, and religion. Many considered them socialists and infidels. Wright and Robert Dale Owen saw in Brownson an intellectual companion and a kindred spirit, as their reprinting in the *New Harmony Gazette* of one of Brownson's articles clearly indicates.[56] Brownson indeed sided with the radical reformers and saw their attempts to meet the needs of the poor and the laboring classes as a "Christian" work, regardless of what they believed regarding Christianity and religion. In fact, he asserted that they were doing what Christian ministers, who were wrong-headedly preoccupied with the world beyond the grave, should have been doing: promoting the cause of amelioration in society.

Brownson, however, never did fully side with these social radicals. He believed they did not see the limits of reason nor did they appreciate the necessity of religion for the promotion of justice in society. He thought their views of marriage and education, moreover, were utopian, being excessively preoccupied with freedom, giving too much authority to the state in matters of education, and not seeing the force of family and tradition in society.[57] Despite his criticisms, however, his favorable association with the *Free Enquirer* crowd had made him by the middle of 1829 a *persona non grata* within Universalist circles.

Brownson's relationship with the Universalists gradually changed in the course of his ministerial career. At the beginning of his career he was a firm advocate and apologist for universal salvation (a single-minded preoccupation of almost all Universalists in the early nineteenth century)—in opposition to Calvinists, New Lights, and other traditional Christians. Even though he supported universal salvation, he did not belong to that school of Universalists (sometimes called "ultra-Universalists") who held that there was absolutely no future punishment after death. He belonged, as did his mentor Loveland,

---

[56] See, e.g., "Of the Cause of Evil," *The New Harmony Gazette* 3 (August 13, 1828): 330, a reprint of "The Essayist," *GAII* 6 (July 19, 1828): 230-31.

[57] "Free Enquirers," *GAII* 6 (March 21, 1829): 89-90.

to the Restorationist school within Universalism.[58] For him, as for all Universalists, there was no eternal punishment, but for Restorationist Universalists all moral evil required punishment as a means of personal reformation, and such temporary punishment would be actualized either in this world or in the next. There is not much evidence in his writings, however, that he entered into any significant discussion with ultra-Universalists on the issue of future punishment. His primary concern was to defend universalism against the attacks of traditional Christians.

Later in his Universalist career, however, Brownson began to have doubts about universal salvation. He indicated in his autobiography that even during his days as a Universalist minister he had begun to lose confidence in the biblical warrant for the doctrine of universal salvation.[59] In 1829, too, he hinted that he had apprehensions about the final salvation of all human beings,[60] but there is little other evidence in his Universalist writings that he had actually denied the doctrine of universal salvation. He had some doubts about the biblical evidence in support of the doctrine and by the end of 1829 he saw it primarily "as an inferential doctrine, rather than as one positively taught."[61] Certainly he had given up the belief in universal salvation later in his life because he believed there were too many biblical passages that could not be explained satisfactorily by universalism and because universalism could not logically support moral accountability. But, these views were not yet evident during his Universalist years.

Throughout his publishing career as a Universalist Brownson sought to expand the very notion of salvation, whether understood as universal or not. He asserted, against some Universalists as well as evangelicals, that the traditional notion of salvation had been excessively restricted to an eternal other worldly form of emancipation from evil. For him salvation was an emancipation from all forms of personal and social evil in this world, and not just a conversion to

[58] Hosea Ballou was one of the significant articulators of ultra-Universalism. On Ballou, see footnote 15. Although Brownson eventually followed Ballou on the theory of Atonement, he did not follow him on future punishment. Punishment for him, especially divine punishment, was never vindictive, but only remedial and reformatory or disciplinary. On the so-called Restorationist controversy within Universalism between 1817 and 1841, see Richard Eddy, *Universalism in America. A History*, 2 vols. (Boston: Universalist Publishing House, 1884, 1886), 2:260-342.

[59] *Works*, 5:32-39.

[60] "Union of Papers," *GAII* 7 (November 14, 1829): 362.

[61] "A Gospel Creed," *GAII* 7 (October 3, 1829): 311-12.

Christ who would assure one's eternal life (which was, he believed, the primary focus of traditional preaching). In fact, as his earliest writings in his diaries show, he was preoccupied, even before he identified himself with the Universalists, with the causes and remedies of social evils.

In the course of his writing as a Universalist Brownson became increasingly more radical in his understanding of traditional Christian doctrines, e.g., the Trinity and the Atonement. In this he was simply becoming attuned to the Unitarianism that had captured Universalism by 1820.[62] Perhaps under the influence of Hosea Ballou's *A Treatise on Atonement* Brownson gradually moved away from traditional doctrines he had held as a Presbyterian and as an early Universalist: the doctrines of the Trinity, the divinity of Christ, and the satisfactory or vicarious theory of the Atonement. Brownson's increasing emphasis on the role of reason and free inquiry in religion was also significantly responsible for his difficulties with these Christian doctrines. For all practical purposes, reason became for him the rule of faith and practice, and reason alone could not accept the traditional Trinitarian and christological doctrines. Even though Brownson retained some belief in the divine inspiration of the Scriptures, he ultimately limited inspiration to basic New Testament teachings, making all other post-biblical ecclesiastical definitions of doctrine subject to the interpretation of reason. The ultimate test of correct doctrine and moral practice became for him the test of reasonableness.

In addition to his attacks on traditional Christian doctrines, he had become increasingly more radical from 1827 to 1829 in his attacks on organized religion, on priestcraft, and on the propensity of all traditional Christians to escape their moral and social responsibilities by fleeing to an other worldly paradise. The attacks were meant to apply particularly to those evangelicals who were engaged in revivalist work and in creating the benevolent empire. But, the attacks were so universal and unnuanced that they could be taken as assaults upon all organized religion, and, indeed, even some Universalists understood his criticisms as manifestations of heresy or an anti-religious spirit.

Traditional Christians and by 1829 some Universalists critics clearly saw that Brownson's thought was moving in a direction they

---

[62] On this development, see Miller, 105.

characterized as deist, infidel, or atheist.[63] His radical and many times generic attacks on traditional Christian doctrines and life and particularly his association with Fanny Wright and the Workingman's Party[64] gave some substance to the charges that Brownson had increasingly separated himself from traditional Christianity and even from the more liberal Universalism. Brownson gave his Universalist critics enough reason for the charges they made against him when one of his articles was republished in the *New Harmony Gazette*, a precursor to the *Free Enquirer*, when he attended one of Wright's lectures in Utica and reported favorably on it in the *Gospel Advocate*, and when he assaulted all ministers, Universalists as well as others, for their inactivity in regard to necessary social and moral reforms. One Universalist critic and fellow editor of a competing magazine, Theophilus Fisk (1801-67), wrote in March of 1829, "I was almost led to rejoice, that Mr. Brownson had renounced his belief in Christianity."[65] Another Universalist—Thomas Whittemore, who had repeatedly opposed the Restorationist Universalism of people like Brownson—was particularly disturbed by Brownson's association with Wright and his joining the staff of the *Free Enquirer* because he believed that by his association with those radicals Brownson had entirely renounced Christianity. He also charged that Brownson was deceptive in his continued association with Universalism and intimated that Brownson had been fired from his Universalist pastorate in Auburn.[66]

In the early part of 1829, moreover, the charge of atheism was leveled at Brownson when he asserted that one could not know the existence of God on the basis of reason alone, that nature alone did

[63] For some examples of Universalists who brought these charges against Brownson, see "Infidelity," *GAII* 7 (April 18, 1829): 121-23; "Gospel Herald," ibid., 123; "Mr. Reese's Letter," ibid., (July 25, 1829): 236-40; and T. Fisk, "A Letter to the Readers of the *Gospel Advocate*," *New York Gospel Herald and Universalist Review* 1 (March 28, 1829): 106-07 and "Gospel Advocate," ibid., 110-11.

[64] The Workingman's Party had its origin in Philadelphia in 1827, at the same time as Ely's organization of the campaign for a Christian Party in Politics. The Workingman's Party aimed to improve the rights and working conditions of the working class. On the working class, see Sean Wilentz, *Chants Democratic: New York City and the Rise of the Working Class 1788-1850* (New York: Oxford University Press, 1984).

[65] Fisk, "A letter," 106.

[66] See in particular Thomas Whittemore, "Orestes A. Brownson," *Trumpet and Universalist Magazine* 11 (November 11, 1829): 82. Whittemore, one of Brownson's constant critics, later asserted that Brownson had "sunk down" to the level of Unitarianism and that that movement in his thought was predictable. See ibid., 15 (February 8, 1834): 130.

not clearly reveal the existence of an all-good Being. Such a view appeared to be inconsistent with Brownson's previous emphasis upon reason's capacities. At this point he had not yet clearly articulated the motive for this view of reason's limits in coming to a knowledge of God, but the view was consistent with earlier declarations that reason indeed had its limits. He held that the origin of the idea of God did not come from reason but in fact came from a primitive revelation that was passed on from generation to generation by tradition. The origin of the idea of God's existence was emerging as an issue that would be a controlling interest for the remainder of his life. At this point in his intellectual development, though, his views seemed to many a radical departure from his previously articulated confidence in reason.

The charge that Brownson was an infidel or atheist missed the point he was trying to make: namely, that reason and nature were incapable of originating the "idea" of God in the human mind because nature by itself was incapable of generating an idea beyond itself. At this point, however, Brownson was not very clear about how this emerging view was congruent with his earlier positions.

Brownson never took criticism lightly, to say the least, but he found it particularly pernicious when it came from fellow Universalists who had supported free inquiry, private interpretation of the Bible, and the irrationality of banning persons from ecclesiastical societies because of their religious opinions. He was incensed, for example, when Universalists excommunicated (or, to be more technically correct, removed from fellowship) Rev. Abner Kneeland for positions they considered incompatible with Universalism. Although Brownson did not know Kneeland personally, he saw nothing offensive in his writings. For those who did not believe in an eternal hell, Brownson charged, it was incongruous that they would excommunicate someone for his religious opinions.[67]

By the end of 1829 Brownson had indeed become more radical in his views of the limits of biblical revelation, the judiciary provenance of reason over biblical revelation, the limits of reason's capacity to know God, the absolute right to freedom of inquiry, and the moral responsibility of all believers for social reform and amelioration, but he had not become an infidel, as his critics and some biographers have charged and as he himself later asserted in his

---

[67] "Rev. Abner Kneeland," *GAII* 7 (April 4, 1829): 106-07.

autobiography.[68] His articles from 1829 reveal clearly his exaspera-
tion with all forms of sectarianism and organized religion. He was
particularly irritated with his Universalist critics who attempted to
limit his freedom of inquiry. He never departed, however, from his
belief in God or in the value and utility of Christianity even though
he had by 1829 severely narrowed the doctrines and institutional
manifestations of Christianity.

By the end of 1829, Brownson himself felt alienated from Universalism, not because of the doctrine of universal salvation but because he felt that many Universalists could not accept the logical
trajectory of their own acceptance of freedom and free inquiry, and
their rejection of a dogmatic Christianity. On November 14, 1829,
Brownson announced that he was leaving the editorship of the *Gospel Advocate* by the end of the year because of the union of the paper
with Dolphus Skinner's (1800-69) *Evangelical Magazine*, another
Universalist paper.[69] Skinner was to become the new editor of the
combined papers and Brownson asserted that Skinner would probably be more acceptable to the readers of the *Gospel Advocate* than
Brownson had been because Skinner had firmer convictions than
Brownson on the divine authenticity of the Bible and the final salvation of all humanity.[70] On November 28, 1829, Brownson declared
that he was no longer a Universalist.[71] On December 7, 1829, he
became a corresponding editor of the *Free Enquirer*, but continued
that association for only a few months in 1830.

Brownson asserted in a few published letters of departure from
Universalism[72] that he could no longer abide by the kind of sectarianism he found even among Universalists. He came to believe that
their doctrinal hangovers from the tradition were inconsistent with
their advocacy of free inquiry. He also admitted that he wanted to be
freed from any creed so that he could in fact be a "friend to man."
Now, freed from religious boundaries he maintained that he could

[68] Henry Brownson, for example, noted his father's "avowed infidelity" during
this period. See *Early Life*, 42. On Brownson's own admission that he had become
an "unbeliever," see *Works* 5:39.
[69] On Skinner, see Edith Fox MacDonald, 133. Like Brownson, Skinner had
read theology with Samuel Loveland at Reading, VT prior to becoming a Universalist minister.
[70] "Union of Papers," *GAII* 7 (November 14, 1829): 362.
[71] "Universalist Hymn Book," *GAII* 7 (November 28, 1829): 377.
[72] "To the Universalists," *Free Enquirer* 2 (November 28, 1829): 38; "To Robert Dale Owen," ibid., 2 (December 12, 1829): 55-56; "Letter[s] to Mr. Doubleday,"
GAII 7 (December 26, 1829): 409, 417; "To the Editors of the Free Enquirer,"
Free Enquirer 3 (January 2, 1830): 95-96.

turn his attention fully to human improvement and concern for the working class, areas of activity, he charged, that his former Universalist friends thought inconsistent with his role as a minister of the gospel.[73] It was also clear from the *Gospel Advocate* that his evolving radical positions, particularly in support of Fanny Wright and the working class, had caused a decline in Universalist subscriptions to the paper and had created something of an economic threat for his publisher, Ulysses F. Doubleday (1792-1866), who had by December of 1829 lost confidence in Brownson's integrity.[74] Brownson indicated, furthermore, that the ideological battles of 1829 had taken their toll upon him; he was tired of the hostilities and anxious for peace. On September 14, 1830, the New England Convention of Universalists issued a declaration of disfellowship, officially excommunicating him from the denomination he had freely withdrawn from ten months earlier.[75]

Brownson's association with Universalism came to an end in 1829, but it was, as he noted in his autobiography,[76] the beginning of his intellectual career. His experience with Universalism helped him define the issues that would remain with him for much of his life, and although he would change and modify his positions in subsequent years, he repeatedly tried to come to terms with a number of questions that had exercised his mind during these early years: e.g., the origin of the idea of God, the roles of reason and revelation, the problem of evil, the nature and means of salvation, the relationship between Christianity and social justice, and the relationship between religion and the state.

---

[73] Brownson was upset with the Universalists who believed it futile for human beings to try to redeem society. For some substance to this charge, see Curtis Johnson, 68; and David L. Rowe, 44, 78, 80, 96, 126-29.

[74] See *GAII* 7 (December 26, 1829): 417. On Doubleday, see p. 363 n. 2.

[75] Hosea Ballou II, on September 14, 1829 headed a committee for the General Convention of Universalists for the New England States which resolved that Brownson had indeed renounced his faith in Christianity and by that renunciation he had dissolved his "fellowship with this body." See "Proceedings," of Universalist Convention, in *The Trumpet and Universalist Magazine* 12 (October 2, 1830): 54; see also, "O. A. Brownson," ibid., 12 (March 26, 1831): 154, and Russell Miller, 183.

[76] *Works* 5:19.

EDITORIAL PROCEDURES

The principal editorial aim in this and the subsequent volumes of Brownson's early works is to provide easy access to representative texts of his thinking on the subjects of religion, philosophy, literature and politics.[77] The current edition also aims to provide as accurate a transcription of the original texts as is possible given the ink-blotted condition of some of the extant copies of the journals for which Brownson wrote, and as readable a copy as is possible, which requires some uniformity and modernization of spellings, punctuation, and capitalization.

The documents for this multi-volume edition were selected on the basis of the following criteria: documents that (1) reflect Brownson's changing philosophy of religion; (2) show the earliest development of his thought, particularly between 1826 and 1835 (years not at all represented in Henry Brownson's edition); (3) reveal his political philosophy, especially his changing views of democracy, popular sovereignty, and the United States Constitution; (4) review major works in American literature (e.g., Emerson's *Nature*), focus on literary criticism, and/or address the need for a specific American scholarship; (5) outline his philosophical positions (his theory of knowledge and knowledge of God in particular) and philosophical evaluations of Cousin's eclecticism, Leroux's socialism, and Kant's transcendentalism; (6) articulate his arguments for religious liberty and separation of church and state; (7) outline his economic theory, particularly his views of the relationship of Christianity to social justice and his understanding of the rights of the working class.

Documents selected for inclusion demonstrate Brownson's sympathies and debates with John Locke, Thomas Reid (1710-96), Samuel Taylor Coleridge (1772-1834), Immanuel Kant (1724-1804), Victor Cousin (1767-1830), Félecité de Lamennais (1782-1854), Pierre Leroux (1797-1871), Jonathan Edwards, William Ellery Channing (1780-1842), Ralph Waldo Emerson (1803-82), Theodore Parker (1810-60), George Ripley (1802-80), Robert Dale Owen, John C. Calhoun (1782-1850), and a host of other philosophical, religious, literary and political thinkers who came into his purview during the period. The volumes include documents discussing the following

---

[77] For the most complete chronologically arranged bibliography of Brownson's works, see my *Orestes A. Brownson: A Bibliography, 1826-1876* (Milwaukee: Marquette University Press, 1997).

topics: revivalism in the "Burned-Over District" of upstate New York, the roles of reason and revelation in religion, the Kantian critique of the limits of reason, the understanding of sin and redemption, the role of religious sentiment, the social nature of religion, the nature and grounds of government, principles of literary criticism, the role of American democracy in divine providence, the rights of the working man to a just wage and the limits of egalitarianism.

The volumes contain various kinds of writings Brownson published in his early years: letters to editors, sermons, extended and brief essays, lectures, pamphlets, and books. Letters to editors generally articulated his point of view on current issues like slavery. Selected sermons are included, all of which were originally delivered orally. They were written with a listening audience in mind and demonstrate something of Brownson's forceful pulpit style, which some of his contemporaries have noted.[78] Brownson was known throughout his life primarily as an essayist. The essays included, dealing with a variety of religious and philosophical issues, are generally those that have a well-developed argument and thesis, but even these extended essays, serialized over a period of weeks and months, suffer from interruptions of time and include a number of digressions from the main point he is trying to make. But, this too is a characteristic of Brownson's style throughout his life as a writer. Shorter essays, usually brief summary statements of his beliefs, have also been included because of their clarity in defining Brownson's religious beliefs at a particular period of his development. Shorter essays at times articulate a position either of self-defense of what he had previously written or contain attacks upon positions with which he disagreed. The volumes, moreover, contain all of Brownson's early published pamphlets. They are pieces that appear to have been delivered orally as public lectures on a variety of topics from capital punishment to the necessity of particular social reforms. Three of his early books, *New Views of Christianity, Society and the Church* (1836), *Charles Elwood* (1840), and *The Mediatorial Life of Jesus* (1842) are included in the collection because of their substantial arguments and demonstration of major changes in his development as a religious philosopher and theologian.

There is little difficulty in establishing the authenticity of Brownson's writings between 1826 and 1844 because he signed most of his own articles. Brownson's authorship for those few articles he

---

[78] See, for example, Adin Ballou, *The Autobiography of Adin Ballou, 1803-1890* (Lowell, Mass.: The Vox Populi Press, 1896), 254-55.

did not sign (or for which he was not responsible as editor[79]) has been determined by examination of his known habits and style of writing, historical references to himself (which occurred repeatedly in his writings when he was responding to attacks or criticizing others), and the actual content which reflects his intellectual position. The documents in these volumes have been accurately reproduced from the original journals, pamphlets, and books in which they were printed; none of the selections have relied upon Henry Brownson's collected works because he at times took liberties with the text.

This edition has made some editorial corrections in the original text. Brownson himself aids in identifying errors in the text. He periodically reread his own published writings, noted the errors that occurred in the printed texts, and then published the errata in subsequent issues of the journals to which he contributed. I have made these corrections in the text whenever there is clear evidence from the published errata that corrections are necessary. All these editorial emendations in the text will be indicated in footnotes that explain the source of the correction.

The transcription of the documents aims at accuracy. It reproduces Brownson's stylistic aberrations, syntax, grammar, awkward constructions, ambiguities, archaic phraseology, and paragraphing. The editor, however, has silently corrected all misspellings and obvious typographical errors, standardized and used consistent spellings for all proper names, and modernized the use of capitalization and punctuation (particularly in eliminating excessive and meaningless commas and em dashes) for the sake of readability. Whenever it is clear that a word or words have been left out of the original text, moreover, they are inserted inside brackets within the text.

Brownson's writings require some editorial annotations that will help the reader identify unfamiliar texts, persons, and concepts to which Brownson refers. These editorial notes, most of which will be placed at the bottom of each page, will be kept to a minimum. Footnotes also locate previously published documents and passages mentioned in the text. Other cross-reference notes highlight major developments, changes and reversals in Brownson's intellectual arguments

---

[79] During his early years Brownson was editor for the following journals: *The Gospel Advocate and Impartial Investigator* (1829), *The Genesee Republican and Herald of Reform* (1830), *The Philanthropist* (1830-32), *The Boston Reformer (1836)*, *The Boston Quarterly Review* (1838-42), and *Brownson's Quarterly Review* (1844). While editor of these journals he wrote most of the unsigned articles.

and positions. Citations of texts and references that Brownson does not identify, moreover, are, whenever possible, identified in footnotes.

Brownson frequently cites and identifies biblical passages in his writings. Whenever he fails to identify biblical quotations or references, the editor provides the biblical source in brackets within the text. Most of the time Brownson used the King James Version of the Bible and that is the text used in this edition. The books of the Bible, moreover, are named and abbreviated here as in the King James Version, and the texts that Brownson frequently quoted from memory have been checked against the actual texts of the King James Version. Whenever he uses a translation other than the King James, he usually tells the reader which one he is using. But, for the most part, he preferred the King James Version and even after his conversion to Catholicism he asserted that that translation was much more readable than the Catholic Douay-Rheims English translation.

Explanatory footnotes are used to define words or phrases that have a technical meaning or are used in a special sense by Brownson, to delineate major philosophical and theological concepts, and to identify references to historical events that are not generally known. These notes will also give some brief bibliographical information for a more extensive examination of the references.

Identification footnotes are confined to those persons and places not widely known. References to Ralph Waldo Emerson, for example, do not need to be identified; but those to Pierre Leroux, the Saint-Simonians, Benjamin Constant (1767-1830), and Americans of less prominence than Emerson (e.g., Abner Kneeland, Hosea Ballou, James Freeman Clarke [1810-88]) are given brief identifying notes. The identifying note will occur the first time the name is mentioned in the texts. If the name is mentioned in subsequent volumes, the identification will not be repeated, but a footnote will make a cross reference to the volume containing the identifying information. All editorial footnotes will be surrounded by brackets (e.g., [Ed.]) to distinguish the editorial notes from Brownson's original footnotes.

Each volume follows a chronological order in arranging Brownson's writings. Some writings, however, will follow a topical-chronological order because they were serialized in journals under the same title over a long period of time. In the years 1826 to 1829 in particular, Brownson wrote a number of such serialized articles that must be read together to understand the flow of his arguments. All texts in this edition are arranged in the following fashion: titles of texts (as those titles appear in my bibliography of Brownson's writings) are given at the beginning of a work, followed by the source of the entry. For essays that are serialized over a period of time, the title is given at the beginning of the initial article, and only the date and pages of the subsequent articles appear within the text—unless the title or subtitle of the essay changes; in that case, the changed title or subtitle as well as the date and pages are given.

WORKS

1.

THE INFLUENCE OF RELIGION
ON PROSPERITY

The Christian Repository 7 (August 1826): 49-58

He shall be like a tree planted by the rivers of water, that bringeth
forth his fruit in his season; his leaf also shall not wither; and
whatsoever he doeth shall prosper.   Ps. 1:3.

The kindly influence of religion on the heart and condition of
man has, by most men, in all countries and in all ages of the world
been received and generally acknowledged. But she has been chiefly
confined to the *shades* of life. Mankind are willing to receive her as a
comforter, to call in her assistance on any occasion of deep distress, or
when suffering under some great and unexpected calamity. But it is
not only in the dark and adverse parts of a man's life that religion is
useful; she is no less salutary in the hour of prosperity than in the day
of adversity.

Those who would confine her influence to the gloom of disappointment or the melancholy of old age greatly mistake her nature.
She is indeed useful in such seasons and without her assistance we
should find it extremely difficult to bear up against the many painful
sensations that then unite to overwhelm us. But to those who are
acquainted with her character, to those whose hearts have felt her
warm invigorating touch, she will ever be a welcome companion.
They will seek her when the sun is clouded, wish her to cheer the
evening of life; but will wish her no less, will find her powers no
weaker in the morning of prosperity.

And then she puts on her lovelier charms and appears in her
more engaging dress. Imagination cannot present a more pleasing
object than the youth animated by the pure emotions of genuine
religion, than the man smiling with prosperity, obedient to her calls
and faithful in the discharge of her offices. "He is like a tree planted
by the rivers of water, that bringeth forth his fruit in his season; his
leaf also shall not wither, and whatsoever he doeth shall prosper."

A more lively and beautiful figure to represent his prosperity
could not have been selected from the whole compass of nature, than
the one chosen by the Psalmist in our text. A tree is an object of

beauty. Few things in nature can awaken more pleasing emotions in the bosom. To see one stand on a barren heath with short and shrubbed branches and withered leaves is, I confess, calculated to depress our feelings and overwhelm us with melancholy reflections. But to see one growing beside the running stream that moistens its roots and replenishes the soil, to behold it bearing its "fruit in its season," giving fragrance, beauty and shade to the surrounding scenery, will fill with admiration every lover of nature. Add the evergreen leaf with the assurance it "shall not wither," and you have a picture on which you may gaze with emotions of delight and tranquility.

To point out the man that is likened unto *this tree,* and show the increase of his prosperity is the design of what follows.

The Psalmist has assisted us in the first part of this inquiry. He begins by informing us he is blessed: "Blessed is the man that walketh not in the counsel of the ungodly, nor standeth in the way of sinners, nor sitteth in the seat of the scornful. But his delight is in the law of the Lord, and in his law doth he meditate day and night" [Ps. 1:1-2]. Such a one, we are informed in our text, "shall be like a tree planted by the rivers of water," etc. He is one then, we may say, who has withdrawn himself from ungodliness, has not mingled with the vicious multitude, nor joined with scoffers, one who studies the law of God, carefully inquires his duty, cultivates the warm and generous emotions of religion, feels them in his heart, and acknowledges them in his conduct; one we may suppose who has enlarged his mind, expanded his heart with benevolence, learned "to do justly, to love mercy, and to walk humbly with his God" [Mic. 6:8]; one whose hands are clean, whose intentions pure, whose conscience void of offence, who listens with interest to the calls of humanity, commiserates the calamities of his brethren, studies to remove the load of common misery, and to enable all to smile beneath the gracious bounty of our heavenly Father.

He is one who has subdued his desires for unlawful pleasures, weaned his affections from things of this world, and placed them on things above.[1] One who puts his trust in his God rests all his hopes of happiness on the will of his Father pays his early vows in the sanctuary, rejoices to come before the Lord, and bows himself before the high God. And, to sum up his character in a word, he is one who

---

[1] [Ed. When Brownson republished this essay in 1829, he made the following editorial comments on this passage: "The expression, this world should be restricted to the vain things of the Jewish age, or if applied at the day, to the pleasures of sense, in opposition to those above, or to the more noble things of the Gospel, which is righteousness." See *GAII* 7 (September 19, 1829): 292.]

avoids vice and vicious companions, loves virtue, reverences religion, and is kind, generous and humane in all his intercourse with his brethren. Such is the man who is religious, such is the man that shall stand beside *the rivers of water,* yield his *fruit in his season,* whose *leaf also shall not wither, and whatsoever he doeth shall prosper.*

Let us then turn to consider the increase of his prosperity, and to show in what manner he is more prosperous than the *irreligious or bad man.*

1. *Prosperity is increased to him because religion has prepared his mind for enjoyment.* If we look into the heart of the bad man, we shall find it filled with a multitude of rough and discordant principles, which are continually raging and opposing each other. We shall see inordinate love of wealth, unreasonable ambition for greatness, a burning thirst for unlawful pleasures and sensual gratification. These are increased by appetite, strengthened by indulgence, and confirmed by habit. Their demands are loud and imperious. Their objects different, and often contradictory. The man is compelled to follow each, which must be done at the expense of its rival. Thus it happens, the satisfaction gained by the gratification of one favorite passion is generally lost in the disappointment it occasions another. A thousand desires are constantly springing in his bosom, so equally balanced in their weight, so nearly powerful in their strength that he no sooner decides to follow one than his purpose is shaken, and he is drawn back by another. Hence he lives in constant turmoil and perplexity. Hence his mind in a state of perpetual fluctuation hangs vacillating between these imperious masters; all which he wishes to obey, but their variety and discordance is such that he seldom yields obedience to any. Or grant some one, more powerful than the rest, has gained the ascendency and reduced the others to submission, a thousand obstacles intervene, which delay or embitter its gratification.

We grant the man wealth; we grant his external condition may appear flourishing; his houses and lands may increase; his fields yield the plenteous harvest. But something is wanting still to complete that plenitude of felicity he desires. His mind, yea his heart, has become attached to his possessions. A mean, sordid, avaricious disposition, ever characteristic of wealth, renders him incapable of happiness, deadens all the finer feelings, cools all the warm emotions of the heart, closes all the small springs of pleasure, which excite and spread joy and delight through the bosom of the good man.

Or is he bent on worldly pleasure? Every lisp of censure carries dejection to his soul, and fills him with the most painful sensations. But the good man having subdued these vain desires hears unmoved the praise or scorn of the world. Conscious of the rectitude of his own heart and the purity of his intentions, all *within* is calm and heaven will take care of that which is *without.*

Still further, the bad man has a never-failing source of uneasiness and deep regret in the improper means he has used to gratify his appetites and passions. The cries of the injured orphan, the complaints of the oppressed widow haunt his sleeping and waking hours! Bleeding innocence torn from the bosom of her parents, from the society of her friends, rifled of her charms, ruined, left bleaching in the tempest of fortune, strikes daggers to his soul! Conscience tells him his guilt is great, his condemnation is sealed. Trembling at the account she reads, horror presents him before the bar of his God. His own heart condemns him, God is greater than his heart! Struck aghast at the picture, "sleep becomes a stranger, food insipid, society wearisome, pleasure disgusting, and life itself a cruel bitter."

But the good man having ever aimed well, trusts the mercy of his God for the pardon of those offences which through the weakness of his nature he may have committed. His past life brings to his mind no instance of cruelty or deception; no enormous crime or act of injustice. He delights to call up the hours that have gone by. He can view them with a placid serenity. He looks around on the present with pleasing tranquility, and forward with confidence and hope.

2. *Prosperity is increased to a good man because he is free from all the terrifying apprehensions of unseen calamities and impending ruin.* The bad man has no source of happiness but the world. All his dependence is placed on the good of fortune; his wealth, his pleasures, his family, or friends. Little experience is sufficient to convince those of the least discernment that these are not durable goods. "Riches take to themselves wings and fly away" [Prov. 23:5].[2] The elements often burst their rage with resistless fury, in one moment hurl with them the labors of years, and leave him destitute. Fame's shrill clarion may sound his achievements, proclaim the multitude of his friends and pleasures; competition may slink to the caverns of envy, and slander to the shades of night. Yet the sun of prosperity will grow weary of gilding the habitation of uninterrupted repose; the clouds of sorrow will arise, the tempest of adversity gather round, and the thunder of disappointment burst upon him. His friends will leave him, his name be enrolled on the black list of infamy, or crowded away with the thousands that are—die and are forgotten!

[2] [Ed. Brownson quotes Prov. 23:5 from memory: "Riches certainly make themselves wings, they fly away as an eagle toward heaven."]

These are ordinary occurrences. These fill his mind with dreadful apprehensions and the most gloomy forebodings. In the absence of *real* he adopts *imaginary* ills and mourns over anticipated woe as though he actually felt its direful hand. But the good man, having cultivated his mind, acquired habits of virtue, has a source of happiness independent of his external condition. He has a fund within himself, a permanent fund, whence he can continually draw fresh pleasures. He has learned all sublunary things are evanescent. He expects they will leave him. He guards against their flight; but prepares himself to meet, unmoved, the shock. But should they leave him, he is not destitute; his peace of mind remains. That rests on the rectitude of his heart, the purity of his intentions, the consciousness that he has ever discharged his duty and been faithful over those things which were placed under his care. This source of happiness no change of fortune can destroy. It remains the same whether she smiles or frowns, and this being the source of his greatest and chief happiness, he can dread no attack from without, fear no approaching calamity or impending ruin. He trusts in his God. "He shall hide him [me] in his pavilion, in the secret of his tabernacle shall he hide him, he shall place him upon a rock" [Ps. 27:5]. Hence, secure from all imaginary ills, from all forebodings of future woe, he can enjoy his prosperity with cheerfulness and tranquility.

3. *But prosperity is still farther increased to the good man by the generous manner in which he uses it.* Reason and religion both assert the fact that everything is good and proper when properly used; that the only evil there is in anything is the improper manner in which it may be used. Hence the bad man by the improper use he makes of his prosperity, converts it into adversity. He allows it to corrupt his temper, debase his mind, produce a feverish and sickly appetite, enervate the nobler faculties of his soul, harden his heart, blind his eyes and deafen his ears to the complaints, sufferings and wretched condition of those around him; to generate that frame of mind which becomes confident of its own importance and superiority; proud and haughty looks, with contempt on others, and secures their hatred and detestation. He hears no one proclaim his benedictions; sees no one happy through his munificence; has no consoling reflection that he has studied to lighten the load of common misery; receives the kind embrace of no worthy, virtuous and affectionate friend. The behavior of all with whom he associates is characterized by cold civility, or disgusting obsequiousness. Hence he languishes in the midst of his studied refinements and vast possessions, envied and envying, unloving and unbeloved.

But on the other hand, mark the good man. Religion has softened his heart, rendered him feelingly alive to the wants and distresses of others. He has not possessed wealth for himself alone, he has made it a common blessing. He has compassionated the sufferings of the wretched; his presence has gladdened the lonely cottage; his bounty rescued the hungry soul from death. He sees a happy land smiling with content, made so by his benefactions. The blessing has returned upon his own head; and the secret delight of benevolence and gratitude has fully demonstrated the fact, "it is more blessed to give than to receive" [Acts 20:35]! He can adopt the language of the once prosperous Job: "When the ear heard me then it blessed me; and when the eye saw me it gave witness to me; because I delivered the poor that cried, and the fatherless and him that had none to help him. The blessing of him that was ready to perish came upon me, and I caused the widows' heart to sing for joy. I put on righteousness and it clothed me; my judgment was as a robe and a diamond. I was eyes to the blind, and feet was I to the lame. I was a father to the poor; and the cause which I knew not I searched out. My root was spread out by the waters, and the dew lay all night upon my branch. My glory was fresh within me, and my bow was renewed in my hand" [Job 29:11-16; 19-20].

4. But lastly, *prosperity is increased to the good man from the happy prospect he has in his children.* The greatest and chief concern of a man's life is his children. To provide for them, to see them walk in the paths of usefulness, fill places of honor and respectability, constitutes a large proportion of the felicity allotted his pilgrimage journey of life. While the bad man has been engrossed in the cares of the world, neglecting the education of his children, vainly thinking to ensure their felicity by worldly splendor, the good man has been faithfully cultivating the minds of his children, suppressing their evil propensities, drawing out the latent virtues of their nature, and with "pious care," endeavored to form them to all that is truly great or good in man. While the bad man has the mortification to see his children grow up with all their natural propensities, unrestrained appetites and passions strengthened by his own indulgence and confirmed by his own practices; while he sees them plunge into excess, sink in the vortex of dissipation, rove in the labyrinths of folly and inconsistency, or fall before the tribunals of justice, the good man sees his grow up in the ways of virtue, walk the paths of wisdom, sing in the bowers of understanding, or ramble over the flowery lawns of religion; sees them shine with lovely graces, endeared by a peculiar sweetness of temper to their parents, attracting the esteem of their ac-

quaintance and the friendship of all who know them. Early impressed with filial piety, they remember him, and do not forsake him in his old age; but study to make his decline of life smooth and easy. Hence "his leaf also shall not wither." He sees his children green, they do not wither away with evil or vicious companions; dissipation does not blast their verdure; and even the storms of the winter of life cannot destroy their freshness. They bud in his bosom in this terrestrial soil, but they shall bloom with unfading glory in the bosom of his heavenly Father in the regions above. Hence the influence of religion on prosperity, hence the superiority of the good man over the bad; a mind free from perturbation, guilt, or remorse, firmly relying on his God, believing his pardon sufficient for the past, praising for the present, and trusting him for the future, a heart susceptible of the highest felicity rendered supremely happy in himself in the love and gratitude of others in the good conduct and bright and brightening prospects of his children. "His wife is a fruitful vine by the sides of his house, his children like olive plants round about his table" [Ps. 128:3].

Such is the influence of religion on the prosperous, and such I presume is the desire of each of my respected auditors. Cultivate, then, suffer me to entreat you, the benevolent affections of the heart, acquire habits of virtue, place your dependence on God, keep his commandments, retreat from vice and the company of the ungodly, and this prosperity shall be yours; you "shall be like trees planted beside the rivers of water, that bear their fruit in their season, and whatsoever you do shall prosper."

2.

AN ESSAY ON THE PROGRESS OF TRUTH

The Gospel Advocate and Impartial Investigator
5-6 (November 17, 1827): 361-62

Mr. Editor: I this week commence a series of numbers on the progress of moral reform throughout the world. I shall continue them if I have leisure and health, until I either exhaust my subject or my knowledge. The importance and interesting nature of this subject, as well as my own method of treating it, will be unfolded as I proceed, hence need not be labored in an exordium. As a motto to my inquiry I select Isaiah, 35:1.

> *The wilderness and the solitary place shall be glad for them; and the desert shall rejoice and blossom like the rose.*

The final emancipation of the human race from sin, misery and death is a source of pleasing contemplation and may justly employ the attention of those who despair of ever finding consolation from the prospective improvement of man while an inhabitant of this sublunary state. At a convenient time, we should not hesitate to wing imagination through regions of ether, and survey a beatified universe bending around the throne of light, bursting amid the rays of Jehovah's love; but the present requires us to consider what amelioration the progress of truth will make in the condition of human society below.

Whatever bliss there may be in store for us in that unseen world to which we are all hastening, the present is all we can call our own. We are now inhabitants of the earth, and our chief inquiry should be how can we render it a pleasing and desirable habitation? I am a believer in life and immortality beyond the grave; but I am not ambitious of being one of that number who forget earth for heaven; who, to ensure the joys of that invisible kingdom, forego the rational pleasures of this.

The present generation owes a duty to all succeeding ones. The course we take will have a greater or less effect upon the morals or happiness of our latest posterity. We live not for ourselves alone; we are connected with all nations, all generations of men. Let us not,

then, because we expect soon to remove to some distant clime, de-
molish or suffer to decay, the institutions necessary to give peace and
felicity to our successors. There are those, who think, if our future
welfare or happiness after death be secured, there is no necessity of
troubling ourselves about our condition here; and if this generation
was the last of the human race, there would be some force in the
consideration. But "one generation passeth and another cometh, but
the earth abideth forever" [Eccles. 1:4]. The parent finds sufficient
inducement to labor, that he may secure his child a competent support; the philanthropist looks through futurity to ages yet unborn,
and, while his bosom swells with the prospect, he invokes the genius
of improvement to transmit them such institutions as shall preserve
external peace and internal tranquility—to transmit them such a fund
of knowledge that the evils with which we and our forefathers have
been afflicted may never reach them.

Is this no inducement to labor? Look back then upon past ages;
what deplorable ignorance has debased the human mind! Man has
been the slave of both civil and ecclesiastical tyrants. The dignity of
his nature has been forgotten amid the bigotry and superstition with
which he has been governed. At one time, he is seen rushing with
ruthless fury against his brother; at another bowing and cringing
before a God of his own manufacture, the property of a fellow lordling,
who supports the luxury of his table with the produce of his blood;
the dupe of designing hypocrites who make him sick that they may
be paid for curing him; filled with a zeal for God, fired with enthusiasm for his law, he is seen dealing forth death upon all whose zeal and
enthusiasm are different from his own. Robbed by the political despot of the right of pursuing happiness and enjoying the fruit of his
labor, divested by the priest of the liberty of conscience and all the
felicity of mental independence, he rises in gaudy ignorance or splendid poverty, in the most abject servitude and the most degrading
superstition. A prey to all the evils of his physical constitution and
the calamities incident to life, rendered thrice doubly severe by his
own folly and the exorbitant exactions of his brethren; war sweeps
off its millions, carries mourning to as many cottages and childless-
ness to as many mothers. Theological wrangling, intestine divisions
and domestic discord destroys what little repose might otherwise have
been received! Say, ye friends of the human race! Do you wish those
evils to go down to posterity? Have you no anxiety to remove these
evils that the wrongs and outrages which you have suffered may not
be entailed upon your offspring?

But if these considerations have no weight with the philanthropist of the day, it only shows the degradation of their minds, the narrowness of their conceptions, and the feeble claim they have to the name they assume; and no stronger argument is required to show the importance of a reformation throughout the world. Those, however, who can join in the prospective improvement of our race while here, reasons sufficient to call forth their exertions, will contemplate with delight the improvement itself and linger with inexpressible gratitude to God on the certainty it will in due time be effected.

The improvement of which we speak or the reformation which we desire is one that will recognize the original equality of the human family, secure to them all the rights which nature has given them, whether as individuals or members of society. The government of the country recognizes many of our original rights and in a good degree secures them. The reformation we seek will base all institutions, whether civil or ecclesiastical, upon this original equality and will call forth all the energies of statesmen, moralists or divines to preserve it. Government will then aim at the good of the governed; political and other rulers will be the servants, not the masters of the people; [rulers] will be chosen for the good of the whole, not of a few, and be supported from a conviction of their utility, not because they have been born to hereditary advantages, or been forced upon us by circumstances over which our partiality for ancient usages would give us no control.

Men will then be free in their persons, free to pursue happiness, and free to enjoy the good of their labors. Amid this freedom, industry will awake and all will be enabled to find a competent support. Temptations to vice will be removed; crimes will become less and less frequent till they finally disappear, and our jails and penitentiaries be thrown open, or converted to abodes of virtue and happiness.

The mind will then have recovered its independence; conscience will not then be bound by the fetters of priestcraft; but it will become the monitor to virtue, the friend of mankind; [it] will entwine around each heart the cords of fraternal affection and no more break a brother on the wheel or burn him at the stake. Reason will have regained her long lost dominions; her mild and gentle laws will extend peace through all her empire and preserve the quietness and felicity of every bosom. The happy children of men will form the cheerful circle around the evening fire, give free exercise to all the kind and benevolent feelings of the heart, with no gloomy personage to destroy their heaven born harmony with his furious declamations and horrid denunciations! Implicit faith in unintelligible dogmas will find no adherents. Each will claim the right of examination; whatever is not congenial with facts, corroborated by universal experience, will be laid aside as a remnant of ancient superstition.

Religion will then rest for its support on a knowledge of human nature, not on the assertions of ignorant or interested men. It will not be a fruitful source of unhappy contention, will not tend to alienate the affections of brethren, nor drive them to the commission of the foulest crimes that ever blackened the page of history; but it will encourage all those good actions, cherish all those kind feelings, render all that mutual assistance which our dependent situation requires.

Such is the improvement we seek, such is the reformation that will be accomplished when men shall have recovered mental independence, and shall dare reason on the nature and propriety of existing institutions; when they shall acknowledge no law but *reason*, no religion but *justice*, no morality but *humanity* in all its forms.
(November 24, 1827): 369-71

The opposition to the emancipation of the human race from the bondage of their numerous masters will be long and obstinate. There are so many notions abroad; so many vague and inconsistent theories are proclaimed by the learned, and enforced by those who claim the direction of the public mind, upheld by those in authority, and eagerly embraced by the multitude; the simple dictates of reason, the plain injunctions of morality, are so readily consigned to forgetfulness that he who comes forward with a plain and rational scheme is in danger of being doomed to suffer the contempt of the ignorant and the persecution of the designing.

The experiment has been fairly tried: to the advocates of a blind and unnatural religion and to the adherents of a cruel and despotic policy, every indulgence has been granted; we have listened with the most profound attention; we have believed with the most yielding credulity and obeyed with the most persevering enthusiasm. The popular instructors, from their first existence, have contended earnestly for "the faith," extolled the purity of their principles, and the wonderful efficacy of their instructions in making society virtuous and man universally happy. Alas! discord has marked their proceedings, confusion their preaching; and notwithstanding man was totally depraved at first, he has been growing worse ever since!

The circumstances of the age call aloud for reform. There has been so much tinsel; so many pretenses have been made; so much noise about religion and divine communications has been heard; that men, whose minds have been enlightened by science, whose hearts are warmed by philanthropy, and whose bosoms bleed with compassion for the human race, have turned with disgust from everything bearing such a recommendation, and sought in nature alone a remedy for infatuated man. They may have gone too far; but every truly enlightened mind will reject with disdain every notion that contradicts the great principles of universal existence or supersedes the necessity of studying them. I am no enemy to religion; but I would listen with attention and examine with the most vigilant caution; whatever is not conducive to our happiness while here, I reject as unworthy our attention. Happy would it be for all men, if they would come to this conclusion. But the obstacles to be surmounted in coming to this are many. They rise like mountains, and we tremble as we survey the broadness of their base and the sublimity of their tops. The errors of antiquity are so numerous and so tenaciously embraced that no wonder timorous souls are despondent. No improvement can be effected while men retain their veneration for institutions merely because they are ancient; nor until many, who now labor with the most persevering assiduity to perpetuate such veneration, shall cease from their pernicious task and turn their attention to ascertain what is beneficial to man in his social and individual capacity. But the struggle to accomplish this will be long and arduous. Princes who hold their power on the precarious tenure of artificial distinctions in the human family will be unwilling to enlighten their subjects. Truth is dreaded by them for they well know the right by which they govern has no existence in the nature of things. Should people learn [that] the God of the universe made all men originally equal, privileged classes would lose their prerogatives, and be reduced to a level with the rest of mankind. Kings would then depend on the suffrages of their subjects for their election. This, the crowned heads of the earth well know. Hence it was [that] they saw with consternation the independence of this country and armed their united forces against republican France. It is the apprehension that truth may enter the dark recesses of their deluded, degraded subjects, that binds together the "Holy Alliance" of Europe; and it is this that drives them to extinguish every ray of liberty that might for a moment illume the darkness of despotism!

Kings and potentates will, from a regard to their own interests, oppose any innovation upon the old order of things. Their power is founded in ignorance, supported by arbitrary and unnecessary distinctions, and has no recommendation but its hoary age. Consequently they have nothing so much to fear as a spirit of inquiry and close investigation. Such a spirit would undermine the thrones on which they are seated and trample in the dust every vestige of their tyranny!

They will, it must be expected, use every exertion in their power to prevent any alteration in the condition of their people.

Our religious education and the nature of our ecclesiastical institutions are much more powerful obstacles in the march of improvements. These form an impediment much more difficult to remove because supported by more stubborn, more numerous, and more complicated prejudices. It is here, too, where reformation is most needed. Whoever has turned over the historic page and traced man through his *religious* career has wandered in the midst of crime through scenes the most foul and horrible that fancy can paint. Man—though doomed to suffer from the physical circumstances of his condition, though he is a child of sickness and distress, a prey to every calamity, affected by every change in this ever changing state—may forget the whole in the magnitude and numberless variety of the evils he has heaped upon him by his pretended *spiritual assistants!*

From time immemorial men have formed themselves into religious associations; and—under the pretense of superior sanctity, of more successfully promoting their own and their brethren's welfare—have presumed to dictate to the world what it must believe and what ceremonies it must observe. To over awe the mind and make it submissive to what all the better feelings of the heart oppose, inspiration has been pretended, and the voice of the Almighty has been made to sanction errors too absurd to be believed on less authority. The vendors of this inspiration have usurped an undue ascendancy over the lives and consciences of men, as degrading to those who obey as it is profitable to those who rule.

Particular churches have been established and the priest has promised heaven to all who unite and denounced the most horrid doom upon all who refuse. A creed was drawn up for the church; the more unintelligible the better because the aid of the priest in its explication becomes thus the more necessary; a system of external duties is enjoined, the more absurd, or the farther removed from common utility the better for its observance thus more clearly draws the line of distinction between those who belong to the church and those denominated the world. All that is required to maintain the purity of one's character is to believe this unintelligible creed and damn all who doubt it; to perform the external duties enjoined, which usually consist in assembling together, making a few grimaces and genuflexions, repeating over, parrot like, a few unmeaning words, in doing penance, supporting the church, and treating with infinite contempt or extreme cruelty all who pay less reverence to such pious *indispensables.* This maintains one's claim to holiness, opens to him the doors of the church here, and of heaven hereafter, gives him a passport to regions of glory, and entitles him to endless beatitude in the mansions of felicity.

A class of men have been produced, fanatics, who have labored with a zeal and perseverance worthy a better cause, which, had they been properly directed, would have done honor to themselves and been of the highest utility to man. But alas! their zeal was not according to knowledge. They have been deceived by an unreal form; they have contended for a phantom; overlooked the great duties of justice and humanity; encouraged a blind worship, for they knew not what; tolerated a bigoted, superstitious religion equally derogatory from God and unprofitable to man.

Antiquity is replete with instruction. So many valuable lessons are taught by her examples that we should frequently recur to her sacred archives. The farther our retrospection runs the more have we to deplore; more prevalent and more absurd is the superstition. Implicit reliance on the priest, augur, soothsayer, sibyl, or whatever name designated their character comprised nearly the whole of man's moral and religious duties. The priests were mere tools of state; whatever they taught was designed to promote the interest of their masters or to advance their own ambitious prospects. Thus it was with the priests of Greece, of Rome, and many of the oriental nations. Their religion was upheld for the express purpose or exacting that submission and that support, which they despaired of otherwise obtaining. And the whole machinery was as much regulated by the state government, as any other department of state police. The philosophers, indeed, discarded the silly and absurd tales of which their religion was composed; they would have labored to enlighten the minds and lead men to the practice of moral virtue, but the infatuated multitude ever true to the hand that oppresses them, were the first to condemn any effort made for their amelioration.

The Jewish theocracy, however useful it might have been in its first establishment, soon became no better than that of other nations. The priests usurped nearly all the power and seemed to regard little else than the receiving of their tithes and other offerings. They uttered, to be sure, the most horrid denunciations if the people thought for themselves or became weary of their hierarchy. If the people worshiped Baal, notwithstanding they themselves had made the worship of the true God too grievous to be borne, they usually succeeded in overwhelming the nation with calamity, and when led away captive by their enemies, told them it was the just resentment of the Almighty for their apostasy. But all this was apparently not because they cared more for one religion than another, only to support that one which best supported them.

(December 8, 1827): 385-87

Jesus Christ about 18 centuries ago appeared. He digested the crude notions of religion then prevalent, elected from the systems already known what was universally obligatory to which he made some new accessions, and finally gave us a religion of reason and common sense as pure, doubtless, as the circumstances of our condition require. His tragical death and the subsequent preaching of his disciples gave his doctrine a rapid and wide extension; but it had no sooner gained ascendancy over the ancient religion than those in authority sought to make it subservient to state policy, dependent on courts and levees.

Christianity was diverted from its natural course and instead of ameliorating the condition of man, making him more happy by making him virtuous, it uncapped the bottomless pit and permitted monsters of cruelty and blood to fill the earth with rapine and war. The sickly wretch substituted for the fair daughter of heaven, never softened the heart, never called into action the virtuous principles of our nature, but allowed the appetites all their force and the passions to rage uncontrolled.

Be sound in the faith, tell a religious experience, and support the church, was a passport through the society of the holy here, and to the regions of the glorified hereafter! This maintained the sanctity of one's character, regardless of moral goodness, and this being all that was required, little more was sought. Justice and mercy fell into disrepute, humanity was unknown, and common sympathy consigned to the land of forgetfulness. Zeal for the church usurped the place of every other virtue. Then were seen swarms of mendicants pillaging the scanty pittance of the villagers for which they gave indeed a few *holy relics*, such as "sanctified rice."

> Tears which saints had wept,
> A thousand years in vials kept.[1]

Then were seen hordes of monks who cloaked every species of iniquity under the sacred garb of piety constantly laboring to increase the wealth and independence of the church. Then, too, holy enthusiasm raged. Mothers, without a complaint, could see their sons, and wives their husbands, torn from their warm embrace, confined

[1] [Ed. Not able to identify quotation.]

in the dungeon of the Inquisition, brought before the *Ghostly Father* or burned on the *Auto da Fe!*

Different in forms, but the same in spirit, are the religionists of the present day. Men, professedly holy, do not hesitate to declare from the desk, the supposed guardian of virtue, that the abandoned profligate is *less dangerous* in society and more likely to be *saved* than the honest upright citizen, renowned for his benevolence and general humanity. Faith is raised over morality and those who style themselves sound in *that* arrogate to themselves all that is correct in theory or virtuous in practice and denounce the most horrid doom upon all who do not bear the same character.

They indeed have an ardent love for God, manifest great anxiety to maintain the glory of his power and the honor of this character. They are ever ready to let him save from endless woe souls which his veracity stands pledged to make eternally miserable. But alas! they have so much to do to assist Omnipotence, they are unable to regard the wants of a neighbor. Or, they have time to bestow a casual glance upon the necessities of a brother, their benevolence evaporates in prayer for this never dying soul, while the body is left to starve!

Men frequently change the name of their sect while they retain the spirit of their former opinions. The primitive Christians, with few exceptions, retained all the distinctive features of the several systems of faith from which they had been converted. A Jewish Christian was in general still a Jew, except in name and the observance of some few ceremonies. Papal Rome was pagan Rome, under a new appellation. Images of gods were replaced by pictures of Christ and his apostles, deified heroes by canonized saints, and the one as it had been with the other.

The beads, crucifixes and holy trinkets, held in so much reverence by thousands of *nominal* Christians, are good evidence that the gospel of Christ, in the manner it was preached, has not much elevated their conceptions of things, or given them any very exalted ideas of God or his service. The superstitious members of the Roman and Greek churches who regard these trifles are no more worshiper of the true God than were the blind votaries of Bacchus, Hercules or Apollo; nor indeed Protestants who place their highest sanctity in the observance of certain days or ceremonies—they are as much idolaters as were the deluded adorers of Wodin or Thor.[2]

---

[2] [Ed. Bacchus, in Roman mythology, the god of wine and revelry; Hercules, in Greek mythology, the son of Zeus and the god of strength; Apollo, in Greek and Roman mythology, the god of music, poetry, prophecy, and medicine, who represents manly youth and beauty; Wodin or Woden (Wodan), the English name for

Most European nations, together with the civilized part of America, embrace unanimously the Christian religion; but it is not infrequently we find the *spirit* of that blessed doctrine exhibited in much greater perfection by the untutored natives of our forests. The *meek and humble* disciple of Christ may blush for his own want of goodness when he marks the native generosity of the savage.

Little research is necessary to show the rational man that the boasted religions of the day bear strong marks of consanguinity to the long since obsolete superstitions of ages we hope may never return.

The religions of Greece and Rome are condemned, and justly. No man of common sense, but discards the deistical notions of the orientals, and the arrogant pretensions of the Pharisees of Palestine; but the most popular sentiments of our time are only a gross compound of them all in which each ingredient retains all its peculiarities. The man that should draw a parallel of ancient faith, particularly of the Pharisees, with the most approved modern notions would be pronounced a severe satirist on the faith, and if he was in the synagogue would soon be cast out.

The directors of our opinions have discovered this identity, and to prevent any evil which might fall upon themselves, have very discreetly forbid the comparison, and prohibited investigation and the exercise of our own understanding. The reformer wishes to convince the people, the notions they imbibe are supported neither by reason or revelation; he is commanded to lay reason aside, and is told the priest, *who cannot lie,* has declared these notions to be inspired. He refers them back to their origin, explains the causes which gave them birth, the reasons which first gained them notoriety, and the circumstances which have perpetuated their existence to the present time; the vengeance of the clerical despot here and the threatened wrath of Omnipotence hereafter is the reward he receives for his benevolent intentions.

The reformer expostulates: "God had made man a rational being, can he be displeased with the exercise of the noblest faculty he has given us? The notions you imbibe, O people! are unreasonable and contradictory; they are dishonorable to God and injurious to man. The consequences of such sentiments are seen in that spirit of contention which pervades every department of society: in the readiness with which parents, for the love of God, can discountenance

the chief god, Odin, of Norse mythology; Thor, in Norse mythology, the son of Odin and the god of war, thunder, and strength.]

their children, and children their parents for the same cause; in the alienated affections of brethren; the hostility, the animosity with which brother attacks brother, and sister rails against sister. O peace! heaven-born world! there is music in thy name, but alas! theological wrangling has driven thee from our bosoms, and banished thee from our dwellings! The domestic circle is invaded and tranquility forsakes the fireside! Malice and rage arm the priest, fanaticism the multitude! Ignorance and cupidity urge them on, and though *Religion* may flourish, *Happiness* is gone. Where is the calm and dignified Christian? Where is the man that dare assert the independence of the mind? Where the society not torn by contending factions? Where the community not distracted by intestine broils and the heart-withering conduct of professed religionists? O whither has wandered the genius of Christianity! Whither has fled the native benevolence and forbearance of the human heart? God of Love! Restore to man the exercise of his reason that in contending for religion he may not destroy everything worthy the name!"

> O the lover may
> Distrust that look which steals his soul away:
> The babe may cease to think that it can play
> With heaven's rainbow; alchymists may doubt
> The shining gold their crucible gives out;
> But Faith—fanatic *Faith*—once wedded fast
> To some dear falsehood, hugs it to the last.[3]

The appeal to facts, to the benevolent feelings of the heart, but enrages the deluded votaries of a blind and unnatural religion, and calls down upon him who makes it the curses and indignation of the ignorant, the superstitious, the bigoted and the designing. "Licentious Innovator!" "Infidel!" "Blasphemer of God and Reviler of the Saints!" are the honorable epithets he receives and the names by which posterity shall learn the extent of his philanthropy.

Men have so long been taught to distrust their own reason, so long heard enforced as the only means of their eternal salvation [to] receive implicitly what the priest shall dictate that the great body of the people have forgotten that all were originally equal and endowed with the same right to judge for themselves. They consider the various notions transmitted them by circumstances of which they never think are absolutely necessary to maintain proper reverence for the

---

[3] [Ed. Thomas Moore (1779-1852), *Lalla Rookh* (1817), "The Veiled Prophet of Khorassan," pt.3, lines 351-57.]

God of heaven; they consider them sacred as the light of Jehovah's throne and they would sooner part with life itself than renounce them. They believe their eternal all is at stake if they do not swallow all the ancient whims however absurd or pernicious—all, all is gone! A place of eternal, inconceivable torture remains as their inevitable doom!

(December 15, 1827): 393-94

The least reflection, one would suppose, might convince the most skeptical that this excessive veneration, this implicit reliance, is the result of the craft of a class of man who wish to revel in luxury without sharing the common burden. That man must be grossly infatuated who imagines the All-wise parent of nature has suspended the eternal weal of his children upon the contingency of their believing certain religious dogmas. The religious opinions of the age may indeed have been transmitted to us from remote antiquity; they may be consecrated by the blood of martyrs and endeared by the memory of our fathers who believed them; but the man who disclaims all authority but reason and all creeds but truth will consider all these external ornaments of little importance and every argument founded upon them he will ever treat with contempt.

The grand secret is disclosed. No man is against reason until reason is against him. People that reason cannot be duped. In order to maintain their authority over our minds priests have told us it is offensive to God that we exercise this noble faculty. Should men reason, the injustice of their practices would be discovered and the solidity of their claims be called in question.

Many of those sentiments which have been outstripped by the improvements in natural and moral science were, no doubt, in their first establishment useful. The first preachers of them considered them true and very likely proclaimed them with the benevolent intention of ameliorating the condition of man. It was probably by the same desire that they were induced to represent them as coming from God; and with the wish of insuring them a cordial reception, they were also led to make it criminal to doubt their truth. But ambitious men converted the precautions, those philanthropists had to preserve their sentiments, to a source of individual aggrandizement, assuming to themselves the prerogatives of the Most High; pretending to be under the immediate influence of his spirit, they declared to the people, "whatever we do, however absurd or pernicious in its tendency, is suggested by the Holy Ghost and you will be torn by demons if you do not believe it."

A traffic in human souls the most deleterious in its consequences was carried on by these spiritual merchandisers; but the people, however much oppressed and borne down by the heavy burdens they had to bear, must not complain because their complainings would be against heaven whose vengeance would flash instant death upon them if they dared murmur against his will.

They brought forward their sacred books, written in a style and language wholly unintelligible to the great body of the people. These books they said were from God, and no one must expect salvation that has the audacity to doubt them. To the complaint from the people that they could not understand these books, they answered, "true, many things in them are hard to be understood, which many wrest to their own destruction, but God has conferred on his servants, *the priests*, the privilege of understanding them; believe what we say, give us of your substance to support us and our children and we will guide you to heaven."

If the people complained the doctrines preached were unreasonable or contradictory, they were answered: what is contradictory to *us* may be perfectly consistent to God, with him doubtless black and white are the same. What to short-sighted man appears unreasonable may be perfectly reasonable with God; with him it may be perfectly reasonable to say infinite goodness may produce infinite evil and still retain the character of infinite goodness.

Thus wearied with undue usurpations, the mind lost its elasticity and finally yielded itself an abject slave to its spiritual master, placed unbounded confidence in what he taught, and obeyed with the most persevering enthusiasm what he commanded. The evil effects of such a state of things have come down to us. The cloven-footed monster which preyed upon our ancestors has come hither to embitter our felicity and to render us gloomy vassals to clerical dominion.

Adventurous spirits from the old world have felled our forests, converted the wilderness into a fruitful field, erected on the fastnesses of wild beasts, cities which bid fair to rival the numbers, wealth, commerce and refinement of any which Europe can boast. Liberty has given additional splendor to our noon day sun; freedom has brightened the fires of our evening skies, and mental independence has given verdure to our fields and beauty to our landscapes. Here the care-worn son of despotic climes has found a home; oppressed virtue an asylum; and bleeding humanity, driven from the courts of tyrants, a retreat.

The enemies of the human race have cut their way to our peaceful shores, have entered our paradise, coiled themselves around the tree of knowledge, and are now presenting us the "death-distilling fruit." The claims, which the inhabitants of the old world are already beginning to spurn, are brought hither to bind the sons of those fathers who taught the world by their example to discard every species of tyranny.

My country! more is thy peril, greater is thy danger than when the gigantic power of a trans-Atlantic prince sent its minions to ravage thy courts and destroy thy women and children. A direful doom awaits thee; the chains of a more dreadful slavery are even now clanking in thy ears; repose not too much confidence in the virtue of thy sons; the mode of attack is secret and the movements of the enemy are silent.

A clerical hierarchy is threatened us and the utmost vigilance is requisite to avert the impending danger. The leaders of the grand enterprise are as crafty as they are ambitious. The missionary cause, like the crusades against the infidels, was thrown out to engage the great body of the people that the engine might move unobserved. The sympathies of the people were enlisted by many a pathetic description of poor heathens dropping into hell; the purse was opened, money was at the disposal of the reverend dignitaries who had shown so much compassion upon the wretched pagans.

They sought, as the next step, the superintendence of literature; they have obtained the management of nearly all the seminaries of learning; and, to make their triumph complete, they established their Sabbath schools, introduced their tracts and other books fraught with their own peculiarities, and thus they could begin with the infant and attend him through all the stages of his education. Immense power has thus been thrown into their hands; and they hold in their hands, to use their own exaggerated expression, "the lever that moves the moral world." In this department their plan has succeeded.

One thing remains to be accomplished—this done, and their plan has succeeded in every part. This thing is to get the supreme control of our political institutions. This, indeed, *remains* to be done; but there is some fear it may be nearer effected than any philanthropist is willing to believe. The proposal that none but *Christians* should be elected to any office; the attempt to persuade the freemen of these states to vote for no man unless he belong to some church, if it succeeds, will pave the way to designate the *particular* church; and when such a measure has succeeded, a majority of the favored church will compose the grand council of the nation. Woe be to thee, O Columbia, when that shall be the case.[4]

(January 19, 1828): 24-26

The preceding numbers may seem rather an essay on the progress of error, but the exposition they contained was deemed necessary to point out the nature of the evils to be removed and to exhibit some of the obstacles which ever have had and probably ever will have a tendency to impede the march of truth. The task was by no means pleasing. To trace the mind in its downward course is an ungrateful employment calculated to arouse the angry feelings and call forth the resentment of those whose lives and errors may be discovered and exposed, without receiving the commiseration of even those who wish to see mankind more virtuous, consequently more happy.

The benevolent heart weeps in sorrow over the follies, the aberrations and inconsistencies of the children of men; it deeply deplores their misery and wretchedness, the severity with which they oppress each other; anxious for their amelioration it raises its inquiries: "Indulgent God! is man eternally ordained to be the dupe and slave of man? Shall he never regain his independence and be free to exert his mental powers in the acquisition of knowledge; be free to study the works of his Creator, and while his bosom glows with gratitude to his heavenly Father, be free to repose with confidence on the paternal affection of the sovereign of nature?" The opposition to this has been already stated. It is aided by all the powers of darkness, but it is hoped the remainder of this essay will evince the "omnipotence of truth," and bring to weary and disconsolate man the joyful intelligence that it shall prevail to the annihilation of error and to the eternal banishment of evils which have so long afflicted the human race.

Nature gave to man the law of liberty and entwined a desire for independence around every fibre of his heart. Amid all the usurpations of tyrants, under all the oppressions so liberally heaped upon him, some secret thought recurs to his native dignity; he rises enraged at the shackles of his slavery; indignant, [he] spurns the thought

---

[4] [Ed. The reference here is to Presbyterian Ezra Stiles Ely's (1786-1861) plan for a Christian Party in politics, which he articulated in a Philadelphia speech on July 4, 1827. The speech, entitled "The Duty of Christian Freemen to Elect Christian Rulers," set out the reasons for the plan. For the text, see *American Philosophical Addresses, 1700-1900*, ed. Joseph Blau (New York: Columbia University Press, 1946), 548-62. Brownson repeatedly refers to this speech as indicative of the "orthodox" attempts to reunite church and state. See Introduction for analysis of speech, p. 22.]

and demands his rank in the scale of being. He may be misled, he may mistake the road to the land of freedom, he may deceive himself in the choice of means to promote his felicity, but he will never relinquish the attempt. His errors shall serve to correct him, and his follies shall teach him wisdom.

A cursory view of the past may be profitable towards enabling us duly to appreciate the present and to form rational conjectures respecting what may hereafter prevail.

The origin of the world is involved in impenetrable darkness; and notwithstanding some may assert it had its birth only the other day; the man who "knows how little can be known" will be convinced that the period is so remote that it is useless to expect any *minute* details of its infantile history. Whether men lived alone or in society in that early stage of its existence, what language they spoke, or what opinions they formed are alike hidden from the sharpest ken of those who live at this lapse of time. What passed before the flood, together with a number of years since, may be delivered over to lawless poets and the lovers of fiction to be peopled with such inhabitants as their prolific imaginations may choose to create. These also who are dissatisfied with the present, and despair of finding anything better in the unexplored regions of futurity may paint to themselves a golden scene in those days long since forgotten. Then perhaps the earth yielded her fruit without culture and man found a rich supply without labor; then perhaps the heavens wore perpetual sunshine and the fields were clothed with continual verdure, uniting at all times the hopes of spring with the enjoyments of autumn; then the air may have been pure and man a stranger to disease may have reclined in the ambrosial abode or basked amid beds of flowers, free from want or satiety, pain of body or remorse of mind; then too the morning may have been vocal with his hymns of praise and the evening may have repeated his devotions to his God; but alas! Very different is the picture since history has usurped the province of fable and too faithfully recorded the follies, the crimes and sufferings of mankind.

The earliest records in our possession represent the inhabitants of the earth as divided into petty hordes, continually making war upon each other, subsisting by the chase, pasturage, some rude agriculture and plunder. They united under a chief in whose abilities they could place confidence, who led them forth to battle but returned them to an equality with the rest when the object was attained or when the war was over. In time of peace the father governed his family without submitting to the authority of a higher tribunal; in cases, however, where the interests of the tribe or nation were involved, the whole were summoned and the deliberations of the most experienced were listened to with profound reverence and their advice followed with little deviation.

Religion was then but little more than that respect due to a superior or that reverence due from a child to its father, together with gratitude to those who were considered benefactors of the community. Under the patriarchal form of government every father was the priest in his own family, as may easily be seen in the history of Abraham. Religion being then free from the doubt and mysticism in which it has since been involved was easily learned and easily practiced, hence the necessity of a person to devote himself wholly to explaining and enforcing it was unfelt.

The relations given of Osiris, Bacchus and Jupiter show plainly enough, what was the early situation of men and also what was the character of the gods they worshiped.[5] Men must indeed be ignorant when it becomes necessary to have a God to teach them agriculture; but it was said of Osiris, a principal deity among the Egyptians, that while king of that country, he had taken unwearied pains to civilize his subjects and to teach them to cultivate their lands. Hence he was represented by the *Apis* or Ox because that animal being the most useful one in tilling the ground was the most proper emblem to perpetuate the memory of him who had taught the art.

The *Oak* was sacred to Jupiter because he first taught men to live upon acorns. Men could not have advanced far in the knowledge of things when they deified a man for showing them acorns were good to eat, nor could this simple act become a proof of his divinity.

Many became gods because they had *killed* some monster, such as the Minotaur the Hydra, etc.[6] It is not however to be supposed that the most ignorant considered these as creatures of the world; they only served them as benefactors of the country to which they belonged or for which they had done them signal services. It is true they were worshiped, but probably at first the worship was nothing more than a decent respect paid to their memories by those who felt themselves under obligations to them for the utility of their lives. But the poets and orators who celebrated their achievements and enumerated their virtues, in their exaggerated strain, represented them

[5] [Ed. Osiris, in Egyptian mythology, the god of the underworld and the dead, and husband of his sister Isis; Jupiter, in Roman mythology, the god who rules all other gods.]

[6] [Ed. Minotaur, in Greek mythology, was the half man, half bull offspring of Pasiphae and a white bull sent by Poseidon to Minos, who confined it in the Labyrinth where it was annually fed human flesh until killed by Theseus.]

as a superior order of beings, inhabitants of the stars or the celestial regions, who had submitted to privation and distress on earth for the benefit of its inhabitants but had now departed, returned to their former place or residence and were looking for sacrifice and offering as due for the benefits they had conferred. Hence perhaps, the first ideas entertained of a superior being; hence originated the fables and absurdities of the heathen mythology.

It is admitted the poets and philosophers, speaking of Osiris, Bacchus or Jupiter address him as "the *greatest* and *best* of beings, the *father of Gods and men*" but this must be understood rather as complimentary than as conveying their real sentiments, for the accounts which the same persons give of their god in other places are utterly inconsistent with such declarations. The words of De la Motte in reply to Madame Davier may be properly introduced in this place: "What! could Homer seriously believe Jupiter to be the Creator of gods and men? Could he think him the father of his own father Saturn, whom he drove out of heaven, or of Juno his sister and his wife, of Neptune and Pluto his brothers or of the nymphs who had charge of him in his childhood, or of the giants who made war upon him and would have dethroned him if they had been then arrived at the age of manhood? How well his actions justify the Latin epithets, *Optimus Maximus*, so often given him, all the world knows."[7]

The idea of one supreme Being, creator of all things seems not to have made any part of the religious creeds of antiquity. The ancients deified men and paid them religious worship. They erected temples to the sun, moon and the hosts of heaven; they dedicated altars to the hidden virtue of mere astrological conceits, and sacrificed to the elements of nature; but the worship of the true God was unknown.

Abraham during the early part of his life was an idolater and his views of God for a long time were extremely defective. The supposition that God required him to offer up in sacrifice his beloved son Isaac argues great ignorance of the perfections of the Deity for which he was justly reproved by the voice that called to him just as he was about to stretch forth the sacrificial knife. Abraham no doubt showed in this act his willingness to obey God and, notwithstanding, he erred

---

[7] [Ed. Brownson may be referring here to Antoine Houdar de Lamotte (1672-1731) and his *Lettre à madame Dacier sur son livre Des causes de la corruption du goust* (1715). Brownson probably refers here to Madame Anne (Lefèvre) Dacier (1654-1720) rather than Davier. In Roman mythology, Saturn was the god of agriculture; Juno, the wife of Jupiter and the queen of all the gods and the goddess of marriage; Neptune, the son of Saturn and god of the sea; Pluto, the god of the infernal regions.]

in respect to the nature of his duty; the readiness he had to discharge it was accounted to him for righteousness.[8]

However exalted were the conceptions which Moses had of the attributes of Jehovah, if he be the author of the book of Genesis he certainly was far from having found him out to perfection.[9] He frequently represents him as moving from place to place, also as being disappointed, grieving and repenting for what he had done; all which when applied to the Deity must be grossly improper; for if he move from one place to another he cannot be omniscient,[10] and if he be disappointed his wisdom must be finite, and if he repent, he cannot be immutable. This is not urged as an argument against the divine authenticity of the book, for the state of the human mind at that time necessarily required an imperfect system; for one that was perfect would have exceeded its powers of comprehension.

(February 2, 1828): 46-47

The most extraordinary increase of divine light which the records of antiquity have preserved is to be found in the system of religion and politics established by Moses, the great prophet and lawgiver of the Jews. To us it is a matter of perfect indifference by what means he received the knowledge of that system, whether by inspiration or philosophical research, whether his ideas of God were wholly original with himself or collected from the opinions of different theologians, whether the ritual he instituted, the sacrifices and offerings he enjoined upon his followers were invented by him or modified from the existing practices of other nations or sects with which he had become acquainted; since it is only at the institution itself we look, and for its correctness and real utility in producing the happiness of mankind we inquire.

Many of the ideas Moses entertained of Jehovah are such as the most enlightened theologians of all subsequent ages even to the present have held in the highest estimation, and are such as the most skeptical respecting the divine authority of the Bible, must pronounce to be in accordance with eternal truth. He called Him an Almighty Being, the Creator of all worlds and all beings, the Father of the spirits of all flesh. He considered Him one and indivisible, without any particular form or likeness by which he could be represented. Thus far Moses and the Christian philosopher agree. The physical character and essence (if the terms mean anything) of God were as

[8] [Ed. Reference here is to the story of the sacrifice of Isaac in Gen. 22:1-19.]
[9] [Ed. The conditional statement on Mosaic authorship indicates something of Brownson's historical-critical sense, the origins of which are not entirely clear.]
[10] [Ed. Brownson must mean omnipresent rather than omniscient.]

clearly understood and as fully made known by him as by any of his successors; for indeed no one that knows his own weakness will ever expect to have any clear conceptions upon a subject so far exceeding the sublimest flight of human thought. With regard to the moral character of God, the same cannot be said. There runs through the whole of the Mosaic economy traces of partiality in the Being it professes to adore, and it cannot be denied, his character is drawn rather from the suggestions of man's dark understanding than according to the light which the beauty, order and utility of nature everywhere sheds with divine effulgence upon our eyes. The right for one nation to extirpate another, not sparing even the women and children, and to possess their land is not now admitted by those who can pretend to have any correct views of justice; and the prince who should profess to have received from God a commission to such effect would be looked upon by all judicious persons either as a gross imposter, designing to turn the religious prejudices of the people to the channel of his own ambition, or as a mad man more fit to be the inmate of an insane hospital than to hold the reigns of government. The case of the Canaanites rests on the same ground for a justification, and it is presumed no Christian believes the moral perfection of *his* God would allow him to issue such a commission at this time, however proper it might have been in the days of Moses and Joshua.

The declaration contained in the second precept of the Decalogue, that Jehovah is "a jealous God visiting the iniquities of the fathers upon the children to the third and fourth generations" [Exod. 20:5; Deut. 5:9], if it be understood as teaching that God punishes the children for the crimes of their parents is certainly opposed to every principle of moral equity, if we, at this period, can be supposed to have any correct idea of the term.

Moses seems to have been too contracted in his views of the Providence of God. His regard for all *His* children. He seems to convey the idea (and it is certain his followers obtained it) that Jehovah held all the world in abhorrence but themselves, and that the children of Israel were the only nation on earth on which he had the least compassion. Perhaps this may be justified. All the world were idolaters and it accordingly became necessary for Moses, who abhorred idolatry, to place the strongest guards possible around his people to prevent them from adopting the odious practice. Hence it might have been necessary to impress his followers with the idea that God hated idolaters. The guard, strong as it was, however, did not prevent them from embracing the idolatry of the nations which surrounded them.

Moses made no distinction between moral and ceremonial duties. The want of this distinction, though probably unfelt at the time his system was established, soon became the occasion of great neglect of the substantial virtues, and very useful in enabling those who had the desire to make the observance of the *form* pass for the *power* of godliness. The externals of religion as they are usually called are nothing of themselves and are to be valued only according to their power of leading men "to do justly, to love mercy, and to walk humbly with their God" [Mic. 6:8].

Moses erred in establishing so many rites and ceremonies. His numerous sacrifices and offerings, whether considered as gifts designed to express the devotion of those who made them or as expiatory, intended to atone for the commission of moral evil and to placate the Deity, evince clearly enough his want of proper notions of the Divinity, and due attention to that kind of worship which a God of absolute perfection must demand of his intelligent creatures. But in this he may be excused, as in the case of divorcement they were permitted on account of the hardness of heart or gross conceptions of the people. Still it may be urged, the effect of so many rites and ceremonies was to draw off the attention of the worshiper from the substance and lead him to depend only on the shadow. The writers of the 50th Psalm, the 1st chapter of Isa. and the 6th of Micha, have adopted a more rational, and it is presumed a more correct, sentiment on this subject, and may be adduced as a strong argument to prove that the ideas of religion among the Jewish prophets had improved or approximated the truth during the lapse of days from Moses to Micah.

The ideas of punishment found in the laws contained in the system under examination seem to have too much of the nature of revenge. The penal code seems calculated to nourish a vindictive spirit rather than that mild lenient, and which experience, as well as the gospel, has proved to be most conducive to the felicity of society and consequently most pleasing to God.

An "eye for an eye" was their proverb among themselves; and their most approved method for redressing a wrong was to inflict the same degree of injury upon the offender, which had this singular advantage, it doubled the amount of suffering by making two evils where was but one before. The same as would be the case, a man burns down my house, I burn down his, so that both our families may be left destitute. The most unreasonable exactions was their demand from those in their power; hence, one reason why they were so much detested by the nations by which they were surrounded. Supposing God hated all the world but themselves and believing he had designed to heap upon all nations except their own the most severe judgements, they arrogated to themselves the province of interpreters of his will and presumed to measure out his justice according to their own ideas of the desert of *their*, and by consequence, his enemies.

The admission of slavery was another imperfection in the Mosaic system. This, however, seems to have been the besetting evil of all the political systems of antiquity; and it must be said, in palliation of the Jewish lawgiver that he made many wise and benevolent regulations to alleviate the condition of the slaves he permitted his followers to hold.

Another defect was in blending his civil and ecclesiastical affairs. This had a tendency to encourage encroachment upon the rights of the people by the priests and to produce a servile or superstitious disposition on the part of the governed. This was actually the case. No priests ever encroached more upon the prerogatives of the people than the Jewish and no people were ever more blindly devoted to their priests than the Jews.

(February 17, 1828): 55-56

It is not intended by pointing out some of the defects of the Mosaic system, to lessen the real value of that institution; but merely to evince the fact that the most perfect of the numerous systems of religion transmitted us from remote ages does not contain that clear and consistent view of the moral perfections of the Almighty, nor that comprehensive, correct and satisfactory detail of the various duties belonging to our individual and social relations which the general diffusion of knowledge at this time would lead us to expect from a system formed under the immediate direction of the Most High.

If Christians are in the habit of admitting the divine authenticity of the Jewish Scriptures, they should also recollect that the institution itself was abolished by the introduction of Christianity. If the institution had been perfect, it should have remained; but inasmuch as a system of religion given by God has superseded this, we are at perfect liberty to consider it defective and to examine the correctness of the several parts or the beauty and utility of the whole in the same manner we would had it been of human origin.

Christ did not hesitate to pronounce some of its maxims incorrect and to give new ones in their place: "Ye have heard that it hath been said, 'an eye for an eye, a tooth for a tooth;' but I say unto you, resist not the injurious." See Matthew 5:38, 39. His decision in the case of divorcement was very different from Moses, and may serve to explain the reason of many other of the laws found in his code. See Matthew 19:7, 8. The disposition of the Jews was so intractable and the state of improvement was such that different laws would have been either useless or pernicious.

But he who loves truth and desires to follow her sacred injunctions will not ask for scriptural authority to convince him that that is wrong which comes in contact with enlightened understanding, or to give him liberty to express his honest convictions when from the best information he can obtain the cause of religion and humanity require it. To conceal fraud is to be an accomplice of imposition and to be silent when we have discovered it is to declare our friendship for the original perpetrators. If we have ascertained that the creeds of our brethren contain error united with truth, we ought to invite and assist them to make a separation that they may reject that which is bad but hold fast that which is good.

There is no intention in the writer of this article, by telling the world there are imperfections in the Mosaic system, to weaken their faith in the Christian religion; but he would, by exciting them to an examination of the subject, induce those who wish to know the truth to study the Christian instead of the Jewish Scriptures. For the Jewish being given to man in a state less improved and less refined admits many things which would be improper under the Christian dispensation.

People have generally imagined the Jewish Scriptures did not contain all the truth; yet all they did contain was truth. As greater error need not be imbibed. This was the very case with the Jews; and, to convince them of this mistake, the apostles labored long and hard. No fact is or can be clearer, than that the new dispensation contains things in opposition to the old. Hence, as Christians, we should form our sentiments from the new. If we wish to be Jews we may study the old.

Divines know these things but they continue to practice on the maxim, "It is no harm to deceive a man to his benefit." The experiment has been tried; but all deception is found to be against the best interests both of the deceiver and the deceived; and though a partial good may sometimes be practiced, yet seldom, if ever, is it sufficient to overbalance the evil. Priests suppose that because we have hitherto been taught that the Bible was every word of it dictated by the Spirit of God, if they should now disclose the truth that some of it does not contain sentiments proper for us to believe, we would reject the whole. Hence, to make people believe the truth, we must preach a certain mixture of falsehood and we must become dishonest for the benefit of mankind. This language is too degrading; it is more than the independent spirit of man can bear. It says to a fellow being, "You are incapable of managing your own concerns; your ears are such you must not hear the truth, but you must have some one to oversee your affairs and preach to you falsehood." Can anything be more insulting? Can there be anything more destructive to everything valuable in the human bosom, or virtuous in human society? And who is the being that presumes to read this language in our ears; is it a God? No, it is a frail mortal, like ourselves, as ignorant and equally liable to err. Let then the lesson return to himself and let him say how he should be pleased to have such language pronounced in his own ears. Honesty is the best policy; and he who has not sufficient independence to speak what he believes to be truth is not fit to be a teacher or to have the least concern with instructing mankind.

From an examination of the Mosaic system it is learned that the best system antiquity could boast would not be called perfect now. Other systems there were, but they were inferior to this and may therefore be permitted to rest in the tombs where for ages they have been inured. The Mosaic was a great advance from the idolatry which preceded it. The prophets made many improvements in the religion left by Moses; but it was still imperfect.

(March 1, 1828): 68-69

On commencing the inquiry into ancient opinions I intended to run over the various systems of religion which had at different times occupied the attention of mankind, and to have marked the gradual improvement of each that encouragement might be afforded to the almost despairing philanthropist that truth was progressive; and it may confidently be expected that the revolutions of the future will accelerate its march, as well as those of the past; but I found myself laboring to prove what few will deny; and also exhibiting that kind of proof which but few would appreciate. The question, "*Cui bono?*" also occurred: What benefit will it be to mankind to call from the tombs, where for ages they have been inured, the ashes of those errors which employed the cogitation of the speculative and contemplative, which fired the zeal of the enthusiastic, or promoted the designs of the ambitious for enslaving mankind and trampling on the ruins of all that is noble or endearing in the human bosom? All that we can say with certainty is that man acquires his knowledge by observation and experience. Time enlarges experience and continual researches extend our observations; hence, every generation may leave its successor an increasing fund of knowledge, which may be transmitted, still enlarged, to later posterity.

In conformity to this maxim, we find antiquity or the remotest period of which we can obtain any record was extremely ignorant.

The true character of God was unknown; man's moral and religious obligations but vaguely perceived and improperly enforced; physical and intellectual science had no name; the true principles of philosophizing or the rules to be observed in our search after truth were undiscovered; hence little can be found to satisfy the mind of the inquirer; he returns in disgust and seeks relief in contemplating the present or expatiating in the boundless expanse of futurity. But as you come down you find an improvement. As men acquire leisure for study, they detect old errors, but generally substitute new ones in their place, which, again, in their turn, give way to others more lately invented.

Formerly men pretended to a great deal more knowledge than they do now; but since we have abated some in our pretensions, I am inclined to believe we are, in reality, more knowing; for there is more truth than poetry in Pope's definition of wisdom, "to know how little can be known."[11] Most of the moral, religious, and philosophical systems which we have received from our ancestors are merely hypothetical. They elicit genius but it is often of an unchastened kind. Their authors had mental greatness, perhaps superior to ours, but they were deficient in science or a true knowledge of nature.

Time was when the priests were in possession of all the knowledge as well as the religion of the community; and experience has shown us very clearly how willing this class of people are to enlighten the great mass of mankind. Now they do indeed labor to diffuse knowledge, but they did not do it until the laity came in possession of it by other means. Had priests pursued the course which the policy of that body suggested as the most proper, we might perhaps, at this time, been bowing down to Egypt's "dok ox"[12] as the fit object of our religious veneration; or, perhaps, fashioning with Aaron the golden calf, as the emblem of the God of nature. But they have been driven from their policy and have been compelled to resign the keys of science, and to relinquish their exclusive claims to the chair of literature. The keys of heaven and hell they are indeed permitted to retain but the great body of the people believe they have neither power to open the one or shut the other.

The ancients may be excused in some degree for the absurdity of their religious systems for they depended wholly upon their priests; and as priests always delight to amuse the credulous by marvelous

---

[11] [Ed. Alexander Pope (1688-1744), an English poet and satirist, author of *An Essay on Man*, ed. Frank Brady (London, 1733-34; Indianapolis: Bobbs-Merrill, 1965), epistle 4, line 261.]

[12] [Ed. Reference here may be to Apis, the sacred bull of the ancient Egyptians, who was considered by many to be the embodiment of a god on earth.]

stories and astonishing miracles, we may suppose they revealed them in all the wild luxuriance of mysticism, and dealt out to the gaping multitude without measure the pious absurdities of their midnight dreams, and the holy raptures of their unlicenced, yet unreproved imaginations. Their dreams and raptures may now supply matter for an evening tale, and may excite our risibility or raise our indignation at their impositions upon their brethren; but they will not gain a moment's credence, or create the least regret that they are never to return. With these remarks we bid adieu to those airy castles and fantastic fabrics which once employed the imaginations and excited the hopes and fears of mankind; for though God may have spoken to them face to face, they were subject to the same law that governs us. The tree of knowledge must wait the nourishment of slow experience before it can expand its branches, afford shade or beauty, yield fragrance or fruit.

Christianity has done much for mankind. But alas! the best system is of no avail to minds still slumbering in the cells of ignorance. Though its rays beam with power, they cannot pierce at once the mighty deep of superstition; nor can their warmth penetrate in a moment the icy heart of the bigot and melt it to philanthropy. It has done much and much is now doing; but it would have done more if men had known at its first exhibition, what bitter experience has since taught, that, though science is not religion, she is the handmaid of religion. There may be science without religion but religion cannot claim much purity nor usefulness without science. But science has flourished under the fostering sun of Christianity, and its reciprocal influence has brightened that sun, expanded his rays, and given him a more agreeable and a more permanent warmth.

One circumstance which now exists promises to be of vast utility in enlarging the boundaries of our knowledge. Philosophers now build on experiment. The fondness for hypotheses and love of theorizing, which so long checked the growth of knowledge, are now in some measure laid aside for matters of fact, and it is now ascertained to be folly to build on conjecture, or to pretend to know that which we have never seen or investigated with any of our senses. True philosophy now attempts to analyze nature, exhibit her various phenomena, but not to explain them. The composition of bodies is ascertained and the changes to which they are liable are, in many instances, predicted. The mind also is subjected to the same analysis; its susceptibilities developed and the various classes of its changes as they are affected by its relation to matter or to itself are defined. The same rule, the same method is finding its way into religion and the most beneficial results may be anticipated.

(March 15, 1828): 87-90

Science has shed her "lucid rays" over many nations and the most abject slaves of ignorance have caught a glimpse, faint indeed, but sufficiently powerful to make them dissatisfied with their condition and to enable them to meditate some amelioration. The invention of the art of printing has furnished the philanthropist with successful weapons to combat the foes of the human race and vindicate the cause of wisdom and virtue. Armed by this invention, he has already shaken thrones, filled the hearts of tyrants with dismay and the courts of despotism with consternation! The mighty fabric of bigotry and superstition, which cost the labor of ages to erect and which were cemented by the blood of millions, already trembled to their foundations before his successful attacks. Several nations have been compelled to throw off the burden of political servitude and others have been obliged to abate the rigor of their institutions and the severity of their laws.

The enlightened benefactors of mankind, a few years since in this country, lighted the beacon of universal emancipation. Europe saw the illumination; France assembled in its rays, increased its effulgence. Did she fall? She reflected splendor as she "kissed the dust." From her temporary defeat we are enabled to learn the rules of our future exertions to avoid the rock on which she split and the whirlpool in which she was lost. The march of liberty may be more slow hereafter than was anticipated but what is lost in severity will be gained in permanency. But France shall rise. The republican principles of her revolution, though now apparently dormant, shall yet spring up and yield a plenteous harvest. Her martyred patriots still live in her bleeding memory and sooner shall the enemies of the human race arrest the sun in his progress or roll back the wheels of nature than prevent the resuscitation of the cause for which they bled and its complete triumph over the tyrannical principles which have for a time obscured its glory!

The overgrown power of the pope of Rome has become little more than nominal. The splendid dome of popery, erected from the spoils of almost every heathen temple and ornamented with the paintings of almost every heathen artist, is nearly demolished. The "bulls"[13]

---

[13] [Ed. Reference is to a papal bull (from Latin *bulla*, i.e., literally a seal). A written papal mandate that carries a seal and is of a more serious and weighty authority than a regular papal brief.]

of the Vatican are now regarded as harmless things, and their thunderings cease to terrify mankind. The church which was not improperly styled the "mother of harlots" has begun her reformation and bids fair to outstrip her daughters in this laudable work. Calvinism has had its day. There have been converts that could gravely declare that man a heretic who did not believe "God has not created all men to like estate but to some has fore-appointed life and to others death and as they were created to the one or the other so they were elected to eternal life or reprobated to misery inconceivable, and themselves thus elected or reprobated were eternally and unchangeably designed and so definite that one cannot be added or diminished, and all this for the manifestation of his sovereign mercy and his vindictive justice." But where is the man that will now boldly advocate in all its native deformity this consummation of absurdity and cruelty, this focus in which all the objectionable parts of the most objectionable theories ever dreamed of by man have concentrated their power?

We have Calvinists in name but they are most of them ashamed of the peculiar tenets of the successful champions of malevolence whose name they bear. Every sober minded man among them is much more solicitous to conceal these doctrines or to give them a more inviting dress than he is to exhibit them as believed by our ancestors. Edwards and Hopkins[14] in our country, men possessing by no means small abilities have endeavored to reconcile the *decretum horribile* of Calvinism with the universal benevolence of God, and notwithstanding they have concluded it is best upon the whole to compel a part to weep eternally in hell that the righteous in heaven may have their bliss consummated; they have borne testimony strong as was in their power to the fact that God is a being of universal benevolence, a truth when once admitted by the mind puts in the background all those imaginary fears and burning hells which Calvin placed in the front.

[14] [Ed. Jonathan Edwards (1703-58), American Puritan pastor and foremost eighteenth century Calvinist theologian, had a major influence on the development of theology in the United States. Samuel Hopkins (1721-1803), American Puritan pastor and a student of Jonathan Edwards, extended and reformulated Edwards' Dortian and evangelical theology in the late eighteenth and early nineteenth centuries. Brownson would show more appreciation for Edwards' theology of the divine light in the mid 1830s, but at this point in his career he, like many other anti-Calvinists, could only identify Edwards with the "horrible" Calvinist doctrine of Predestination, a doctrine, he believed, that violated divine benevolence and human freedom.]

The Church of England, though originally Calvinistic, or nearly so, now pays very little attention to the doctrine of election and reprobation, except it be to discountenance it. She indeed retains her thirty-nine articles[15] but they have not much control over the sentiments of the clergy in general.

The Methodists sprang up in the last century and although in point of doctrine they have done little more than to declaim against the horrid tenets of the reformer of Geneva[16] they have by their unwearied exertions done much to benefit in many places the lower classes of mankind, these unfortunate persons whom the clergy of more popular churches have generally treated with neglect.

These are indeed trifling considerations when our minds take in the vast family of man, but as they show that the most enlightened religious institutions are purifying themselves, we catch the hope that they will soon be prepared to instruct the more ignorant and to shed the rays of truth upon the benighted parts of our earth. They show the spirit of investigation is abroad and however powerful or obstinate the enemies it has to encounter it will never return till wreathed with laurels of victory. These apparently minute consequences show us there is a redeeming principle in human society and however slow may be its operations it will finally produce a glorious renovation.

The last century has done much and should the same exertions be made and be attended by the same success for one hundred years to come the world will appear almost entirely different from what it was one hundred years back. The work is begun and the first obstacles are surmounted. The path now before us is plain, and as the wheel of improvement acquires celerity from its own motion, the remaining part of the road will be run with more quickness, ease and safety than that already traversed.

The labors of our predecessors though apparently feeble produce astonishing results and instead of wondering why we are no further advanced we should rather wonder why we have progressed so far. A few centuries back the world was in darkness and "gross darkness covered the people," a senseless jargon disturbed the schools,

[15] [Ed. Brownson refers to the set of doctrinal formulae originally accepted by the Church of England in 1563 (revised and put in final form in 1571) to define its dogmatic position in relation to the religious controversies of the sixteenth century.]

[16] When I attribute the doctrine of election and reprobation to John Calvin, I would not be understood as asserting that the sentiment originated with him, for I believe it was held by Luther in a light not less abhorrent; but as we know the sentiment now only as a part of the antiquated system of the Genevan Reformer it may receive his name.

a philosophy was taught which had little effect but to render more imperious the gloom of ignorance which brooded over the nations. War in its grossest forms and in its most malignant aspect was multiplied to an extent which threatened the world with depopulation. This "horrid monster" is now made to wear a milder garb and much is done to render his march tolerable. That philosophy is discarded and a new one commenced which rests on experiment not conjecture for its authority. That jargon is no longer heard and our seminaries have learned it is their province to teach their subjects *things* rather than words.

Improvements in navigation have brought all nations within the vicinity of each other. Commerce has made us acquainted with all. The art of printing will convey to all, almost instantaneously, the discoveries of each. Hence what we gain cannot be lost. Our discoveries and improvement are embodied in so many books and read in so many different languages that nothing less than a universal conflagration can destroy the whole.

True, many nations are yet ignorant, barbarous and savage, and exhibit a faithful picture of what all once were, but missionaries are flying with the wind to each; and though what they carry is of no great consequence they will open with them a communication, make us acquainted with their language, manners and customs and enable us to transfuse through their ignorant mass those truths which at once correct the head and amend the heart. It is thus the arts of the enemy shall operate to his own ruin and the efforts made to extend the dominions of priestcraft be the means of its final overthrow. One, however, would naturally suppose there was a shorter and more direct road to the desired object. But all men are not philosophers, but few reflect seriously on the propriety or impropriety of the measures they adopt. The majority of mankind are borne along the tide of things as passion or belief gives the impulse, without attempting to correct their progress or even to inquire where they are likely to land. Men are governed more by their prejudices than by their reason and these are generally so obstinate that nothing short of miscarriage can subdue their power. Experience is surely a dear school but we have a great many who will learn in no other way and some not even in this. Hence the march of truth has sometimes been by a circuitous route. The obstacles which impeded her footsteps were not always to be surmounted at once. She has many times apparently slackened her progress and permitted the fables of men to pave for her a way to certain victory. Such is the missionary scheme contemplated either as to the motives of its founders or the measures adopted to carry it into execution. Contemptible indeed is the motive. It is no other than to spread those unintelligible doctrines, sometimes strangely called the "doctrines of grace," among the heathen—those doctrines which must excite the ridicule or disquiet of every man's mind that is freed from the leading strings of his mother. Contemptible and worse are the measures adopted to prosecute this scheme. But I will not mention them for may posterity never learn how grossly depraved were the most popular religionists of the 19th century. The selling of Joseph into Egypt was not commendable in itself considered but the consequences were good, and the same perhaps may hereafter be said of the missionary scheme. The same perhaps too of the petty institutions of Sabbath schools. When the first lessons taught are veneration for the church which adopt them. These and all similar measures will finally produce a reaction. Woe then to the pride of their abettors for it shall receive a deadly wound!

Truth is the pebble in the lake and however small at first are the circles or however slow they may succeed each other, they will continue till they have spread over the whole surface. Truth has already disclosed to the once despised inhabitants of the southern half of our continent the balm of personal liberty and national independence; she armed them against the tyrants that oppressed, she led them to victory and though her triumph be not yet complete she will finally spread a richer wealth over the sand than the silver of Potosi or the gold of Mexico could purchase. The wrongs of Montezuma[17] shall be avenged and science flourish over all the territory beheld by the disgraceful conqueror of the Inca of Peru.

Greece shall emerge from the gloom of Turkish vassalage; science and literature revisit the land of Plato; liberty triumph again on the plains of Marathon, and be maintained by the justice of Aristides.[18] Nor here shall end the march of Truth. India shall behold her effulgence, cast aside her idol gods, recognize the original equality of the human family, treat them all as brethren, and worship with gratitude the common Father of all. The Minstrel of Zion shall retake his harp from the willow and heavenly music shall re-echo from the mountains of Jerusalem. Nor ye sable sons of Africa shall truth forget to light the darker features of your doom. Distant, yes, ye degraded men, distant is the day, but come it shall, to restore to you the rights to which nature and nature's God entitle you, and give your long

---

[17] [Ed. Montezuma (1479?-1520), the last Aztec emperor of Mexico, was dethroned by Hernando Cortez (1485-1547), the Spanish conqueror of Mexico.]

[18] [Ed. Aristides, a fifth century B.C. Greek statesman and general, called "the Just."]

abused country its place among the nations of the earth. Ye wanderer's of Arabia's desert, and ye tribes that roam the forest, a glorious sun shall shed his enlightening beams upon your desolations. Showers shall distill their genial influence upon your land, and the desert shall be glad with the rest, and the wilderness and the solitary place rejoice and blossom as the rose. The Genius of Emancipation is hurrying over the world; he bears on his wings the long wished for relief, and fast as the wheel of improvement can move, it shall be borne to you.[19]

Such are the suggestions of hope, such are the conclusions warranted by a review of the past and the contemplation of the present. Philanthropists, awake! your exertions shall be crowned with success. Regard not the proscriptions of the ignorant and the designing. Disapprobation from those who are incapable of perceiving the value of your labors, and from those who have no desire to witness the renovation you wish to produce, you must expect, but be not discouraged. Posterity will reap the fruit of your toil, and the unbounded felicity which you may transmit to future generations will fully compensate you for any sacrifices you may be compelled to make. Let your voices be heard! Ye friends of Truth, of science, of liberty, and religion in its purity, break your long silence, let the echo of your voices ring back from every quarter—man shall be free! Tyranny, whether civil or ecclesiastical, shall be annihilated, wars shall cease, contentions end. Peace and unbroken harmony shall reign wherever the voice of man is heard, or wherever the sun emits his golden beams.

[19] [Ed. Brownson's ideas on slavery changed very little from the time of his youth. He abhorred slavery, but his idea on policies for the abolition of slavery and the emancipation of African-American slaves changed periodically. For his views on slavery, see Arthur M. Schlesinger, Jr., *Orestes A. Brownson: A Pilgrim's Progress* (Boston: Little Brown and Co., 1939), 17, 58-59, 79-80, 90, 113, 161, 240-46, 252, 287; Thomas R. Ryan, *Orestes A. Brownson. A Definitive Biography* (Huntington, Indiana: Our Sunday Visitor, 1976), 32-33, 135, 405-06; and, for his Catholic period exclusively, Madeline Hooke Rice, *American Catholic Opinion in the Slavery Controversy* (New York: Columbia University Press, 1944), 111, 118-22, 129-30, 152. There is, however, no systematic study of the evolution of Brownson's thought on slavery.]

3.

A SERMON. ON ZEAL IN RELIGION

The Gospel Advocate and Impartial Investigator
6 (March 29, 1828): 97-101

They have a zeal for God but not according to knowledge.
Rom. 10:2.

It is not infrequently alleged against liberal Christians, against those who profess a rational religion, that they are cold and indifferent respecting the spread of their peculiar tenets; they do not take that deep interest in the great schemes adopted to spread the gospel as do their orthodox brethren, nor as it seems proper they should. Many of my friends tell me Universalists may with advantage borrow some of the orthodox zeal. So I have thought and so doubtless thinks every one who estimates a man's religion according to the noise it makes. But more extensive observation on the practices of different religious societies, together with a careful and dispassionate perusal of ecclesiastical history, has taught me exertions may be made, zeal may be manifested which is rather prejudicial than useful in the true church of Christ.

Whoever has made himself acquainted with the history of past ages and attentively traced the rise and progress of events, whoever has diligently marked the various machines, the numberless engines put in operation during the current century, will find sufficient testimony to corroborate the assertion of the Apostle that men may have a zeal for God but not according to knowledge.

The Jews were a *zealous* people. They were strenuous supporters of the glory of God and extremely tender of the honor of religion. But no rational man believes they advanced the one nor vindicated the other by their indiscriminate slaughter of women and children, because their husbands and fathers were idolaters, as in the case of the Canaanites.

Samuel was a zealous prophet. No one ever accused him of supineness nor of any want of fervency in the cause of religion, but what man of common sympathy does not regret it should have led him to saw in pieces the accomplished king of the Amalekites?[1]

David was a zealous king and in general to be admired for his piety and devotion, but who believes that he honored God or advanced the real interests of religion by placing "under saws" and "under harrows" the captive Amalekites?[2]

In that age of general ignorance when none but partial views were entertained of the Deity, when the laws of humanity were undeveloped and liberality in religion unheard, some excuse may be formed for conduct which enlightened reason condemns. But the zeal which distinguished the Jews in after ages is not much to be preferred. For myself I as little approve that zeal which on the Sabbath day disarmed the multitude and made them an easy prey to the Syro-Grecian forces, and think Matthias fully justified in abolishing the custom.

No one can doubt the extent or the warmth of the zeal which characterized the Pharisees, but who approves it when it compassed sea and land to make one proselyte, especially when it made him twofold more the child of destruction than themselves? They exemplified their zeal in various ways. They gave proofs of its power by crucifying the great founder of our religion, by their unwearied persecutions of the apostles and primitive Christians. Everybody believes Saul going with letters from the chief priests to Damascus had zeal in abundance. But the threatenings and slaughter he breathed against the followers of Jesus of Nazareth, the consent he gave to the death of Stephen will make every enlightened Christian pause before he pronounces eulogium on religious zeal.

But this was Jewish zeal. This we are willing to admit is not according to knowledge. Here trace then the zeal of the *Christians.*

No one doubts the zeal of the council which condemned the sentiments of Arius, as heretical, and himself to banishment; and all equally admire the one which a few years after recalled him and established his sentiments as the religion of the Empire. Constantine must have been a prodigy of religious zeal. Who could not have been surprised to see the short time since heathen prince, now demolishing every heathen temple, forbidding his subjects on pain of death to sacrifice to the gods of their country or to practice the religion consecrated by its antiquity and rendered memorably dear by having been the religion of their fathers and of their own childhood. But every philanthropist must regret the foundation laid by this zeal for the

[1] [Ed. See 1 Sam. 15:1-33.]
[2] [Ed. See 2 Sam. 12:31; 1 Chron. 20:3.]

great corruption of Christianity known by the name of the great papal apostasy.

Theodosius,[3] no doubt, had a great anxiety for the spread of *evangelical* truth when he wished to bring all mankind to a uniform faith, to believe just like himself. But the pagan that was doomed to death if he followed the dictates of his own conscience, the Arian that felt the weight of his vengeance if he dare assert what everybody believes, that a father is older than his son, never rejoiced that he fostered a zeal so fatal in its consequences.

St. Dominic,[4] founder of the Inquisition, was no doubt zealous for the favor of God and the purity of his religion. But I would rather he had been the coldest lump that ever quenched the Christian's fire than he should have constructed a machine so sanguinary in its operations.

Peter the Hermit[5] of Crusade memory had zeal enough and to spare when he traveled over Europe and roused up the slumbering spirits of her sons and fanned the dying embers of their devotion to the flames of enthusiasm. But myriads who were led by him to rescue the holy sepulcher from the hands of infidels but perished in the attempt would, if they could have arisen from their untimely graves, have exclaimed with emphasis "Peter thy zeal was not according to knowledge."

But this was a Catholic zeal no one should expect anything better from that corrupt church. Well then trace the Protestant zeal.

John Calvin was a Protestant divine, one of the principal reformers, a man of an enlightened mind and in general of agreeable manners, but alas, Michael Servetus[6] burning over a slow fire made of green wood could tell how *hot* was his zeal.

Henry the 8th of England was a Protestant, zealous, as 72,000 persons slain for daring to contradict him can well testify. The edict

---

[3] [Ed. Theodosius I, Roman Emperor from 379 to 395, helped create the orthodox Christian state by outlawing Arianism, forbidding sacrifice, and almost prohibiting pagan religions.]

[4] [Ed. Saint Dominic (1170-1221), founder of the Order of Friars Preachers (Dominicans), was not, as Brownson claims, founder of the Inquisition. That institution was created after 1232 when Emperor Frederick II issued a heresy-hunting decree and entrusted the task to state officials. Pope Gregory IX (c. 1148-1241), thereafter, claimed the office for the church and appointed Dominicans as papal inquisitors.]

[5] [Ed. Peter the Hermit (1050?-1115) was the most eloquent preacher of the First Crusade inaugurated by Pope Urban II in 1095.]

[6] [Ed. Michael Servetus (1511-53), a physician and anti-Trinitarian heretic, was burned at the stake in Calvin's Geneva.]

of Elizabeth and of William as well as the law obtained by the Westminister divines may be adduced as examples of Protestant zeal.[7]

Our *"pious ancestors"* who fled from the persecution and corruption of the church of England were zealous for God. Few persons would, like them, for religion have left their homes, the scenes of childhood and youth, their friends and everything endearing to the memory or soothing to the heart to explore a savage wilderness and to become subject to all those privations and distress which were consequent upon the first settlers of this country. But alas the Baptist that was banished or the Quaker that was hung deeply deplored their pious frenzy and no doubt devoutly prayed that it might be tempered with a little more knowledge.

But if we come nearer home within the sphere of our own observation we shall discover no abatement of zeal, though the laws of the country prevent its rising to that degree of excess which it did formerly. We grant the orthodox zeal. We see the exertions they are making, we have witnessed their "missionary societies," their "education societies" their "cent societies" and their "mite societies," etc. Our minds have imperceptibly been carried back to the days of their ancestors and we have almost involuntarily exclaimed "Woe unto you scribes and Pharisees, for ye compass sea and land to make one proselyte and when he is made, ye make him twofold more the child of Gehenna than yourselves" [Matt. 23:15]. But enough: we bear them record they have a zeal for God, but as we believe not according to knowledge. And if it be said we have not this zeal we plead guilty to the charge, or rather we acknowledge the truth of the assertion, but deny that there is any guilt in it, for we have no wish to possess a zeal which if not restrained by wholesome laws might carry us to such extravagance that our associate or our fellow being must ever deplore its lamentable consequences.

True we have issued no pious "bulls" for the introduction of silly tenets into our common schools. Nor have we petitioned our legislature to prevent people who are [away] from home on [their own] expense, from returning on the Sabbath to see their wives, their children, their fathers or their mothers.[8] We have not appointed meet-

---

[7] [Ed. References most likely are to Queen Elizabeth's (1533-1603) Uniformity Act of 1559, which reestablished Protestantism in England, to King William III's (1650-1702) tightening up of the penal laws that excluded Catholics and a few others from public life in England, and to the Westminster Assembly's (1643-49) decrees which created a uniform Presbyterian confessional statement of orthodoxy and a catechism that was widely used by orthodox Presbyterians.]

[8] [Ed. Sense of this sentence is unclear in the original.]

ings every evening in the week, we have not requested our friends to suspend all business to hear our preaching or praying, nor have we run from house to house and from shop to shop, abusing the good sense of the people and denouncing endless woe upon all who have the audacity to dissent from our assertions. We have not frightened little children by telling them "God hates them" that "Jesus Christ will frown upon them," that "the Holy Ghost will forsake them." We have indeed never shocked the feelings of our youth by telling them "damnation is written in their forehead," that "God Almighty has sealed their everlasting doom" nor have we insulted grey hairs by praying God "to shake them over hell." Our zeal has never carried us so far, and probably for this plain reason, we do not believe the interests of religion require such extravagances. There is a great difference between the orthodox and ourselves, we are sensible of it, but we believe that it flows as a direct consequence from the different views we have of the character of God.

Our religious creed recognizes no violent emotions. Like its author it "can weep with those who weep and rejoice with them who rejoice," but it seeks to moderate the passions, to soften the affections, to enlighten the understanding that may produce a rational and permanent devotion. And we can no more change our practice than we can our sentiments.

But it is alleged, "Universalists are indifferent to the great interests of religion." If by the great interests of religion be meant justice, candor, liberality, or real love to God, and good will to man, the charge is denied and we appeal to experience for a justification of the denial. We do not say Universalists are better than other people, but we ask an instance where our societies are more deficient in the practice of those virtues which endear human society than their orthodox neighbors? I will ask the lone wanderer, the friendless child of affliction and sorrow, the shelter less son of charity, whose house has received him from the pelting storm? I will ask the aged, the decrepit, grief-worn son of poverty, whose bounty has relieved his wants? Whose compassion has soothed his aching heart? Whose kind attention has made him forget his wants and his sorrow?

But "Universalists do not take that unwearied pains to spread their sentiments which do their orthodox brethren." If by this be meant that we are not particularly anxious all men should believe our peculiar tenets, we grant it, for we have yet to learn there can be no religion where our views are not embraced. We feel a deep interest in the spread of true religion; we rejoice to hear the widow and the orphan are relieved from their distresses, but we believe with the apostle John, "he that doeth righteousness is righteous even as he is righteous" [1 John 3:7].

But it is still said "Universalists have no concern for the souls of men." If there can be no concern for the welfare of the souls of men unless it be expressed by exclamations of wrath and indignation we acknowledge we have none, for we are determined never to attempt the absurd practice of frightening men into religion, nor shall we ever submit to the indecency of preaching the gospel of Christ in a fit of anger.

We, to be sure, have never paid great attention to the cure of the soul, we have never expressed great concern for its welfare, nor have we told people we were willing "to spend and be spent" in making their peace with God when we would without remorse rob the body and take the last cent from our hearers, to pay us for our kind endeavors to propitiate the God of heaven in their behalf. True we have not sent out our unemployed preachers, our theological students and other agents to solicit funds to save souls from hell for we have yet to be convinced that money in so much valued by the Almighty that he will accept it in exchange for the souls of men. Nor, indeed, have we made many lamentations over those who have not joined our church for we are not certain they would be more safe by coming within our enclosure. It is I believe a prevailing sentiment among Universalists that a man's salvation depends more on *himself* than on his *neighbor*, more on his *actions* than on his *opinions*, more on his God than on anything else whatsoever.

"Universalists support no foreign missionary establishments. They give no assistance for carrying the gospel to the heathen." True, we as a body support no missionary establishment now in existence for we know of none which we believe deserving any support from sober people. We have not assisted our orthodox brethren in carrying the "gospel to the heathen," for we do not believe that is the gospel which they would carry. And we do not deny that we have little anxiety that those sentiments which alienate friends, divide families and sow the seeds of discord at home should be transplanted to those people who, all know, are miserable enough without them.

That we are opposed to sending the *gospel* to the heathen we deny; but our actual strength has hitherto been insufficient to send any missionaries, and in fact we have no more than we could employ at home; and while the moral and religious aspect of our country remains unaltered, we think we can find sufficient employment for all the preachers we have to better advantage and with less expense near-by.

But again "Universalists do not encourage Bible societies." We do not. And we think we are justified in the course we pursue for we have no very high opinion of the plan on which they are conducted, nor do we discover any great necessity for them. Most people, in our country at least, are able to procure a Bible, and in our opinion the loud talkers about circulating the Scriptures would do better to *say* less about extending them and *read* them more.

But "where are the Universalists Sabbath schools?" We have them in some places, but as we discover a sectarian spirit we do not generally support them. So long as we are able to give our children education without soliciting the charity of our neighbors, we think it better to let them have other days to acquire their learning, and everybody knows that six days out of seven is as much as any children ought to study. With regard to a knowledge of the Bible our children may be compared with the children of orthodox families and we think we shall have no cause to blush at the result.

"Your churches are lax, you do not pay sufficient attention to discipline, you have many bad members." We shall not attempt to defend the moral character of the members of our societies, nor should we consider them any *too good* if they are admitted to be as good as the members of other societies. As for discipline we prefer lenity to severity and would always rather reform than destroy a man's character.

"Universalists neglect the ordinances and do not regard the Sabbath as holy time." We have never wished to be of that number which "strain at a gnat and swallow a camel" [Matt. 23:24]. We observe the ordinances, but do not consider them the whole of religion. They may be convenient means, and properly explained and administered they may be useful. But we have always considered "justice and mercy more acceptable to the Lord than sacrifice."[9] We observe the Sabbath, but are of the same opinion with the great Founder of our religion, that the "Sabbath was made for man, not man for the Sabbath."[10]

But in general "Universalists do not express that deep concern for the spread of the gospel and they seem to consider religion of less importance than others do." You may converse with Universalists, their acquaintance with the Bible, the unwearied pains they take to inform themselves can best tell how important they deem religion.

---

[9] [Ed. Brownson conflates Hos. 6:6; Prov. 21:3, and Matt. 12:7. However, Matt. 12:7 is drawn from the two Old Testament sources.]

[10] [Ed. Mark. 2:27 parallels Matt. 12:7, but has a different ending, which Brownson uses in the quote.]

The number of our periodical papers and the theological works issuing from the various free presses in our country can very well assure our orthodox friends that we are not indifferent to the spread of our sentiments. And they may be assured, though our operations are not excessively noisy, we are not inactive. But people are not always consistent with themselves for we are also told we are "too active," that "our dangerous heresy spreads to an alarming extent."

But enough; a thousand objections may be raised against the best sentiments ever proclaimed and numerous failings may be discovered in the practices of the best Christians that ever lived; and perhaps it would be well for us all to learn from this consideration that it is our duty to cultivate mutual forbearance and endeavor to cherish sentiments of good will and fraternal affection with each other. Zeal in religion is proper and desirable if it proceed from a good heart and be directed by an enlightened understanding.

We consider our sentiments true; we feel that interest for their spread, that anxiety for their extension and universal prevalence which every sober well informed man must feel that truth should triumph over error. Our sentiments are professedly free and liberal in their nature, and we believe them of importance to the world; but we dare not derogate from their dignity by resorting to low and puerile measures for their advancement.

Our sentiments are learned by slow patient inquiry and close investigation. They are not acquired amid the excitation of passion, nor amid the turmoil and bustle of a crowd; they are not enforced by frightful grimaces and unwarrantable exclamation, nor are they endeared to the heart by bitter invectives against those who think differently from ourselves. They do and will keep pace with the march of intellect. As the traces of the dark ages wear away, as the shapeless specters engendered by the dreams of superstition disappear, human nature will be better understood, the character of the Almighty will appear more beautiful and desirable, and rational sentiments of religion will find a more cordial reception by the human heart.

Liberal Christianity under God has done much for the emancipation of the human understanding. To this must be attributed the labors we discover among our orthodox brethren to soften the asperities of their creed and to give them a more smooth and inviting appearance. No man who is ambitious to hold a claim to common sense or common consistency can now be found who will maintain in all their native deformity the peculiar views of Calvin and Luther.

True inquiry has shed her hallowed influence over almost every rank and condition. From the various commotions we discover on every side, we indulge the cheering hope that the day is not far distant when reason will exert her sway and religion become acceptable to God and profitable to mankind.

Though we may be accused of supineness we see all the movements we wish, all the exertions [we are] making we desire or believe to be proper. And should the same continue to be made and be attended by the same success for fifty years to come as they have for that time past, the frightful stories which shocked our infancy will be rehearsed only as memorials of an age never to return.

What remains for our brethren is to be careful to maintain that purity of conversation, that propriety of conduct which shall give dignity to their faith and permanency to their efforts. In this department of the Christian's life there is no danger of too much zeal. To be anxious to maintain a life free from reproach in obedience to the dictates of reason and the injunctions of revelation is truly lamentable; and this I hope to see the chief object of every professed liberal Christian, of every Universalist. As his creed does not limit the sphere of his good offices to any particular party he should be careful to enlarge his benevolence and extend his philanthropic exertions.

As his creed is rational let him never degrade it by a resort to measures irrational or absurd for its support. As he believes he received it from God let his conduct correspond to the purity of its celestial origin.

We do not approve of indifference in religion nor do we believe we are more indifferent than others. We view the measures adopted by the orthodox as calculated to inflame the passions, produce a splenetic or enthusiastic disposition rather than to convey any real good to any human being. It is, therefore, though we have zeal, it is not their zeal; though we make exertions, they are not their exertions; though we use means, they are not always such means as they adopt. It is (or ought to be) our study to be consistent with ourselves. We view the Christian religion as the inestimable gift of God to man, entrusted at first to a few but designed its operations to benefit the whole. It stands opposed to all other systems of religion ever promulgated; it exhibits the character of our heavenly Father; it reveals the moral perfections of his government, our duty and our final destination. Coming from a source so high and so excellent, containing truth so glorious and so important, it demands the exertions of our noblest powers and sublimest human faculties. We dare not excite the passions, we dare not awaken animal feeling or call the ravings of fanaticism the legitimate offspring of Christianity.

That zeal which is according to knowledge is a sober, dignified, rational zeal. It steals with a gentle, permanent warmth through the heart without intoxicating the brain. It softens the heart by enlarging the mental faculties; purifies the affections by enlightening the understanding.

This is not the work of a moment. Like everything else it must be acquired by time and assiduity. Study and investigation are requisite in forming an acquaintance with any of the sciences. A superficial knowledge may indeed be obtained without much labor but it is worth not much when obtained. Religion is the science of living well, the most important but the most difficult of all the sciences to learn. It comprises so vast a number of subordinate branches, so many apparently extraneous pursuits, that it must be the business of one's whole life to become properly proficient. We therefore discard the idea that it can be obtained in a moment, that in the course of a very few seconds the vilest and most abandoned profligate may become a saint of the first class.

We say to the man desirous of obtaining religion "be calm, be considerate, rationally and candidly review your past life." We present him the gospel, we address ourselves to the reasoning powers and by arguments drawn from the fitness of things and the nature of the case, we endeavor to convince him of the wrong he has done and to persuade him to reform. In this we use not the whirlwind, nor do we hurl the bolts of an incensed Deity, because experience has taught us whatever effect such violent proceedings may produce, they are generally not very agreeable.

We cast our eyes forward to ages yet unborn. Their faith will depend much on the opinions we adopt and the manner in which we maintain them. To them we would transmit the religion of Jesus pure, noble and desirable as it came from its author.

We would ever wish to possess that zeal which is according to knowledge and to acquire it. We study to ascertain the truth of the creed we adopt and the propriety of the course we pursue. Hence we proceed no farther than we proceed safely. All the systems of religion ever practiced except ours have either fallen or are beginning to fall into disrepute. Notwithstanding the zeal with which they were propagated and defended many are now destitute of even a name. We wish ours to be permanent. It is our desire that it may extend to the remotest corners of the peopled earth and be perpetuated to the latest posterity. Wherever it is known, wherever its influence is felt, we desire it may be the harbinger of peace, that it may like the day star be followed by the enlightening and invigorating beams of the glorious sun of righteousness. We look forward with joyful anticipation to the period when all shall bask in the rays of that glorious sun of truth, which our sentiments shall usher in, and while we drink the purest bliss from the prospect we wish to hasten the period by cultivating the temper which we believe will then be most approved and acquiring that moral character which all will then possess.

But to conclude, to our brethren we say be not indifferent but be not impatient, you cannot be healed before the moving of the waters. The various agitations of the public mind augur well. The signs of the times are indeed flattering; but see then that when your Lord appears ye are not found drunken with passion nor slumbering in cold indifference. Yours is the cause of truth. It shall prevail. Not all the powers of earth or hell shall be able to prevent its march and its final triumph. Be careful you do not degrade yourselves by your own earnestness. Be active but act with the understanding. Be devotional but let your devotion be the result of reflection and sober thought. Kindle your zeal with the fire from off the altar of reason and teach your piety to bow at the shrine of wisdom and knowledge.

The passions may be excited, the person may fancy himself elevated to some lofty height, but alas the power that reared is short lived, the ferment of passion soon subsides, and its deluded victim was elevated only to fall the lower to sink in a more frigid zone than before. Brethren bear with you this reflection, that he is the best Christian who relieves the wants of the oppressed; he will most effectually support the real interests of religion, who encourages free inquiry, studies to enlighten the mind and to maintain a sober and dignified walk through life. Amen.

4.

THE FAITH AND CHARACTER
OF THE TRUE CHRISTIAN

Gospel Advocate and Impartial Investigator
6 (April 12, 1828): 113-17

And the disciples were first called Christians at Antioch. Acts 11:26.

In the earliest records of mankind, religion holds a prominent rank. It was so early in its adoption and so general in its extension that many have pronounced man naturally a religious being. Some, rejecting this hypothesis, contend that religion owes its origin to revelation from God made to man during a state of innocency, which has been perpetuated through successive generations and extended to different nations by the aid of tradition and the dispersion of mankind.

Others again resort to reflection and experience and conclude that man first obtained the idea of a God and the utility of worshiping him from reasoning upon his works, and duly considering the nature and variety of the circumstances of their condition. In support of this it is remarked that in the infancy of our knowledge our religious ideas were vague and unintelligible and our practices absurd and often pernicious; but as knowledge increased, as the laws of nature became better and more satisfactorily developed, our ideas of God and his worship became more rational and more salutary in their influence on the morals of society.

But whether mankind first imbibed the idea that religion was necessary from instinct, from revelation, or reflection, this much is certain—they have made but little proficiency in this most interesting science without the extraordinary influences of the Spirit of the Most High.

Few, since the age of history, have denied the utility of some kind of religion; but alas! it cannot be concealed that this offspring of love, designed to cheer our gloomy path and smooth the asperities of the road of life, has too often been degraded from the dignity of her station and prevented from executing the benevolent office with which she was entrusted. She has too often been compelled to second the schemes of the ambitious and cover with her sacred garb the insidious designs of those who wished to aggrandize themselves or their party by the depression of the rest. And even amid the knowledge and refinements of the present age, this heavenly messenger has been obliged to lend her name to sanction the ravings of fanaticism, the effervescence of passion, the zeal and enthusiasm of sectarian ambition. But we are permitted to hope that the time has nearly arrived when she will assert her dignity and extend to all that kind assistance which she is empowered to give.

A little short of two thousand years ago there appeared a personage who, by his example and precepts, and the subsequent preaching of his disciples has made the most important revolution in the opinions and practices of mankind ever before known or ever hereafter to be expected.

Previous to his appearance men had made many valuable discoveries and many useful improvements. The Jews had taught the unity of the Deity in a clear and conspicuous manner. The attributes of Jehovah were, in a good degree, rationally explained; the immortality of the soul or the resurrection from the dead had been suggested and believed by some; a retributive providence founded on man's accountability had been defended; moral philosophy in the pagan school had been closely and successfully studied; but the great mass of mankind were deeply sunk in ignorance and superstition. A fashionable atheism was in high repute in many places, riot and obscenity disgraced the temples of the gods in almost every instance. While those who held a more rational religion degraded it by their mean sophisms, by their superstitious attachment to the minor parts of religious worship, and unwarrantably passing over the more important and more benevolent duties.

Something was requisite to correct the abuses everywhere prevalent to give additional light to the religious world and to religion itself a more imperial sanction that it might rest upon a more permanent basis, be more extended in its authority, and more benevolent in its influence. To effect this was the end the great founder of our religion proposed to himself and to this desirable object he adapted his preaching. Success attended his labors; but amid the convulsions of the church and government of the distracted and unhappy people of the Jews, where he made his first appearance, he found the most severe opposition, the most virulent persecution; [he] was accused of blasphemy against God, and of conspiring against the Roman government to which they were subject, was insulted with a mock trial, and finally perished upon the cross.

But his miracles, together with the purity of his life, the benevolence of his character, the excellency of his doctrinal and moral precepts, the dignity and sublimity of his preaching, had collected a number of disciples who became confirmed in what he had taught them by his now appearing to them risen from the grave. They joyfully embraced his doctrine; and animated by the cheering influence of the Holy Spirit, which they received from heaven, they began to proclaim the resurrection of their so lately crucified master and to enforce what he had directed them to teach. Churches or congregations of believers were collected in several places, as in Jerusalem, Samaria, Antioch, and others. As the religion they taught was different from all others, it became necessary that it should be distinguished by some name. While they were but few the term disciple, among themselves, answered every purpose of designation; but increased in numbers and beginning to have an extensive intercourse with the rest of the world, a name more specific in its import was required. Hence, at Antioch, they took the appellation of their master Christ; "and the disciples were called Christians first at Antioch."

In after times they have been distinguished by other appellatives, such as Catholics, believers in one universal church under one visible head; Episcopalians, or those who contend for the regular succession of bishops and the hierarchical government; Congregationalists or Independents, such as maintain the sovereignty of each separate congregation; Unitarians, those who strenuously contend for the unity of God and the subordination of the Son; Universalists, those who maintain that all mankind will be raised to a state of progressive holiness and happiness; and various other names designed to express some peculiarity in faith or practice. But with these we have no concern at present, it being our object to point out the true Christian and delineate his character.

It may be asserted without adducing any proof, because all will admit it, that the true Christian is a disciple of Christ. A disciple is a scholar or one who learns. The disciple of Christ is one who learns of Christ, believes what Christ taught, and practices the duties he enjoined. What Christ taught and enjoined is the religion of Christ or Christianity; an examination of this will enable us to ascertain the character of the true Christian.

All systems of religion resolve themselves into two parts, theoretical and practical.

With regard to the theory of the Christian religion, there is much difficulty, and perhaps some uncertainty; which unhappily have given rise to many painful contentious and aggravated controversies that

have ended in the separation of brethren. The occasion of this difficulty is found chiefly in the fact that almost every man commences
the study of the doctrine with preconceived ideas, which it becomes
his main object to defend. We generally have determined in our minds
what Christ *ought* to teach before we come to him for instruction,
and his words must be turned to speak our own sentiments, which
indeed would be correct if we were masters, but since we profess to
be his disciples, we ought to shape our opinions according to his
directions.

There may be another cause: Christ did not deliver his doctrinal
precepts in that connected, systematic form which we moderns are
apt to imagine essential to a body of divinity. It may here be remarked that our master does not seem to have designed so much a
regular system of divinity by his instructions, as he did to give wholesome rules for our practice. Hence the theory of his religion is to be
learned from casual allusions and perhaps must be collected from his
practical observations.

Our great and ever blessed Master was not ignorant of human
nature; he knew how extremely difficult, if not absolutely impossible, it is to bring all mankind to a uniform faith; he seems therefore
to have anticipated a contrariety of sentiments, and to have adapted
his instructions to the circumstances of each. He doubtless knew if
he laid down a series of doctrinal propositions, time in its operations,
might obliterate their meaning, and render them useless or pernicious. He knew also that language was continually fluctuating, and
might easily be made to speak that which its author never designed
to teach. He knew how exceedingly fond men were of establishing a
creed; how prone they were to raise faith over morality and to substitute correctness of opinion for a life of benevolence and humanity.
And indeed, notwithstanding his precautions, the consequence which
he most disapproved has actually followed. What would have been
the case had he been as particular in teaching men what they should
believe, as he was in directing them what they should do? As he
knew what would be the consequences of his instructions, and as it
was his great object to produce righteousness, he chose never to gratify
idle curiosity with doctrinal ideas or theoretical speculations, at least
no farther than it was necessary to lay a permanent foundation for
his moral superstructure. He never expressed so much solicitude about
what particular opinions we should imbibe as he did about what
actions they should perform or what course of conduct they should
adopt. Good works are always useful; faith is nothing only as it adds
to a man's comfort and stimulates him to benevolent exertions; so far

it is necessary and so far Christ regarded it, but no farther. This regard for faith the true Christian ever cultivates, but always bears in mind "faith without works is dead" [James 2:17].

The unity of the Deity was an article already in the creed of Christ's countrymen but it certainly receives additional sanction from his authority. "Hear O Israel the Lord thy God is One Lord" Mk. 12:29. The Apostles also bear witness to the same sentiment and seem to have maintained it in all their preaching. Hence they assert there is "One God the Father of our Lord Jesus Christ, etc."[1]

The benevolence of the Deity together with his universal providence was clearly taught by our great master.

That God is benevolent is what every reflecting man does and must admit. Infinite in wisdom, illimitable in power, there is no conceivable inducement for him to be evil. Whatever he desires his wisdom is at hand to devise the best possible means for its acquisition, and his power is ever ready to carry his plans into execution, and as we have been unable to find in the depths of wickedness a being sufficiently malignant to desire evil for the sake of evil the conclusion is evident, God must be benevolent. But this sentiment is put beyond the reach of doubt by the language of him who spake as never man spake. "If ye then being evil know how to give good gifts unto your children, how much more shall your Father which is in heaven give good things unto them who ask him?" Mk. 7:11.

God's universal providence is taught by the operations of nature and to these operations Christ refers his disciples for proof of the same, to the sun which rises on the "evil" and the "good," to the rain which falls upon the "just" and the "unjust." Observe the fowls of heaven. They neither sow nor reap. They have no storehouse; but your heavenly Father feedeth them. Are not ye more valuable than they? Mark the lilies of the field. They toil not; they spin not. Yet, I affirm, that Solomon, in all his glory was not adorned like one of these. If then God so array the herbage which today is in the field, and tomorrow will be cast into the oven; will he not much more array you, O ye distrustful. Therefore say not anxiously, as the heathen do, what shall we eat; or what shall we drink, or wherewith shall we be clothed? For your heavenly Father knoweth that ye have need of these things. Mt. 6:27-32.[2]

[1] [Ed. This is not an exact quote of 1 Cor. 8:6.]

[2] Campbell's translation. [Ed. Brownson refers to Alexander Campbell's (1788-1866) *Sacred Writings* (Buffaloe, Brooke County VA, 1826), a revised English translation of an 1818 British edition of the New Testament. On Campbell's translation, see Roland H. Worth, Jr., *Bible Translations: A History Through Source Documents* (Jefferson, NC: McFarland Co., 1992), 152-55.]

The doctrine of rewards and punishments is very clearly stated and the principles on which they will be dispensed forcibly illustrated in many observations which may be collected.

The righteous will be rewarded because they have performed acts of benevolence and humanity, and the wicked punished because they have neglected them. Or, in a word, the doctrine rests upon the fact that man is an accountable being and that he must in the day of judgement give an account of every foolish or improper action and of every idle word. See Matt. 12:38 [36].[3]

Where the day of judgement will be we are not particularly informed, neither is it a matter of much importance that our information should be more specific; for since we are assured the servant that knoweth his Master's will and doeth it not shall be beaten with many stripes and the one who knoweth it not, though he do things worthy of stripes, shall be beaten with few, we are permitted to believe the decision will be according to our deserts, and as we know the punishment comes from a kind and compassionate Father, we need be under no apprehension that it will be greater than our best good requires.

Forgiveness of sin on condition of repentance is another doctrine taught and illustrated by our great master.

It is taught in the prayer he has left us "forgive us our debts, as we forgive our debtors" [Matt. 6:11]. It is illustrated in several of his parables, particularly in the parable of the prodigal son; by which we are taught the most abandoned sinner may return and find the affectionate embrace of his Father and his God. The same truth is contained in the object of his mission, which was not to call the righteous but sinners to repentance. That is, he came to reform the world, to recall the guilty sons of our race from their wanderings and restore them to the bosom of their God. Found also in that ever to be remembered declaration, "God so loved the world that he gave his only begotten son to die that whosoever believeth on him should not perish but have everlasting life" [John 3:16].

That all will finally repent, return and come to Zion in such a manner as not to be cast out is pretty clearly taught by his asserting all things were delivered into his hands, that he had power over all flesh for that purpose and that *all* which were given to him should come once not to be cast out. See Matthew 11:27, John 6:37-40, 12:33.

---

[3] [Ed. Brownson refers to verse 38, but the correct citation is verse 36 in the King James Version.]

He taught the resurrection of mankind from the dead and exemplified it by rising himself.

The particular condition of those that shall rise is not revealed but we are assured that in the resurrection they will be spiritual, immortal, like the angels, and will also be the children of God because children of the resurrection. See Matt. 22:35, Luke 20:35-37, 1 Cor. 15:22, 42-55.

As it respects himself, Christ uniformly taught he received his authority from God, that he was commissioned by the Father who was greater than he, to whom he was subject and to whom he directed his prayers.

These seem to be the leading points in the theory of the Christian religion. To these the true Christian pays attention and from these he draws the conclusion God is one, even his Father, the Father of all, providing for all his children; forgiving all upon the condition of reformation, giving his Son to bring all to repentance, assuring them though they die they shall live again, and because their Savior lives they shall live also.

My brethren will allow me to remark here that in all we can discover in the preaching of Christ we can find nothing that is contrary to natural religion. Natural religion indeed could never have soared so high but when the author of these sublime sentiments discloses them or to continue the metaphor brings them within our reach. Natural religion embraces them with the warmest affection. When we find a revealed religion thus corroborated by natural, we have strong presumptive evidence of its truth and utility.

The practical part of the Christian religion is more plain because more important. This consists of two parts, our duty to God, and our duty to mankind.

[1.] Our duty to God is that we love him with all the heart, mind, and strength. This may surely be ascertained to be our reasonable service. God is our Father, the fountain of all excellence, the source whence we derive all our enjoyments. He is our friend, our benefactor, our Redeemer, and our everlasting Savior. All that we are, all that we have, all that we can possess is the gift of his love, the effect of his munificence. However great the happiness we enjoy, however valuable our possessions, we received them from him, and it is no more than reasonable that they should endear the character of him who bestows them, and render us grateful to the Being that has shown us so tender a regard and such powerful proofs of his fatherly affection.

Worship to God in order to be acceptable must be in "spirit and in truth." It must be the spontaneous offspring of grateful affection, seated in the heart. The performance of his worship is not confined to any particular place nor to any prescribed form because none are necessary. God is everywhere present and wherever the creature is there we may find the Creator, and in whatever manner the heart is grateful will its gratitude be accepted.

Christ established no rites or ceremonies because he would not countenance superstition. He however permitted his disciples to baptize and he himself instituted the sacrament of bread and wine. The first was only an initiatory performance which served as a witness or seal of one's profession, but made him, in itself considered neither more virtuous nor vicious. The last was a memorial of his own sufferings and death and might have a tendency to refresh the minds of his followers and perhaps bind them more closely to each other with the cords of brotherly love.

Worship to God is proper and is enjoined by our Savior, but he has left us no prescriptions respecting it any more than that it must be the incense of the heart. From which it is inferred, every act which does not make the heart better or convey some good to some fellow being will not be acceptable. The mode must be left to time and circumstance to dictate. Christ has left us a prayer, but it is to be considered rather as a specimen than as a form; designed to serve as a guide, to teach us the nature of the petitions we should prefer to our heavenly Father.

Christ's own example is the best instruction we can have relative to this department of our duty; by studying this and endeavoring to imitate it, we shall be preserved from falling into gross mistakes or irretrievable errors.

Remark then his deportment, always meek, always sober, always dignified. No violent emotions were discovered; no rapturous exclamations were heard. No bursts of zeal, or fiery enthusiasm were seen emitting their destructive flames. Mark his prayer, it breathes a calm, sober, and rational devotion. It speaks a good heart and an enlightened mind. See him in the garden on the eve of his departure. His soul was exceedingly sorrowful, unto death; his prayer was affecting, it discovered feeling, it told deep devotion and pious resignation, but it was sober and rational. He possessed in this hour of trial, in this moment of severe affliction, that same fortitude and self-command which he always maintained. From the whole of his character, we may collect this truth, that to worship God acceptably, it requires the exercise of all the powers and faculties we possess. The heart must feel, but the head must direct; the affections must be engaged, but reason must guard their operations. We must pray fervently, but not enthusiastically, and in all our expressions, in all our modes of worship, in all our devotional zeal, in all our pious affections, we are to maintain a calm and considerate manner; a propriety of address, an unostentatious manner, yet that dignity of deportment which to enlightened minds will ever be deemed most becoming rational beings in the presence of their Creator.

I cannot avoid remarking in this place how different is this description from the character of many of the professed followers of our great and ever to be revered Master. I say nothing of their doctrines, for of them, I have already spoken; but to what extravagance do some people run in their ideas of the worship of God! From the loudness and boisterous manner in which they pray, one is led to conclude that they suppose their God is deaf and cannot hear or is asleep and must be waked. But, brethren, let us compassionate their mistakes and watch diligently over ourselves lest we run to the same or a worse excess.

2.[4] The other department of practical religion regulates our conduct to each other. This belongs to ethics, and can be only slightly touched in this place.

I confess myself highly pleased with the morals of Confucius. So far as I have learned them, they elicit an enlightened mind and a benevolent heart. I admire many things to be found in the writings of the pagan philosophers. Plato has sublime flights. Cicero has many maxims that should be engraven on the tablets of the heart, and I can never read Seneca without feeling my heart softened, my virtue confirmed, and my philanthropy increased. But to me these all fall far below the practical observations of Jesus of Nazareth. Notice forgiveness to enemies: What heathen philosopher ever taught this? Most of them represent that not to resent injuries is the result of meanness and pusillanimity. How much better the sentiment of him who knew what was befitting man! "Ye have heard that it hath been said, thou shall love thy neighbor or friend, and hate thy enemy; but I say unto you, love your enemies." The reason assigned is that we may be the children of our Father who is in heaven: See Matt. 5:43, etc. This duty might also be inferred from the nature of our relations and the fitness of things; but he who has once forgiven an enemy will require no argument to induce to forgive again.

---

[4] [Ed. Brownson began numbering here with number 2; there is no number 1 in the original. Frequently he fails to provide proper numbering in his texts.]

Forgiveness stands opposed to revenge; and we are taught that the true Christian should never indulge in resentful feeling and by no means a vindictive disposition. He is commanded not to resist the injurious; but if a man strike him on the right cheek, to turn to him also the left; that is, he is to be always placable in his temper and forbearing in his manner.

Notice as the next trait in the Christian's character, universal benevolence. The national character of the Jews was illiberal and cruel; but very different is the case with the disciple of Christ. He is taught that all mankind are brethren, all are neighbors, and he must love them as he does himself. No peculiarity of nation, language or manners, is allowed to break the social tie, or dissolve the moral obligation; no sectarian interests must prevent reciprocal kindness and mutual good offices.

The Jews and Samaritans were bitter enemies, alienated by prejudices of religion and country; yet to the lawyer who asked, "who is my neighbor?" Christ proposed the example of a Samaritan assisting a Jew for his imitation. "Go," he would say, "wherever you see a fellow mortal in distress, ask not to what country he belongs, ask not what religion he professes, ask not whether he be a friend or enemy; but bind his wounds, heal his broken heart, and take care that he suffers no more." Would to God the sectarians of this day had a little more of this philanthropic spirit.

3. But to conclude: As a general rule, the Christian does to others whatever he would wish them to do to him. No rule can be better adapted to popular practice than this. It is short. It is no burden to the memory, yet it is sufficiently comprehensive. It may always be at hand, and, if observed, it will solve any doubt that may arise. We have only in our minds to exclude circumstances, and self-love will generally give a correct decision.

We may sum up the character of the true Christian: he is one that loves God and worships him in a sober and rational manner; one who, though he may contend for faith, does it only because he believes it will be subservient to good works; one who recognizes all mankind as brethren, bound on the same voyage, destined to the same haven, and beloved by the same Father; one who compassionates the follies of his brethren, weeps over their calamities, reproves their vices, but omits nothing of his kind offices or good wishes. He is the sober, devout worshiper, the universal friend and consistent moralist. May we all bear his character and receive his reward.

5.

THE ESSAYIST

The Gospel Advocate and Impartial Investigator
6 (April 12, 1828): 117-18

It has long been the practice of a large majority of professed Christians to decry the works of nature and to consider the contemplation of the physical phenomena with which we are surrounded as unfavorable to genuine piety or as not essential to our forming proper notions of the Supreme Being whom we are bound to love and obey. Perhaps no idea has ever been imbibed which is fraught with more real iniquity to the interests of true religion, or one that has done greater disservice to the cause of rational piety.

Christianity unfolds to us truths which the study of nature could never have discovered; it brings to us a knowledge of the moral perfections of the Deity, which our limited capacities, unassisted by revelation, could not have reached; but it does not supersede the necessity of improving, to the extent of our ability, every means presented by the natural world for exalting our conceptions of its Author, or for correcting and enlarging our views of our service to him or of our duty to ourselves and to our brethren.

The relation of the Creator to his creatures is immutably the same; and it was that their relations might be more distinctly seen and the advantages accruing to us from a knowledge of them might be more duly appreciated, that infinite wisdom condescended to make us the disclosures contained in the Christian revelation. But to neglect the study of them because we have the additional light required to make the study pleasing and profitable is certainly contrary to the design of Christianity as well as no small ingratitude to him who has bestowed upon us the invaluable favor.

The revelation God has made us in his word does not contain *all* the knowledge we need; it contains only that *part* which could not be acquired without an extraordinary communication from him to whom all things are known. This revelation supposes us to be acquainted with the material world, to have obtained all the information the exercise of our natural powers can give; and then bestows itself as a free bounty, as an addition to the fund already accumulated. If we neglect the natural sources of knowledge, if we do not improve the means nature has placed within our reach, we cannot relish the bounties and excellencies of the free gift which our heavenly Father has made us.

Revealed religion is not opposed to natural religion, but is natural religion enlarged and sublimated. It commences where natural religion stops and carries or extends it to perfection. Natural religion lays or rather is the foundation; revealed [religion is] the superstructure; and the attempt to support revealed independent of natural religion is as absurd as to attempt to rear a fabric without a base. What Deity has taught by his works is eternal truth, and could our minds take in all his works and ascertain all their relations to themselves and to their Creator, we should need no greater knowledge. But this we cannot do. Heaven has therefore kindly in compassion to our wants enlarged our vision and enabled us to discover some things which our natural eyes could not discover. But because we can now see more things than we could before, shall we refuse to look upon those things and learn the utility of those objects which were within the bounds of our vision? Revelation is to the mind what the telescope is to the eye. The telescope certainly strengthens the natural powers of vision and enables us to see objects more distinctly and at a greater distance. It also enables the eye to discover objects which were before invisible; but what should we think of the man who, having once felt the pleasure of looking through it, should put out his natural eyes that he might see only with the telescope? Not less the folly in one, who, because he has felt the natural powers of his mind assisted by revelation should destroy those powers or refuse to exercise them that he might see only by revelation. As in the first case the telescope would be useless, so in the latter would be the revelation.

Absurd as this may seem, it has been frequently the practical convictions of professed Christians. Hence those numerous denunciations against the exercise of human reason, against the study of nature, and the acquisition of human wisdom, which have been so often reiterated from the lips of the professedly pious. Hence, too, those systems of faith and practice, at which human nature is sickened, that have been propagated with unremitting zeal and industry. Hence, too, those violent persecutions for the love of God or the honor of his religion, which crimson the page of history and make us almost wish ourselves infidels. Had those who persecuted with unrelenting malice during those ages which we would forget studied nature as much as they did their own opinions, we might now contemplate their zeal and labors with satisfaction.

But what kind of religion must we conclude that to be which proscribes mental improvement, which condemns every advance in natural and moral science, which hurls its anathemas against everyone who has the boldness to mention some of the phenomena of nature, which by his studies or his experiments he has discovered? Can we wonder that unintelligible dogmas were implicitly believed? Shall we wonder how men could believe that "three is one," that "the Lord is co-eval with his father," that "the sacred host might be indefinitely multiplied and each part contain the whole and entire body of Christ?" That "the sign of the cross, or the counting of beads could avert danger or procure blessings?" No; we rather wonder why greater absurdities did not gain credence. These follies are now discovered to be such, but there is still reason to complain that men are inclined to believe, if they have the Bible in their house, they have all the knowledge they need. I do not say but a man may have genuine piety who has never read any other book, or who has never contemplated the works of nature; but if he has had the means of making himself acquainted with the discoveries of science, the majesty of God displayed in the heavens, his power and wisdom in sustaining, his beneficence in providing for the countless millions of beings he has created, I say if he has been so situated that he could pursue those studies and has not done it, he has great reason to distrust the sincerity of his piety.

(May 10, 1828): 151-52

The Christian revelation has disclosed to us many noble and valuable truths, truths which give us a more exalted rank among the creatures of God, which make us capable of rising to a higher pitch of excellence and of receiving more sublime satisfaction from contemplating the works of our Almighty Father. But this revelation was not made to the brute creation; it could do them no good, for they are incapable of relishing its beauties; but it was made to rational beings and demands the exercise of all the powers they possess. It might as well have been made to brutes as man if we by voluntary resigning the exercise of our reason make ourselves the same.

Revelation is not to be depreciated; but revelation comprises not more than half the truly excellent system of religion called Christianity. The supernatural relations recorded in the Scriptures give us indeed very exalted conceptions of the Deity; but he who is unacquainted with the volume of nature, though he may have read the Bible a thousand times over will be a stranger to those sublime emotions which a view of the magnitude, variety, order and harmony of the universe would constantly inspire.

The Scriptures declare Jehovah to be infinite in power; but no man from reading this declaration can have so clear or so forcible a demonstration of Almighty power as he can from viewing the works of nature. To justify this assertion let anyone compare the emotion the reading of this sentence excites in his bosom, with the one he feels when he contemplates the endless variety with which the earth is adorned, when he views the majesty of the ocean, the dashing of its waves; when he marks the excessive height of the firmament, listens to the roar of thunder which seems to shake the distant heavens, or when borne on the pinions of astronomy, he sees suns rise on suns and systems of worlds on systems, till wearied thought lost in the sublimity of the scene, he exclaims — "Great are the works of the Lord; they have no bounds."

The Bible pronounces the wisdom of God to be infinite; we early assent to the proposition and suppose it must be true because the *Bible* declares it; but the very moment we begin to survey the Creator's works, observe the nice design and unbroken order which everywhere prevails, the numerous proofs of contrivance seen in the adaptation of one thing to another—conviction flashes upon the mind, we *feel* the force of demonstration, and prostrating ourselves before the altar of wisdom are lost in silent admiration.

Revelation pronounces the author of our being good and gives us a clue by which we can trace his benevolence through all his works; but it is to his providence, his mode of dealing with his children, and to the blessings he actually bestows upon them we must ultimately appeal for that irresistible conviction which fastens upon the mind and calls forth the gratitude of the heart. It is in his works that the Creator is beheld and his character ascertained. I do not mean we could have learned him in these, had he not given us a revelation in his word; but having received this, our vision is now extended and while we contemplate nature through its medium, we shall discover the evidences required to demonstrate the perfection of the Deity[;] [that perfection] must be collected from what he has done.

Let no one think he will dishonor God by learning the greatness, beauty and utility of his works. There is no danger of our forming too elevated conceptions of the Deity or of ascribing to him greater perfection than he actually possesses. As he is known only by what he has done, we must become acquainted with his works if we would have correct views of his character. Every page we read in the great volume of nature will more forcibly impress our minds with a sense of his unlimited power, wisdom and benevolence. Study then his works, whether you view creation as an immense body created and sustained by the Deity, or attempt the analytic investigation of any particular portion you will find cause at every step to pause and adore the Creator.

This study would have a tendency to enlarge the mind, to expand its ideas of benevolence, and to correct those selfish views which degrade too many of our race. The great reason why so many narrow, contracted systems of religion have been imposed upon us is because their advocates never considered the immensity of the Creator's works; but confined themselves to a few topics in theology, without inquiring how their descriptions would agree with that character of God which is displayed in the vast assemblage of beings and things which we denominate the universe. Had the manufacturers of our creeds kept a steady eye on the number of inhabitants on the earth in each generation, had they considered that about eight hundred millions of inhabitants enter on our earth and pass off again in about thirty-three years, that each of these beings was created by the same almighty power, and supported during his stay here by the same ever watchful providence, with about the same degree of loving kindness, I cannot but think they would have discarded that exclusive spirit which they have labored so industriously to infuse through our hearts. Had they considered of this vast number of beings that each individual is made capable of exalted felicity or deep anguish, they must have been shocked to have preached a doctrine which banished all from happiness to eternal pain except a few, say eight or ten million, who happen to agree in the essential articles of certain creeds. What benevolent soul can read over the "Confession of Faith" of the Presbyterian church and not feel his blood run cold. My God! What havoc does it make of the human family! How liberally does it people the kingdom of Satan! Seven hundred and ninety millions of the present race of pagans it consigns to destruction without mercy. Roman Catholics, Greek Church, heretics, infidels, infants and idiots, all, *all* go to hell. How solitary a place must be the kingdom of righteousness! Away with a doctrine fraught with such ungodly sentiments. If true, they would clothe heaven with sackcloth and if possible make demons howl with joy.

To the advocates of this unnatural creed the balm of kindness should ever be extended; for while they retain one spark of the native benevolence of the human heart, or exercise the least reflection, they must mourn in bitter anguish in view of the horrid destruction which they suppose the Creator will make in the felicity of his own dear children.

(May 24, 1828): 167-68

The sentiment which consigns to endless wretchedness a large proportion of the human family may be readily enough received by those who have never examined it; but whoever will take the trouble to investigate its claims upon our credence will find that it presents but a gloomy picture of unlimited goodness and is poorly calculated to reconcile one to his maker, to himself, to life, or to mankind generally.

The sentiment, however, is such as might naturally be expected from rude and uncultivated minds—such as are under the influence of strong passions, influenced by a sense of deep personal injuries. We readily love those we consider our friends and just as readily hate those we deem our enemies. As towards the one we generally manifest ourselves with kindness; so towards the other we show ourselves harsh and revengeful. Hence we need not wonder that those who fancied a God like themselves and adored a Divinity fashioned after their own image should imagine him under the influence of similar passions, and affected in a similar manner towards his friends or his enemies.

Men in their savage state set no bounds but their ability to the favors they would heap upon those who had shown a tender solicitude for their welfare; and too many have dreamed that God would do the same. As men in this state are always implacable in their hatred and will pursue revenge to the extent of their power, they foolishly imagined God would heap excessive tortures upon their and by consequence his enemies. It often happened they suffered severely from the injustice of their fellow men without the means of redressing themselves. It was then they called upon their imaginary Deity to avenge them; but not seeing the wished for judgements overtake their oppressors here, they created an ideal world and consoled themselves with the reflection that they should be recompensed in the blissful fields of Elysium while their enemies should be hurled to the depths of Tartarus to weep and howl forever.[1]

This sentiment gained a more ready acceptance and a more general extension from its congeniality to the various passions which in the infancy of knowledge and refinement would actuate the human breast. Every man considered himself a sufferer and his sufferings here he believed would be a sure claim to a recompense hereafter. Hence each hoped for himself. But each would fancy his neighbor

[1] [Ed. In Greek mythology, Elysium was the abode of the blessed dead and Tartarus was the abyss below Hades where Zeus confined the Titans.]

happier than himself and his happiness he believed was owing to his injustice, consequently his portion in the world to come must be pain and bitter anguish. Hence envy, a passion so common to us mortals, was soothed, and gratified its malignity by picturing to itself the reverse which would soon take place with respect to the object of its malice.

Such was doubtless the origin of the doctrine under consideration and such the passions which have had a tendency to perpetuate it. So long as men continue under the influence of hatred, revenge, or envy, they will doubtless draw the same conclusions. It is no matter of surprise that while men knew little more than to pursue the chase, plunder a weaker neighbor, or torture an enemy, that sentiments so much at war with the economy of Divine Providence should find supporters; but that now, amid the general diffusion of the sciences, and under the light of Christianity there should be any to advocate it is certainly an anomaly in the march of improvement.

How often do men who have been favored with a liberal education assert that "no man can be happy in another world, unless he believe in Christ in this." A sentiment like this exposes itself to the severest censure at first sight inasmuch as it sets all justice at defiance and laughs at impartiality. Faith is the assent of the mind to the truth of a proposition. The assent is not voluntary but the result of evidence which irresistibly convinces the mind. Any proposition demanding universal assent must be presented to all with sufficient evidence to produce the conviction in each mind of its truth. Now everybody knows that the Christian religion has never been communicated to one half of mankind. How could those believe it who never so much as heard that there was such a system of religious notions as Christianity?

Of the four hundred and ninety million of pagans now on the globe, perhaps not a thousand have ever had an opportunity of believing in Christ. Shall the rest be condemned for not believing when to believe was never in their power? And what justice is there in such a condemnation? About one fourth of mankind die in infancy; these were incapable of believing, what shall be their doom? The rule says: "no one can be happy in another world, unless he believe in Christ in this life." Infants we know cannot believe, consequently they must be miserable, or the rule is false. The rule is unjust because it makes one miserable for not doing that which he had no power of doing. It is partial because it does not present itself to all with the same degree of propriety. The rule can never claim the shadow of a reason for its support, until mankind shall be placed in exactly the same circumstances and the proposition they are required to believe with the evidences of its truth presented to all alike.

Were the views of some, who make very great claims to theological knowledge correct, how small a part of the human family will ever be happy! These theologians justify themselves, or attempt to justify themselves, by saying men are such exceeding great sinners that they deserve to be made endlessly miserable. Let it be so, and who can escape, since all mankind are sinners in about the same situation? Stronger arguments than any presented must be produced before any rational man will believe that a part will go to eternal blessedness while the rest shall be dragged down to infinite despair. I say divide not the child.

(June 7, 1828): 181-82

The gospel of Christ enjoins upon all its advocates the most unbounded charity and the same is enforced by the general economy of Divine Providence, as it is everywhere administered; it is therefore unjust to censure too severely those who may still cling to opinions long since superannuated. There can be no doubt but many who profess to believe in the doctrine of endless misery persuade themselves that they are sincere in their professions, notwithstanding they are unable to reconcile a sentiment so horrid in its features to the light of nature or to support it by the authority of revelation. They however seldom take that particular view of it which is requisite to enable them to draw just conclusions respecting it.

There is scarcely one among the warmest advocates of this strange doctrine who would not revolt at the idea of making one of his children as miserable as he could for a hundred years, and should we insinuate that a believer in endless misery would, without any compunction of conscience, make even his most bitter enemy endure the supposed torments of hell for only one year, he would accuse us of doing great injustice to the benevolence of his heart. It is a fact that this class of people are not destitute of those kind and social feelings which are the ornaments of our race. They can weep with those who weep and rejoice with those who rejoice; they can mingle their sympathies with their fellow beings and no doubt from their hearts pray most fervently that the calamities of mankind may be averted and happiness become the lot of every individual. They love their families and smile with gratitude to God for the prosperity of their children; they are as quick to perceive cruelty as any other people; they sigh at oppression; and, when not influenced by their peculiar creed, are in general ready to succor the distressed. How happens it, then, that these people, who evidently belong to the human family, who show by their conduct that they are subject to the same passions, emotions and affections with the rest of mankind, should adopt a creed so repugnant to every kind or social feeling?

They are men not deficient in ability. In the ordinary concerns of life and indeed on almost any subject not connected with their peculiar faith, they generally decide according to the dictates of common sense. May not their early education have produced that species of insanity which discovers itself in only a particular association of ideas while it leaves the mind perfectly sane on every other subject? I have read of many persons and in fact have known some of this description. Meet them, they appear rational; converse with them on ordinary subjects, they will answer you correctly and not infrequently carry on the conversation to your entire satisfaction; but if you chance to light upon the particular association of ideas which has disordered their minds, and the maniac raves in all his wildness and incoherence.

Now, I have often found it so when conversing with believers in endless misery. Speak about their property or such like things, their perception is acute, and I do not generally discover any great deficiency in their logic; but touch the doctrine of endless misery and they are wild. Reason, which before was clearly enough discerned, now loses its power and as if ashamed of defeat conceals itself from observation.

I was once relating with affected calmness to one of these persons the circumstance of a parent's killing his children. The parent had only two children, sweet little cherubs they were! The father had often been seen to caress them with fond delight and been heard to instruct them with much anxiety for their future welfare; but just as their minds began to unfold like the blossom and they were becoming capable of profiting by the directions he gave for their conduct, he violently seized one by the arm—he remembered that when the child knew no better, it had disobeyed one of his commands—he dashed its head against the wall; the child he apparently loved lay lifeless at his feet! "Was not this," I asked, "a most righteous parent? And do you not, sir, justify his conduct?" He answered as any man with the feelings of a man would have answered. "Justify him? No; the deed is too horrible to be named. The father might have suitably chastised his child for its faults, or for disobedience after he had come to the years of discretion; but to have taken the life of his child, and that for something done when it knew no better, cannot be too severely disapprobated." This was well enough; but when I came to ask him respecting the propriety of supposing that God would make nine-tenths of his children eternally miserable, and he could justify the deed, when he condemned the parent for simply taking the life of *his* child. He said "God had a right to make all miserable; that his justice required him to send all to hell; that his honor as a sovereign required him to make them miserable as long as," I perceived his brain was disordered and turned from him regretting with myself that strange infatuation under which so many labor. Alas, said I, how long shall men ascribe that character to God, which if borne by a human being, they would utterly detest? When will men learn to study nature and consent to be guided by the directions of common sense? If men would reason upon the same general principles, let the subject of consideration be what it will, all would be well.

(June 21, 1828): 196-98

One of the great defects among theologians now, as it was formerly among philosophers, is the using of words without the conveying of any distinct idea. One can scarcely read a book on divinity that does not lead him into the mazes of unintelligibility or occupy his attention with mere sound without sense. In works written professedly for amusement, if the sound be agreeable, the objection may pass without any severity of censure; but in those designed to instruct it is certainly a very great imperfection.

Men sit down to write often with no other qualification for the task than that of merely making a book that may be respected for its size. Having no definite ideas themselves, it is not to be expected that they will communicate any to their readers. Hence it is that we may read hundreds of volumes and remain as ignorant as we commenced. There are many writers who have almost inundated the literary world, of whom we can say little more, than that they have collected a great variety of words and put them together in such a manner that they may mean anything or nothing. There are readers, too, whose mouths are full of quotations, who have a certain number of phrases, which they mistake for ideas, and vainly imagine because they can repeat them with a good deal of facility that they are quite well informed.

These remarks are so evidently true that none who have accustomed themselves to reflect on the subject will need any arguments to induce them to acknowledge their force. I shall, however, illustrate them by some few examples selected from the many I might adduce. There is one phrase frequently met with in theological books and as frequently heard from the mouths of those who think they know something about that great Being, who, though invisible, yet manifests himself in the government of the world and the bounteous provision he makes for all his sentient creation.

This phrase is the "*Glory of God.*" I do not say that this phrase is susceptible of no definite meaning; but I do say that those who most frequently use it have no distinct idea of its import and they in general throw it out as an apology for the absence of an argument or the want of thought. To me this appears evident from the manner in which the phrase is applied. "God," it is said, "always seeks his own glory and his administration is so ordered that it will promote his highest glory. God will be as much glorified in the endless damnation of sinners as he will be in the endless felicity of the elect."[2] Now let any one examine these expressions and what idea does he obtain? Surely, if any, one at which those who use them would be alarmed.

Take the first: "God always seeks his own glory." Surely if there be a *selfish* man on earth, he is one who is continually laboring for the acquisition of glory. Those who use this expression are decidedly of the opinion that all sin consists in *selfishness,* in one's laboring to promote his own interests without any regard to the welfare of others. And if it be said that his own glory is the end which Deity everywhere proposes to himself, it cannot be alleged that he regards the happiness of his children any farther than such regard tends to produce the end he has in view, and as all his labors (if I may be allowed the expression) terminate in himself he can be considered in no other light than as a selfish being. If all sin consists in selfishness and every being is sinful in proportion as he is selfish, the conclusion to be drawn respecting our heavenly Father is such as would justly startle anyone, however fond he might be of saying "God always labors to promote his own glory."

It will not do to say that the glory of God and the happiness of his creatures are the same, or are inseparably connected. This, though it be a fact, does not alter the case in the least; for it must be conceded that if the happiness of his creatures was opposed to his glory, they must be sacrificed to its augmentation. Now this does not represent Deity as promoting our happiness for its own sake, but that he may make himself more glorious; neither does he *will* our misery, but as he cannot make himself glorious without it, he does not scruple to send us to eternal woe.

Should an earthly sovereign act upon such principles, we should not consider him worthy a crown, much less should we call him the father of his people. His character would be justly reprobated by

---

[2] [Ed. Reference here is to the theology of Samuel Hopkins, whose emphasis upon disinterested benevolence included the maxim that one should be willing to be damned for the greater glory of God.]

every man of wholesome principles. But can any man apply to the heavenly Father that character which he would detest if borne by a human being or indeed would he call such a character glorious? By no means. Hence I conclude that those who use this phraseology have not settled its meaning, and consequently do not get any definite idea from it.

Take the other expression: "God will be as much glorified in the endless misery of sinners as he will in the salvation of the elect." This is only a modification of the phrase which we have dismissed and if it convey any idea at all it supposes the happiness or misery of mankind, in itself considered, as a matter of perfect indifference to God; but as he finds it more for his glory to make some happy than it would be to make all miserable, so he does it; and as it would not be sufficiently glorious to make *all* happy, he, for his glory, makes the rest miserable. Now the sovereign who should sacrifice one half his subjects for his own glory would be looked upon as a monster in cruelty, and it cannot be that those who say God has "by a decree for the manifestation of his glory, predestinated some men and angels unto everlasting life, and foreordained others unto everlasting death" have any definite ideas of the terms they use; for such a decree would make him anything but glorious in the eyes of his intelligent creatures. If it be said that our mode of judging among ourselves is improperly used when judging of God or of what is glorious or inglorious in him, I answer, we can reason only "from what we know" and to refer us to some unknown method of determination is only to confess our ignorance, and to build our hypothesis upon something that is unknown when it bears no analogy to anything known is to betray a disposition that should ever be branded with disgrace. Any course of conduct which would degrade a human being cannot with the least shadow of reason be supposed to exalt the character of the Deity when attributed to him.

(July 5, 1828): 213-15

No subject demands more serious attention than that of punishment. Much has been written upon it, thousands have endeavored to correct our views respecting it, but still there is great want of knowledge upon it. Mankind have from time immemorial believed that there was some necessary congruity between crime and the infliction of pain for it, which they have called desert, but with what degree of propriety they have generally neglected to inquire.

The idea that man deserves punishment for the commission of crime should be closely examined. Punishment, according to the common sentiment, implies the inflicting upon an offender a certain quantity of pain for a certain quantity of crime without any regard to the good of the one punished, merely because it is supposed there is a fitness in the thing itself. It is supposed that justice would be very angry if one should do an improper act and not receive for it a severe chastisement. For instance, should a man murder, but before he received any punishment should reform and become a worthy man, it would make no difference; but justice would require that a certain degree of pain be inflicted, say his life taken in exchange for the person he had killed.

Now every person who thinks must perceive that the punishment in this case does no good so far at least as the murderer is concerned. It neither restores the murdered to life nor makes the murderer a better man because he had already reformed. If his life is taken it can do no good to society because it deprives society of one of its members. Suppose the person has not reformed, punishment has no view to his reformation for it looks only to the crime committed, consequently must be retrospective in its influence. What benefit will this retrospective influence confer? Or what satisfaction will the infliction of pain give to justice when no good results? Nothing is more evident than that punishment merely for crime committed does no good and to say the least it is useless or unjust.

"But if we are not to punish for the past, may we not punish with a view to reform an offender?" Punishment for reformation is a contradiction. There is no such thing. Punishment is vindictive; it looks only at the crime committed and is measured according to the real or supposed heinousness of the offense. The infliction of pain for the purpose of reformation is not punishment; for its object is not to redress the wrong done but to render the man who receives it virtuous. It now appears with other means for rendering men better and must be solved according to its power of effecting its object. No matter how bad the man has been, no matter how black with crime, this is no part of the inquiry, is no criterion by which the quantity of pain to be inflicted must be determined, but how much will it require to make him a good man is what must be ascertained.

The question now occurs, is the infliction of pain a proper means to be used in reforming a moral being? Some would answer in the affirmative, but I cannot. Reformation is effected by enlightening the understanding; but how inflicting pain on the body can convey light to the mind, I am unable to perceive. The understanding is enlightened by the perception of new truths or by obtaining clearer views of old ones; but blows upon a man's back seem a strange means to enable him to perceive truth with which he is unacquainted, or to render clear what he faintly discerns, or impressive what floats idly in the brain.

If I do wrong it is because I am ignorant. I am deceived with regard to my true interest. You wish to reform me, present me the truth, convince me by argument that what you propose is for my interest, and you need be under no apprehension. But the moment you begin to inflict pain upon me you sour my mind, you render me extremely distrustful of the value of your proposition, and in most cases you will render me determined not to give it any attention. What mighty advantage can that which this man proposes confer upon me? I ask, if what he asserts is so very important, so very useful to myself and others, what is the reason he has no arguments but his superior physical strength by which he can make my mind receive it? Has reason no power? Has truth no might with itself? Or why this violence, this pain inflicted upon my body, or mind? If this man is really my superior in knowledge and virtue, how happens it that he is unable to make me perceive his superiority or desire to possess it? The truth is, every man that uses any other force than truth, or any other means for my reformation than sound argument calculated to convince my mind of the necessity of a reformation in the particulars he enumerates violates my natural sense of right, and renders abortive whatever benevolent designs he may have formed.

The most powerful means of reforming an offender is to convince him he has done wrong, to show him what is right, and point out to him the path he must take, and the course of conduct he must pursue to avoid the evil and obtain the good. In doing this the language of kindness will be the most effectual. The offender must not be branded with infamy, but be treated as a brother, entitled to all the kind offices enjoined by fraternal affection. Jehovah requires us to love him; the means he adopts are certainly worthy our imitation. He brandishes not the forked lightening; he commands not with a voice of thunder; he crushes not the wretch by his superior strength; but unfolds his character to us; convinces the mind that he is deserving our love; we perceive he possesses all the attributes necessary to engage our affection; "we love him because he first loved us" [1 John 4:19].

If it is not allowed to inflict pain on a being for reformation, may it not be for example? Does not punishing guilty persons have a tendency to deter others from the commission of crime? This view of punishment is frequently taken and there are no doubt many who really believe that if the guilty were not punished, vice would prevail beyond all bounds. But we ought to be exceedingly cautious how we "do evil that good may come" [Rom. 3:8]. It has already appeared, that to coerce or punish a man for what he has done without any reference to the future is unjust. It is only retaliatory and retaliation is forbidden by the New Testament. "If a man strike you on the right cheek turn to him also the left" [Matt. 5:39; Luke 6:29]. The infliction of pain or the application of force for the purposes of reformation is but ill calculated to effect its object. To inflict pain on one man without any regard to his own welfare, merely for preventing some other person from the commission of crime, cannot be considered a very good example to present to society. It is unjust as it respects the individual who suffers and I confess myself unable to perceive what salutary effect examples of unjust suffering can have on the morals of society.

Punishment for example reads a very unwholesome lesson to the spectator. It says to him, "this man suffers unjustly today; and if you do the same act he has done, *you* shall suffer unjustly tomorrow." Now, a much more effectual way to prevent crime is to enlighten the mind, and a person can most easily be deterred from vicious practices by convincing him it is for his true interest to be virtuous.

There is one view more to be taken of punishment, punishment for restraint. This is not properly punishment; but there is no doubt force may be justly applied to restrain a man who is in the act of violence. This, however, must be admitted rather as a matter of self-defense, and requires no more pain to be inflicted upon the offender than is absolutely necessary to prevent him from committing the act of violence he has commenced or is about to commence. There must be no wish to make him miserable but we must do all we can to prevent the restraint we lay upon him from being painful. Hence I conceive there are no just principles on which punishment can be defended. Desert is a word either of no meaning or of one not to be admitted. Man, by transgression, brings misery upon himself; punishment increases it, and consequently must be unjust.

But may not God punish? No: not unless for the good of those he punishes. In this view the innocent man may be the subject as well as the guilty, if it be for his good; a guilty man can be the subject of it in no other. The conclusion to which I arrive is that all punishment from man is unjust; all coercion from one individual to another or from society to its members, except in case of absolute necessity for the restraint of actual violence, cannot be allowed. Punishment from God to his creatures may perhaps be sometimes inflicted, but not justly if we know anything about justice. All vice undoubtedly produces misery; but not as a penalty, but as a necessary consequence. Hence, if we would be happy we must be virtuous.

(July 19, 1828): 230-31

All mankind desire to be happy; all labor continually to gratify this desire. Whence, then the cause of failure, for fail mankind do? Misery rears her horrid front, and scatters her noxious effluvia through every atmosphere. All countries, all ages, all ranks, all conditions bear the impress of her footsteps and exhibit the insignia of her triumphs. Why is this monster permitted to prey upon us? Why are we the subjects of her lamentably permanent reign? "Man is born to suffer; he must submit to the dominion of Misery," say the desponding and faint hearted. "He must be miserable here that he may be happy hereafter," say our divines and all those who know more of heaven than they do of earth, and are better acquainted with Jehovah than with men. "God, as a kind and beneficent father, has, in his wisdom, deemed it proper to inflict terrible evils on his children that they may know how to appreciate enjoyments," it is said, and from time immemorial this stupid doctrine has been preached to justify tyrants in their usurpations and priests in the maintenance of their craft. Did a people suffer from a despotic government, they were dissuaded from choosing a milder form for it was better they should suffer; they would feel so much the more happy when they were relieved. Did the priest make us miserable (reader, pardon the supposition), did he make us sick with the silly tales he told, miserable by the dreams he made us believe, and wretched by robbing us of the bread we wanted for our children? Why, all was well: we should be so much the more happy *when* we become happy.

If God makes me miserable today, what surety have I that he will not make me the same tomorrow? If God makes his children miserable who shall make them happy? Poor consolation indeed, to be told that our sufferings come from God. From him we had hoped to receive good. To him we had hoped to fly as a place of refuge, as a shelter from the storms of affliction which beat upon us. But if he send afflictions, if he hurl the bolts of adversity, what is there left? What hope? What tower of defense? "O, the misery we suffer will do us good, and make us happier; it is only a blessing in disguise." So forsooth, we reason, ingenious to perpetuate our sufferings. Grant that good sometimes follows evil, does not evil sometimes follow good? And why not say that our enjoyments are evils in disguise? Whatever produces agreeable sensations, we call good; and we call ourselves happy in proportion as these sensations are predominant. Evil and misery are the reverse. To say evil may be good and misery may be happiness is to confound all distinctions, to destroy all knowledge, to deny the superior desirableness of any object, of any pursuit or of any act. Pain is not pleasure. No sophistry can make it so. Pain is an evil; no matter whether the pain proceed from real or imaginary objects, whether it be unavoidable or removable, temporal or eternal, it is an evil, an absolute evil, proportioned to the intensity of the sensation. It is the opposite of all I call good, the destruction of which my experience teaches me is for my happiness. Hence, to me it is an evil. I do not know what it may be to other beings, or what I may receive from it in some other world; but here, while it lasts it is an evil.

"Whatever is, is right," says Pope, but Pope had a much better faculty at making rhymes than ethics.[3] There is evil in the world. Everybody suffers more or less. Everybody desires to be happy, yea, labors to be. Why, it is asked again, are they not? Is it because we are doomed to be miserable? Who doomed us? Or who has stamped us with such a curse? Jehovah? Breathe it not, think it not. It is a foul slander upon his character. The Bible declares "Jehovah is good," and who does not know that goodness cannot produce evil, nor subject its offspring to its dominion? If God be good he is not the cause of our sufferings and to charge them upon him must betray our want of respect for his character.

"But our sufferings are punishments from God," some will say. But for what does *he* punish? For our vices? Why so? What is vice? It is a wrong action; but what is a wrong action? One which brings misery. Why does it bring misery? Because it is wrong? No; but it is wrong because if brings misery. To punish one, then, because he has done wrong is only because he had brought *some* misery upon himself to make him *more* miserable. That is, if a man burn down his barn, he must have his house burned; or if he cut off one hand, he must lose the use of the other; or if he break another man's head, he must have his own broken! O, fine principle! This would multiply suffering as fast as any one could wish. But why does God punish? Could he not prevent crime? Or does he choose to permit, or allow, or, as others say, compel its commission that *he* may have the inexpressible pleasure of punishing it and *we* the favor of feeling a great deal better when we get over it?

Why then do we suffer? The cause is in ourselves. Deity has made us as he saw fit, it is not ours to find fault. He made the world as he liked; that is none of our business. He has established a certain fixed order, which I call the order of nature, or certain laws which may be called the laws of nature. Why he established these laws I

---

[3] [Ed. *An Essay on Man*, Epistle 1, Line 294.]

know not, I ask not. But this much experience has taught me, when we obey these laws we are happy; when we disobey we are miserable. The cause of our suffering is not in the bosom of Jehovah; but in our deviating from the order, the laws which he has established. The cause of our deviation is ignorance. Every man pursues that course he believes will lead to enjoyment. He fails only because he took a wrong course. Show him the right and he will pursue with a zeal and perseverance proportioned to his desire for happiness.

The reason, then, why we are not happy is because we are ignorant of the means of bettering our condition. We have been studying nursery tales, when we should have been learning the best means of procuring food, clothing and shelter; have been poring over musty volumes of legendary lore when we should have been examining things contiguous to us, or objects connected with our welfare; endeavoring to propitiate the gods when we should have been conciliating the affections of men; and disputing about angels and demons when we ought to have been studying ourselves. All we want is instruction. Let nature be our instructor, her lessons our delight, and we shall be happy. Let men study to be honest, industrious in some useful calling, benevolent to their fellow creatures. This will be more profitable than obsolete creeds, silly tracts, foolish catechisms, or stupid folios of polemical theology with the whole list of et ceteras. Yes, let us pursue this course and all will be well and happiness become the birthright of our children.

(August 2, 1828): 249-50

What shall be *done*? Not, what shall be *believed*, is the question which now presses upon us and imperiously demands a serious answer. What shall be done? Not to purchase *heaven*, or bribe the favor of the Almighty; but *what shall be done to produce and perpetuate the rational enjoyment of the human race*? Something *must* be done! The circumstances with which we are surrounded forbid us to be idle or inactive.

Ignorance is collecting her forces, cupidity is calling her armies into the field, a terrible conflict is just ready to take place, not between rival religious dogmas, not between the votaries of different systems of faith, but between truth and error, between folly and common sense, between the friends of civil and religious liberty and the advocates of ecclesiastical domination and clerical vassalage. The clergy and their minions and their dupes are determined to perpetuate the gloom of the dark ages where it exists and reproduce it where it has been dispelled.

Americans have boasted their love of liberty, the freedom of their civil and ecclesiastical institutions; they have said to the old world, *"Mark our example and follow it."* But ah me! This boasting must soon be dismissed, this invitation to other countries to compare their governments with ours must not be indulged unless we call forth our sleeping energies and drive from our hitherto happy land the clerical monster which now threatens us with his ghastly reign.

The noble emotion, the conscious dignity we once felt at the mention of our country's name and at the recital of the toils, sufferings and achievements of our fathers will give place to shame for our supineness, or deep regret that we cherished a viper to destroy us. There is, there can be no want of proof *that our liberties are endangered,* that we, like Spain, are to be devoured by monks, priests, and the *pretended lovers of God* unless we combine to prevent a doom so horrible.

What shall be done? Shall we, who bid defiance to kings, and made thrones tremble to their base, shall we, who first set the world an example of a free government founded on the inalienable rights of man, now submit to the disgrace, the degradation of a spiritual hierarchy? Shall we who half a century ago were so jealous of our rights that we would rather involve our country in all the evils of war than pay a trifling tax lest we should countenance a doctrine which might encourage tyrants to oppress us, now contribute immense sums to the ignoble leaders of a barbarous superstition to enable them to overturn our political edifice and trample the rights of conscience in the dust?

My religious sentiments are sufficiently known. Whether I am orthodox or heterodox, dissenter or conformist is no man's business, nor do I care what religious creed my countrymen adopt. All that can be desired on this subject is that every denomination have the privilege of expressing their own opinions and the liberty to support them by such arguments as they possess. Let everyone tell his own belief or keep it to himself just as he please; but let no mortal presume to censure another for the opinions he may adopt. Let truth and error both rest on their own resources, and there will be no danger of truth's losing the victory. Truth needs no protection to be able to cope with error, hence laws in her favor are unnecessary. If any doctrine needs the aid of government to maintain its standing, it may be fairly presumed that it has not truth in its favor, consequently to grant it protection is the same as to nourish falsehood, we want no law in favor of any particular sentiment. Truth spurns such aid and to grant it to falsehood would be highly pernicious. Hence we want no law religion, or which is the same thing, neither the cause of truth or human felicity requires any such establishment.

But there are many in this enlightened country, yea, some from the desk, have dared pretend it is necessary we have a religion established by law. Such pretenses are mere mockery. Do we want the scenes of persecution, of blood, of death in its most appalling form which the old world has beheld *brought* hither to convert our paradise into a hell filled with impious monks and hypocritical priests? If not, let us cease from supporting any of the misnamed benevolent societies of our country. Let every liberal, every enlightened, and philanthropic minded man take a decided stand against the high-handed measures with which this country is replete. The courts and splendid establishments are beginning to have too much influence over our people, and we think because England, or some other country subject to an arbitrary government, has a religious establishment, we must; and so we can be like other nations. Let this influence be pointed out and discouraged. Let the superiority of plain republican institutions be faithfully shown; let the value of freedom be felt, the arts of the hypocrite and the wretched conduct of hireling priests be held up to public contempt, and the danger with which we are threatened will be averted.

To accomplish this it becomes necessary that there be exertions used. The press must be active. Truth must be told and the unsuspecting awakened to a sense of their danger. Let minor differences among liberal Christians be forgotten, and let them cordially unite to preserve mental independence, free inquiry, and rational liberty both civil and ecclesiastical. The call for union is imperious; the object is sufficiently important and the interest is the same. Let these men of liberal feelings and wishes combine to overthrow Dr. Ely's *Christian party in politics,* by discountenancing every criterion of decision which does not refer solely to a man's *moral* worth.[4] By doing this, something will be done and this something can and must be immediately done or all is lost.

(August 9, 1828): 262-64

Nothing is more important to the elevation of the human character than philosophy. But philosophy has a thousand enemies. Mankind, or a large proportion of them, have a thousand prejudices and in most cases they are prejudiced against it because they know nothing about it. There are numerous systems of something or nothing called philosophy, advocated with much zeal and no little ingenuity,

---

[4] [Ed. On Ely, see Introduction, p.22.]

to which all but learned fools ought to be opposed; but to real philosophy no man who knows anything can be opposed. The opposition which the great mass of the people have hitherto exhibited against the name and its study has arisen from mistake; from not knowing what philosophy is or what it requires of its votaries.

Philosophy is simply a love for wisdom or knowledge. A philosopher is one who loves, desires, or seeks after wisdom or knowledge. The true philosopher is not a systematizer, is not one who forms theories or who builds upon hypothesis or conjecture, but one who endeavors to examine the phenomena of nature and represent them as they are. He seeks to learn what is and what valuable use can be made of the circumstances which surround us. He is and ever must be a character which every friend to human happiness must love.

Men have called themselves philosophers when they were little entitled to the appellation. They have builded for themselves in the fields of imagination certain airy castles, which they have called substantial dwellings; have spider-like spun from their own resources systems which they have dignified with the name of philosophy. Such things are nothing, or worse than nothing. Philosophy has nothing to do with systems; it rejects all systems and depends solely upon observation. It observes facts or is a knowledge of facts. Its provinces are the world without us and the world within us. It studies, it examines the various objects around, the relation of one body to another, and the laws by which matter is regulated in its changes either of time or place; how various bodies may be combined or brought within apparent continuity, or separate those which appear contiguous etc. It looks within, and endeavors to ascertain the several emotions, passions and affections of which the mind is susceptible; the relation of the mind to external objects, its power of affecting them, or being affected by them. In a word, philosophy attempts to discover all the phenomena of the material world. With the world of spirits it has no connection, that world being the peculiar province of faith.

Formerly men attempted to establish theories or systems. They attempted from the examination of certain particulars to draw general maxims which should apply not only to the particular phenomena examined but to all others which they supposed to have a general resemblance. But this is no mode of philosophizing. It is now abandoned. And philosophers, or those who deserve the name, adopt no maxims or lay down no general laws as being established any further than the particulars examined warrant. Formerly, those who were called philosophers attempted to explain the phenomena which they discovered and to account for their existence; but this belongs to faith. It is not the province of the philosopher. All he can do is to represent things as they are without telling how they came to be so. He can tell the relation one body of matter holds to another, trace one occurrence to another, or a consequent to its antecedent; which last if it be uniformly followed by the same event he denominates a cause, i.e. if two events uniformly appear in connection, one the precursor and the other the successor, he denominates the first the cause producing the second; not because he sees in the one any physical connection or force producing the other, but from the fact that they always appear in the relation of antecedent and consequent. In relation to *matter*, the philosopher when he discovers a body seeks to ascertain the number of smaller bodies which are apparently contiguous of which it is composed. This is called analysis. If he cannot separate it or discover any new combination of different substances, his investigation stops; he has gone the length of his chain. In relation to *events*, or the changes matter undergoes, or the changes he has discovered it to be capable of undergoing, he traces each train of consequences to the remotest antecedent in his power to examine and then stops. What is the remotest antecedent cause or power which produced the whole he does not pretend to tell. That again is the business of faith.

Every man is a philosopher in proportion to his desire after knowledge and the number of facts he has examined, or the facts he has established by observation or experiment. The difference between the ploughman and the most learned is not in the different modes of judging they adopt, not in the power of the one over the other of accounting for an event or an appearance, but in the number of particulars they have examined, in the number of facts they have discovered or in one's having seen more things as they *are* than the other. The simple man, untaught by schools, knows as well why an apple falls to the ground when broken from the tree on which it grew, as a Newton or any philosopher, though he may never have heard of gravitation.

We are gravely told all heavy bodies have a tendency to fall to the earth, to its center, and this tendency is the attraction of gravitation. But this does not account for the phenomenon. If it be asked why a body falls to the earth and it be answered because of the power of gravitation, it is only saying the body does fall. For if it be asked again what is gravitation, it can only be said it is the tendency which bodies have to fall to the earth, and we are back where we were before; but if we ask how these bodies come to have such a tendency, philosophy can give no answer. Here, faith must answer. Thence we see the philosopher, the ploughman and every other class must pursue the same path, viz observation and experiment. All that either can do is to tell what *is* in the department of nature he has investigated, and the sum of the facts he collects constitutes the amount of his knowledge. He is the greatest philosopher who has observed the greatest number of facts.

Knowledge is necessary for our happiness. By acquiring knowledge, we not only open to ourselves a new source of enjoyment in the acquisition itself, but become acquainted with the best means of satisfying our wants and of contributing to the happiness of society. Let every man, then, be a philosopher.

Some object to philosophy because it makes men irreligious. We might say the person who first ascertained that the churning of cream would produce butter was an irreligious man, and that he who discovered that cultivating and sowing the earth is necessary to procuring a crop of grain was an irreligious man. But who would believe us? They might indeed have been irreligious, but nobody believes that their discovering these facts ever made them so. The same remark may be applied to every discovery in philosophy.

True philosophy does not travel out of this world. It may not teach the existence of a devil. But though philosophy does not affirm the existence of such a being, it does not deny his existence. For philosophy never presumes to assert or deny the existence of those beings or things which are beyond the limits of its province.

The line of distinction should be drawn between faith and knowledge. To regulate the former is the business of the priest; to assist us in acquiring the latter is the office of the philosopher. If the priest is careful to regulate faith according to the suggestions of philosophy, he may unite both characters in himself. He may be a priest and a philosopher. In this case, it will appear evident that philosophy will not destroy one's faith or make him irreligious. But, if the preacher enjoins a religion contrary to all facts we have discovered, contrary to all the facts we do or can possess, why, let mankind be irreligious; we think they will do as well as those who embrace such a religion.

(August 30, 1828): 278-79

As faith by the majority of mankind is deemed to be more important than philosophy, this number will be devoted to its consideration. I speak of religious faith. The objects of this faith are the existence of God, his providence, the accountability of man to him, and a future state of happiness or misery. To discuss these subjects or to inquire their truth or falsity is not my present aim; nor indeed do I know that I possess any *infallible* criterion by which I can *positively* pronounce anything concerning them. Each of them lies beyond the boundaries of *my* knowledge, though I do not wish it to be understood that I consider there are no reasons which can justify our belief of them, but that we can never positively know them. They are therefore matters of faith and rest for the most part on that kind of evidence which we are but ill prepared to collate in this mode of existence.

Such being the character of the principal articles of religious belief, or such the foundation on which they rest, we seriously inquire their importance? What is their utility? How far shall we make them the principles of our actions, or the rules by which our actions should be governed? To give a clear and satisfactory answer to these questions is neither easy nor safe in the present state of society. But fear is something with which the writer of this essay is unacquainted and to be told the subject is difficult is only giving him an additional motive to attempt the removal of its embarrassments.

What is the importance of religious faith? Mankind have ever since the age of history embraced all the articles I have enumerated; experience informs us what *has* been its importance, and the tale it unfolds is too mournful to repeat. But two classes of benefits can be expected from adopting a religious faith: One is happiness in the other world, and the other greater felicity here. With regard to the first class I can only say it has reference to a world I have never explored and to a mode of existence of which I am totally ignorant. Whether the opinions I adopt in this world will have any effect on my condition in the next or not is something which I cannot know till I "shuffle off this mortal coil." I may believe this thing or that but it will make no difference in the truth respecting it.

The second, "to produce greater felicity here," demands our attention for we cannot consistently be indifferent to anything which is advantageous to us poor mortals while traveling throughout his world. This class of benefits may be numerous. It should be closely examined, not with a prejudiced, but with an impartial eye. We want the truth but have no anxiety to deceive or be deceived. Is a belief in the articles we have enumerated essential to the happiness of mankind here is the question. How shall it be answered? Shall we appeal to the experience? Shall we ask what effect this belief has had on the nations which now sleep beneath our feet? What can that tell more than they were miserable? We may speak of wars, of outrages, and sufferings, which it makes us weep to recollect; but though a religious faith was the apparent cause we may be answered, they were occasioned by the abuse of such a faith and notwithstanding such in almost every instance has been the consequences, we may still be told it is owing to the abuse of faith and we have no means of disproving the assertion. Mankind have been miserable with a religious faith but we do not know but they would have been more miserable without it. They are miserable now, they are quarreling about faith; but they might quarrel about something else if they had no faith.

Another consideration is important. How many articles shall we adopt? All above enumerated? But why stop here? Why not do as mankind always have done, add a thousand more? Or who shall prevent the world from doing the same hereafter? Mankind never have agreed. Christians, though they nominally admit all I have stated, explain these articles so as to mean things diametrically opposite, and each tells the other he will be damned if he does not believe as he does. How shall this evil be prevented? We all appeal to the Bible, but the Bible either gives us no information on the subject, or may be and actually is so interpreted as to give about equal support to contradictory systems. For instance, one believes the Bible proves a devil, another believes it does not; one believes the Bible proves all but a few favorites will be eternally damned, another believes it proves all will be eternally happy; one is confident the Bible declares God is angry every day, and another one is equally confident that the Bible declares God is love and that anger rests in the bosom of fools. Hence our difficulties multiply. For if we agree what shall be the common source of our faith, we each claim the privilege of interpreting the books according to our own understandings, of turning the streams which flow from the common fountain into the channel of our own particular opinions. If we agree on the number and names of the articles we are to believe, we can easily find means by our exposition of these articles to damn each other for the glory of God and the good of souls. What shall we say? Shall we give up all faith? By no means. Why not? What is its utility? Its utility is the comfort or consolation a belief in a God and a future state may afford the suffering son of humanity. But does every system of faith do this? No: if such was the case one system would not be preferable to another. But no system but one which represents God as boundless in his goodness and promises an eternal state of ceaseless bliss can do this. Such then is the system we will patronize.

But shall we make this system a rule of our conduct? Yes, if we understand it. But as we are liable to mistakes, it will be the more safe to act only as experience has determined to be most for our felicity. To attempt to convert everybody to our belief is not very wise. It immediately produces a sectarian spirit, which, if we know anything, we know cannot be beneficial to ourselves or others. One important consideration is necessary in reference to our contending for faith; what we believe may be true or it may not, and our anxiety to circulate it should never exceed the ratio of good it will produce.

But it may be asked, is not faith necessary to please God? I know nothing about that; the only way I know of pleasing God (if he can be pleased) or which it appears most rational to believe will be pleasing to him, is that we do good, i.e. do justly, love mercy, and endeavor to make our brethren of the human family happy.

So far as reason goes in this matter, it informs us religious faith is a subject between the individual and his God, that is, it is an individual concern with which society has nothing to do. "But should not preachers endeavor to inculcate their own views or to establish their own religious faith?" The preacher's office is to point out to us what we should *do*, and persuade us to its performance. But what he believes has nothing to do with this. Faith in religious dogmas is no part of man's *duty*, and should be considered rather as indifferent, yet may be proposed to an audience for their adoption or rejection. The reasons by which it is supported may be presented, the advantages supposed to flow from it clearly stated; but here the preacher must stop, another step carries him beyond his province.

My opinion is nothing, but my conviction is that faith is less important than philosophy; that if we would be happy we must pay less attention to the examination of religious dogmas than heretofore, and devote more to the investigation of those subjects which are within the limits of our means of observation.

(September 13, 1828): 295-96

The language of reason has been so long neglected that mankind dare not hear it; and nothing is more startling to a vast portion of our unfortunate brethren than to be told the paths they are required to walk is plain, smooth, impeded by no remarkable obstacles, and leading through a pleasant champaign, adorned with flowers and variegated foliage, but broken with no enchanted mountains, and inhabited by no mysterious beings who challenge to combat. My two last numbers[5] were designed to correct the pernicious influence of former education by informing the inquirer after truth that all he has to do is to make use of his senses, to exercise his eyes, his ears, his power of discovering objects as they are; not to exert his imagination to find out what on certain assumed premises ought to be. They were also

---

[5] [Ed. See the previous two entries in this text and *GAII* 6 (August 9, 1828): 262-64 and (August 30, 1828): 278-79.]

designed to call the attention from those things which we cannot know in this state of existence and to place it upon those things which are within the sphere of our observation and are immediately connected with our happiness or misery in this world.

I am a professed Christian. I consider the morals enjoined by Jesus Christ to be excellent; the doctrines he taught, to wit, the character he gave of our heavenly Father and the hope he gave his followers of a future state of happiness are certainly very pleasing to everyone who is depressed by adversity or suffering under the numerous casualties of life. But whether these doctrines are true or not I cannot *absolutely* know. I may believe, but my belief is not knowledge. Now the whole economy of nature evinces very clearly that what is most necessary to our preservation and felicity is within our reach, unencumbered by the numerous difficulties which surround those which are less important. Philosophy or as I have explained it a knowledge of things as they are, being within our power to a certain extent at least so far as we can examine is more important than a religious theory which consists of opinions respecting certain beings and worlds which may or may not be, that is, so far as we can at present by the aid of our senses know.

I am no enemy to religion. I value my religious faith and would use all the means in my power to convince others it is true. But my religion consists more in doing than believing. For I *believe* it is more acceptable to the Lord for us to do justly and be merciful than to offer sacrifice, however sweet may be the incense or rich the perfume. If I am deceived in this conclusion I have one advantage, the actions my belief enjoins, experience proves to be useful to man while here; and if I do not serve God by this conduct, I have the satisfaction of contributing to the happiness of his children, and if I do not secure a heaven in the invisible world I at least enjoy one here. Hence to me reason says "give up no certain for an uncertain good. You know not whether your conduct will have any influence on another world, but you do know it has an influence upon your enjoyments in this. And since you cannot be certain whether you can make yourself happy hereafter, neglect no opportunity to prolong your existence and increase your felicity in the world where you find yourself."

This precept obeyed, the whole of man's attention would be turned to the answering of two important queries: First, how can I preserve my existence to the latest possible date? Second, how can I make this existence a source of the highest happiness of which my constitution is or can be made susceptible? The preservation of life being the first object, we should be led to inquire not what religious creed shall we adopt, but what things shall we avoid as injurious to life and what shall we seek to gain as beneficial? Here opens a field of inquiry. Nature must be examined. The qualities of the articles fit for food must be ascertained and the best kind determined and the quantity which will have the best effect fixed. We must become acquainted with the medicinal properties of everything that we may know how to cure the diseases which might at times attack the human body or mind. And this would also require an acquaintance not only with the diseases themselves but with the causes producing them; whether they be in our diet, our climate, our mode of life, the nature of our pursuits, in our action or indolence, etc. This inquiry would in fact lead us to study everything which can be known; and when we had ascertained this, we should be prepared to answer the second, how can I make my life a source of the highest felicity which I am capable of receiving.

The answer to the first is the answer to this second. For it will be found that nothing which has a tendency to shorten our life can be productive of our happiness. The first inquiry must necessarily ascertain the influence which any body of matter can exert over us or rather the relation of the human body to every object which does or can affect it, and also the nature and tendency of every pursuit and of every action about which man can be employed. In these inquiries experience is our only guide.

Religion will not be forgotten. But from holding the first it may be reduced to a subordinate rank. What this rank is it is not my intention now to discuss; but I wish mankind to know that religion demands our attention only as it is subservient either to the preservation of our existence or the enlargement of our felicity. Jehovah has revealed to us all that we can suppose he designed we should know and this is all comprised in the golden maxim, "do by others as you wish them to do by you." That is, we should always be just and merciful for we always wish others to be so to us. God himself is unknown; he dwells in thick darkness, surrounded by the deep counsels of the Divinity which no man can approach, much less penetrate. To attempt to scan him is utterly vain. Our optics cannot reach him; we have no sense by which we can detect him and no power by which we can fathom his wisdom or ascertain the depth of his designs. Had it been necessary we should have known more of him, it is rational to suppose he would have more fully disclosed himself. But as he has not chosen to do this we must be content with the study of those objects which are within our reach.

The Bible is a valuable book. It contains many glorious truths, *truths* which it is important we should become acquainted with. But these truths are but few in comparison of the whole number it is important to learn. The Bible tells us what we ought to believe respecting another world, what will be our condition there, and what relation we shall hold to the Father of spirits. This disclosure may be of use to us. But the only use yet discovered is that when we become weary of this world, and sickened with its scenes, we can please ourselves with anticipating a new and better world. This anticipation is, no doubt, frequently the source of joyfully sublime emotions and very often makes ample amends for the scorn and injustice of the world. To destroy or to wish to destroy in any man's mind this anticipation, this hope of bliss to be, is not, cannot be a proof of kindness or a mark of anything but a desire to sport with the feelings of the unfortunate by gratifying our own vanity.

Perhaps the remark is not exactly correct that the only use of religion is the hope, the consolation it affords the unfortunate, or rather some may apprehend it is not. It is supposed by most who have written on this subject that religion is the foundation of every virtue. This I do not believe because I do not believe that virtue is what religionists generally define it to be. According to the opinions of those who honor themselves with the title of orthodox, virtue is not merely a good action but a strong desire to obey the will of God. An action, according to these persons, doctors perhaps they ought to be called, an action is not good because it produces pleasurable emotions but because Deity has commanded it. Hence murder, suicide, or any act however destructive to others or to ourselves might be called good, providing God had commanded it. I shall not stop to inquire whether this be correct or not, but simply observe that it is not in the power of Deity to make evil good, and as we can never have positive knowledge of what Deity commands, it will be best to consider that a virtuous act which experience shows us has a tendency to produce happiness; and that it is good, not because Deity has commanded it but because it is beneficial. Placing virtue on this footing, my remark respecting the use of religion will be found to be correct so far as this world is concerned.

This number closes the Essayest. When I commenced this series of articles, I intended they should contain a regular dissertation on natural religion; but ill health prevented, accordingly they consist of only detached articles on subjects which I hope have not been wholly uninteresting. If they shall remove any encumbrances to free inquiry, give new confidence to the aspirant after truth, or afford some hints which will serve to guide him in his progress, the object for which they were written will have been obtained.

6.

A SERMON

The Gospel Advocate and Impartial Investigator
6 (June 7, 1828): 177-81

*Because with lies ye have made the hearts of the righteous sad whom I
have not made sad; and have strengthened the hands of the wicked,
that he should not return from his wicked way, by promising him life.*
Ezek. 13:22.

The human character is stamped with variety. No two in the vast
family of man can be found who in all respects correspond to each
other. Every countenance has its peculiar mark or marks by which it
is easily distinguished from every other. The diversity of the minds of
men and even contrariety of their opinions are no less strongly designated than that of their external appearance. Uniformity is a mere
creature of imagination; nothing like it is to be found in the works of
nature; and the attempt to produce it is as vain as to attempt to
destroy that power which sustains the universe.

But perhaps we may blunt the points of contact, may render by
our labors our social intercourse more agreeable and more beneficial.
We may perhaps persuade men to bear with each other's opinions
and not be disturbed because each claims the privilege of believing
according to the dictates of his own understanding. We hope to persuade them to the disuse of those harsh speeches and opprobrious
epithets, which are so frequently thrown out and applied to moral,
honest men; especially in matters of religion we hope they will become mild and forbearing. The essence of religion is charity; its design is to spread liberal sentiments and liberal feelings; but strange as
it may seem, there is no subject about which there is so much contention as religion and no people are so illiberal as religionists.

There are a number of passages in the Scriptures which contain
awful denunciations against false teachers. Each sect, believing itself
right, is ambitious to apply these passages to those it believes to be
wrong. From the passage selected for the theme of our discourse it
appears there were in the days of the prophet Ezekiel several false
prophets who made the hearts of the righteous sad with the lies they
told and strengthened the hands of the wicked by promising him

127

life. Now, if these did as the prophet says they did there is no want of proof that they were false prophets; hence the passage becomes very convenient for party purposes and has been strapped around the necks of every new sect from that time to this.

There is a sect existing now,[1] a sect increasing in numbers and influence, a sect that pays very little attention to the traditions of the elders; generally relying on the Bible and common sense for the support of their sentiments, its members have the audacity to question the correctness of many things long considered as sacred truth, the presumption to worship God after the manner which many denominate heresy and to allege the testimony of Scripture in their vindication. Those who have long considered themselves sound in the faith are *sad* when they hear this sect assert that all the kindred of the nations shall be blessed in the seed of Abraham, and their hearts are sorely grieved when they hear it proclaimed that "as in Adam all die, even so in Christ shall all be made alive" [1 Cor. 15:22]. This doctrine is so repugnant to their own that they cannot bear it; and despairing of effecting its overthrow by sound argument, they attempt to vilify it by giving it a bad name. All they have to do is to assume to themselves the position of the prophet: "This doctrine is a lie. We are the righteous. Our hearts are sad that it prevails. Therefore, woe unto you false teachers for with lies ye have made the hearts of the righteous sad."

But still farther: "The preaching of this doctrine prevents people from uniting with *our* church; therefore strengthens the hands of the wicked that he should not return from his wicked way by promising him life out of our inclosure."

Now the advantages of this kind of logic are not easily to be appreciated. You have only to pronounce a man a "vain talker" and St. Paul himself will command you to stop his mouth, or to denominate him a heretic, and you have Scripture that the man who is a heretic after the first and second admonition should be rejected. This mode of reasoning saves a world of trouble. It need not labor to prove the point in dispute because it has the *right* to assume this as true, and by one or two cant phrases it can put the proudest of the advocates of a new doctrine to the blush, and show that all the soundness of their reasoning is nothing. Another advantage, by no means to be overlooked, is the self-gratification it affords the *pious* and the ardent devotion thus raised to God. They are gratified to find them-

---

[1] [Ed. Brownson is referring, of course, to Universalism. On the growth of Universalism in the 1820s, see the Introduction, pp. 14-16.]

selves proved to be the righteous; and are exceedingly thankful to God that they who oppose them are the wicked, denominated such by the Holy Ghost. Their hearts cannot refuse the tribute of gratitude to the Deity, to find he has so clearly, by words which cannot be misunderstood, pointed out the wicked and false teachers. "God knew there would be vile reprobates in the latter days, who by their lies would make the hearts of the righteous sad. And indeed it has come to pass. *Our* hearts have been sad and our bosoms filled with sorrow to see the wicked triumph. We have done all in our power to check heresy of every kind. Formerly we had a *holy* Inquisition and we called to trial all whom we suspected of deviating from the path of the faithful. From time immemorial we have established our schools and seminaries of learning for the purpose of giving a proper bias to the young and tender mind. We have drawn up our creeds and pronounced them the standards of faith; we have warned the people of the danger of the awful consequences of rejecting them; we have been careful to render every new sect as odious as was in our power, and we have labored diligently to destroy the influence of every heretical teacher. We have been sure to exclude from our communion all we feared were inclined to embrace those dangerous innovations, which ungodly men are always making, and we have uniformly delivered over to Satan all who dared embrace their damnable heresy."

"Latterly we have sent out our agents to cry from house to house and warn people of the danger of the church. We have also sent them, time after time, through town, village, hamlet and country to implore funds to support the gospel against the ungodly. We have established missionary societies, Bible societies, education societies, and have left untried no measure that we believed might put a farthing into the treasury of the Lord. False teachers have ridiculed us and told us that our trouble was unnecessary. So much money is not wanted. Christ and his apostles did not require it. Our hearts all the time have been sad; for we knew money was necessary to save *precious, immortal souls* from hell. But thanks be to God, he has borne clear testimony against them who with lies sadden the hearts of the righteous; and we cannot but hope these light afflictions will work for us a far more exceeding weight of glory."

Notwithstanding, Young[2] tells us "to recriminate is just," we shall not exercise the privilege; for we would never fight against truth; and if these assertions contain anything that is true, let it have its due influence. I know our text is frequently applied to Universalists. It

[2] [Ed. Not able to identify Young.]

had no original application to them, nor can it have, unless it be proved that Universalists are guilty of the conduct condemned by the prophet. Universalism is not very well calculated to strengthen the hands of the wicked; for it declares misery is ever attendant upon transgression. And how a sentiment, which declares that all men shall become holy before God and consequently happy, can sadden the hearts of the righteous is more than I am able to perceive.

I intend to make an application of this text, but not to any particular creed; for I care but little what men believe, if they are liberal in their feelings and virtuous in their conduct. There are indeed many creeds, very zealously taught, which every rational man must reject; but let them be proven false by fair argument. There is no need of giving them a bad name. Convince the people they are false and they will have no disposition to retain them. But to my text.

The first inquiry demanding our attention is who are the righteous? There need be no controversy respecting the answer to be given. The righteous belong exclusively to no sect, but are found in all. They are those who in all their intercourse with their brethren are remarked for their probity, their honor, and their benevolence; those who in judging of the characters of others, judge them by their conduct, and not by their faith; those who value men for their moral worth, for their usefulness in society, and not for any extrinsic qualifications they may happen to possess. They do not consider themselves more holy because they belong to a certain sect, or because they make great pretensions to goodness, for they know men may attach themselves to different societies; they may by accident be thrown among those that are good, while themselves are bad; also that it is the easiest thing in the world for a man to pretend to be holy, and it generally happens that those are loudest in their pretensions whose claims are the most ill-founded. They therefore esteem themselves only for those acts which are by experience found to benefit mankind; in the performance of these acts they study to be industrious and successful. What, may we ask, is most likely to make the hearts of such persons as these sad?

Nothing is more grievous to the righteous man, nothing makes his heart more sad than to see the hypocrite triumph, than to see a man whose conduct in almost every instance is exceptionable styled a saint merely because he says he believes what the majority call truth, or because he belongs to a society which the multitude are taught to consider holy: to hear such a man applauded and to see him held up as a pattern for our imitation while the honest, the virtuous man who makes no pretensions and says but little about those things of which he knows nothing, is cast aside as nothing worth, does indeed sadden the hearts of the righteous and of every friend to human happiness. To hear every moral virtue decried from the desk and the man who practices such set down as more dangerous than the abandoned profligate; to see a something independent of all practical goodness made the standard of acceptance with God and of respectability among men is enough to make everyone who wishes well to society mourn; for then the hands of the wicked are strengthened that he should not return from his wicked way. What can be the utility of my endeavoring to be a virtuous man? Why shall I be anxious to discharge any moral obligation, if I am no better for it? Why need I care what my conduct is when it is perfectly immaterial what I do, and since I can be saved without any labor? I can believe and he that believes shall be saved.

And do we not hear this? Do we not see it? And does not the history of every age of the church prove this sentiment, this mode of procedure to have been her distinguishing feature? Have not the hands of the wicked been strengthened by such a mode of determining a man's worth? And have not the hearts of the righteous been made sad? Antiquity may sleep; we will call up only the present age. What is the popular sentiment of the day? It is not that *morality* is no mark of piety? And is not the man who is zealous in contending for articles of faith, who pays liberally to support the church, who countenances with his purse the various plans of Christian enterprise for evangelizing the world deemed a good and holy man; though unfeeling in the extreme to the poor of his own neighborhood and relentless to all who do not think like himself? And is not a wild fanatic who keeps community in continued uproar deemed a much holier man than the cool, dispassionate preacher who studies to make men better? And would it not be considered almost impiety to compare the latter with the former? In a word, contend mightily for the faith, be zealous in supporting the church, and be severe against dissenters is ticket good enough in the popular opinion to carry any man to heaven.

This is what makes the righteous sad, this is what strengthens the hands of the wicked, and what gives him confidence in his wickedness; and unless mankind possess a redeeming spirit, religion will ere long be hissed from the stage; and the sun of revelation will set and man be left dayless, hopeless in the night of skepticism and despair.

My brethren: The evils of which I complain are evils of no small magnitude. I could weep over their devastations, but tears are useless. There has been weeping for ages, but few however have dared attack the cause and those few have been branded with the vilest epithets and stigmatized as the enemies of God and his religion. Let the stigma be continued. We equally despise the curses and the blessings of those we may offend. We care not for all the obloquy or reproach which mistaken zeal, ignorance or priestcraft can heap upon us. The cause of these evils is found in a great measure in petty religious associations. The organization of particular churches for *spiritual* purposes is the most powerful demon that has labored to disorganize all other societies, to arm man against his fellow man, to banish the social virtues from the bosom, and to destroy the peace and tranquility of the domestic circle.

Brethren: Much as you may deplore the evils with which human society is infested, much as you may lament the pride, arrogance and hostility of different religious societies, you can never remove them but by the abrogation of every established creed, and the demolition of every partition wall; and this *must* be done if we have to abandon the building altogether. But understand me: I am not declaiming against religion, but against the abuse of it, against making it a cloak for villainy, a mask for the hypocrite, against converting or rather perverting it to a creature of whom Virgil might say, "*Monstrum horrendum, informe, ingens Cui lumen ademptum.*"[3] But to the argument.

Self-love is common to man and it is not always easy to distinguish it from selfishness. But society condemns the selfish man and the disgrace attached to the character generally keeps the individual on his guard; but when he joins a party it is deemed honorable, nay, important, that he should support the interests of that party. This is only a modification of selfishness and often a modification not much for the better. Hence by encouraging the selfish passions these parties destroy the moral principles of a man and make him in the end a mere tool of this own or another's ambition.

A church is formed; a line of distinction must be drawn between it and those denominated the world. Believing themselves to be God's peculiar people, it is perfectly natural that the members of a church should consider themselves more holy than the children of the world; and in the same degree as they think themselves better, they will think others worse. The world becomes disgusted; this excites a pre-

[3] [Ed. The quotation is from Virgil's *Aeneid*, 3.658, referring to Polyphemus, the Cyclops. Latin for "a horrible monster, lumpish, huge, from whom the light [eye] had been stolen." I would like to thank professor Stephen Beall of Marquette's Classics Department for identifying this quotation for me.]

tended holy contempt in return, and thus on, till all harmony between them is lost.

Members of churches may unite firmly together while danger is apprehended from without; but freed from that fear and they begin to quarrel among themselves. The posts of distinction are established; hence one continued struggle; some pulling others down to prepare the way for their own elevation to the heights of priestly ambition. But setting this aside; the ungenerous prejudices imbibed against the world are attended by the annihilation of everything which makes society worth possessing. "We are the people of God; we have been born again; you must certainly acknowledge we are better than the children of the devil." Hence the pride natural to the human heart is fostered and with it are encouraged many rough and not much to be desired principles. The members of the church become arrogant and selfish importance takes the place of that meek and humble spirit which ever characterizes the followers of the lowly Jesus.

But again: amid this pride and this arrogance, various religious factions take their rise. A man finds it is popular to belong to some society of this description, but unable to gain that particular applause he desires, he starts the leader of a division with sentiments and practices different in some particulars from others as a shorter path to his favorite object than the common beaten track. Hence different churches are formed with different creeds and different modes of worship, the members of which will be generally tenacious of their own peculiarities, and opposed to each other, and treat each other with animosity proportioned to the tenacity with which each clings to his own faith.

Another objection to churches as they exist is they are calculated to place the sanctity of a man's character not in acts of substantial virtue, but in the zeal and fidelity with which he serves his party; this is a necessary consequence. Were the conduct of a man made the criterion by which his religious worth should be determined, this being about the same among all sects, and as good out of the church as in, no substantial reason could be assigned why one of these associations could be called better than another or why any one should be supported. But tell a man, "you join *our* church, believe what we tell you, and pay us liberally for the care we take of your soul, and eternal felicity shall be your reward, and eternal misery your doom if you do not"; if you can make him believe you, be assured every faculty he possesses will be exerted in favor of the party to which you belong. Another man who believes differently from you places another in the same situation, and thus you may have all religious churches in miniature. Both these persons believe they are right. Each believes he shall be saved; each believes the other will be damned unless he is converted to his own opinions. Benevolence may now come for her share of the work. Each says of the other, "could this man be induced to embrace my faith, it would be of vast importance to him; hence whatever means I use for his conversion, if successful, will be of infinite advantage to him and I shall cover a multitude of sins." Now begins the contest. Every art is tried; every engine is put in motion; pity, flattery, threatening, pain, and slander, all are successively repeated and nothing can equal the rage and violence which follows if either be disappointed. During the struggle, religion falls and infidels sit laughing over its expiring gasp.

These things make the hearts of the righteous sad and strengthen the hands of the wicked that he should not return from his wickedness.

But still farther: as one of the most powerful objections to the propriety of having churches, they check improvement and tend to perpetuate ignorance. Establish a church and certain qualifications must be demanded in those proposing to unite. These qualifications must be such in the opinion of the church at least as to entitle the candidate to a seat in heaven. This consideration will serve as a check to any farther progress. The person becomes about perfect in his own opinion, thinks he shall be saved if he is no better than he is already. But to believe the creed of the church is absolutely necessary to becoming a member. Study and investigation may increase one's knowledge or increase of knowledge may create doubts and finally change his faith. But this will not do. A man who changes his faith must be dealt with. The change will weaken his attachment to the church; he will become lukewarm; he will enfeeble the exertions of others; perhaps corrupt their principles and destroy their usefulness in the church; hence he must be excluded. And after having a long string of curses patched upon his back, he is *piously* delivered to Satan for the love of God and the good of his soul.

Now, when a man knows that if he should change his faith he would wound the feelings of his friends and perhaps be excommunicated, he will not take much pains to inform himself; but will settle down where he is and in the end become a poor superstitious vagabond or a bigoted fool.

Every church which presumes to adopt a creed to which its members are required to conform says to the human mind, "hitherto shalt thou come but no farther." It supposes itself in possession of the whole truth and another advance is not possible. The only rational argument that can be assigned for the organization of churches, or rather, the only ground upon which they can be consistently maintained is that by mutual assistance their members discover truth. But the bar to this is placed at the entrance by telling the candidate what he must believe and what he must not presume to doubt, for if he does he can no longer be considered one of their number.

But I forbear. The sum of my objections against churches is that they encourage hypocrisy, uphold a man when he should not be, and destroy one's character when entitled to respect; that they divert our attention from what should engage it; that they tend to degrade morality, to damp our social feelings, to contract the sphere of our good offices, to confine our charity to those of our own way of thinking, and to limit our benevolence to what is barely necessary to uphold our associates and condemn all others. That they make things which are of little value to be all important, create a universal buzz about what is of no advantage to society at large, leap the common bonds of brotherhood, and cause humanity to weep at the contest they always produce.

Instead, therefore, of applying my text to any particular doctrine or dogmas, I consider the formation and support of churches with articles of faith and modes of worship to which all the members are obliged to conform is what in our day makes the hearts of the righteous sad, and what strengthens the hands of the wicked. I would therefore abandon them and labor to place mankind upon a footing of equality, to enable each to stand or fall according as his conduct is virtuous or vicious.

Perhaps it will be supposed by some that the Scriptures oppose the order of things I wish to introduce, but in reply I remark, I know no command in the Bible for the organization of churches as they now exist. If the example of the apostles be adduced and it be alleged that they formed churches, admit it to be true; but this proves nothing more than that they deemed it necessary to organize them then, but that is no argument that it is necessary now. Were they of divine appointment, we should have had a command to that amount. The apostles practiced circumcision and some other rites which we do not consider ourselves bound to perform. Hence their example proves nothing.

But some may ask, "If you abolish churches, how will you support religion?" Leave it to stand on its own basis, to be embraced for its own intrinsic merit, not from any gaudy tinsel with which man may decorate it. Some perhaps may ask, "how will you support ministers?" That, we answer, is a matter which concerns the ministers themselves. Mankind will voluntarily support as many as they believe will do them any good, more would only be pernicious were they maintained; let the surplus go to work.

To conclude: the object of every human pursuit is happiness. Religion is one of the means, perhaps one of the most successful means employed to gain the desired object. So far as it produces this, we cherish it, but no farther. God did not make us that we might be religious beings, but he made us religious beings that we might be happy. Whenever our religious practices do not have this tendency we should seek a reformation. A reformation we need, and for one, brethren, pray; and pray in faith, too, for the wheel of improvement is silently performing its revolution; that stone is cut from the mountains; it grows, and ere long it shall fill the whole earth and banish all jarring interests and confused notions of religion from the abodes of men. Amen.

7.

A SERMON. ON THE NEW BIRTH

The Gospel Advocate and Impartial Investigator
6 (August 16, 1828): 257-62

Except a man be born again he cannot see the kingdom of God.
John 3:3.

Christian auditors: I have selected for our consideration this morning a subject in which we are all deeply interested: one which the religious part of community deem the "one thing needful," the qualification absolutely necessary to secure our immortal peace and felicity in the world beyond the grave, one which is the burden of self-styled orthodoxy and the beginning, middle and end of nearly all the sermons which they deliver for the benefit of our souls. This all-important subject is the doctrine of the *new birth* or spiritual regeneration. As your speaker is a dissenter from the commonly received notions on this extraordinary birth, he claims the privilege of laying before you a brief statement of the reasons for his dissent, together with his own belief respecting the doctrine really taught in our text.

With a view of accommodating the plain, simple doctrine of Christ to the fanciful notions of the oriental philosophy, the gnostics, even in the days of the Apostles, denied the sufferings and humanity of the Savior, alleging that both existed only in appearance. They thus laid the foundation for those long and aggravated controversies which distracted the primitive church and gave rise to those absurd creeds and dogmas which have continued from that time to this to pervert the common sense of mankind and to fill society with discord and suffering.

To avoid the imputation of ignorance, the language and many sentiments of the heathen school were borrowed and the simplicity of Christ was lost amid the unintelligibility of Plato. That the new religion might not appear deficient in point of dignity and want no proofs of its celestial origin, the paganizing Christians converted the whole into mystery, which neither themselves nor others could understand. Hence originated various absurd and contradictory dogmas, such as a "Three-One God," the "Incarnation of the Son," the

"Procession of the Holy Ghost," Transubstantiation, etc. and from causes no doubt similar has originated the popular opinion of the doctrine under examination. To this doctrine, according to the common belief, we object.

1. That it is unintelligible. A proposition demanding our assent should be cognizable by the human mind, should be plain, easy to be understood. Make to me a proposition which I do not, which I cannot, and which I know I cannot understand, it is folly in you to demand my assent; and if I pretend to believe it, I encourage suspicions of my discernment or of my want of honesty. Now, the notion in question is in the highest degree unintelligible. The most learned of its advocates can say no more of it than that it is a certain perceptible, mysterious, inexplicable impulse supposed to come from the Holy Ghost. All that he who professes to have experienced it knows is that he has a certain feeling. All beyond this is mystery, a land of shadows or of frightful monsters. Who produced this change, no one can know. How it was produced is not in our power to ascertain, nor indeed what it is when produced. Now a proposition with the imposing importance with which this is clothed, we think, and we believe justly think, ought to present itself in a tangible form that judgement may be passed upon it according to its merits. But exert all your faculties, it escapes detection. It bids defiance to reason, laughs at the exercise of thought, and tramples all intellectual greatness in the dust. We must not attempt to examine, for we cannot touch it, must demand no evidences of its truth, for none can be given; it is neither to be proved nor disproved; if believed it is received without reason, and if maintained it is without argument. Now a sentiment of this description cannot, in the eyes of rational or honest men, have strong claims upon our credence, but ought to be treated with indifference.

2. We object to this dogma as commonly believed because we know nothing about the properties of the Holy Ghost, its alleged cause. We know little about causation. All we know is that when we see one event always precede another of a given description, we pronounce it the cause. But that the antecedent, or what we uniformly term the cause, does actually produce the consequent or effect is more than we can in a single instance ascertain. All we can say, is, so far as our experience goes the appearance of the same antecedent has been followed by the same consequent. This antecedent may or may not be the cause of the consequent. We are accustomed to believe it is, though we must not, in these cases, say a thing *positively is so*. But if we see only one event, if we cannot discover its antecedent, to at-

tribute this event to any specific cause is as much as to acknowledge ourselves ignorant of the cause producing the phenomenon in question. The antecedent or cause must be known, must be perceived as well as the effect or consequent, or else we shall be unable to say that there is any relation existing between the thing perceived and the thing or event to which we ascribe it. The presence of the sun has, so far as our experience has anything to do with the case, always been followed by light. Now, supposing we had never seen the sun and that no one ever had seen it but all had beheld the phenomenon of light, should we, I ask, be warranted in saying the sun is the cause of light? If we did say so, would it not be a full acknowledgment that we did not know the cause of light? Whenever we attribute an effect which is known to something for its cause which is unknown, it may be taken for granted that we have no knowledge of what is its cause. We must see the cause as well as the effect before we pronounce it the cause, and if we do not see or perceive it by any of our faculties, the name to which we attribute the effects stands for nothing but our ignorance.

Now the Holy Ghost is a being of which the faculties of the human mind can take no cognizance. We know nothing of his properties, we know not the effect his influence would have on the human heart; consequently we know not whether the impulse which we feel is such as he would give or not. If it be said the effect is such as the Holy Ghost would naturally produce, I answer, we know nothing about it. It may be so; but as I have never been able to ascertain the qualities of the Holy Ghost — as I have never seen him in connection with this impulse, it would be absurd for me to say that he is its cause.

3. Another objection to the popular opinion of this subject is the discordance which the same popular opinion exhibits. Though nearly all *orthodox* Christians agree that it is absolutely necessary to their final salvation, yet there is nothing like agreement among them respecting what it is or how it is produced. Every proposition which presents itself to all alike, with the same clearness in itself and with the same evidences of its truth, is understood and judged of in the same manner. Everybody who has seen the sun, as it appears in the heavens, will pronounce it of a circular form. All that have seen it, have drawn this conclusion, and for this simple reason that it presents itself to all alike. But when we see different opinions about any subject, whenever we hear disputes, and especially if the disputers are characterized by a large share of bitterness, we may justly conclude

there is in the minds of the disputants, if not in the subject, some uncertainty, or at least some obscurity.

The new birth, if true, is a subject in which the eternal interests of the whole family of man are involved. The evidences of its truth should be universal, immediate, so clear and decisive that not a single dissenting voice should be found. The subject is alarming. How few of mankind have ever heard of it! How many less have believed in its utility! Millions and millions, both before and since the coming of Christ have died in total ignorance of it; and still we are told all must be eternally damned if we do not undergo its operations before we die! How liberal are these theologians to the devil! How readily do they rob Christ of his purchased possession! We tremble at the awful catastrophe, if the doctrine be true. We ask what it is?

One says the new birth is a radical change from nature to grace. Alas! I am as ignorant as before! How is it produced? He answers it is produced by the irresistible influence of the Holy Ghost; but that influence you can resist. When will he produce it? The advocate of the dogma replies, "when you repent and believe; but know, that in consequence of your corrupt heart you cannot repent and believe until the Holy Ghost does produce it."

Another calls it the implantation of a principle or a small sprig of grace in the heart, which, if duly cultivated, will make one as perfect as the Father in heaven; but notwithstanding this perfection today, the person may wilfully sin tomorrow and go to hell after all. Another says it is a ray of light which the Holy Ghost lets into the mind. But unfortunately the light thus let in not infrequently makes one man a Baptist, another a Presbyterian, perhaps one a Methodist, and, sometimes, one a Universalist. "But did you say this light ever made one a Universalist?" asks the Presbyterian. "That is a false light, a strong delusion sent by God that he may believe a lie and be damned." "Did you say," cries the Baptist, "that this light ever made one a Presbyterian? That is a delusion of Satan for it taught me that immersion is the only true mode of baptism, and the Presbyterian sprinkles." "And I am sure," thunders forth the Methodist, "that this light never taught Baptists or Presbyterians the doctrine of election and reprobation for it taught me salvation is possible to everyone; but it bade me be particularly careful not to allow my daughter to wear a ribbon on her bonnet, especially if tied in a bow."

O ye believers in the new birth, agree among yourselves what it is, what it teaches, and how it can be produced, and we will listen to your arguments, if you have any, in its support.

4. I object to this doctrine from the different conduct of those professedly under its influence. Now I do not say that this mode of judging is infallible; but since I have no other means than the man's own words to determine whether he is "born again," or not, I must judge him according to his profession. Some persons who profess to have been born again are very kind, are honest and virtuous citizens, while others love the soul, will do much, that is make many prayers to save that soul from hell while the body is left without assistance. Some are led to murder, as in the case of the assassination of Henry IV of France, of Archbishop Sharp of St. Andrew's of Scotland,[1] and in the circumstance of those who hung witches and Quakers in our country. Sometimes the Holy Ghost makes his subjects very happy, sometimes very miserable, and not infrequently compels them to the commission of suicide. But it is alleged that these were not influenced by the Holy Ghost, but were deceived. Be it so. If a man can deceive himself or others in this case, I conclude there must be some defect, either in the quality or quantity of the evidence, consequently the subject cannot be very clear nor very well established. I shall therefore claim the privilege to doubt yet longer.

5. We object to the common view of the subject under consideration that its demands are unreasonable and if complied with are useless. This new birth is contrary to the laws of nature and not necessary to enable them to perform their operations. It is not only contrary to nature but proposes itself as a change of the characteristic principles of man, as a *radical* change of his nature. It is then undoubtedly a preternatural thing and one of which we can form no rational opinion. A subject above our comprehension cannot be proved by arguments we can comprehend, consequently should be delivered over to those beings who can know something about it.

By a change of nature we must understand some alteration of the constituent principles of either mind or body. But mind and body are intimately connected. I know not any change which can be effected in one, without producing a corresponding effect in the other. My nature is such as God made it. He has either made it right or he has not. If he has made it right, a change will make it wrong. If he has not made it right, it is either because he did not know how or because he did not act agreeably to the suggestions of wisdom; but as

---

[1] [Ed. Henry IV (1553-1610) was assassinated by the fanatic Ravaillac on May 14, 1610. Anglican Archbishop James Sharp (1613-79), a firm and bitter opponent of Presbyterianism in Scotland, was brutally murdered by a party of Fife lairds and farmers after he had supported some rigorous measures to abolish Presbyterianism in Scotland.]

neither of these can be admitted without being lost in the abyss of atheism, or foundering upon the rocks of infidelity, nothing remains but the conclusion that he has made us right, consequently we need no change of nature.

Man has by nature all the faculties requisite to be all that God can, in justice require him to be; has all the faculties which belong to him as man; and if the Deity is not satisfied with the being he has produced, it is his business, not ours, to make us to suit himself. All that can be demanded of us is that we exercise the powers we find allotted us in the best manner possible. This will give us all the knowledge, holiness and happiness we need. With this consideration we should be satisfied. To desire some additional faculty, whether moral, physical or mental is but a plain murmuring against God for making us as he has—a serious complaining because we are not more exalted beings, which ill becomes us in the presence of our Maker.

A revelation from God, to enable us to understand and obey the laws of nature is desirable if we cannot obtain the requisite knowledge by any other means. Such a revelation, we, as Christians, consider the Bible. If that is sufficient, we need no other. If it is not, we can only say, God has given us a defective book, and whether this reflects honor on the character of Infinite Wisdom or not I leave for the candid to judge.

Every revelation made from God to man must be made in a manner we can understand so that there can be no room to doubt that God has made it, and with evidences, too, sufficient to convince others, or it can be of no use to any except to the one to whom it was first made. This is not the case with the dogma in question. The believer in it cannot convince others of its truth, nor prevent even himself from having the most serious doubts, until he succeeds in stifling the voice of reason, and in sinking himself beneath the degradation of a brute. And after all, so far as we can discover, the man who has experienced this boasted change, who has been brought from nature's darkness into God's marvelous light, knows no more about God, man, beast, or anything else, than he did before.

Boast of this new birth as much as you will, let its praises be sung in every temple of orthodoxy, and be responded by every fanatic, bigot, hypocrite and ignoramus in the world, and we still ask, and ask with emphasis, too, *what are its mighty fruits?* Shall I be pointed to acts of benevolence, of kindness, of humanity, to the widow relieved of her load of accumulated afflictions, to the orphan, fed, clothed and sheltered from the inclemencies of the weather and the more merciless cruelty of those whose God is the "root of all evil?"

Shall I be pointed to the angel of relief it sends to the lowly cottage; to the prison to smooth the captive's fate; to the house of sorrow to heal the broken heart and dry the mourner's tears, as its legitimate fruits? Would to heaven its advocates could do this! But alas! I see the consequences of this *godly* change in rent societies, in the alienation of friends, in the want of love in the father or mother for the child, in the want of filial and fraternal affection in families, in the wranglings, backbitings, calumnies, discord, and persecution which embitter our peace, and make life itself almost a curse. Great God! Shroud these consequences with a veil of impenetrable darkness and grant that thy children, by pretending to less wisdom and virtue, may acquire more.

I have seen the professors, the pretended, and for aught I know justly pretended, possessors of this *radical* change. I have marked their conduct; I have seen revivals of *religion;* I have seen young and old, male and female, crying, telling how bad they had been and how good they intended to be. My heart rejoiced. I thought God was indeed to work. I looked for righteousness; but ah me! I found nothing in these new converts to distinguish them from what they were before, or from the rest of mankind, except their bigoted, intolerant, fanatical or pharisaical conduct. This charge is weighty, but if you will use your eyes and ears you will easily find a justification for all I have said. With this conviction fastened on my mind that the change is neither reasonable nor useful, and fastened by facts I have seen, and which every one may see, I could willingly consign the dogma to the shades of eternal night.

6. So far as human observation extends, we can rationally attribute all that men feel in these cases to physical causes. There need be no doubt that all the sensations men pretend to have in this new birth are actually felt. I have had similar feelings; and so far as I could communicate them, they were, by those who considered themselves judges in such matters, pronounced genuine. I then attributed these feelings to the Holy Ghost.[2] But more familiar acquaintance with the human heart and the laws of the human mind has convinced me that what I then attributed to supernatural agency may be easily resolved on natural causes.

Before one is born again, he is told and generally convinced, that the new birth is absolutely necessary to his eternal welfare. With this

[2] [Ed. Brownson had something of a conversion experience when he was thirteen or fourteen years of age and again at nineteen when he became a Presbyterian. The Presbyterian session pronounced his experience genuine. On this see the Introduction, pp. 4-6.]

conviction there will be a strong desire to obtain it. Now overwhelm the mind with all the thunders of Sinai; play upon his imagination with all the lightnings of God Almighty's wrath; make the astonished, trembling victim of divine fury, see the world on fire, the flames ascend and involve heaven and nature in one vast sheet of liquid blaze; make him hear globes fall on globes, suns dash on suns, systems on systems, till all is one boundless ocean of rolling fire; point him to the awful Judge upon his throne, with a countenance that turns the burning ocean pale! to the nations of the dead trembling before their God; let him see the saints welcomed to the palace of their king amid the shouts of ten thousand angels; let him hear the awful sentence pronounced against himself and others, "Depart ye cursed," while devils drag them down to infinite despair! Uncap the bottomless pit, present him the horrors of hell, the pains, the groans, the anguish, the shrieks, the tortures, the agonies of the damned; roar out in a voice of thunder, "there, *there*, sinner see thy doom, thy eternal dwelling place!" Well may the thunderstruck mortal be under "concern of mind."[3] Well may he, if he believe this frightful exhibition, feel a *load* at his heart and in the voice of frantic fury cry out, "What shall I do? How can I escape? How save myself from a doom so awful, horrible, beyond description?" Change your tone. Speak the soft, suasive accents of love, of tenderest compassion; open a dying Savior's veins; let him see the blood freely flowing for his salvation; let him see Jesus dressed in robes of mercy, rushing towards him, bearing relief in his hand; strike the heavenly choir; let the music of heaven pour a balm into his wounded heart and infuse a gentle thrill through his soul. The scene is changed. His grief, where is it? His sorrow? It has flown. His remorse? the blood of a God has washed it away. The scene is changed; his fright is over; his fears are gone; he is calm; he is filled with joy; angels sing; trees clap their hands; all nature is vocal with the praise of God. He is born again; he is a new man; old things have passed away; all things have become new. Glory in the highest. Poor man! 'tis fancy nothing but the freaks of a bewildered imagination. Fancy saw the world on fire; fancy saw the Judge; fancy screamed over the burning lake, the torments of hell and the wretchedness of the damned. Reason had nothing to do with it; but the fright was no less real on that account. What followed was also the work of fancy; there was no reason in it; but the joy was no less really felt because it was the production of imaginary scenes. The

---

[3] [Ed. "Concern of mind" was a stage in the process of conversion. On this, see Brownson's "Patrick O'Hara. Chapter VI," *The Philanthropist* 1 (July 23, 1831): 141-43 and William J. Gilmore, 60-67, 102-09.]

constitution of the human mind, with the nature of the circumstances exhibited, is all that is wanting to account for the different feelings which are manifested. The description I have given is but a common process. The first thing requisite is to make the person believe he is in an awfully dangerous situation, that heaven frowns above and hell yawns beneath. In the next place the person must by the fears thus excited be driven to beg for help. The priest who excited can allay his fears. This is done by pointing to a Savior, reading promises of God's love, singing some pleasing tune with words adapted to his condition. The poor creature is asked how he feels, answers, he feels better: every countenance is lighted up, he sees nothing but smiles playing around every one who speaks, hears nothing but praises to God or congratulations to himself or his friends for his miraculous escape from hell, he is in raptures.[4]

All this is a natural process. The means used are adequate to the end; and if there be anything marvelous, it is, how any can *hold out* against these powerful means impelled by high steam pressure as they are in seasons of revivals. The orthodox clergy, half of them must be mere ignoramuses, or they might have made us all undergo the new birth long ago. To get up a revival is the easiest thing in the world. It only wants a little praying, fasting and crying, with exhortation, preaching hell, telling dreams, and a remarkable experience; and some young or old child will take fire, and the clergyman, if he knows anything, may keep it burning as long as there is anything to burn.

I may add that the new birth, in the opinion of its advocates, is produced by means at least within the control of the priests. Councils have met, committees have been appointed, deliberations have been held, votes have been taken respecting the best possible means to produce a revival of religion, or in other words, to produce the new birth. Now if they supposed these sensations, called the new birth, were produced by the Holy Ghost, would *they* attempt to produce them? Or do they suppose the Holy Ghost too weak or too ignorant to go on alone with the important work? They tell us, indeed, that the Holy Ghost works by means and they have lately, I believe, decided that he shall not use such means as he has for some years past, for those means have been the occasion of much scandal and very injurious to the cause of orthodoxy. But enough! The Holy Ghost usually employed in these seasons is a creature of human manufacture and may be dismissed with the whole catalogue of orthodox

[4] [Ed. "In raptures" is another stage in the conversion process. See Gilmore, 60-67, 102-09.]

follies, till the reappearance of the dark ages. Universalists have not
much success in producing revivals for they have abjured the devil,
and laughed at the eternity of hell torments; consequently they are
unable to avail themselves of the assistance of either. This is all as it
should be. The new birth, as it is commonly represented, is unintelligible. The agency by which it is supposed to be produced is unknown and not to be ascertained. The dogma is unreasonable, productive of no good but of much evil and may fairly be attributed to
the weakness and credulity of the human mind, and to the exertions
of a set of men who love to sport with the ignorance and passions of
mankind. Such are the reasons why we dissent from the popular opinion. What remains now is to explain our text and give our own opinion respecting what kind of a change reason and the Scriptures require in mankind.

All the text means may be easily ascertained by adverting to the
circumstances under which it was spoken. Christ was appointed to
establish a kingdom, a new order of things, which should produce
righteousness in the earth and cause the most distant isles to wait for
his law. He began to unfold the principle on which his government
was founded and to establish them by the performance of miracles.
Nicodemus saw the miracles Christ performed; he had no doubt that
God aided him, "For," says he, "no man can do the miracles which
thou doest except God be with him" [John 3:2]. But a difficulty
occurred: Nicodemus was a Jew; he had been taught and he believed
Judaism was from God. Was the doctrine Christ taught the same as
Judaism? If so, what need of miracles to establish it, since it was
already established? If not, why teach another? Christ does not give
him a direct answer, but informs him that no man, unless born again,
can enjoy the blessings of his kingdom; i.e., "no man, unless he re-
nounces Judaism, Paganism, or whatever system he has formerly
embraced, and receives, as a little child, the doctrines I teach, can
share the benefits of the order of things which I am about to establish
in the earth." The phrase "to be born again" may be understood by
adverting to the practice of the Jews with their proselytes. When
anyone renounced paganism and wished to become a Jew, he was
received either as a proselyte of the gate or as a proselyte of justice.[5]
If received as a proselyte of justice, he was baptized and taken into

---

[5] [Ed. Rabbis distinguished between the half proselyte, called *ger tosahu* (i.e.,
settler proselyte) or *ger ha-sha'ar* (proselyte of the gate), who observed some of the
basic principles (but not the ceremonies) of Judaism. The full proselyte, called *ger
tsedeg* (righteous proselyte), was the person who converted out of love of Judaism
and who accepted all its laws and ceremonies.]

the church or congregation of the Lord as it existed under that dispensation. This event, to wit, the conversion and baptism of a person, was considered as the most important epoch in a man's life. He was taught to date his existence from it, he was called a *new man*, and the change itself was called *being born again*. Now all the phrase could mean in the mouth of a Jew was simply a conversion or change of faith. The phrase I consider was proverbial and when Christ used it to Nicodemus, he intimated, without expressly denying Judaism, that he must be converted to another faith. Christ reproved Nicodemus because he did not understand him, which he could not have done had he taught him a new dogma similar to what is now called the new birth. Christ's exposition, in which he refers to being "born of water and of the spirit," plainly indicates that he had the treatment of proselytes in his eye and in his mouth the expressions commonly used respecting them. Being "born of water" referred to the water used in baptism, and being "born of the spirit" showed the distinguishing feature of the gospel and the nature of the change required. The new birth, change, regeneration or new creation so frequently spoken of in Scripture had reference to conversion or change of faith, to the renunciation of Judaism or Paganism, and the reception of Christianity. This I consider to be the true meaning of the text. Christ would say, "though you have been born a Jew, you must be born a Christian, that is, you must become a Christian, before you can share the blessings of the gospel," and this we must all admit.

The change required in us is that we "cease to do evil and learn to do well." This change is effected in a natural way by acquiring that knowledge of God and ourselves which a thorough acquaintance with the doctrine Christ taught is calculated to give. The doctrine Christ taught lays the foundation for correct conduct and gives us proper motives or persuasives to the performance of our duty. The spiritual influence is the power or energy which this doctrine exerts over the mind of a believer.

The design of Christianity is to make us better. This it attempts by giving us not in a supernatural, but a natural way, a knowledge of what we ought to do in order to have a commendable practice or to pursue a proper course of conduct. By teaching us what is proper for us to do, it points out the path we are required to walk; and by teaching us the character of God and unfolding to us our future destiny, it prevents us from going wrong. This instruction is found in the Bible, in nature, in our own observation and experience. Hence, these are what we are to study and what they teach we should follow.

Thus, Christian auditors, I have, as briefly and conclusively as I could, gone through my subject. The subject is embarrassed with difficulties, not only from its abstruse nature, but from the delicate feelings we all have, or have had respecting it. It is unpleasant, as well as ungrateful, to oppose the errors of our brethren and recall them to the purity and simplicity of the gospel. But this must be done or our holy religion will fall to rise no more. The indiscretion of its friends has already given it a blow, the evil consequences of which will require the labor of years to remove. The age of miracles has gone by. We live too late by some hundreds of years to have unintelligibility pass for knowledge or mystery for evidence of truth.

Infidelity has availed itself of our folly in contending for absurdity and is already erecting on the imprudence of professed Christians an empire of skepticism alike ruinous to religion, to civil order, and individual happiness. What has been tried amid the effulgence of science at the tribunal of reason and found wanting must be relinquished. The advocates of religion must be foremost in the encouragement of science and the cultivation of rational sentiments or they will lose their influence and be cast aside as the refuse of the earth.

The dogma we have been examining is replete with so many absurdities, enveloped by so much mystery, and followed by so many evil consequences that each should be ambitious to stamp it with the marks of his disapprobation. Let Christianity shine once more in its native purity and simplicity. Let its ministers discard all the foreign ornaments it received from the barbarous taste of the dark ages and its temples will be crowded by the wise, the virtuous, the scientific and the pious.

Let preachers point their hearers to what they can do to make themselves and their associates happy. Let the people with unanimous voice inquire what good work we can perform and be resolved to persevere in its performance, and the abstruse and often unintelligible points of polemical theology may be dismissed. Men may become virtuous, holy, and useful to their brethren, society be filled with peace and joy, earth itself be converted into the paradise of God watered by the pure streams of the river of life.

Brethren: we say, and say it with confidence of its truth, all that is required of you, is to "*do justly, to love mercy, and to walk humbly with your God*" [Mic. 6:8]. Do this and rest with the fullest assurance that the God who has given you while here so many proofs of his loving kindness and fatherly protection will be no less mindful of you wherever he shall be pleased to continue your existence. *Do this*, we repeat, and rest in the hope that you will triumph in the hour of death and be received with joy amid the acclamations of heaven into that world where sin, imperfection, sorrow and death are unknown; where praise to God and love to man shall dwell on every tongue and fill every heart and bosom forever and ever. Amen.

8.

A SERMON. ON THE SALVATION OF ALL MEN[1]

The Gospel Advocate and Impartial Investigator
6 (August 30, 1828): 273-78

For the grace of God which bringeth salvation to all men has appeared.
Titus 2:11.

The point of doctrine labored in this discourse is that the grace of God will in its final operations produce the happiness of all mankind.

Grace is favor. In our text it implies that benevolent, that compassionate disposition of Almighty God, which he exhibits in the redemption and final salvation of sinners of the human family and that declaration which he has made to us by his son Jesus Christ, by which he assures us that he is determined to bestow on the objects of his love all the happiness, which the nature he gave them is capable of receiving.

We institute no inquiry why we are made as we are, or why we are incapable of receiving no more happiness, or why we are capable of receiving so much, but conclude that Infinite Wisdom allotted us that rank in the scale of being, which he considered best, from which we have no right to dissent. Hence our inquiry naturally resolves itself into three parts:

1. What happiness are we capable of receiving?
2. Is it consistent with what we can ascertain of the moral perfections of Deity to bestow this happiness?
3. Will he bestow this happiness upon all who are capable of receiving it?

1. In answering the first, we shall not say man can enjoy a degree of happiness equal to that of Jehovah. Man is finite; consequently, the highest felicity to which he can attain must be finite, proportioned to the limited powers of his nature. His happiness may be

---

[1] [Ed. Sermon originally published in *The Gospel Preacher; Consisting of Original Sermons by Universalist Ministers*, vol. 1, December 1827 to December 1828 (Providence: John S. Greene, 1829), 108-16.]

complete, but it is still the happiness of a man and not of a God. By complete I mean as perfect as his nature will bear, that is, as perfect as in his original constitution he could receive. Deity may enlarge this capacity; this capacity may also continue to enlarge through all eternity, but whether so or not, we shall not now inquire. Man may also have fallen from his original perfection, and by transgression may have lost his relish for many pleasures which at first were suited to his taste. But restoring him to that primeval perfection and giving him all the felicity which naturally attaches itself to that state is giving him nothing which does not properly belong to him as man. Hence if we can ascertain that original state and what happiness is connected with it we can, at once, answer our first question.

This state is commonly supposed to have been a state of innocence and active virtue. "It may be so easily perceived that without any unusual exertion of the imagination, we can figure its revival. All the duties to God and man that are neglected we may fancy performed; all the crimes committed we can conceive forborne." Man would then be restored to his moral perfection and this restoration will present the idea of what is generally supposed to have been his primeval condition. He is endowed with all the faculties requisite to love God and be benevolent to his fellow men. He requires no new principle to enable him to perform all the duties to his God, obligatory on his station and all the offices of justice and humanity due to his brethren. If he have fallen from such a state, let him be restored, or let him be placed in such a state and he will then receive all the felicity, the consciousness of having discharged his duty, supreme love to God and a cheerful submission to his will can give — increased, no doubt, by the interchange of those kind feelings and good offices which enrapture the heart and raise it in gratitude to God for the blessings he receives.

This state supposes, first, the absence of all those painful sensations which we receive from external violence, from the wrongs and outrages of mankind, the beating, oppressing and enslaving of one another; from the cruelty of tyrants, from the rapacity and devastation of armies, from private murder, assassination, and the long catalogue of crimes which under various names and in various forms embitter the peace of society and banish tranquility from the domestic circle.

Secondly, this state supposes the absence of all that internal pain which is produced by transgression, all the compunctious stings of conscience occasioned by guilt or by folly to which we may add a large share of the sickness and distress which we suffer; for most of them are in some way or other chargeable upon ourselves, to our imprudence or to some impropriety of our conduct. Hence in such a state we should be free from nearly all the evils of which we now complain, and if we may add an indestructible body and a sound constitution, which we hope to receive in the resurrection, and which some suppose was possessed by man before transgression; we may say man, without making any material alterations in his moral nature, is capable of being perfectly free from pain. Let the *degree* of happiness be what it will, we readily discover that we are susceptible of a condition far above inconceivable woe.

How much happiness one might feel who faithfully performs his devotions to his God, who trusts him in every situation, has the approbation of his own conscience, the peace and tranquility of a good heart and the complacency of believing whatever he does, is pleasing to his heavenly Father and beneficial to his brethren, I cannot tell. But from the little experience I have had in such things, I conclude it must be great. The most virtuous can best tell how great. This much I say, I wish for no greater than I believe such considerations can give. To me it would be a paradise. I should recline in the bowers of Eden, feast on the tree of life, and drink the pure waters which flow from the temple of God.

2. *Is it consistent with what we can ascertain of the moral perfections of the Deity to bestow this happiness?*

I presume not to scan the Almighty. All I know of him is what he has revealed of himself. The volume of nature, stored with knowledge for all mankind, stands open for the perusal of all who wish to be instructed. On each page is stamped the impress of its Author in characters so plain that he who runs may read, on leaves so durable that no time or circumstance can efface or render the writing illegible. Here let us read: The first section is devoted to his power, which is seen in the immensity of his works, their magnitude and innumerable variety. The second displays his wisdom, in arranging the whole in the most beautiful order, instituting the best and most salutary laws for its government, in preserving harmony amid all the complexity of its parts and causing it to pursue with undeviating accuracy, the path he at first prescribed for the scene of its operations. The third combines the two first, and shows them resulting in benevolence, or exhibits every part adapted to some useful purpose, to the convenience or pleasure of the sentient creation. With this conclusion, the Scriptures of truth harmonize. An apostle sums up the moral character of God in short terms, "God is love" [1 John 4:8; 4:16], nor materially deficient is the testimony of the Psalmist, "God is good unto all, and his tender mercies are over all his works" [Ps. 145:9].

From the union of infinite wisdom and infinite power, unbounded goodness is naturally produced. I grant that I am unable to ascertain the extent of God's wisdom or of his power, but it would be folly in me for this reason to limit either. As far as I have been enabled to extend my observations, I have seen these attributes equal to any purpose of him who possesses them; hence I infer they are infinite; and if infinite, Deity can have no want, or imperfection. Whatever he desires, his wisdom devises the best means for its accomplishment and his power at once carries it into execution. With these attributes and the nature which possesses them, he must be perfect, and if perfect, he must be happy. Hence my idea of God is that he is a happy being. If he be happy himself, it is natural to infer that he is delighted with happiness in others or pleased with the production of happiness in his creatures. This proves him a good Being.

Now that disposition which delights in the misery of others, so far as we have any knowledge of it, is an unhappy disposition. We never know a man to take pleasure in afflicting his neighbor unless he is in some degree of uneasiness himself. Man has sometimes murdered his brother, but it was because he believed his brother's existence was prejudicial to his own. And I think I may lay it down as an invariable law of human nature that we never voluntarily disturb or wilfully destroy the peace of others unless we are unhappy ourselves. Hence the most virtuous are not only the most happy, but the most happy are the most virtuous.

From the fact that God is happy, perfectly happy, I infer his perfect goodness. If good, he must delight in goodness, must be pleased with the production of happiness. For his creatures to become happy, they must become good, and this will make them more like God; consequently a good and happy creation must be more pleasing to him than a wicked and miserable one. Scripture speaks the language of reason when it represents God as having "no pleasure in the death of the wicked" [Ezek. 18:23], "not willing that any should perish" [2 Pet. 3:9], but rather all would turn and live. If God has no pleasure in death, we may suppose he has pleasure in life. If he delight not in the misery of his children, we may reasonably infer he delights in their felicity. Hence I see no reason why our question may not be answered in the affirmative. It *is* consistent with the moral perfections of the Deity to make his creatures happy.

Perhaps it will be said man has sinned and his iniquity has rendered him obnoxious to the justice of God. This is conceded; but it is inquired, what is justice? It is nothing else than God manifesting himself in a particular manner or towards a particular description of individuals. Disguise it by what name you please, it will retain the traces of its derivation; it is goodness, or at least so intimately connected with it that if Deity were not just he could not be good; nor could he be good if he were not just. The fact is no being can be just without being good, nor can one be good without being just. Justice is so far from being opposed to the bestowment of this happiness that it exerts itself for that purpose, and is one of the principal means Jehovah uses to effect it.

But it is still alleged, "God's honor, as a sovereign and a lawgiver, stands pledged for the execution of the sanctions annexed to his laws." This we grant; and we verily believe that his honor will never be tarnished. God is not honored by disobedience, but by obedience. The bestowment of the happiness we have proposed is only in other terms reducing man to a willing obedience to the laws of God. If, as cannot be denied, I honor God more by my obedience than disobedience, so much more shall I honor God by the reception of this happiness than I should by remaining in a state of sin and misery.

But it is said, God told the sinner, "In the day thou eatest thereof, or transgressest, thou shalt surely die" [Gen. 2:17]. Very true: and the long catalogue of sufferings which blacken the page of history or which depress the spirits of mankind fully verify the prediction. But there will be no inconsistency in God should he induce the sinner to reform and then bestow on him all the happiness he is capable of receiving.

There are doubtless some who think the existence of evil now may be considered as a sure indication that it will eternally continue. But such persons would do well to consider the original design of God in creating mankind was to make them happy. This is evinced by the capacity or pleasure he has given them and the external supply he has so munificently contrived for their gratification. Evil, though perhaps inseparable in the present mode of existence from it, yet in no instance that we can discover does it form a part of that original design, and it must be overruled so as to coincide with it unless we suppose God may be disappointed. But as this argues imperfection in perfection itself, it cannot be admitted. Therefore, though we may not be able to determine the origin of evil or the bounds of its existence, we must conclude that in some way or other it will be made subservient to the original design of God. Hence we infer the existence of evil now does not necessarily afford conclusive evidence that it must always exist.

It is also alleged that God is holy, is opposed to all unholiness and without holiness shall no man see him. Men are unholy. "How then can he consistently with his moral perfection bestow this happiness upon them?" To which we answer, in the same degree as God is opposed to unholiness, he must love holiness, and as he is represented as determined to destroy unholiness, no man can dream it is inconsistent with his moral perfection to produce holiness. If it be, tremble, ye believers in total depravity; for according to your own concessions, you must be completely unholy, and be assured that God will never contradict himself for the sake of making you holy. But nature, reason, Scripture and everything else declare it cannot be contrary to holiness to produce holiness. And as all we ask is that men become holy in order to be happy, the objection falls lightly to the ground.

But men are not naturally unholy. My nature is as it should be. By nature I mean that constitution of mind which everyone possesses or which God gave man when he made him. This is human nature. This nature Christ took upon himself and yet he was not unholy. All the unholiness we have is our evil practice. This was all the unholiness Adam had. His transgression did not corrupt his nature nor does our transgression corrupt or render our nature unholy. Our *practice* is wrong; let this be corrected and all will be well. A change in man is undoubtedly required, but this is only that he may "cease to do evil and learn to do well" [Isa. 1:16-17]. No man in his senses can suppose holiness will ever object to a change of this kind. Therefore, it is consistent for God to bestow the happiness we have supposed upon the unfortunate children of men.

3. *Will God bestow this happiness upon all who are capable of receiving it?*

We trust we have prepared the way to answer this question and to answer it with effect and we hope that after this day we shall have no occasion to resume it.

We have already shown that the bestowment of this happiness is consistent with the attributes or moral perfections of God. It is only making mankind holy and since God is holy it can never be inconsistent for him to bestow it, and if it be not opposed to their happiness, which it cannot be, then we may naturally conclude he is perfectly willing all should receive it. The bestowment of it would be a due manifestation of his gracious disposition, and the withholding of it when he had it to give would be a certain proof of his want of affection for his own offspring. One of three things must be admitted: God can bestow this happiness and *will* not, or would but *cannot*, or can bestow it and will. If you say he can, and will not, you impeach his goodness, and if you say he would, but cannot, you limit his power. But either being atheism in effect, nothing remains but the last conclusion, he can and will make his children holy and happy.

Only two objections can be raised against this conclusion. The first is the existence of misery in this mode of being. "For," says the objector, "either God can make all mankind happy here, and will not, or would, but cannot"; and proceeds to the same conclusion, which is contrary to fact. But the objection has no weight because, if we suppose that the evil we now suffer may have an end, or be succeeded by endless felicity its existence may be no argument against the goodness of God. Should it continue eternally we have no proof of the goodness of God. For we know evil is not good, that is, evil, absolute evil; but a temporary suffering like that we have in this world may upon the whole be for the happiness of mankind. If it be not, we say God should, if he could, destroy it. By allowing that evil will have an end, we perceive clearly that God may be good notwithstanding its existence.

The second objection is: God would save all mankind or make all holy if it were not inconsistent with his righteous government. Now whatever government Deity may have established, he can have established no one that is inconsistent with his holy nature. And as we have already shown that holiness cannot be opposed to the production of holiness, the objection may be dismissed. We therefore say, God can bestow this happiness and will.

The fact is, the attributes of God can never, according to our perception of them, be harmonized upon any other plan than the final happiness of all mankind because in this inquiry each and every individual is to be considered a distinct and separate creation. For should there be only one individual who would, taking the whole of his existence into consideration, receive a preponderance of misery, Deity, so far at least as that individual is concerned, would prove himself unkind. Had but one man been created, what may we suppose, knowing God to be love, would have been his destination? Happiness to be sure. The same conclusion must be adopted, let the number created be swelled to any amount. Should it be said that we are reasoning upon assumed principles; we answer, we reason upon what we know. We indeed do not know the whole extent of the attributes of God, but the conclusions we adopt accord with what we do know of them. To draw a different conclusion, we must be referred to what we do not know, which can never be called a sure method of reasoning.

2.[2] We infer that God will bestow this happiness because in our original constitution we are made capable of receiving it. All are alike in this respect. Every man is susceptible of all the happiness we have supposed. All have a desire for it; and this desire is the first principle developed in their nature. "It grows with their growth and strengthens with their strength." God does not mock his children. He does not implant in their bosoms desires which he intends never to satisfy. Hence it is reasonable to infer that when he gave this desire, he intended to satisfy it; and as no power can thwart his intention it must be satisfied, consequently the happiness must be conferred.

3. We draw the same conclusion from the superior worth of a holy and happy creation over a wicked and miserable one. God, it is said, seeks for himself the highest possible glory. But he has made his glory and the happiness of his creatures inseparably connected. God declares that he had no "pleasure in the death of the wicked" [Ezek. 18:23], and everybody knows it would be absurd to say God is glorified in that which gives him no pleasure.

A sovereign is glorified when all his subjects are obedient to his laws and are happy in consequence of their obedience; for this shows him to be a good sovereign, not only good but wise, because he presents his instructions to his subjects in such a manner as to secure their approbation. The same may be said of God, our sovereign. He is glorified when his laws are obeyed and receives the highest degree of glory when this obedience makes his subjects happy. Obedience to his laws proves him to be a wise and powerful sovereign; happiness in consequence of obedience proves him to be a good sovereign.

"But may not a sovereign punish?" Yes, but if he is powerful, wise and good, he will punish on the same general principles as he governs, viz. for the good of the punished. Certainly to us that sovereign would appear the most glorious who so adapted his punishment to the capacity of the criminal and the nature of his crime that he should be reclaimed, and anything but glorious, would the one appear, that should punish eternally without doing any good to the punished, to himself or others.[3] Hence as the glory of God requires all mankind to be obedient and happy, it is inferred that all in due time will be.

[2] [Ed. Brownson had no number 1 within the third question in his original text.]

[3] Punishment according to the strict sense of the term is inadmissible. For punishment seems always to imply something of retaliation, which is contrary to the doctrine of Christ and of the principles of enlightened humanity. Deity has so ordered it in the dispensations of his providence that certain actions or a certain

4. We infer the same fact from the consideration that man has within himself those seeds of improvement, which, if allowed to expand, would in a period much short of eternal duration reach the felicity we have supposed. See that helpless infant in the arms of its nurse. Who would imagine that feeble mind would ever have power to scan the celestial orbs, determine their revolutions, and returning disarm the riven bolt of its fury and direct the harmless fire? Yet such was a Newton, such was a Franklin. Allow that mind to continue its expansion for a thousand years without any interruption, and how vast the sum of knowledge it must have collected, and how much greater if you permit its exertions to continue eternally! The most prolific source of our misery is our ignorance. Time would obliterate this, and experience would teach us that the only way to be happy is to obey the commands of God and thus we should be induced to obey.

5. We believe God will confer this happiness upon all mankind because he has declared it to be his will. Negatively, he is "not willing that any should perish" 2 Peter 3:9. Positively, "He will have all men to be saved and come to the knowledge of the truth" 1 Tim. 2:4. "Having made known unto us the mystery of his will, according to his good pleasure which he hath purposed in himself, that in the dispensation of the fullness of times he might gather together in one, all things in Christ, both which are in heaven, and in earth, even in him" Eph. 1:9-10. These declarations clearly show that it is the will of God that all men should be happy, be raised or gathered together in Christ, which are only different ways of expressing the same thing. Now, since it must be admitted that God works all things according to the council of his own will, we conclude it will be effected and men be holy and happy.

6. We infer the fact that God will bestow the happiness we have supposed upon all men from the consideration that he has actually adopted measures for that purpose. These measures are found in the system of divine grace which he has communicated to us by his Son

---

course of conduct does invariably produce painful sensations and ends in misery or death. But this is not to be considered a punishment but a necessary consequence of such actions and should touch us to avoid them. Why Deity attached pain to certain actions we do not know; nor can we assign any other reason why any action is wrong than that it produces painful sensations. These sensations have a tendency to alter our conduct and lead us to the performance of those actions which are salutary in prolonging our existence and in enlarging our felicity. For a full view of the author's sentiments respecting punishment see "Essayist No. 6," Gos. Adv. [Ed. *GAII 6* (July 5, 1828): 213-15 (pp. 108-11 above).]

Jesus Christ. This grace we are assured in our text brings salvation to or more properly saves all mankind. This grace contains the will of our heavenly father. Jesus is appointed to see it executed. "And, we have seen and do testify that the Father sent the Son to be the Savior of the world" 1 John 4:14. If it be God's will that the world, or all mankind should be saved, and if it be true that he has sent his Son to execute this will, that is, to save the world, will not the world be saved? Or shall we say that God has been unwise in the choice of means? God has all means under his control. He can produce means or he can perform a work without means; but since he has chosen means to accomplish his will, it would be a derogation from his wisdom or his power to say that the means adopted are not adequate to the end he had in view. Therefore, we conclude that the purpose of God will be effected and Jesus finish the work he was commissioned to perform.

7. And lastly, this conclusion is adopted because it is supported by the positive declarations of Scripture.

I shall notice in this place only a few passages out of the many that I might enumerate. See Matt. 1:21: "Thou shalt call his name Jesus, for he shall save his people from their sins." This passage positively asserts that Jesus shall save *his* people from their sins, which is the same thing as bestowing the happiness for which we contend, and the only inquiry is, who are his people? Inasmuch as we are told he shall save them from their *sins*, we infer his people are sinners. Matt. 11:27: "All things are delivered unto me of my Father," settles the question whether all mankind or only a few are given to him. For if it be contended that all things do not comprehend everything, we may with propriety reply, it at least comprehends the most important things, and it would be a strange perversion of language to say a phrase of such broad import should not include all mankind; or had reference only to the minor parts of creation. John 18:2: "As thou hast given him (Jesus) power over all flesh, that he should give eternal life unto as many as thou hast given him." This verse read in connection with the other two clearly proves all for which we contend. Here it is asserted that the Father hath given the Son power over all flesh and that the object for which this power was entrusted to him was that he should give eternal life to those that were given him. Now if he had power over all flesh, all flesh must be in his hands or under his control, and if he will save from their sins or give eternal life, which is the same thing, to as many as the Father hath given him or over whom he hath power, and he has power over all, it is evident he will save all mankind from their sins.

John 12:32: "And I, if I be lifted up from the earth, will draw all men unto me." Jesus was lifted up. The promise therefore remains that all men shall be drawn unto him.

Acts 3:21: "Whom [Jesus] the heavens must receive, or retain, until the times of the restitution of all things, which God hath spoken by the mouth of all his holy prophets ever since the world began." The word here rendered *restitution* implies, not merely being placed back in a former condition, but signifies being raised from a previous bad or unhappy state to a good or happy one. Hence this passage contains a full and unequivocal assertion of the doctrine for which we contend. No exposition can to a rational mind do away its force. Here then we rest. Reason, nature and Scripture in unequivocal language demand the discontinuance of sin and misery, and imperiously require the universal production of righteousness and felicity. It shall be done. The last enemy, death, shall be destroyed. Christ shall deliver up a reconciled, a happy universe to the Father, and God shall be all in all. AMEN.

9.

A SERMON. ON THE MORAL CONDITION
OF MANKIND

The Gospel Advocate and Impartial Investigator
6 (September 13, 1828): 289-94

*Is there no balm in Gilead? Is there no physician there? Why then is
not the health of the daughter of my people recovered?*   Jer. 8:22

I wish my hearers not to misunderstand the discourse I am about
to present them. I speak not of another world. I lay down no rules to
ensure endless felicity in a future state of being. Heaven is not exposed to sale nor can our labors bribe the Almighty to give it. On his
grace we depend not only for a future state of existence itself but also
for the particular degree of happiness we may hope there to possess.

The minds of the people have been misled. They have been taught
to believe that the peculiar advantages of religion are confined to
another mode of being and that the rewards of virtue are delayed till
after the resurrection. It is time to correct this mistake; and to let
mankind believe that religion is designed to benefit them while here
and that they have no need to look beyond this to another, and as yet
unknown, mode of existence for the reward of being virtuous. What
influence our faith and conduct may have on our happiness or misery in another world we do not, we cannot, at present ascertain. The
Bible, which is our guide, nowhere teaches that future life is dependent on our exertions here nor does it in any place inform us that
happiness in the kingdom of eternal glory beyond the grave is the
reward of anything we may have believed or done while subjects of
earth. It not only does not declare it to be a reward but does not even
represent our faith or works as being its cause or occasion. Hence
what we do should be valued according to its utility here and not
from any supposed advantages to be derived from it hereafter.

It is time to speak plainly. The circumstances of the age require
it. The mighty exertions of the self-styled orthodox, the means they
use to acquire wealth, power and a courtly establishment for themselves, the prospects, the delusive visions they present to flatter the
hopes or excite the fears of the thoughtless and the credulous, impe-

riously demand plainness of speech and correctness of instruction. The philanthropist must no longer be induced by the fear of giving offence to soften his sentiments, to conceal what might appear objectionable or to present them but partially to the world. The truth must be told, and told too with such independence of mind and clearness of manner that the hypocrite shall tremble, error be driven from its last retreat that virtue may have new confidence and benevolence additional ardor.

Mankind are infected with a moral malady. A powerful and malignant disease has spread its baleful contagion from time immemorial and continues its rage, little wasted by time or exertion. Something is wrong. The head is sick, the heart is faint, and wretchedness extends its dreary reign over all ages and all countries of the world. Time swallows in its vortex the labors of man, and crumbles the proud monuments of his industry and ingenuity. Vice prostrates his greatness and transgression corrodes his heart and points the sting of conscience. Community feels the wound; the social affections are destroyed; the warm, endearing sympathies of the bosom are deadened; friends are alienated; both private and public life lose their charms and are filled with bitterness, contention and discontent.

Is there no remedy? No balm in Gilead? No physician? Doomed are we to plunder and devour each other? Stamped are we with some fatal curse that man must destroy the happiness of man and live on the misery he makes? Shall rapacity forever continue to glut her vengeance? Shall iniquity in all its death-like forms stalk the earth, or, rising on the pinions of hell, scatter blight from her shaggy wings upon our brightest prospects and dearest joys? Forbid it, Great God! And let man inquire what remedy he needs and study to apply it effectually.

My Brethren: It is our object this day to inquire if we can find a remedy by which this powerful disease of whose existence we are all of us but too sensible can be removed and man be restored to moral health.

The cause of the disease must be ascertained before we can with any prospect of success prescribe a remedy. To ascertain this correctly we must perfectly understand the moral constitution of man, how far dependent on his physical and how far separate; how far the mind is influenced by physical objects, and how far the heart is corrupted by circumstances over which man neither in his individual nor collective capacity, has any control. This is a degree of knowledge to which we cannot pretend. Our knowledge of human nature is extremely limited and we cannot understand it fully without a perfect acquaintance with all other beings and things which are in existence. This we cannot hope ever to possess for such knowledge would make us omniscient. But some knowledge respecting ourselves we can obtain. From Scripture we learn "the creature was made subject to vanity" [Rom. 8:20], and all experience establishes the position that our capacity is limited and our knowledge imperfect. A limited and imperfect being like man, propelled to action by wants and appetites not to be resisted, must naturally in many things go wrong. He would judge improperly, execute imperfectly; nothing would be done right: hence the cause of the disease. It, so far as we can ascertain, originated in the weakness of man, the imperfection of his understanding, and in the paucity of his knowledge, or rather in his absolute want of experience.

Man desires to be happy; experience has demonstrated the fact that the order of nature is such that if every man would pursue his own best interest the whole would be happy. Why we ask does not every man pursue his own good? It cannot be said that it is because he is so depraved. Depraved, men no doubt are; but we have never seen any so depraved as to hate their "own flesh." Men adopt various methods to lessen their misery and to increase their enjoyment: some succeed and some do not, but we have never seen persons adopting methods for the express purpose of making themselves miserable; nor do we ever see people who desire to be unhappy. What then is the reason we pursue so many destructive paths? The answer is easy: every man desires to be happy, and would be, if he knew how. Hence the reason why we go wrong is because we are deceived; we err in our judgement; we make false estimations of things; and, acting under the influence of these wrong impressions, it is morally impossible for us not to go wrong.

Man, in his infancy, was without experience; knew not aliment from poison; could not predict the consequence of his actions nor ascertain whether the immediate and remote result would be the same or not. Driven by hunger and thirst he must be active; impelled by new wants continually accumulating, he was obliged to extend the sphere of his exertions; and laboring without knowledge, without the light of experience, without guide except his appetites, he was a blind man groping in the dark and no wonder if he ran foul of obstacles which impeded his progress, or stumbled upon objects which impaired his health, or prevented success? Such being the condition of man in his infancy, error was the result, and as one error paves the way to another, he continued to err, till habit fixed him in a course of aberration as wretched as it was far from the truth.

If ignorance be the cause of the evils which prevail in society, little discernment is requisite to know that TRUTH is the needed remedy, the balm in Gilead; and the knowledge and practical application of it, all that can be required to restore society to the soundness of moral health and to the strength and activity of virtue. Jesus was commissioned to save his people from their sins. This he does by teaching them the truth. "This is eternal life, that they may know thee, the only true God, and Jesus Christ whom thou hast sent" [John 17:3]. Solomon the wisest of men says, "wisdom is the principal thing," and he exhorts his subjects to "get wisdom and with all their getting to get understanding" [Prov. 4:7].

Had mankind at first known the course they should have taken; had they known what was requisite for their happiness, they would have been happy, or if not, we could assign no reason for the errors they have committed, and we should be utterly unable to exonerate God from the charge of involving his children in miseries too great to be endured, and too dreadful, we should think, to proceed from a being of boundless benevolence. He made us as he saw fit. It does not become us to ask why he has made us as he has; but if he has made us such creatures that we are doomed to go wrong, to injure ourselves and others, when we know better, and when we have also no inducement to do it, reason justifies the assertion that such creatures reflect no honor upon their Creator.

The Deity has placed us here; for what purpose we know not; but from Scripture and from reason we conclude it is for a purpose not inconsistent with our own good. Experience has evinced the fact that the only rational objects of desire or the only end to which we should direct our labors is the preservation of our lives and the increase of our enjoyment. This desire we have and towards this end we invariably direct our labors. We fail, why? Because the end is unattainable, or because there is any absolute necessity for our sufferings? We answer no; but because we, being ignorant and inexperienced, made a wrong choice, took from mistake the wrong road, lost ourselves in the wilds of misery. Experience is the school in which we must learn to correct our errors and the study of nature the science that must govern our future exertions.

It is not to be understood that we never do anything which we know to be contrary to our own interests. The contrary is the fact; and too often have we to lament that men do not do as well as they know how. But ignorance is still the remote, though *habit* may be the immediate, cause. Our modes of thinking and acting are adopted at an age when the powers of the mind have scarcely begun to expand

and when we seldom reflect on the tendency of any course of conduct. The child from the prompting of nature acts and must act; but from his want of knowledge he acts to no end. He does what he sees others do, or what is within his reach, or what others, ignorant as himself, command or induce him to do. Thus habits are formed; an improper bias is given to the mind whose influence is felt for years, if not till death. The passions, or rather the appetites are thus sharpened and receive a power which enables them to overcome the suggestions of the understanding and not infrequently to lead the intellectual man captive, notwithstanding he is armed with knowledge and defended by experience. See Paul to the Romans, chap. 7.

This is the process. The cause is ignorance; the ignorance of the person when the improper habits are formed; the ignorance of parents and guardians who give him his first impressions and the ignorance of the society in which he lives and of that which existed before him. We are at no loss to discover that truth applied to our condition would remove the disease of which we complain and recover our health. By being cautioned in early life against the influence of habit we should be on our guard and in after life we should from our knowledge resist the habits with all the power given us, and in the absence of temptations we should fortify the mind and render it invincible to the shafts of appetite or too ardent passion. Instruction also would be more useful; for parents, guardians, and teachers would feed the mind with truth not as they have done hitherto with error. The impressions the child, the youth and the man would receive from association would be more favorable; in a word, everything would have, if knowledge should become prevalent, the same tendency to make us virtuous that it has had in the reign of ignorance to make us vicious.

Our reasoning is correct, for it rests on the maxim sanctioned by experience and revelation. "Train up a child in the way he should go and when he is old he will not depart from it" [Prov. 22:6].

But is truth within our reach? And if it be, what is the reason it has not long since been discovered and applied to the healing of the nations?

These questions are important and shall be answered separately. Is truth within our reach? But this provokes another question: what is truth? Truth, so far as we know anything about it, is a knowledge of facts or simply the observation of things as they are. This observation may be extended to everything which can come under the observation of our senses; and though we can never know everything, it is confidently believed we can know enough to remove most of the evils of which we complain.

Jehovah is declared in the Scriptures to be good; but what opinion should we form of him if we believed he had made us a prey to all the deleterious consequences of ignorance without putting into our hands or within our reach the means of instruction, or without intrusting to us the power to acquire that knowledge which he has made necessary to preserve our existence and produce our happiness? Cruel indeed would seem his conduct; severe in the extreme would appear his treatment of his children should he make them ignorant, make misery the consequence of ignorance and then prevent us from acquiring the knowledge we needed. Tyranny could not be better defined nor a malignant being be more clearly characterized. But experience, the best instructor in things pertaining to earth, has answered the question; the skeptic may listen and lose his doubts. Knowledge has been obtained; we have risen high from our original degradation and to the limited information of the primeval savage we have added many useful and valuable improvements. Many of the evils which haunted our ancestors have been made in particular places; and, from what individuals have done, we are led to infer of what the whole species is capable. Our bosoms swell with noble emotions; we feel a conscious dignity when we contemplate the acquisitions to the sum of human knowledge which many of our brethren by their unwearied exertions in the fields of science have made, the evils they have lessened or removed and the increase of happiness they have given. I glory in the name of MAN. I feel grateful to Almighty God for the noble faculties he has allotted to the rank of existence to which I belong, for the wide field he has given it to explore, and the increasing delight afforded by every new discovery or improvement. The Christian loves mankind and could embrace them all in the arms of his affection. He only regrets that so many are still bewildered in the mazes of ignorance or groping their way in the gloomy walks of misery. Could he impart to mankind a desire for knowledge and kindle an ardent zeal for the acquisition of wisdom how soon would their sorrows die away and their sufferings be succeeded by a feast of intellectual delicacies, pure and permanent as the God whence they emanate.

Much is said of the spirit of the age, much of the free inquiry which prevails, and the ardent desire for knowledge which is manifested. This is well if he actually feel such a desire and act under its influence. But let us not be deceived by sounding words or pompous phraseology. Our love for wisdom may evaporate in praises for the spirit which we imagine prevails and our exertions may end in flattering the noble minded philanthropy which we may fancy some to possess. Knowledge is not obtained without labor. The senses must be used, we must think; must reason; must reflect. But unfortunately too many choose to roam the fields of imagination rather than to traverse the plains of reality, to exhibit the fairy visions of fancy than to trouble themselves with sober facts or the cool result of demonstration.

Every age has boasted its ardor for truth, its zeal for knowledge and its tender regard for the interests of humanity. Every age has done something, may we make our boasting good and leave to our successors less to reform than was left us by our fathers. There is fear that many are ambitious to be thought the advocates of free inquiry, the patrons of science and the promoters of useful knowledge and pure religion, who nevertheless seldom think, but waste all their supposed good intentions in merely reciting the names which are approved without attempting to understand their import.

We are placed here to be active; nothing in the world where we find ourselves is gained without exertion. But if we act, and act understandingly, with a knowledge of the propriety of the actions we perform, we shall be amply paid for all the sacrifices of ease and tranquility we may be compelled to make. The most excessive labor we can endure is less burdensome than the mere weight of idleness. What becomes necessary to ascertain is what shall we do? What is proper to perform? What institutions shall we support? What innovations in the old order of things shall we make? How can we separate the good in what now is from the bad connected with it? How abolish what is injurious and perpetuate what is beneficial? Such are the inquiries which press upon our attention and which must be answered correctly before mankind will have reached that degree of perfection which will banish the evils with which we are now acquainted.

To answer these questions is not in my power. They involve a knowledge not only of all the sciences now discovered, of the arts invented, of the improvements made in each; but also a complete knowledge of everything man is able by the most assiduous application to learn. We must endeavor to find the true path, go as far as we can and leave to our posterity to complete the acquisition. Some directions to aid us in the acquisition of knowledge is necessary.

The first thing for a man to study is himself, that he may ascertain what are his rational wants and what are the powers which are allotted him. Certainly I do not mean to be understood that the character of the Great and Good Being on whom we are dependent for all we are and all we can enjoy is not to be studied. I have been a skeptic; I have run over the arguments of unbelievers, but to me the logic of the heart has peculiar force; and if it will not readily silence an opponent, it has more power than the mere logic of the head to silence those angry disputants which a man sometimes feels within himself. I am so far from wishing men not to think of this Being that I believe a large share of their happiness depends on the contemplation of his character and pious resignation to his will. But Deity is known through the medium of his works. We must read him in man, trace his wisdom as displayed in the nice design which runs through the whole of our organic structure, must mark him in the succession of day and night, in the changing seasons, see his beauty in the green robes of spring, in the flowers and foliage of summer, and the golden sheaf of autumn; behold his glory in the heavens and his goodness in that rich supply which he has contrived for our wants. To know God is to know his works, and as man, at least to us, is the most important of these works, it is proper to begin with him and learn what he is and of what he is capable.

The second rule to be observed in our inquiry after truth or knowledge is to draw the line of demarcation between things which we can and things we cannot know. The only inlets of knowledge are our senses. What is not cognizable by these it is useless to study; for unless Deity should enlarge our senses or increase their number we should not be the wiser after studying a thousand years. We must avoid then disputes about spiritual beings and immaterial substances. Some suppose God is immaterial; it may be so; but we have no perception of his immateriality. We know him only by material objects and can worship him only as that Being in whom we live and move.

Those things which are within our means of examination we are to study; to them we may devote our time without fearing it will be misspent. It is only when we attempt to explore regions beyond the reach of sense we fail and lose our labor; and one thing is already discovered, *that which is most useful to us, is most easy to learn*; though it must be confessed that ignorance has been so fond of mystery that through her misrepresentations it so happens that what in itself was plain is now difficult although highly useful.

The last thing that I propose is that we learn to doubt; that we guard against credulity and place a higher value on matters of fact than on the deductions of theory or hypothesis. We must doubt our own infallibility, learn we are liable to err, to mistake the subject and sometimes the evidence by which a position is supported. This will teach us modesty in proposing our own opinions and candor and impartiality when speaking or judging of the opinions of others.

We must be cautious about believing every tale or placing credit upon every idle relation of occurrences which took place at a distance of time or place for which no one stands voucher, and we must always remember facts are better than opinions and truth is worth more than theory; hence those things which belong to our own sphere and to our mode of existence are to be studied before those which belong to any other. These rules observed in our inquiries, we can set no bounds at present to the acquisition we may hereafter make nor can we imagine the eminence to which the human race may arrive.

But if knowledge be the balm to heal our wounded hearts and to restore us to moral health, and this knowledge be within our reach, why has it not been hitherto attained? It is with regret we answer this question. We would ever treat mankind, however unfortunate, with tenderness, and towards individuals, however injurious their conduct may have been to the general interests of mankind, we would indulge no sentiments but compassion for their ignorance and grief for the misery they have occasioned.

The various systems of religion which have been promulgated, cruel and absurd dogmas which have been enforced, may be alleged as a strong reason why this moral disease has not been removed. Religious systems were not the cause of our sufferings. We were unhappy before they were invented and we adopted them vainly hoping to find relief. The remedy has proved worse than the disease. I need not point to the wars, to the popular commotions they have occasioned. I need not refer to the partialities and prejudices, to the irreconcilable animosities existing between kingdoms and empires embracing different religious creeds; nor need I rehearse the imprecations of Mahometans upon Christians nor the bitter reproaches which Christians cast upon Mahometans; nor need I refer to the violent persecutions of one sect towards another. These are themes of popular declamation, and you have all heard them repeated with all the force of human eloquence. These are but the most obvious effects of the evil deeply rooted in the bosom of society.

The evil consequences of these systems may be traced through all the complexity of our actions and be found to be, through the influence of habit, almost the governing principle of our lives. They penetrate the inmost recesses of our hearts, generate our thoughts and direct the train of our reflection.

Mankind newly settled here adopted the best religion they could. Gross in their perceptions and sensual in their wishes, they painted their gods like themselves. Rude and uncultivated in their manners and vindictive in their dispositions, they imagined despots for gods, placed a tyrant upon the throne of nature and paid a worship of fear and painful sacrifice. Priests were called to propitiate the tyrant and conciliate the affections of the gods. These priests were pleased with the sacredness attached to their character and the influence and emolument they received from the supposed importance of their office. Hence they became fond of their station and used all their art and machinations to secure it.

I do not wish to be one of that number who are constantly crying "priestcraft," and full of bitterness to the clergy; but the evils this class of people have heaped upon us are more than I can or wish to enumerate. But they acted naturally, just as any other persons would have acted in their condition. It is not mine to look into the heart, to explore the inmost recesses of thought, and condemn or acquit our fellow beings of guilt for the miseries they have brought upon themselves and others. I neither praise nor blame the priesthood. I speak of the consequences which flowed from their institution.

When religion was first deemed important it was vague, inconsistent and often arbitrary and cruel. Formed by the persons who afterwards lived upon its revenue, it had no idea of the equality of the human family, but considered all as doomed to eternal wretchedness that did not embrace it. Such being the fundamental principle, such the basis on which religion commenced her fabric, can we wonder that the superstructure should be imperfect, unequal and improper? Inequality increased among the wretched children of men; a privileged class arose to fatten on the labors of the ignorant, the timid and the credulous. The priest leagued with the despot, and both physical and mental liberty was borne on the winds to some lone retreat. Luxury began to rear her palaces, she spread her tables with the most costly viands and richest delicacies, consumed the wealth of a province at a meal, and laughed at the destruction she made. On the other hand, poverty—cold, unfeeling poverty—branded the multitude with the stamp of inferiority. The great neglected, the powerful oppressed, the pious taught them ignorance and the rich enslaved them. The higher ranks divided into factions: cabals and intrigues made them furious, and the poor were compelled to decide the quarrels of their oppressors by the loss of their lives.

Pride, vanity and luxury were the characteristics of the great: poverty, meanness and discontent of the lower orders. The priest saw this division, saw he was leagued with the great and determined he would prevent innovation. He despatched his emissaries to the little and the great. The great, the higher class, supported him from policy; the poor were flattered or frightened. To the poor the priest came with his face of sorrow and eyes suffused with tears. "Ah me," said he, "what a weary land is earth, full of briars and thorns; misery is the lot of mortals here; vain the attempt to be happy. Wealth is a mere bauble; power is a vexation, and pleasure is worse than mourning. God had wisely made these distinctions in society; he has, through his providence, appointed some to masters; but there could be no masters without servants. He has appointed some to declare his will, to be priests; but there can be no priests without altars and sacrifice, and no preachers without hearers, consequently you must learn to obey, listen to us and believe what we teach. God has commissioned us to pray for your souls and to labor for your everlasting welfare. You are unhappy now: ah, thank God for that, you will be more happy hereafter. You are poor: blessed are the poor for they are entitled to the protection of the gods."

Thus they endeavored to silence the murmurs of those discontented wretches who wished for a better order of things and to reconcile the unfortunate to their sufferings. Instead of exhorting the soul to be free, to exert itself to remove the evils which it suffered, they amused it with the fairy tales of Elysium, with splendid descriptions of its peaceful groves, its shady walks, its beautiful and delightful employments. Instead of firing the soul with a desire to be happy by the removal of its evils, they taught that evil was unavoidable and to complain would be to murmur against heaven.

They discouraged free inquiry and stamped a fatal anathema upon the exercise of thought, called off the attention from virtue, and made holiness consist in paying the priest, in the observing of unmeaning rites, in reverence to certain days, and in the belief of certain unintelligible dogmas about unknown beings and invisible worlds.

Innovation was prohibited on pain of the excommunication of the priest and the wrath of the Almighty. All the sciences which enlighten the mind or give vigor to intellect were condemned as the suggestions of the devil and all the books which were not panegyrics upon the priesthood were committed to the common hangman to be executed.

Such have been the arts used, such the impositions practiced upon us. The disposition generated by these; the pride, indolence, contempt, fanaticism and intolerance produced by these are the disease and the reason why our moral health is not recovered.

REMARKS

Thus, kind auditors, I have gone through my subject. We have considered the moral disease with which we are afflicted and have, I believe, ascertained a remedy within our reach and assigned a substantial reason why the remedy has not been hitherto applied.

The moral malady of which we complain originated in our ignorance or in our want of experience and not, as has been supposed by many, in our depraved disposition. Our duty and our interest are the same: as we all pursue what we believe to be our own interest; as we cannot suppose that mankind go contrary to their own interests because they are averse to performing their duty, we conclude they avoid their interest through ignorance. This being the cause of the impropriety of our conduct it is perfectly plain that all that is required is knowledge and acquaintance with our own interest and the means by which we may pursue it. Hence, knowledge or wisdom becomes the principal thing and the first object demanding our attention.

We have also found [that] the reason why mankind have progressed so slow in the acquisition of truth is because it has been the interest or the supposed interest of a privileged class to keep the great body of the people in ignorance. Here we find reason to deplore the mischief done by various systems of religion and the evils perpetuated by the selfish conduct and artful managements of the priests. And here your speaker would add a remark to prevent his objections to religion and priests from being misconstrued. Nothing which he has said is intended to injure the true or the Christian religion, but what he has said is designed to disclose the mischiefs done by false, degrading or superstitious systems of religion. Christianity is believed, but Christianity has been abused; it has been corrupted and perverted to the basest purposes. Its doctrines have been wrongly interpreted, have been so explained that this heaven-born system has become no better than heathenism. We must labor to reform it; bring it back to its pristine purity, and no man of sense will refuse to give it a cordial reception; but no philanthropist, who understands himself, will have aught to do with it while encumbered by the heaps of rubbish it accumulated during the dark ages.

The mind must be free. Christianity if *forced* upon us cannot be beneficial nor indeed can any religion or any sentiment which is adopted through compulsion. Labor, then, brethren, to free the mind from its mental bondage; give it liberty to range at pleasure and be under no apprehensions that it will prefer falsehood to truth. May the Almighty aid us by the wisdom of his councils and by the influence of his spirit in our endeavors to meliorate our condition. AMEN.

10.

MISSIONARIES

The Gospel Advocate and Impartial Investigator
6 (November 13, 1828): 301-02

In our last we considered the tendency of Sabbath Schools as they are now conducted; we shall, in this, remark on the missionary scheme for we are determined to expose the arts of the designing and the hypocritical whenever we discover them.[1]

The missionary system, when first started, appeared to most Christians as truly desirable; and if it was opposed, it was only because it was believed to be impracticable. To the benevolent soul filled with the love of Christ and burning with desire to spread his kingdom, it was painful to see almost a whole world ignorant of the Bible and strangers to the glorious doctrine of Christ. When to this was added the belief which many had that those of the heathen who died unacquainted with Christ must be eternally miserable, it was not hard to kindle a zeal for missionary enterprise not to be easily extinguished. The object, in the opinions of professed Christians, was most glorious; the end such as they could pray for with all the pious, ardent, benevolent and philanthropic desires which the religion of our Savior ever inspires [in] the soul of his true follower. Those who started the plan were thus enabled to enlist all the best and most active feelings of the Christian, to engage the kind wishes of society generally, and to command not a little of the CASH necessary to the grand undertaking.

The spark immediately caught for Christendom was already combustible; it spread almost like a conflagration; our country was overrun and all its energies engaged; and as much of its circulating medium secured as its holders could be prevailed upon to part with. Some ventured to say the plan was impracticable; some wished to know whether the agents soliciting funds were *responsible*, or whether the managers of the grand enterprise could give any *surety* for the

---

[1] [Ed. Reference is to "Sabbath Schools," *GAII* 6 (August 30, 1828): 285-86, where Brownson opposed the establishment of those schools because they were purely sectarian, taught the erroneous Dortian theology, and because they simply supported clerical despotism and were used by clerics to form a Christian Party in politics.]

wise disposal of the money given them, and some even dared hint there might be something concealed in this grand undertaking; that the managers might have some designs of *personal* aggrandizement and concluded by observing that it would be better to convert the heathen in our own streets before we tried those of Hindostan;[2] and that if we had anything to spare for benevolent purposes, there were objects enough near home where we could ascertain whether our benevolence was beneficial or not. But alas for the temerity of each of these classes! They were branded with the vilest epithets: "enemies of God," "opposers to the spread of Christ's kingdom," "infidels," "Atheists," etc. They received a torrent of abuse and were looked upon by the more *holy* part of community as awfully abandoned, as almost needing the aids of the missionaries for their conversion.

Such were the feelings, such were the circumstances with which the mission scheme was commenced in this country. It was all the rage to convert the heathen. But who was there to go? The Rev. doctors, who had so pathetically described the perishing condition of the poor heathen, who pleaded so warmly and so affectionately in their behalf, could not think of leaving their homes, their friends and the dear people of their congregations to sound the gospel in the heathen lands. But a few beardless boys, young and ignorant were sent out, and at once the world was to be converted. The measure has been conducted for some years, and what, we ask, is the result? As for the conversion of the heathen to Christianity, present appearances are not very encouraging, nor are we informed of anything of consequence that has been done.

The reports we receive assure us that the heathen are not yet converted, but the missionaries are praying earnestly they may be; not many converts are yet made, but it is expected there will be some soon. The missionaries do not preach much, for the people do not appear anxious to hear, but there is no doubt they will hereafter be extremely desirous to be instructed, particularly when the meek and unassuming deportment of the missionaries shall be more generally known. Bibles and tracts are indeed distributed, but they excite only ridicule and serve for wrapping paper or fuel for the *fire.*

Such is a fair estimate of what has been done abroad. Except at the Sandwich Islands.[3] Here the missionaries found a credulous old

[2] [Ed. A nineteenth century identification of India.]

[3] [Ed. A former name for the Hawaiian Islands. For one historical assessment of the foreign missionary movement in the United States, see Charles I. Foster, *An Errand of Mercy: The Evangelical United Front, 1790-1837* (Chapel Hill: The University of North Carolina Press, 1960), 208-22.]

king or chief whom they could flatter. They wheedled him into their plans by learning him letters, which they said it was their benevolent design to teach his subjects. They told him wonderful stories about the country they had left, told him what kind of religion they embraced, and even went so far as to prevail upon the old king to be baptized. A change in the religious profession of a court generally produces a change in the opinions of most who are influenced by it. Accordingly quite a large number were baptized "in the name of the Father and the Son and the Holy Ghost." This and the observance of the seventh day (first day) and paying the priest is all we presume they have learned of Christianity, for if they are as stupid as the missionaries represent them this is nearly all they could understand.

But we know of but little the missionaries have done; they generally tell of all the success they have and as they have not told of much, and as they continue to solicit funds, we conclude they have not much unless it be *personal sacrifice* whereof to boast.

Having given this sketch of their proceedings, we shall now state our objections to the missionaries and the plan of sending them to convert the heathen.

We object to the missionaries as being generally incompetent. Messrs. Fisk and Parsons[4] were sent from Vermont to Palestine to teach the doctrine of Christ. We say nothing of the strange thoughts which arise at sending men from Vermont to teach the doctrine of Christ in the very country and on the very spot where Christ lived, preached and died. But these were two young men of no great acquirements, to say the least. But they knew the Orthodox creed, the New-England Primer and some little fashionable religion, that is, damnation to all who do not support missions. These men, thus duly qualified, were sent to Palestine; but was the Christian religion unknown there? O no; there was then at Jerusalem a learned bishop, who, a few years before in London, was justly considered a prodigy of human genius and learning; and yet we send out boys to convert him, for he is not Orthodox. So much for Palestine. They know more about Christianity there than we do here; all the knowledge we have of Christ came from that country, and yet we suppose them so ignorant that those who have little or no knowledge can instruct them.

With regard to Hindostan, if we may credit the best information we can get, nearly the same remark will apply. It is well known that the British have an establishment in that country, and that a large part of it is subject to them. The English East India Company are

4 [Ed. Unable to identify Fisk and Parsons.]

rich; they have the gospel and can easily give it to their heathen subjects if they choose. Our missionaries have not, we believe, traveled
much out of the reach of British authority. It is a very kind thing to
beg from the poor of our own country to convert British subjects;
but some how or other, our good folks like their mother extremely
well. Those who were competent, who have gone to that country,
have been employed [a] considerable part of their time as agents for
the government. Those who were incompetent have cut a sorry figure beside the Brahmin, whose theological books and whose theological knowledge are not, to say the least, far behind ours. In general
those we have sent were more remarkable for their zeal than their
knowledge, and some of them, if not too indolent, would make much
better farmers or mechanics than missionaries.

(November 22, 1828): 381-82

Another objection to missionary enterprise is the ungenerous
prejudice excited against the heathen by the misrepresentations of
their character and sentiments, which are encouraged. There is no
doubt that the heathen are wretched enough; no doubt they are deplorably ignorant, but he must have little acquaintance with mankind who can believe one half that is told respecting them. We would
be the last to apologize for the superstition, the last to adopt the
absurd notions of those whose conversion the missionaries have attempted. Our readers know our sentiments too well; we have too
strenuously contended for knowledge and too earnestly stated the
importance of correct instruction to be so understood. But we do
not believe the condition of the heathen is one half so bad as it is
represented.

Every nation is apt to make its own laws, religion, manners and
customs the standard of right. By it they compare whatever they discover in others, and pronounce it correct or incorrect as it agrees or
disagrees with their own. Our own education is generally the criterion by which we determine the worth or correctness of anything
which we find among others. The religion, laws, manners and customs of the Hindoos are very different from ours, but that is no
certain reason they are not as good.

We are no advocates for the religion or popular superstition of
the Hindoo; but we do not believe it one half as gross, nor the people
one half as stupid as missionaries represent. Our missionaries, one
half of them, were never far out of sight of their mother, the church
or seminary, until they found themselves bound for Hindoostan or
some other pagan country. Landed upon these strange shores, amid
objects entirely new, among a people different from those they left,

speaking a different language, using different forms of religion, seeking heaven by rites and ceremonies different from those enjoined by
the "Westminister Catechism," or the "Confession of Faith,"[5] they
stare around, "Why, the people must be fools or stupid wretches to
act so different from what they do in *our* country!" Full of these
impressions made by the novelty of the thing, they write home to
their friends that they have fallen among "man-eaters, awful wretches,
deplorably ignorant, who never read the New-England Primer, nor
heard a Calvinistic sermon in all their lives. What besotted creatures
these Hindoos are! What monstrous superstition prevails among
them! What horrid gods! Good God, how ill-shapen! Here is a god
having the body of a man with an elephant's head upon it!" O
Hindoostan! How art thou fallen! Land of the ancient
Gymnosophists,[6] instructress of Zoroaster, Pythagoras, Plato and others, whither hast fled thy ancient renown!

The Hindoos are superstitious. Nobody doubts this; so are many
Americans. We need not travel to the land of Brahma to find superstition. We have enough and to spare nearer home. "The Hindoos
worship images." Be it so. Who believes that the Hindoo who pur-
chases those images at the warehouse supposes them to be gods?
Christians have images, or at least the most numerous denominations, but no one who thinks a moment can believe there is a human
being so benighted as to suppose an image, which either himself has
made or seen made, is the God that created the worlds. Missionaries
may say so but no man in his senses will believe a word of such stuff.
The Hindoos, like all who have images, consider them as symbols, to
remind them of their duty, of the particular divine being they are
supposed to represent, of some memorable circumstance in the history of their God, of his Incarnation, etc. as Christians have their
beads, crucifixes and paintings of the passion of Christ, pictures of
the twelve apostles and of the Holy Virgin Mary.

[5] [Ed. The Westminister Catechism and the Confession of Faith were the
creation of the Westminister Assembly (1643-49) and were generally used as criteria of orthodox Presbyterianism.]

[6] [Ed. Gymnosophists were an ancient Hindu sect of ascetic philosophers
who wore little or no clothing.]

We have before us one of the sacred books of the Hindoos, *Bhagvat Geeta*,[7] which contains an account of the sublime mysteries of their religion. We intended to have made some extracts from it and probably shall when we have time and room. This book is nearly as ancient as our Bible, and if one may judge of the original from its translation, the theology it inculcates is not essentially different from that which has long prevailed in the Christian world. Here is much sublimity and much incomprehensibility, much that is absurd, but much that no inspired writer has ever exceeded. The nation that could produce it must have been deeply learned, and those who read it and practice what it enjoins cannot be said to be irreligious or to have no knowledge of God among them. The theological opinions of the Hindoos may be easily ascertained from the remark of a Brahmin who, on hearing repeated from Pope's Essay on Man,

> All are but parts of one stupendous whole,
> Whose body Nature is, and God the soul,
> . . . .
> Warms in the sun, refreshes in the breeze,
> Glows in the stars and blossoms in the trees,
> Lives through all life, extends through all extent,
> Spreads undivided, operates unspent, etc.[8]

started declaring the writer must have been a Hindoo.

Their moral precepts are such as would do honor to any people. Their manners are much refined. No people are more polite, or in general more friendly. One fact speaks volumes in their praise: they patiently submit to have the missionaries live among them. Should we, just, holy and refined as we are, tolerate Hindoo missionaries that should come among us to convert us to Brahminism? We persecute one another. One sect does all it can to prevent another from propagating its peculiar notions: what should we do if men should come among us declaring the Christian faith a fable, calling us ignorant, benighted wretches, and should begin to preach and to circulate their tracts and other pious productions for the purpose of con-

[7] [Ed. The Bhagavad Gita, "Song of the Blessed Lord," is sacred literature for the Hindu. It expounded the duties of caste and the yoga doctrines of devotion to the Supreme Spirit. Brownson could have had access to Sir Charles Wilson's (1750-1836) English translation, *The Bhagrat-geeta* (London, 1785). On the Bhagavadgita, see *The Encyclopedia of Religion*, ed. Mircea Eliade et al., 16 vols. (New York: Macmillan Publishing Co., 1987), 2:124-28.]

[8] [Ed. *An Essay on Man*, Epistle 1, Lines 267-68; 271-74.]

verting us to the religion of Hindoostan? Lord save us from an exhibition of rage and madness like the one which would be immediately seen.

But the "Hindoos are ignorant." Who has said so? Someone just as ignorant who probably never conversed with half a dozen of them in his life. They may not know all we know, but they may be acquainted with many things of which we are ignorant. But "they are deceitful, dishonest," etc. Who makes the assertion? And where will you find a nation of which this cannot in some degree be said? A traveler who should pass through this country might perhaps make an observation not more in our favor.

But why all this rage to convert the heathen to Christianity? Are we to suppose all are to be damned who die ignorant of it? Some may say so, but those who do we consider stand in the greatest need of missionary labor. God saves all that are saved and can as well save a man with a Hindoo faith as with a Christian. We would civilize all that are uncivilized; we would give, had we power, all the knowledge there is in the world to every individual; we would if we could place every man in the path of investigation, give him an opportunity to examine all religions, and leave him to embrace one to suit himself. We do not consider ourselves at liberty to force any religion however good upon anyone.

11.

REPLY TO "L. C."[1]

The Gospel Advocate and Impartial Investigator
6 (October 25, 1828): 342-43

Mr. editor: I noticed in the last number of the Advocate, a communication, signed J. C. which contains some animadversions on the 7th number of my Essayist.[2] I am no controversialist. I generally lay my thoughts before the reader; if he be induced to examine the subject on which I treat, my object is gained. I have no disposition to proselytize.[3] I wish mankind to think; if I can induce them to exercise their intellectual powers freely and fearlessly for themselves, I am contented if they shall then choose to abide the convictions of their own minds, whether their convictions correspond with mine or not. I consequently feel no alarm when my positions are attacked; if truth be elicited, it is well, whether it be with me or with my opponent.

Your Missouri correspondent writes in a spirit truly Christian and deserves to be answered in the same. He will, therefore, I trust, take no offence if I point out some mistakes respecting my reasoning into which he has fallen and some untenable positions which he has himself labored to establish.

He begins by quoting my assertion that, "All mankind desire to be happy, all labor continually to gratify this desire." This he admits to be a fact, but laments that it is so, thinks it wrong for mankind to pursue happiness, and that the reason why they are not happy is because they pursue happiness. I did not state that it was *right* for mankind to pursue happiness, nor did I advocate the principle that happiness is the "chief end of man"; but I do not believe it wrong for a man to desire his own happiness or to take all proper measures to produce it. Indifferent we cannot be; we must desire happiness or misery. Whichever J. C. may choose, I shall prefer happiness for myself

---

[1] [Ed. Title should be J. C., as is evident in the body of the text.]

[2] [Ed. See "'J. C.' Versus 'Essayist,'" *GAII* 6 (October 11, 1828): 326; the seventh number of the "Essayist," to which J. C. objected, is in *GAII* 6 (July 19, 1828): 230-31 (pp. 112-14 above). This was the same essay that Fanny Wright admired and reprinted in *The New Harmony Gazette* (August 13, 1828): 330.]

[3] [Ed. Brownson used the noun, proselyte, for the verb, proselytize.]

and if my preference would effect anything I would prefer it for the whole world.

J. C. says happiness is a wrong object of pursuit. It may be so. He says, "seek the Lord." This is very well. But why seek the Lord? "Seek the Lord, and ye shall live" [Amos 5:4], says the sacred writer. This is correct, we desire to live. How shall we gratify this desire? Answer, seek the Lord. J. C., if I understand him, is decidedly of the opinion that if we seek the Lord we shall be happy. We desire to be happy. How, on J. C.'s principles, shall we gratify this desire? Answer: Seek the Lord. Here happiness may be the motive or desire which prompts to action and seeking the Lord the means to satisfy this desire. This agrees with the doctrine of my Essayist. I there stated that happiness was the object all mankind had in view and the reason why they were not happy was because they mistook the road. J. C. calls this reasoning incorrect. He says we should seek the Lord instead of happiness and then we should be happy. The reader perhaps will discover the difference.

The difficulty in J. C.'s mind appears to be this; he thinks if we pursue our own happiness we are selfish beings, and if we seek the Lord for the purpose of benefiting ourselves we are criminal. I reply to this objection because the principle involved in it is not sufficiently understood. The Bible uniformly requires, exhorts and commands us to seek the Lord. But what reason does the Bible assign why we should do this? "Acquaint now therefore thyself with him and be at peace" [Job 22:21], is I believe, the sum of Scripture testimony on this point; and uniformly, so far as I have any knowledge of the Bible, it proposes the good that shall come unto us as the reason why we are to seek the Lord or make ourselves acquainted with him. Paul exhorts his brethren to look to the glorious "reward," the "prize," and even Christ is said to have "respect to the reward." And indeed if this principle were not admitted, all the exhortations and threatenings, all the promises of happiness for well doing and misery for evil doing would have no effect.

Men mistake on this subject. Self-love is proper when properly understood. Selfishness which leads a man to promote his own happiness, regardless of the happiness of others, is improper and I believe generally has the effect to defeat its object. This I condemn. But approve self-love, for without it we could not obey the commands of Christ. "Thou shalt love the Lord thy God." How can I discharge this obligation, if I have no love for myself? I cannot love God unless I perceive him to be lovely, and this loveliness is elicited by his goodness to us, "we love him because he first loved us" [1 John 4:19].

"Thou shalt love thy neighbor as thyself" [Lev. 19:18; Mark 12:31; Luke 10:27; Matt. 19:19]. Now suppose I had no love for myself, how much should I love my neighbor if I loved him as I did myself?

The truth is every man should love the Lord. The process to produce this love — we desire happiness; when rightly instructed respecting the character of God, we find this happiness secured to us; we therefore love him, why? Because we have discovered him to be good to us. We do not love him because we wish him to make us happy (J. C.'s reasoning on this point is correct) but because we discover he has made us happy. The measure of good we receive from him will, in all cases, be the rule by which our hearts will judge his goodness. In this view of the subject, love to God and desire for our own happiness are not inconsistent.

J. C. thinks me too orthodox because I advocate the principle that we should seek our own happiness. I do not know what is orthodox in Missouri but here it is orthodox for a man to be willing to be damned.[4] J. C.'s principles in one view of them would lead to the same result. A man must love God. For what? Because he is good? Because his mercy endureth forever? Because he first loved us? No: For what then? I know not. But J. C. would say, for what God is in and of himself, abstractly considered I suppose, independent of any benefits we receive from him. This is theory; let him who can, reduce it to practice. If I must be miserable till then, the orthodox hell will prove true.

I would I could persuade the whole world to love God; but I know no other way to do it, than by convincing them, if they wish to be happy, they must, as one of the means to produce it, study the character of their Father and love to him will follow as sure as they hear his true character. I therefore am unable to perceive any discrepancy between my reasoning and the reasoning of the Bible on this point.

Again: J. C. pronounces my assertion, that "the reason why we are not happy, is, because we are ignorant of the means of bettering our condition," incorrect. On this point, I refer J. C. and the reader to my sermon "on the moral condition of mankind" in the 19th No. of the Gospel Advocate; and for the kind of knowledge that I consider necessary, to the last number of the Essayist in the same number of the Advocate.[5] I have said all there I wish to say on this ques-

---

[4] [Ed. Reference here is to Hopkinsianism, the doctrine of Samuel Hopkins that the glory of God is manifested in the human willingness to be damned, i.e., a perfect manifestation of disinterested love.]

[5] [Ed. See *GAII* 6 (September 13, 1828): 289-94, 295-96 (pp. 122-26 above).]

tion with regard to the means of producing happiness, and it is unnecessary to repeat it here. The passages of Scripture quoted by J. C. are irrelevant because they are designed to show that the philosophical knowledge boasted of by many in the days of Christ was insufficient to produce happiness; but should never be urged against the acquisition of a correct knowledge of the gospel or of things with which we are surrounded. They have been so urged, and J. C. may learn the consequence if he will peruse the history of the church during the dark ages, or even look at the church as it is now. But even J. C. practically admits the truth of my assertion. He endeavors to point out my errors: he says mankind are not happy because they have been seeking a *wrong* object, and even he endeavors to correct this mistake and proposes a new object of pursuit, which he says will produce happiness, viz. we must love God. But how can we love God without knowing him? And how can we know him without being taught his character? And if by being taught his character we love him and are happy in consequence of this love, how can we say that knowledge is not wanting to make us happy?

The next objection to my article is that I call it a slander upon the character of God to say that our sufferings come from him. Perhaps I am wrong in this. However I think the reasons assigned for my opinion in the essay are sufficient. God is our Father, our Friend, and our Benefactor. I cannot bring myself to charge my miseries upon him. I believe all that God gives is good. But our sufferings are the result, not of what he gives, but proceed from our want of something more than we have that is from our imperfection. Knowledge would, I think, remove, in a great measure, this imperfection and supply or enable us to supply our deficiencies. Perhaps some pain will always remain; but it may be, as J. C. supposes, over-ruled for good.

J. C. attempts to answer the question why God permitted evil to exist; but this is not the question. Why did God make such a world as he has is the question, but who has a right to ask it? I have not, and shall not therefore attempt to answer it. J. C. may be right in his answer; whether so or not is out of my means of ascertaining. The world is as it is. It is our business to make it as comfortable to all its inhabitants as our ability will allow. Certain actions and certain situations are favorable to the preservation of our lives and the increase of our felicity. Others produce a different effect. So much we know and it is not difficult to decide what should be our course in reference to either of these.

(November 8, 1828): 358-60

Mr. Editor: I have considered several of J. C.'s objections to my Essayist, and, I trust, sufficiently vindicated myself as far as I have replied. Some things remaining in his communication, will form the subject of this article. There have been numerous disputes respecting self-love and disinterested benevolence. All I know about either is that all mankind desire to be happy. One of two things must be true: mankind are miserable because suffering is inseparable from this mode of existence, or mankind are miserable because they are ignorant of the means of bettering their condition. The first seems to me to be a severe reflection on the character of our heavenly Father, and also too desponding to teach men desirous of enjoyment. The old doctrine that we are miserable here that we may be happy hereafter is not much better. I therefore adopt the latter conclusion that mankind are miserable because they have not yet learned to make themselves happy. This conclusion appears to me preferable because it encourages us to hope for happiness here and also to inquire how we can produce it. This may be wrong, but if it be, it is an error that cannot harm me here, and as for hereafter, God, I trust, will take care of that.

J. C. considers my assertion that, "when we obey the laws of nature we are happy; when we disobey we are miserable," true so far as it goes, but thinks it does not go far enough. The instances of suffering he mentions may, or may not, be exceptions to my rule. We have learned to avoid some evils; some we have not as yet; but who dare say that in the progress of truth in the development of the resources of the human mind we may not learn to remove many evils which now afflict us? J. C. says infants suffer. This is true; but does he mean to infer these infants suffer when they know how to make themselves happy or when they obey the order of nature? If ignorance were the cause of suffering I should think the infant is the one most likely to suffer. I do not say the infant suffers because it is a criminal, but it suffers because it has not power to make itself happy and those who have the care of it have not learned to prevent its sufferings. J. C. may say with truth we have not yet learned this but dare he say we never shall?

The other particulars which he enumerates have no bearing on the subject, or at least, present no objections to my assertion to be the case of the Son of God. He was harmless. He suffered. Why? Because he was ignorant? No; but because others were. He died to bring us to God, to give us eternal life, "and this is life eternal that they might *know* thee the only true God and Jesus Christ whom thou hast sent" [John 17:3]. We were ignorant; he suffered that he might enlighten us. Ignorance was then the reason why the Son of God suffered; for had not mankind been ignorant, there would have been no need of his death; and had not the rulers of the Jews been ignorant of his real character they would not have put him to death; or in other words, had mankind obeyed the laws of nature, had they observed the order of nature requisite to their happiness, there would have been no need of the sufferings of the Son of God. The other cases mentioned by J. C. may be resolved on the same principles.

Individual ignorance is not always the cause of individual suffering. Suffering or misery proceeds, in my opinion, from the imperfect state of society. Man is to be considered in the aggregate or in his collective capacity as well as individually. I do not say that knowledge, however great, possessed by an individual only can make that individual happy. For should he understand the laws of nature himself and be determined to obey them, he would find his intention thwarted by the ignorance of others; and if he never disobeyed himself, he would, from his connection with others suffer from their disobedience. Hence, when I say, "if man would obey the laws of nature," I mean that if ALL mankind would obey them, all would be happy.

J. C. will, I trust, appreciate this sentiment. He, with every one else, may see his duty clearly pointed out. Knowledge is wanting to make us happy. We must ascertain what will make us happy: whether it be the love of God, the belief of the popular dogmas of the day, or anything else. We must ascertain this for ourselves, and not for ourselves only, but for every individual, and when every individual comes to this knowledge all will be saved from the miseries of which we complain. We may not reach that point but the course suggested by the observations here made would if acted upon enable us continually to approximate the desired haven. If this will not make mankind perfectly happy, it will at least lessen their evils.

Again: I notice in this place a sentiment J. C. advocates at which I glanced in my other communication, viz. that the existence of pain and suffering was necessary to a proper development of the character of God. That is to say, if there had been no suffering, God's mercy could never have been exhibited in relieving it, and had there been no sinners, there would have been no Savior for sin. Now I have long been familiar with this kind of reasoning, but have always been unable to perceive its force. We may as well say, had we never been sick with a fever, we should have had no physician to cure us; had a man never broke his leg, the skill of the surgeon in amputating it would have been unknown; if a man had never broken his skull, the value of trepanning would have been a secret; but for me, I had rather have a whole head if I never learn the value of the surgeon's skill, and if I never have a fever, I cannot perceive any great disadvantage I should suffer from not having a physician.

"Had we not been sinners," some will say, "we should have had no part in the gospel of Christ." Well, what then? What is the gospel of Christ? It relieves us from sin. So far very well, but nothing gained; for allowing the gospel of Christ does no more than remove the disadvantage of sin, it places us in a situation no better than we should have been in had misery been unknown. If it gives more, very well; that *more* might have been worth just as much without our previous suffering. Upon the whole, I know nothing we should have lost had we been always happy. I value the gospel of Christ; but its value arises from its power of relieving us from our sufferings; without the existence of these sufferings it would have had no value. Hence, it would have been no loss to us to have been ignorant of Christ and his gospel providing we had been equally ignorant of suffering. I value a good physician, but were I never sick, I should not. The whole subject, therefore, resolves itself into the following question, which is best, to be sick and have a physician, or to have good health, and consequently never need a physician?

J. C. advocates the sentiment or seems to advocate it that mankind will be more happy in consequence of having been sinners. I do not like this sentiment. In reference to it, I would say "Let us do evil that good may come [Rom. 3:8], let us continue in sin that grace may abound" [Rom. 6:1]. J. C. quotes, "That as sin hath reigned unto death, so might grace reign through righteousness unto eternal life by Jesus Christ our Lord" [Rom. 5:21]. But what does this passage prove? Surely not that mankind will be more happy because they have been sinners. All that it proves or can prove is that mankind will, through the goodness of God, receive from the gospel of Christ more happiness than they ever received of misery from sin.

Lastly: J. C. objects to the assertion of mine, that "an action is wrong because it brings misery." This is no more than I expected. Mankind have always, for ought I know, believed as J. C. does, that an action brings misery because it is wrong and that it is wrong because it disagrees with the eternal standard, Jehovah." But this is no definition at all. No two men have the same views of this "Eternal Standard," consequently no two men will agree what action is right or what is wrong. Hence has originated the various absurd systems of morals which have had little other effect than to render men immoral.

J. C. may be right. Whether he is or is not is more than I know; I wish to know why an action is right or wrong. I determine according to my perception of things. Why do I approve an act? Because it is beneficial. Why should I oppose an act? J. C. says, because it agrees with the will of God. The question is not yet answered, what is the will of God? Who does or can know the will of God? The Calvinist believes it is the will of God to make a part of his children eternally miserable; the Universalist believes it is the will of God to make all mankind eternally happy. Which of these is correct? If I do not mistake the reasoning, or rather the phraseology of J. C. he would say the Universalist. But, *why* does he say so? Because, he would doubtless say, the God who would will the happiness of all mankind is *better* than the one who should will the misery of a part. But why better? Because he wills more happiness is the only rational answer that can be given. Sum up this reasoning and what is the result? The will of God is good because it produces happiness; or God is good because he wills happiness; an action is right because it agrees with the will of God; an action is right because it brings happiness. This is the only conclusion to which we can arrive.

Vary the question: suppose it was the will of God to produce misery, say he labored to make mankind miserable, what would be right for us to do? Constituted as we are, with our present love for happiness, would J. C. say it would be right for us to imitate God, and begin to carry devastation to the possessions of our neighbors, and to labor to inflict on them all the misery in our power? If he should attempt to act on *such* a principle I should wish him to do wrong. If this reasoning be correct, and I believe it is, the answer is, an action that agrees with God, an action that agrees with God is right not merely because it agrees with God, but because God is good. If God were not good, an action that should agree with him would not be good, consequently would not be right.

J. C. is right in effect, but not in principle: in effect because the will of God is right; not in principle, for if the will of God were different from what it is, agreement with it would be wrong. I have been thus particular on this point because it is not sufficiently understood, and because I think many of the absurd systems, whether religious or moral, which have had a tendency to destroy the peace and happiness of society, have originated in the mistake into which J. C. and most casuists have fallen.

I define that to be good which has a tendency to produce pleasurable emotions and is good in proportion to its power of producing these emotions. That which has a tendency to excite painful emotions, I call evil. Now, as it is certainly right to pursue good, consequently any action which produces happiness, is right, and any one which produces painful emotions, is wrong, and wrong because it produces misery or painful emotions. Pursue J. C.'s principles and they will amount either to the same thing, or to something from which he would revolt as quick as myself. He directs our minds to our heavenly Father. This is as it should be because acquaintance with him will result in our good. He would exhort us to ascertain his will and conform to it. This is right, for the will of God is good. So much for J. C.'s communication. I have run it over and answered it as I deemed proper. I thank him for calling my attention to the essay in question. I wrote it in haste when depressed by sickness. A reconsideration has not made me regret any sentiment or any expression which it contains. If J. C. is dissatisfied with my reply to his animadversions, he will have the goodness to express it. I will read attentively whatever he or anyone else may please to write on this subject. I shall not promise, however, to write any more myself on this subject. I have said the sum of all I have to say, and to pursue the principles I have suggested through all the minuteness of detail, would tire the reader and answer no good purpose.

I close, Mr. Editor, with one remark. To us the preservation of our existence is the first object of our research, and to make this existence pleasurable together with the existence of every other being, our second. Search the Lord, and ye shall live; acquaint thyself with him and be at peace.

12.

A SERMON. ON ENDLESS PUNISHMENT[1]

The Gospel Advocate and Impartial Investigator
6 (November 22, 1828): 369-74

*The wicked shall be turned into hell and all the nations that forget
God.*   Psalm 9:17.

That a portion of mankind will be eternally punished in the
world to come has long been taught and extensively believed. I have
no wish to dissemble my feelings. Neither the antiquity nor general
prevalence of this dogma has given it any charms for me. Endless
misery! The idea is big with horror! I will not boast of my love to
mankind; I do not know that I have more love for them than have
the rest of my brethren; but I cannot contemplate this awful spectacle without having my bosom agitated with the most painful emotions. It casts a somber hue over the fair face of creation, tinges every
object on which the eye can rest with deep impervious gloom, damps
all the warm and generous emotions of our bosoms by the melancholy it encourages, blasts our dearest hopes, overwhelms the mind
and makes the soul dark by the tremendous woe it presents as the
termination of our weary pilgrimage.

Endless misery! To groan eternally beneath the wrath of Almighty
God! The thought is repugnant to all the better feelings of the human heart. *I shall see my brother in hell!* The very thought strikes a
dart through my soul, and compels me to consider well the grounds
I have for believing that mankind were born under circumstances so
inauspicious to their happiness, that they must have their feelings
continually harrowed up by a reflection so painful, or that heaven
will ever blight all our fond wishes with a malediction so awful!

However strong may be the prepossessions of my hearers, they
will not deny that the disagreeable nature of such a dogma, the dark

---

[1] [Ed. Brownson periodically defended Universalism against those orthodox
Christians who brought forth numerous biblical passages that seemed to support
everlasting punishment. See, e.g., "A Sermon. On Future Judgement and Punishment," *GAII* 7 (January 10, 1829): 1-7, for another one of Brownson's substantial
attempts to argue against the doctrine of an eternal hell. In that sermon he refutes
the orthodox interpretations of Matthew 25:46 on "everlasting punishment."]

cloud it hangs over the works of Almighty God, the despair and indescribable anguish it produces in every heart that believes it, are sufficient reasons for us to examine carefully the arguments which are offered in its vindication, and candidly to inquire if we are bound to give it credence. Its claims to admission into our religious creed should be closely investigated that, if it prove true, we may sit down with a knowledge of our doom and deplore the severity of our condition and the awfulness of our end, or if it prove to be a chimera of heathen fancy or a dream of a bewildered imagination, we may rejoice in our God and contemplate with gratitude and delight the productions of his hand.

Painful as may be the task, I have determined to discuss this subject by presenting to your understandings, my brethren, some of the many objections which, to my perception, interpose between this sentiment and truth, and compel me to believe it an idle fear, produced by terror, and fostered by ignorance and credulity. I have, what I consider, strong objections against the idea that God will ever punish one of his creatures eternally. Your attention, my friends, is earnestly solicited, whether believers with me or not, while I exhibit them.

1. I object to this doctrine because it is *unmerciful*. This objection is true if the common ideas respecting this punishment be correct. There is no mercy in the doctrine; there is no mercy near it; it presents pain the most excruciating and an amount of suffering which baffles all numerical skill or mathematical calculation. Mankind speak of this punishment; preachers, the professed servants of Christ—priests who are continually proclaiming their own goodness and reminding their hearers how much they love their souls, can preach about it—say millions and millions of the human race will be eternally miserable, yea, send two-thirds of their own congregations there with as much *sang froid*, as they can see one of their friends sit down to a table indifferently spread! Worse than all, some will go so far as to express a degree of exultation in considering how happy they shall be in heaven when they can behold their ungodly neighbors bound and fettered in the dungeon of infinite despair! But this is the result of fanaticism or of not duly considering the punishment of the wicked either as to its intensity or as to its duration.

We are indeed told the punishment will be awfully severe in degree, and interminable in duration; but few ever consider it in the light they should, or take that particular view of it which is absolutely necessary to enable them to form correct notions respecting it. They look at the wicked, think they ought to be punished, say they will be miserable, call their misery endless; but still do not in reality believe it to be so great, nor does it appear to them one half so severe as would appear a hundred years of intense pain such as a person, providing he could live, would endure in a heated furnace. They make nothing of consigning a man to an endless hell, but very few of them would justify that judge who should sentence a man to burn a hundred years in a furnace, providing it was for the highest misdemeanor known in our statute books. But this punishment, to burn a hundred years in a furnace, to be all the time full of quick sense, to have the limbs swell with pain, the body to writhe and contort with anguish, to call for mercy, to plead for a moment's intermission of pain, but to plead in vain; this punishment, I say, however great, however shocking to every benevolent principle of the human heart, is a mere drop in the ocean compared to that which is threatened the wicked; notwithstanding its disproportion to any crime which man can commit, it would lose itself before the miseries of the damned would be fairly commenced.

Endless punishment! Ages after ages may pass away, the pain is but begun! The wicked may rave in fire and gnaw their tongues in anguish for centuries, which shall out-number the sands of the globe multiplied by all the stars of heaven thrice told, and still be no nearer the end of their sufferings than when they commenced! Horrid thought! Consider the intensity of the pain the wicked must endure; consider the endless ages he must groan beneath the curse of an offended God, and calculate, if you can, the amount of suffering which one individual must endure! Should there be but one individual soul eternally damned, the pain he would endure would exceed all the miseries which the whole human family have felt since the creation of the world. Count all the sighs, the groans, the pangs which have ever been inflicted upon the human race, by all the evils with which we have been afflicted, whether private or public, moral, physical or theological, since the ill-fated hour when Eve plucked the forbidden fruit, and the whole would be but as dust in the balance when compared with what only one individual must endure through the unceasing period of eternity!

But add to this amount of suffering that of the number which must be damned according to the popular sentiment of the day, and weep at the sad catastrophe, the widespread ruin of the creation of God! If, what is every day thundered in our ears, be true, that "no one can enter the kingdom of God in the world to come, who has not believed on Christ in this," by far the greatest part of the human race will be consigned to the regions of eternal woe.

The number of inhabitants which people the earth at this moment may be estimated to amount at least to eight hundred millions. Four hundred and ninety millions of these are pagans. These have never believed on Christ, for of him they have never heard; these all go to hell to infinite despair! One hundred and thirty millions are Mahometans: these are disbelievers in Christ, and consequently must be consigned to Pluto's gloomy reign, to bathe in the roaring Phlegethon.[2] Seven millions are supposed to be Jews: these are disbelievers in Jesus the Son of God; they, then, to the Tartarean gulf must be hurled by the infinite wrath of God. The remaining one hundred and seventy-three millions are nominal Christians; of these one hundred millions are Roman Catholics. These, by Protestants, are denounced as idolaters, consequently in the road to hell. Of the remaining seventy-three millions, thirty millions are Greeks and Armenians, not much better than Roman Catholics, consequently only forty-three millions are left as Protestants, and these comprise a number of different sects, which must, by the orthodox, be considered no better than the heathen. But to compromise the matter as well as the nature of the case will allow, from the whole number of Christians take seventy millions which must be damned for the want of soundness in faith. From what remains take all infidels, that is, such as do not believe in Christ, though they live in Christian countries; from the professedly orthodox all hypocrites and all who have not discharged the duties enjoined, and you may possibly have ten millions who will be saved!

Allow these estimations correct, seven hundred and ninety millions of the present race of inhabitants will weep eternally in hell, in the place where God lets his anger rage and the weight of his wrath be felt! But a generation lasts only thirty-two years, consequently every thirty-two years hell receives an accession of seven hundred and ninety millions of inhabitants. Count now the generations since the coming of Christ, the number from his coming to the creation of the world, make allowance indeed for difference in population, but calculate the number if you please that must now be tossing in the Stygian wave,[3] if the popular dogmas of the day be true. How many millions must be now groaning beneath the weight of Almighty anger! Consider now the pain each one of these must endure, the num-

[2] [Ed. In Greek mythology, a river of fire, one of the five rivers surrounding Hades.]
[3] [Ed. Stygian refers to the river Styx and represents the infernal, dark, and gloomy.]

ber also that must suffer, and say if mercy does not revolt at the sight and weep at this devastation of the human race?

2. Endless punishment is UNJUST. This punishment is said to be inflicted for transgression. But it is a principle I need not labor to prove that all punishment which is disproportionate to the crime committed is unjust. All punishment or pain inflicted which exceeds the wrong done or which it is intended to redress is cruel and no man in his senses will pretend it is just to be cruel.

Tell me not, as I have been told, that the sins of mankind are infinite; speak not of an infinite offence; the thing is impossible. Sin is the violation of a law. To be infinite it must not only be a violation of an infinite law, but it must involve an infinite evil in its consequences. But man cannot be culpable for violating a law which he cannot understand, and who does not know that a man cannot understand an infinite law? To say that our sins necessarily involve an infinite evil, is to say that of which we are profoundly ignorant. Were it a fact we should indeed tremble for no being in the universe could remove it.

Sin is the act of transgression; but there cannot be such a thing as an infinite act. An infinite act! It is one that has no bounds; but is not every act bounded by the power of the actor? An infinite sin! It is one that no being can control. Jehovah himself would be unable to manage it. Such a transgression would hurl Deity from his throne, dash the universe in pieces and clothe the mighty void with eternal night! Infinity! There can be but one Infinity. God is infinite, but he cannot produce a being that will be nor perform an act that will not be finite; for he cannot multiply himself nor produce anything greater than himself, nor perform an act which shall not be bounded by his power. Certainly, then, if God cannot perform an infinite act (and he cannot unless he perform something greater than himself) how much less can man, weak, frail man, be guilty of doing infinite things!

Say not that sin deserves endless punishment. What is desert? A word of no meaning or of one that is improper. We are sinners; all mankind are sinners; all have come short of the glory of God; there is not a just man upon earth that doeth good and sinneth not, but what then? They deserve to be punished. What do we mean by this expression? I have done wrong; be it so; what shall be done? Here is a man that has seduced unsuspecting innocence, robbed her of her charms, her virtue, of her life, clothed her bereaved parents and friends with sorrow and disgrace. A baser crime man cannot commit, a blacker wretch cannot breathe; what does he deserve? Punishment? Why? Will it restore the victim of his guilt to life, to virtue, to innocence, to the embrace of her friends? No! Will it soothe the anguish of the aching heart? Will it assuage the fond parent's grief, wipe the falling tear and heal the wounded spirit? No! What good then does his punishment? Does it, can it alter the past, or undo what is already done? It cannot. The wrong is done, the crime is committed, and should you burn the criminal eternally in the fire of hell, the wrong would not be redressed, the crime would remain committed. Consequently, as far as the past is concerned, the punishment does no good.

Justice requires no one to labor in vain and will never sanction the infliction of suffering, which, to say the least, is useless. We grant the man in the case supposed is guilty, horribly so, but what shall be done? Justice answers all that can be done. Two things are required: first, that the wrong done be repaired; second, that the one who has done the wrong be reformed so that he will never do the wrong again. Justice requires all the good that can be done, but no more. It does not demand impossibilities. Now no pain however severe in degree or long in duration can alter what is done, therefore justice does not require man to suffer on that account.

We must make all the reparation in our power. What will be the best? If the hearts of the injured are right, the best satisfaction they can receive will be to know that the wretch, who has blasted their hopes and pierced their hearts with grief and anguish has become a good man, a virtuous citizen who shall study to atone for his iniquity by a well ordered life devoted to the welfare of his brethren. The greatest punishment I should wish inflicted upon one who had injured me is that he should become reformed, and determined to pursue a virtuous course. To me this would be much more pleasing than it would to see him groaning under the curse of Omnipotence forever.

Whatever punishment is necessary to reform the criminal may undoubtedly be inflicted. Justice is not averse to the infliction of pain when it can be a benefit to him who suffers it; but justice cannot inflict injury on any being or cause one to suffer more than will be for the sufferer's good. Some have imagined that Deity must punish to vindicate his own honor. But this is an assertion that ill becomes man to make. What! Deity involve himself in such a dilemma that to maintain his honor he must sacrifice his own offspring, make his own dear children eternally miserable? Where was his foresight? Why did he not provide for his own honor without involving the destruction of his family? Or shall it be said that God who is good, whose tender mercies are over all the works of his hands, is honored by the cries, groans, shrieks, and horrid lamentations of his children in hell, that his glory is increased by peopling hell with wretched victims to the ruin and devastation of the world he has made!

But, it is said, Deity has given us a law; man has violated this law and God has a right to punish him! It does not become me to discuss the RIGHTS of the Almighty. Doubtless he has a right to do or doubtless he *will* do whatever he please. With this we must acquiesce, let it be good or bad. But when men attempt to pull aside the veil which hides futurity from our sight and to tell what shall transpire during the undefined period yet to come, I wish, so long as they reason from conjecture, they will allow their conjectures to rest upon some data which are already established.

I pretend not to have found out the Almighty to perfection. All I know of him is what he has been graciously pleased to reveal of himself. Nature assures me that GOOD preponderates in his character, that he causes his sun to rise on the evil and the good, and that he sendeth rain on the just and the unjust; and Scripture unequivocally declares him to be LOVE, good unto all, and his tender mercies over all his works; that he chastises in mercy, that he correct us as a father corrects his children, for our profit, that we may be partakers of his holiness. See Heb. 12. Allowing then that we have broken a law which he has given us, what will he be most likely to do? Send us to eternal woe? He may do so, but justice, if we know anything about it, would dissent from a sentence so horrible.

But again, what is justice? If the character of God is any criterion by which we can decide this question, it is just to do good; consequently it is just for God to confer happiness on his creatures. If he can make his creatures happy, and be just, he must be unjust if he make them miserable. If he was just when he gave man a law, he gave it for man's good. If man has violated it, Deity cannot justly punish for any purpose except for his good. The evil consequences of sin are felt by the sinner, not by the Deity. The injury which sin does is done to the creature not to God; consequently, for God to punish this sinner, when the punishment is calculated to increase the injury done to the creature, would be unjust. God wills the happiness of his creatures; he gave them a law to make them happy; they, ignorant of their own good and the design of God, violate this law; Deity makes them endlessly miserable by way of punishment! Is this consistent with his will or the design of the law he gave them? It is a fact that all have sinned; all have made themselves miserable. For God now to inflict endless misery upon us—what would it be but making his character resemble that of the parent who because his child had been so foolish as to burn off one hand should now cut off the other?

Because we have made ourselves miserable, Deity in rage declares we shall never be happy; because we have burned ourselves a little, God now resolves to burn us eternally! This may be justice, but it is the justice of a fiend and should be stamped with the anathema of every benevolent being.

3. This punishment, if endless, must be not only unmerciful and unjust, but entirely USELESS. This has doubtless already been made to appear. It does not undo the wrong that has been done; it does not benefit the one punished, if endless, and who shall we say it does benefit? This punishment must benefit either God, the righteous, the wicked, or be useless. Benefit God! What mean we? Benefit God! How? He is omniscient. His eye pierces through nature and grasps every event that does or can take place. What can he learn? He is omnipotent. He spake. Creation, the universe, with all its furniture of worlds and innumerable grades of beings, which inhabit it, assumed its order and commenced its course. He can speak and the universe shall disappear, and empty space reign where it was. He makes the winds his car and the whirlwind his chariot. He can seize the lightning in his hand and stun creation with his voice! Does he need the assistance of man, of MAN, weak worm of the dust!

God is good. He is omnibenignant. His tender mercies are over all his works. He opens his hand and satisfies the desires of every living thing. The eyes of all wait upon him and he giveth them their meat in due season. Needs be that man should groan eternally in hell to make himself better? God is happy; his happiness depends not on his creatures. It arises from the perfection of his own nature. Can that be augmented or diminished? What benefit then can the eternal punishment of the wicked do to HIM who knows no want, who is infinite in all his attributes and perfect in all his ways? It cannot make him wiser, stronger, better nor more happy. It then does no good to God. He does not punish for his own good.

Perhaps for the benefit of the righteous? Of the righteous! Say, thou righteous man, whose heart is filled with the love of God and expanded with benevolence towards the human race, say, dost thou require the unceasing wailings of thy brethren in hell to lull thee to repose in the blissful vales of heaven? Look, Christian thou who art born again, thou who hast hope in God through the gospel of his Son Jesus; look, behold thy brother in that fire! See, do you mark the progress of the flames? See his limbs how they swell! How his body writhes and contorts with anguish! Do you hear him call for help, for mercy? "Spare, help, man, friend, brother, enemy, help, snatch me, I die!" Do you hear? Can you rejoice at his woe? Look, mother, there is the fond one of thy bosom, see him rolling in that lake of fire and brimstone; see! he raises his hands, he calls, he screams to thee to help him. Canst thou clap thy hands at the sight? Canst thou shout hallelujah at the sight of his misery? Thou canst not. Man has a sympathy for man. We are not happy, we cannot be happy, at viewing the misery of our brethren. All experience proves that the happiness of those with whom we associate adds to our own. Such is our disposition while here. The best are the most sensibly affected with the sufferings of others; they weep at the sight of their misfortunes; they pray constantly that heaven may avert their calamities and raise them to a state of holiness and happiness. Can they, when raised to heaven, when permitted to join the holy throng of angels and beatified spirits around the throne of Almighty God, when freed from sin and sorrow, receive additional felicity by looking from their heights of happiness down to the pit of despair where the wicked lie fettered forever and ever? The sight of misery now agitates their bosoms with the most painful emotions; the better they are, the more painful are these emotions. Shall we say that when they are made *perfect,* their bosoms will become so suited to the sufferings of their brethren, their hearts so hardened to human misfortune, that they will rejoice at the sight of misery inconceivable? They are different now, and if it be true, as we are told, that there is *no change after death,* they cannot be happy by hearing the deadly groans of the damned in hell! The endless punishment of the wicked, then, can be of no service to the righteous. They love God because they perceive him to be lovely. They are happy because they love God, not because they witness the unspeakable torments of their brethren.

Say, then, endless punishment will be beneficial to the wicked, what, to those who are made endlessly miserable? Impossible. A temporary punishment might possibly be of some advantage, but endless misery be of advantage to him who suffers it! Whoever dreamed of such an idea? As well might heaven be called hell, and hell heaven; as well might evil be called good, bitter be called sweet, and darkness be called light. Endless pain a benefit to him who suffers it! Such a thing cannot be. We dismiss the thought. The punishment does not benefit God; it does no good to the righteous who are saved; it can do no good to the damned in hell.

Shall we suppose that a God who is good, who doeth all things for the best, will inflict such inconceivable woe upon his own offspring when it is entirely useless? Shall we say that God has made a place, filled it with tortures beyond the power of description, that he will confine millions and millions of our race in its gloomy dungeon, as long as he shall maintain the throne of heaven, or thunder his commands through the universe, when no good can result to himself, to those who are punished, nor to the righteous who are saved? We cannot; I repeat it we *cannot* we cannot harbor a thought so derogatory from the perfections of our heavenly Father, or so destructive to those he has endowed with life and a capacity for enjoyment.

4. Again: endless punishment is contrary to the revealed will of God and the general scope and design of the gospel of Christ. It is contrary to the will of God. God assures us in his word, that he is "not willing that any should perish" [2 Pet. 3:9]; that "he has no pleasure in the death of the wicked" [Ezek. 18:23]; that "he will have all men to be saved and come to the knowledge of the truth" [1 Tim. 2:4]. The general scope and design of the gospel is that in Christ, shall "all the nations, families, and kindred of the earth be blessed";[4] that "Jesus gave himself a ransom for all" [1 Tim. 2:6]; that "he by the grace of God should taste death for every man" [Heb. 2:9]; that "the ransomed of the Lord shall return and come to Zion with songs and everlasting joys upon their heads; obtain joy and gladness, and sorrow and sighing shall flee away" [Isa. 35:10]. Nothing is more evident than that Jesus was given to be the "Savior of the world"; that he had every requisite qualification to "save his people from their sins"; and of no fact in Scripture can we be more certain than of the one that God designed in sending his Son into the world that the world through him should be saved; that Jesus designed this and that he died to accomplish it. Shall we say that Jesus will fail in the work he came to perform? That God will be disappointed? That all the hopes formed by the angelic[5] hosts, when with acclamations they announced the Savior's birth, shall be blasted? That all the fond expectations of the saints in every age of the church, shall meet no better reward than to witness the indescribable anguish of those for whose salvation they have offered up the evening and the morning prayer? No, it cannot be. Jesus shall do the will of his Father, accomplish the work that was given him to perform, see of the travail of his soul and be satisfied, make an end of sin, finish transgression, bring in everlasting righteousness, fill the universe with the love of God, and permit every son and daughter of Adam to sing in triumphant strain, "O death, where is thy sting? O grave, where is thy victory?" [1 Cor. 15:55].

[4] [Ed. See Gen. 18:18; Gal. 3:8, which Brownson paraphrases.]
[5] [Ed. "angelic" replaces Brownson's original "evangelick."]

5. But lastly, we object to this doctrine because it is not taught in the Scriptures of truth. Endless punishment is either a doctrine of revelation or it is not. If it is, the passage or passages which teach it can be easily produced. No such passage ever has been shown, nor can it be. The Bible does not contain it. We challenge the world to produce such a passage and promise to renounce our belief in the impartial goodness of God whenever it shall be pointed out.

If the doctrine of endless punishment be not taught by the Bible, it rests on no authenticity worthy of credence. Nature disclaims it, reason disdains it, and the whole providence of God imposes upon the assertion of its truth an unqualified negative. It rests either a Bible doctrine or we have no evidence of its truth. What passage can be brought from the Bible—my text? What does this prove?

"The wicked shall be turned into hell, and all the nations that forget God" [Ps. 9:17]. Be it so. What is hell? A place or state of endless misery. Very well. Who are the wicked? All mankind. There is none good, no not one. There is not a just man upon earth that doeth good and sinneth not. The *wicked* shall be turned into hell: all are wicked, consequently all must be turned into hell! Universal damnation must then be the portion of the human race, not a solitary soul can ever be permitted to escape the flames of endless fire. The wicked SHALL BE turned into hell, not *may be*, but *shall be*. There is no condition in the case, no chance for escape. All, *all* without exception must be eternally miserable if hell mean a place of endless punishment. But this argument proves too much, therefore nothing. Some will go to heaven or Scripture is a dream. Hell, therefore, cannot mean a place of endless misery. It does not. It means literally in the Old Testament, the grave, and figuratively, mental agony, pain or sorrow. David thanks the Lord that he had delivered him from the *lowest* hell; which evidently means that he was freed from some pain or calamity which he had suffered. The wicked shall be turned into hell and all the nations that forget God: the plain import of this is that the wicked shall suffer for their wickedness that there is no peace to the wicked. Such is the fact disclosed by experience. Vice ruins the individual who practices it; vice and impiety overwhelm every nation, where they take up their residence. Where now are the boasted nations of antiquity? Where is the busy population which once thronged the land of the Nile? Where the learning, the science and refinement of Athens, and the proud independence of Sparta? Where is the wealth of Tyre, the commerce of Sidon, the haughty greatness of Rome, once mistress of the world? Gone! Vice found its way into the heart of their governments, enervated the arm of justice, and plunged them into barbarism and disgrace! The night-bird now shakes his shaggy wings over the ruins of Balbeck and Tadmour. Jerusalem is demolished and the unhallowed plough has passed where stood her holy of holies. Such is the fate in which vice involves the individual or the nation which encourages its progress. Be wise then, O children of men! Avoid vice as the bane of your felicity, for know it is the unalterable decree of heaven that transgression shall always be attended with pain, and the cup of iniquity be mingled with gall and wormwood. But that this punishment shall be endless, shocks all common sense. One word from the Almighty is sufficient to make all these poor trembling wretches that orthodoxy out of the abundance of her charity consigns to hell, holy and happy. Shall that word be denied? One look from God could annihilate their sufferings and fill their hearts with joy and employ their tongues in hymns of praise: shall that look be withheld? God saw a ruined world weltering in its blood; he saw; he had compassion; he provided means for its salvation: shall those means prove ineffectual?

One drop of the Savior's blood could wash away the stains of that guilty multitude, make them pure, holy and happy; shall that drop be withheld?

Jesus loved the human family. So great was his love, so tender was his sympathy, so powerful his compassion, that he wept, mingled his tears with ours even when he was about to exert his power to relieve our sorrows. He could lay down his life for us; will he forget those for whom he died? Will he so steel his bosom against us that he will inflict those very sufferings he died to avert? Angels made the heavens resound with acclamations of joy on the prospect of man's salvation; will they forget us and turn their cold, averted looks as we are dragged down to the eternal pit? No, no, forbid, Almighty God! If there is goodness in thee, if thou hast justice or mercy, we will throw ourselves upon thee and rest assured that in due time the world shall know thee, all tongues join to celebrate thy praise, and a beatified universe resound with paeans of triumph over sin, death and misery, forever and ever. AMEN.

13.

AN ESSAY ON CHRISTIANITY

The Gospel Advocate and Impartial Investigator
7 (January 10, 1829): 7-9

So much has been written on the subject, which it is proposed to discuss in the following essay, that I have no expectation of offering anything new to those who have examined it. I lay no claim to extensive researches or profound erudition. I write not for the scholar nor for the theologian who has devoted his life to the study of Christianity. My labors are designed for a different class of mankind, for those who depend more on their own reflections than they do on what they read, who study nature more than they do the ponderous tomes of polemical theology or of ancient systems of faith. I wish to aid such as these without diverting their attention from those avocations on which the subsistence of society immediately depends; to throw out some hints which may serve to guide their inquiries and direct the train of their reflections; to supply food for their meditations, and to lead them "through nature up to nature's God."[1] In a word my object is to unite religion and common sense, two kindred spirits which have a natural fondness for each other, though unfortunately, the folly or perversity of mankind has long kept them separate.

The world has been overrun with systems of religion, which have commanded the applause of the multitude, without adding anything to the knowledge or happiness of mankind; numerous theories have been advocated with all of human ingenuity; some perhaps have cast a few rays of light upon the dark habitation of man, but the sun of their glory has set in gloom, or been obscured by the clouds of bigotry which have been raised, or hidden by the storms of persecution which have been too often hurled against the heads of poor defenseless mortals. So many systems are now prevalent that inquiry is distracted and choice baffled. Pardon me, it is not my intention to add another, but if possible out of the surrounding chaos to bring something like order.

I have no wish to divide mankind nor am I so vain as to attempt to unite them. Diversity of sentiment always has prevailed, and, for

---

[1] [Ed. Pope's *Essay on Man*, Epistle 4, Line 331.]

aught we know, always will. This may be regretted, but probably without reason. It prompts inquiry; gives energy as well as activity to the mind; prevents that monotony and that general stagnation of the intellectual stream, which would result were mankind all of the same opinion.

Man is formed for action. When deprived of the privilege of exerting his power, or when condemned to the abode of indolence, he wastes away without usefulness to himself or to others. Idleness is the heaviest burden he can bear; and entire freedom from care, anxiety and every kind of employment, probably the severest curse that could be inflicted to blight his being and to deprive him of every claim to rationality. He is not only capable of action, but his highest felicity is derived from the exertion of his active powers. But, to call forth this exertion, you must present him with some inducement to act. We soon become disgusted with the same routine of pursuits or of pleasure. Any object, no matter how good or how useful in itself considered, loses its value in our estimation the moment the charms of novelty have faded and it becomes generally known and generally received.

Religion is admitted to be a thing of inestimable value, but it must vary its form, change its dress and its pretensions, hold out different rewards and punishments, or it will fail to interest the heart and command the attention. Our fathers had a religious creed, the best, no doubt, they could discover or receive; but to tell us that we must be satisfied with that creed because it satisfied them is to confess our ignorance of human nature as well as to suppose we have made no advances, that our minds are fashioned in the same mold with theirs, that our thoughts run in the same channel, and that our wishes point to the same objects, and that our desires will rest contented with their acquisitions. Such a supposition betrays a want of attention to what passes in our own minds and in the minds of others.

The Christians reverence the Bible, consider it an infallible rule of faith and practice; the Mahometan reveres the Koran, the Hindo the Vedas, the Parsee the Zendavesta, each prefers his own Bible and stigmatizes the others as infidels, obnoxious to the wrath of God. This, at first, might seem a real calamity, which has befallen the human race; and indeed we cannot withhold our regret that each should be so intolerant to the others. But perhaps more mature reflection will lead us to admire the impartiality and forbearance of the Great Father of all, who permits his children to choose their own mode of worship, and does not tie them down to the same tedious form, nor to the use of the same phraseology.

Christians are anxious to convert the world to their own faith; each sect is ambitious to have all embrace its peculiar creed: hence a spirit of proselytism prevails, and a continual collision of conflicting dogmas and contradictory interests is exhibited. And though I have imbibed neither from nature nor from my religion much zeal for proselytizing, I do not regret such is the case with the world. If any one of the numerous denominations of religionists should gain the ascendancy, and like Aaron's rod swallow the rest,[2] the cause of truth and humanity might suffer; but while they are contending the mind is acquiring strength; its mighty energies are awakened, called into action, and even from the collisions of erroneous theories truth may be elicited. Society is all life and vigor. And though the scene may seem painful to the casual observer, a close inspection will discover the angels of science, of virtue and felicity, rising from the midst of the contention and joyfully hovering over the contending parties. It is only necessary they should contend with less animosity; but angry and rough as their disputes are, it is better than it would be for man-kind all to believe just alike. At first, no doubt, the novelty of the thing would make it extremely delightful, but that charm would soon disappear and intellect would fall asleep for there would be nothing to keep it awake. Society would become dull and uninteresting for there would be little to give it life or mental activity.

I have therefore no wish to reduce all mankind to the same opin-ion. It is better they should disagree, as life without variety would be a "dull dunce" scarcely worth possessing. The most that can be de-sired is that they should be persuaded to lay aside that animosity which embitters their controversies, and a little of that exclusive spirit which characterizes their conduct. If they could be persuaded to im-pose a curb upon their impetuous passions which too often run away with their senses, and consent calmly to investigate their own and others' opinions, it is highly probable their disquisitions would be attended with less confusion and with more advantage to the cause of truth. The philanthropist may labor with propriety to blunt the points of contact, and to enable each individual to support, or strive to support, his own creed without infringing the rights of others. I have this object in view and if I accomplish it I shall think my labor will not be in vain and my readers' time will not be misspent.

In our inquiry, we shall attempt to cultivate an acquaintance with human nature rather than with the Divine, and to smooth the rugged features of the earth rather than to ensure heaven for our

---

[2] [Ed. See Exod. 7:10-12.]

souls hereafter. The value of a system of religion will be determined from its utility to man; and its correctness in a great measure from its agreement with the various phenomena of nature in general and with man in particular. Man himself is to be considered not merely as an animal that is born to propagate his species and then return to his native dust. He lays claim to nobler and more sublime faculties. He is an intellectual being, capable of many elevated conceptions and noble achievements. He is not confined to the little spot of earth where he dwells; he can send his thoughts abroad, cull the pleasures of distant regions and regale himself with the intellectual riches of every age. He can rise from this contracted globe where destiny has confined his body to contemplate worlds where his feet have never wandered, and to hold communion with that great and good Being, who, though invisible himself, displays the glories of his Divinity through all the wonderful productions of nature.

Not merely as intellectual but man should be considered as social. He was not born to live alone. Society is his element out of which he sickens and dies. His whole history demonstrates that he is bound to his brother by many strong and indissoluble ties. So numerous are his wants, so complicated are they in their nature that life to an isolated individual would be rather a curse than a blessing. To live and be happy, man must be in society; he must co-operate with his brother and the evils which mocked the individual may be successfully combated by their united strength. Man may indeed retire to the desert, he may lodge in the cave, he may drag out a loathed existence, but it will be useless to the world and loathsome to himself.

In addition to an intellectual and social, he should be considered a religious being. Whether he be indebted to nature or to education for this quality, it is evident from experience that he possesses it; and the philosopher that should overlook it, in his moral disquisitions or in his attempts to discover a correct system of ethics would but half perform his work. Man, wherever beheld, no matter in what age or in what country, recognizes an Over-ruling Power, on whom he is dependent and to whom he believes himself to owe allegiance. And indeed, such is his situation, such the constitution of his nature and such the character of his wants, of his hopes and fears, that a large share of his happiness has been found to flow from a consciousness of this dependence and the acknowledgment of this allegiance. Sensible of the mutability of every sublunary object, convinced that it is in vain to trust the "arm of flesh," that his brother is one thing today and another tomorrow, he asks for some more powerful arm on which he can lean and find support, for some Being who is the same "yesterday, today and forever" [Heb. 13:8], into whose bosom he can pour the various emotions by which he is agitated, and to whose wisdom and goodness he can commit the disposal of all that concerns his felicity.

And to these characteristics, let it be added that man is also a progressive being. The brute creation may have knowledge; the beaver may elicit skill and foresight in the erection of its house and the provision of its food; but the beaver of today is probably no wiser nor more provident than the beaver of four thousand years ago. Not so with man. One generation improves upon another. The infant not only arrives to the wisdom of manhood, but man himself can add to his own acquisitions the stock accumulated by his predecessor, and transmit it to posterity to be still enlarged by those who succeed him.

In this process a man's knowledge does not die with him and the intellectual stores amassed by one generation may survive its ruin and form a capital for the commencement of the one to follow. Thus the human race may go on increasing from one generation to another, for aught we know, till time shall be no more. This, while it encourages our exertions, may check our vanity and forbid us to suppose we have attained perfection or that it is improper for others to innovate upon what we have embraced or attempted to establish.

On man, in reference to each of these characteristics, shall we keep our eye while reviewing the various notions of Christianity which have prevailed; and that each of these may show itself in harmony with the others will constitute our guide in discovering a system worthy our adoption.

No. 2. The Trinity (January 24, 1829): 20-23

In prosecuting the Essay on Christianity I shall not be governed by the *order* of inquiry which was stated in the notice I published, but shall commence with the Trinity, though my readers may be assured each of the subjects, mentioned in that notice, will be discussed in the course of our inquiry.

The Trinity, from the prominent rank which it holds among doctrines reputed Christian, from the high degree of importance which it is supposed to possess, as well as from its own abstruse nature, is justly entitled to the first place in a disquisition of religious dogmas. A belief in this dogma is considered by a large proportion of the Christian world as not only essential to the holiness of one's life, but absolutely necessary to avert the wrath of God and to save the soul from eternal perdition. It is considered the grand pillar of Christianity, the chief cornerstone of that spiritual temple which the prophets, the apostles and the pious in every age of the church have been ambitious to erect. As everyone wishes for happiness both here and hereafter, none can reasonably refuse to examine a dogma possessing such a powerful recommendation and such imposing claims.

It is truly lamentable to the philosophic and to the benevolent mind that mankind should have so long wandered in search of truth without once getting into the right path, or that they should have wasted so much time and exhausted so many brilliant geniuses in fruitless attempt to investigate subjects which must forever elude the reach of our senses or the power of our comprehension. Had mankind at first known what subjects they might have studied with profit and what they could not, or in other words had they at first known the circle which bounds their observation or which fixes the limits of their knowledge they had been at this time far advanced in the acquisition of wisdom. Had this been known the human race would never have been perplexed with so many absurd theories of religion as have spread over the earth with little other effect than to scandalize the Divinity and make enemies of brethren. The time which has been employed in the vindication or in the refutation of vague and contradictory dogmas might have been usefully employed in the development of the various phenomena of the natural world and in the acquisition of useful knowledge.

But ignorant of nature, man disdained to consult the objects which were contiguous to his situation, impatient of knowledge he could not submit to the slow and tiresome process of observation and experiment, but with a boldness honorable indeed to the sublimity of his mind, he rashly leaped into the empyreal sphere, determined to survey the throne of the Almighty and from its lofty eminence to give laws to the universe. Unmindful of earth he was engrossed with heaven, neglectful of his own constitution and of the conduct necessary to procure his own and his brethren's happiness, he attempted to explore the depths of the Divinity, and to scan the counsels of Jehovah. Inattentive to the importance of knowledge which might be made subservient to the purposes of life, he invoked the genius of faith, and deemed it the summit of his hopes, and the purity of his life *to believe*. The evil consequences of this grand mistake are not to be numbered. Inquiry has been diverted from her legitimate course, and the mind has been wasted and the understanding destroyed, to learn that which, if learned, would be useless, but which must forever mock his impotent exertions.

Ignorant that "the proper study of mankind is man,"[3] he vainly asked and attempted to answer the question, "what is God?" The question is involved in impenetrable darkness. Thousands of answers have been given, but all are equally unsatisfactory. Whether the mighty Energy, the mysterious Power which pervades the whole of nature and enables the universe to present its various and ever varying phenomena, be a Being separate from matter or inherent in it; whether it produced and arranged the vast machine, or be the result or aggregate of all the laws by which matter is actuated; whether it acts by intelligence or a blind necessity—are questions which baffle all our powers to answer, and which is the correct, man cannot by all the faculties nature has given him ever ascertain.

If then he knows so little of God how can he pretend to explain the mode of his existence, or state the number of persons who participate [in] his Divinity? From the study of nature he cannot ascertain that there is a God, much less that God exists in a three-fold form, or in other words, that there are three persons in the Godhead, Father, Son and Holy Ghost, equal in power and glory, the same in substance, perfectly distinct and independent of each other, and yet constituting but one God. Nature never taught this, or that part of nature which is open to *our* view never taught and can never assure us it is true. If true, the evidences of its truth are not found among things which we know, nor with which, by our own powers, we can become acquainted.

The subject is enveloped in thick darkness, an impervious veil hides it from our sight, and to investigate it we require the aid of another sense, one which can detect the spiritual world, converse with immaterial existences, tell us what they are, how they are made, and what forms they bear. But such a sense we have not.[4] Some may pretend to it, but man, as such, does not possess it, and has no reason to expect that he ever will. From nature there is no evidence in its favor. It is not a doctrine of nature and consequently is not supported by natural reason. But this is no argument against its truth. It may however be a strong argument why we should not believe it. But as we cannot be so vain as to suppose that whatever is, is present to our sight, or that we know all the possible modes of being which may

[3] [Ed. From Pope's *An Essay on Man*, Epistle 2, Line 2.]

[4] [Ed. By the 1830s, Brownson indeed held that there was a religious or a spiritual sense, and admired Jonathan Edwards' sermon, "A Divine and Supernatural Light." On this see, "Channing's Discourses," *The Christian Register* 12 (January 19, 1833): 10, and "Norton on the Evidences of Christianity," *Boston Quarterly Review* 2 (January, 1839): 86-113, especially 99-104.]

exist in the infinitude of space; it would be in the highest degree absurd for us to pronounce any being a fictitious one, merely because, in our observations, we have never seen it.

But it is proper that in this place we caution ourselves against a practice which many theologians seem highly to admire. The argument addressed to our ignorance is too often used and many, when endeavoring to support dogmas which refuse the cognizance of sense or which extend beyond the province of reason, are extremely apt to infer their truth from the fact that we do not know them to be false. But though our ignorance may be a good reason why we should not pronounce a thing false, it is a poor one indeed why we should call one true. Every man who affirms a position should offer in its support affirmative evidence, and his failure to do this may always justify the conclusion that he has none to offer. And no man is bound by the laws of evidence to believe an assertion because he does not know it to be false. He that makes the assertion must prove it or we may reasonably reject it.

Our ignorance respecting such a being as a "Triune" God is no argument against the truth of the assertion that there is such a Being, neither is it any argument in favor of such assertion. If there be no facts to prove his existence we are under no obligation to believe; and if we must be sent to endless woe under these circumstances for such a disbelief, we shall doubtless go without guilt or remorse. But if the dogma in question contradict facts which we know or which are plain to our senses, we are not only not bound to believe but absolutely bound to reject it.

It is impossible for the same thing to be and not to be. I have two books before me; they are *two*; and I should consider myself justified in telling any person he was deficient in common sense or common honesty who should assert they were *one*. For such an assertion is at war with the plain testimony of my senses and I know it cannot be true because it denies the existence of one book which I know lies before me. Should the Trinitarian tell me that God is three persons, and yet but one person, I might justly reply, your assertion is false, for it is impossible in the nature of things that *three* should be one, or that one should be three. And if he should vary his phraseology, yet express the same thing, if he expressed anything, I should be warranted to make the same reply.[5]

---

[5] [Ed. Brownson does not understand the traditional Christian doctrine of the Trinity. The doctrine asserts that there are three persons, or subjects, in one nature (not one person).]

The Trinitarian indeed complains of the paucity of language and declares that he is unable to find words to express his ideas of this sublime mystery. It may be so; but perhaps the difficulty is he has no ideas to express. Language, I believe, is adequate to express most, if not all, of the ideas the human mind can conceive; at least I have found no difficulty. I have always been more troubled to obtain ideas than I have to find words to communicate them. The Trinitarian is much attached to his peculiar dogma; he is extremely desirous of making it intelligible, but it is beyond the power of man to make a thing which is not, intelligible by any form of words which he can devise. No matter how much labor he bestows upon the child of his affection, if nature has not made it reasonable, he cannot make it so. The probability in regard to the Trinity is that it is unintelligible and unreasonable or contradictory.

If the Trinitarian will assert there are three Gods, his assertion is tangible. It becomes a matter of fact and testimony may be adduced to establish its correctness. But if he assert these three Gods, or rather three individuals, are but one God, he asserts that which implies a physical impossibility.[6] He may say these three individuals are of the same substance, or that the same substance which constitutes the being of one, equally constitutes that of the three; but this assertion would destroy the idea he would wish to convey. Identity of substance may be understood of sameness of kind, that is, the substance which constitutes the being of three men may be the same or of a like kind; but this definition, if admitted and applied to the Trinity, would prove there were three Gods, as much as it does that there are three men, who have a common nature, or who participate the same substance; and it would make it just as improper to call the three divine persons one God as it would be to call the three human persons one man.

Identity of substance, in its strict sense, implies that three individuals have not a like nature, do not partake of similar substance or one same in kind, but one actually the same in every particular of which we can form any conception. Say here is a lump of clay. The potter takes one third part of this and makes it into one vessel; out of the remaining two-thirds, he makes two more. Here was one lump of

---

[6] [Ed. The real problem with Brownson's understanding of the traditional doctrine of the Trinity is that he, like many others in the post-Cartesian era, had taken person as a self-conscious individual whose consciousness is the center of identity. The three "persons" in God, as the tradition understood it, are not three active "subjects," in which case there would no longer be any mystery of the one divine nature.]

clay divided into three parts and made into three distinct vessels. It would not be absurd to say these three vessels are one or the same in substance, understanding the sameness to be in kind, and not in the identity of particles.

But we cannot apply this reasoning to God. We know nothing of his substance. He is said to be immaterial, and consequently indivisible. Might we hazard an idea on a subject so inscrutable, we should say it is impossible to suppose three distinct persons to partake of that which is necessarily one and the same wherever it be found. For we cannot conceive of any distinction which can exist between the persons. Say God is pure spirit and that the whole of this spirit, however widely diffused, constitutes the whole of the Divinity. This Divinity is God. Call it Father, call it Son, call it Holy Ghost, or call it what we please, it is the same individual, the same indivisible God or Divinity. The Trinity is nothing but a word and the distinction for which the Trinitarian contends is a distinction in expression only and not in reality.

Does the Father possess any attribute which does not belong to the Son? Or do the Father and the Son possess anything which does not belong to the Holy Ghost? Every Trinitarian answers no. How then are they distinguished one from the other? It is in vain to talk of a distinction without a difference. And the Trinitarian but tramples upon his natural apprehension of things whenever he attempts to advocate both the oneness and the plurality of the Godhead.

If he would say the three persons in his God were one in design, one in their general pursuits and in their labors, whether of creation, of providence, or of salvation, he would be consistent in this respect. His unity and plurality would go very well together; for though they were many in one sense, they might also be one in another sense. But this would be Tritheism, and the Trinitarian abhors the idea that there are three Gods as much as does the most strenuous Unitarian.

Any conclusion different from this will destroy all distinction of persons in the Godhead, and the Trinity will dwindle down to different displays of Almighty Power, Wisdom or Goodness. That is, if we look at God as the Creator of the world we term him Father; if as redeeming the world from sin and misery, we term him Son because his dealing is with the sons or children of the Father; and if we look at him as by his power or life-giving energy raising us from the death of sin to the life of holiness we term him the Holy Spirit. Perhaps reason could not discover any inconsistency in our statements if we should assert this, but alas for the Trinitarian his dear *something*, I know not what, would be no more.

But it is unnecessary to dwell longer upon the reasonableness or unreasonableness of the dogma under review. Its advocates do not pretend that it is a doctrine of reason. They consider it a Bible doctrine; and as such they contend for its truth. Before we proceed to an inquiry whether it be really taught by the Bible or not, I must be indulged in a digression for the purpose of disposing of some questions which naturally arise out of the state of the case. And I may as well tell the reader in this place as in any other that I am not very fond of system; and that my way of presenting my essay in detached parcels, will permit me to attend to the questions which are excited, by the way, rather than to discuss them all at once.

The Trinity is an unreasonable dogma or, at least, it is not taught by reason, and it actually is, if it mean anything, opposed to our natural apprehension of things and seems to contradict some of the first principles which are the foundation of all reasoning. But without deciding in this place whether it be reasonable or unreasonable, we are provoked by the assertion that it is not a doctrine of reason but of the Bible, to inquire how far this sacred book is to be considered authority for a doctrine which is unreasonable. To answer this inquiry, we must answer several others which we propose to do, before we proceed farther in the examination of the Trinity.

No. 3. On the Use of Reason (February 7, 1829): 36-38

It is a singular circumstance that we should be under the necessity of settling the question how far we shall consider the Bible authority for an unreasonable doctrine and we should not have been reduced to this situation had it not been repeatedly urged that reason has nothing to do with matters of religion. Both the advocates and the opponents of reason seem to have misunderstood the subject in dispute, or at least, each other. The mistake has doubtless been occasioned by the ambiguous manner in which the word *reason* is used. Thousands cry out against the use of reason and perhaps as many exclaim in its favor, who, if they had understood each other, would have been agreed.

The term *reason* is susceptible of different meanings, according to the manner in which it is used. It may be used to signify the thinking faculty, whatever it be, or that power by which we perceive the relation of different propositions and by which we are enabled from certain premises to deduce or infer certain conclusions. It is often used to signify the same or nearly the same as argument; the thing sought or desired to prove a point or position. And not infrequently it implies the motive or cause of a thing or effect, as we say, the *reason* why such a thing is. But when I term a doctrine unreasonable, I mean that it is inconsistent with our natural perception of things or our own experience. Reason I consider that faculty by which we perceive the relation of different propositions and which enables us to determine whether the relation supposed to exist between them does exist or can exist without destroying either. We know that twice one is two, and we know also the assertion that twice one is one is false, therefore unreasonable. We know, so far as our experience extends, that it is the nature of love to make its object happy. We should therefore not hesitate to pronounce the assertion false or unreasonable that should say love will of its own accord inflict misery upon the object of its affection. From the term *love* we obtain a determinate idea, and if we convey any idea by the same term, except the one appropriated to it, that idea should bear another name. "Deity loves his creatures." By this we mean that he is delighted with his creatures and is pleased to make them happy. This is what we mean by love. Now, should anyone say that Deity will make these same creatures endlessly miserable, I answer, reason assures me he can never do this unless compelled, till he cease to love. I am positive in this conclusion because I know the nature of love. I know it never will make its object miserable unless compelled by a power it cannot control. Should I be told this indeed may be true so far as it regards man, but may be false when applied to Deity, I still reply that it can be no more false when applied to God than when applied to man. If we mean the same thing by love when the term is used of God, as we do when used of man, my conclusion is correct. If something else be meant, that something else is not love and should not be expressed by that term but by some other.

Reason should always be heard, and no system should receive a moment's attention, but to be discarded, that contradicts it. The only difficulty in the case is to ascertain what is reason. Reason must undoubtedly have some data. But what are the data from which we are to reason? "The voice of God," says he who claims intimacy with Jehovah. "God has spoken and it is the sublimity of human reason to believe." But I cannot assent to this proposition, in principle, though I might admit it in some of its details. Should I hear a voice from heaven asserting that the two men I now see walking are but one man, I should not believe it, because I have the testimony of my senses (the strongest evidence I can have in the case) to the contrary. Should the same voice declare to me, love and hatred, joy and sorrow, good and evil, pleasure and pain, are the same, I should not believe it; because my own experience irresistibly compels me to believe contrary to such declaration.

"But this," it is said, "is to set up one's own reason against the declarations of God." The remark is incorrect. We do not set up our reason against God. Have not I the testimony of my senses that I *see* two men walking? And have I anything more than the testimony of my senses that I *hear* a voice from heaven declaring the *two* to be but one? I have not; and if I believe one rather than the other, it is only because I choose to believe the testimony of one sense in preference to another. If I believe there are two men, I believe what I see, in preference to what I *hear*. I do not disbelieve that I hear the voice; but I disbelieve its correctness. But how do I know the voice I hear is the voice of God? Do I see God? If I did, and should hear him assert that which contradicted the plain testimony of my senses, I could not believe him. But God has not made such a declaration and if he be a Being of truth he cannot. But should he make such a declaration, humility might induce us to conclude there was some misapprehension in the case, or some play upon words. Deity might use language in a sense different from what I did, and the apparent falsity of the declaration might result from my misunderstanding the declaration.

We have the Bible. We are told the Bible is the word of God. Be it so. We have no disposition to question its inspiration or its divine authenticity. But for the sake of illustrating our argument, we will assume a case. Say then it is ascertained that water is a compound of hydrogen and oxygen, that it is ascertained by a variety of experiments which have established its certainty as positively as anything we can establish. Now should the Bible declare water to be a simple substance, which should we, which ought we, according to the nature of evidence, to believe? Believe that water is a compound is what I should do in such a case though ten thousand Bibles declared to the contrary.

All faith must arise from intuitive perception, experience or from testimony.[7] Intuition is undoubtedly the strongest evidence we can have. This is what irresistibly compels us to believe our own existence, to trust the intelligence of our senses and which at first thought, without any process of reasoning, leads us to admit it is impossible for the same thing to be and not to be, that a whole is greater than a part, etc. The evidence of experience is the next in order. This comprises whatever we have seen, heard or felt. And unquestionably it is easier for me to believe that which I have seen, heard or felt than it is

[7] [Ed. Brownson here shows his dependence on John Locke's *An Essay Concerning Human Understanding*, ed. A. D. Woozley (1689; London: William Collins Sons and Co., 1976), 378, 379-415.]

for me to believe what another tells me he has seen, heard or felt. I may, perhaps, believe on the testimony of another the stories which have lately been told about the Sea Serpent, but had I seen the Serpent myself I should certainly have stronger evidence of his existence than I now have. Hence I am to believe the testimony of my own senses in preference to the senses of others, and perhaps the testimony of a man I know and have always known to be a man of truth than of one who lives at a great distance of time and place, whom I have never seen and who I do not by any personal acquaintance know to be a man to be depended upon.

The Bible comes under the third class of evidence. It is the evidence of testimony, not of experience nor of intuition. Consequently [the Bible] can never authorize us to believe what contradicts our experience or our intuitive perception. "But," it is replied, "God cannot lie, therefore whatever he says must be true." We grant it. "But have we any right to inquire into the reasonableness or unreasonableness of what the Bible teaches?" Certainly: for, though God cannot lie, man, who can and often does lie is the only authority we have for believing the Bible is the word of God. I do not mean those to whom the Bible was given had no stronger evidence than the testimony of a fallible mortal for believing it the word of God, but that we, who live at this late day have no stronger evidence than human testimony.

It may be alleged numerous miracles were performed to establish the truth of the declarations of Scripture. This will not be denied, but we have not seen those miracles and we have nothing more than the testimony of individuals whom we have never seen, and whose names in many instances we do not know, that any ever did see them. The testimony which the Bible affords is the weakest kind of evidence and can never be admitted when confronted by stronger. We should make a distinction in this place. A thing may be beyond our reason and not opposed to it. In all cases of this kind the Bible is infallible. Other things may be opposed to reason; we know no authority sufficient to establish the truth of such things. A thing which contradicts our intuitive perception or our experience, we should at once pronounce false. Should it be asserted that a part is equal to a whole, that black is white, or that pain is pleasure, we may pronounce such assertions unfounded. But should it be asserted that Jesus Christ rose from the dead, we cannot pronounce it false, because we do not know that it was true, we know not but there is a law of nature which may produce such a result; and if the testimony is such as would command our assent in other extraordinary cases, we are bound to believe. Let this distinction be preserved and there will be no difficulty. What contradicts reason or experience, our intuitive perception, or our own knowledge we are to reject, Bible or no Bible: what is beyond our reason or experience, may or may not be true. We shall in our essay consider the Bible decisive on all questions of this nature.

No. 4. On the Use of Reason (February 21, 1829): 54-56

This distinction between things above reason and things contrary to reason, though by no means new, is not sufficiently understood. Whatever relates to another world, or to a mode of existence different from what we can discover here is above or beyond reason, it is said, and so far as relates to the fact that there is another world, or that there are beings different from any discoverable here, the remark is undoubtedly correct. But declarations made to us here respecting that world or those beings are subject to the empire of reason. Should it be said those beings are good and yet delight in cruelty, we should not hesitate to pronounce the assertion unreasonable and false because we know a good being does not, cannot, while he retains his goodness, delight in cruelty.

It is undoubtedly the province of the Bible to give us information respecting the character of our heavenly Father, and some hints respecting our final destination, but in regard to each of these there are certain laws which even the Bible must not transgress. If the Bible tells me there is a God, this is a simple declaration; one which, to say the least, reason does not contradict. The authority I attach to the Bible requires me to believe it. Should the Bible declare this God unchangeable, I should believe it, because I have no reason to think otherwise. But should the Bible assert this same God repents or changes his resolution, I should not believe, or at least I should not believe both assertions, because I know from the nature of things both cannot be true. It is the province of reason to determine which of these two are correct or which we should believe. The data from which reason must decide this question is still the Bible, compared with what we see in nature.

We know from experience that a man never changes his mind or alters his resolutions unless he has some motive to induce the change or alteration. And this motive is the result of something which was not seen or duly considered at the time the resolutions were formed. But could we suppose this man to have been possessed of infinite knowledge, so that he could clearly perceive whatever contingencies might or could happen; and could we suppose him also possessed of illimitable power, so that he could prevent anything from interfering with his plans, we should be unable to perceive it possible for him to change his purposes or alter his resolutions. If the Bible then assert that God is Omnipotent and Omniscient, I must assent to the declaration that he is unchangeable; consequently the assertion that he repents, or is changeable is unreasonable and false according to its own declarations.

The province of reason, as far as the Bible is concerned, is to consider the testimony or evidence by which its authority is established; to decide how far or to what subject this authority extends, and also the reasonableness or internal consistency of the declarations which it makes. The Bible asserts that God commanded the Israelites to extirpate the inhabitants of the land of Canaan. Now the man who believes the Bible would be under the necessity of believing that God actually commanded one part of his children to destroy another part, did not the same Bible tell us God is love, a kind and beneficent Father, who is good unto all, and whose tender mercies are over all his works. Now, we know, a being that is love cannot delight in the destruction of the objects of his love; we also know a kind father would never command one part of his family to kill another part; we must, therefore, either deny that God ever gave any such command, or give up the idea that he is love, or that he regards with affection all his works. Resort, in case like this, must be to nature; we must ask ourselves which is the more probable, that God should command one man to kill another or that an ambitious prince or leader should give the command, and, for the sake of giving weight to his command, should say he received it from God?

Should I be told that the Bible, as many supposes it does, declares the larger part of mankind will in another world be made miserable by their Creator, and that the Creator loves all his creatures, I should not believe both propositions; for they are absolutely in contradiction to each other. We know perfectly well what a good being will do to those he loves if he have the power; and we know God would not, unless compelled, make those he loved miserable. If, then, it should be found that Scripture makes assertions thus in opposition, we can believe only one to be true. The nature of the case may indeed leave us to believe either. If I choose to believe God is good, I must believe he will make those he loves happy, if he have the power; but if I choose to believe that mankind will be made eternally miserable, I shall believe that God is either a very bad or a very weak being.

It is then the office of reason to compare this book not only with the volume of nature, but with itself; and if there appear to be erroneous or inconsistent readings, they must be corrected from the best evidence the nature of the case affords. The Bible can never impose silence on reason, for it must itself submit to the supremacy of reason. Without reason, man could not derive profit from the Bible; and just as little profit would he derive from it, if he had reason but refused to exercise it. I do not mean to lessen the worth of the Bible nor deify reason, but to place each on its proper foundation. It is as much sacrilege to detract from the worth of reason as from the worth of the Bible. Both are attributed to God, and both ought to be agreed; but if on close examination there should be found any discrepancy, the Bible, not reason, should yield.

No person should consider himself under obligations to believe anything which is unreasonable. He may believe in the existence of a God, though reason may not discover his existence; in a future state of existence, though reason does not teach it; because reason does not *contradict* them, and they may be proved by testimony. All that reason can do is to examine the witnesses and determine whether they are worthy of credit. If the character of the witnesses is good, if they have the means of knowing, and appear capable of telling what they know, reason undoubtedly assents to what they depose. But if they disagree among themselves, reason either rejects the whole or selects such items from their depositions as appear to be correct.

The Bible declares there is a God. I believe this declaration, and do not consider myself at liberty to doubt it, from the dependence I place on the Bible. But if I could discern anything in nature which manifestly contradicted this declaration, I should not consider myself bound to believe it, but to reject it. In a word the Bible must bend to facts and not facts to the Bible, should there be a disagreement (which by the by I by no means assert).

Whenever, then, we wish to speak or write about another world, we are to consider the Bible our guide, but we are free to inquire the consistency or inconsistency with itself, of whatever it asserts. Whenever we reason of this world the Bible is to be tried so far as the past is concerned by experience; so far as it regards the present, by what we now see; and what may relate to the future must be left to the revolutions of time to determine, whether it be truth or falsehood.

I have been thus particular in these remarks because I am anxious the subject should be understood. Men have long worshiped the Bible more than they have their Creator; and if you say one word which induces the ignorant devotee to think you do not bow at the shrine of his idolatry, you see him following with the despicable language of the man of Mount Ephraim "ye have taken away my gods and what more have I left?"[8] Every man should thank the hand that takes away his idols, for he will never discover the true object of adoration while the false is in his sight.

Many read the Bible, as they pray or say grace; not from any benefit they expect to derive from perusing it, but because they think it a *command* or a *duty*. Whenever anyone takes the Bible to read, he should have clear perception of what he proposes to himself as the object of reading it. He should read for information, but he should ask himself on what subjects he requires information. Not indeed to teach him the moral virtues, for these being found in our relations to each other, and to the world of matter with which we are connected, require us to study ourselves and others together with the world within and without us, not the Bible. We need no Bible to tell us we ought to be just. Common sense teaches this. The Bible or nature either may tell us what justice is; but as justice, and indeed all the moral virtues, must vary in some degree with circumstances, the Bible cannot, unless it specify every possible condition in which a man can be placed, give us directions. The study of nature then will probably teach us more correctly and more fully what is proper to be done than the Bible, which must adapt itself to the age in which it is given, without making the necessary provisions for the ages to follow. If we wish information respecting God and a future state, we may read the Bible and depend upon what it says, providing it assert no absurdity or thing inconsistent with itself or with what we know. I conclude, therefore, that the Bible is no authority for an unreasonable doctrine, though it may be for a doctrine which is above or beyond reason.

NO. 5. ON INSPIRATION (March 7, 1829): 68-69

It is wisdom never to contend for more than can be maintained. When the Christian assumes a position from which the batteries of the infidel dislodge him, he is in danger of losing the ground to which he has a just claim. He should therefore examine carefully his own strength that he may not by the exorbitancy of his claims provoke a severer combat than he can sustain.

The Bible is an ancient book. It contains many good things, much knowledge of the human heart, and discloses many important facts. It also, if we determine as we do in other cases, contains much that to us appears, at best, very doubtful. This book is said to be inspired, written under the immediate influence of the Spirit of God. If this be a fact, and the Spirit of God, as we all believe, cannot

---

[8] [Ed. Judg. 18:24. The entire text reads: "Ye have taken away my gods which I made, and the priest, and ye are gone away: and what have I more?"]

dictate error, it must be contended that everything in the Bible is truth and nothing but truth. But whoever will read the Bible with a little attention must admit that it contains many things which cannot be believed by a man of common sense. It does contradict itself. It does contain doctrines subversive of the best interests of mankind and dishonorable to its reputed author. I speak of the whole Bible including both the Old and New Testaments and mean that passages may be found which come under this description.

There are those who contend that every word of the Bible is given by inspiration, that every word was dictated by the spirit of infallible truth. If this position be correct, there must not be a single mistake nor a single contradiction in the whole book. But is this a fact? In Genesis, God is said to "tempt Abraham" [Gen. 22:1]; and James tells us, "God tempteth no man" [James 1:13]. One or the other of these positions must be false. It is impossible for the same thing to be and not to be. Consequently impossible for God to tempt Abraham if he tempts no man, and false to say he tempts no man if he tempted Abraham.

The Bible says God is "unchangeable," that with him is "no variableness nor shadow of turning" [James 1:17]. It also says, God "repented that he made man" [Gen. 6:6]; that he "repented him of the evil he thought to do and did it not" [Exod. 32:14]. It, in the sixth precept of the Decalogue, represents God as commanding the Israelites that they shall not kill; and also represents him as commanding them to extirpate all the inhabitants of the land of Canaan; to leave none alive, lest they become corrupted with the vices of the land. The author of the second book of Samuel, informs us that the "*Lord* moved David to number Israel and Judah" [2 Sam. 24:1]. But the first book of Chronicles assures us it was *Satan* that provoked David to this wicked act [1 Chron. 21:1]. One or the other of these assertions must be false for both cannot be true. One would scarcely suspect the author of these contradictions to be the Spirit of God. I should think man might thus contradict himself without any supernatural aid.

It must be admitted I think that a man under the Spirit of God is incapable of error or of falling into mistakes. The Apostles, it is contended, on the day of Pentecost, received the gift of the Holy Ghost and that they were then qualified to proclaim the gospel. If we admit then they were inspired, is it not singular they should have been so ignorant as to suppose the gospel was limited to the Jews when nearly the last instructions they received from Christ were that they should "go into all the world and preach the gospel to every creature?" [Mark 16:15]. But when Peter was sent for to instruct Cornelius he had to witness a miracle before he could be persuaded; and he had also to relate the wonderful vision he had seen in his trance before he could persuade the rest of the Apostles that he had done right in preaching to the gentiles.

John, in the last chapter of his gospel, mentions a mistake into which the brethren had fallen. Just before the ascension of Christ, Peter had asked what a certain disciple who was leaning on Jesus' breast should do. The answer was, "If I will that he tarry until I come what is that to thee? Then went this saying abroad among the brethren, that that disciple should not die; yet Jesus said not unto him, He shall not die" [John 21:22-23]. Was not the brethren then mistaken? And if John had not corrected the mistake, might we not now be laboring under the same erroneous impression?

It is an indisputable fact that the primitive Christians concluded or expected that the end of the world, the destruction of the material heavens and earth, would take place at the same time the Lord should come to execute vengeance on the city of Jerusalem and the nation of the Jews, that is, within the lifetime of that generation that heard Christ proclaim his gospel. And that the Apostle Paul fell into the same opinion is easily collected from his first epistle to the Thessalonians. Nothing is better attested in the history of the church than that the believers about the time Paul wrote this epistle were exceedingly alarmed that they neglected their business and concluded the end of the world was at hand; and from various passages scattered through the epistolary part of the New Testament, it seems evident that the Apostles urged this consideration as one motive to induce the multitude to embrace their doctrine, promising them, in case they believed that they should be saved from the overwhelming ruin. But the alarm grew too great and Paul's second epistle to the Thessalonians was written to allay it by assuring the church that it should not be so soon, though still intimating the day was not far off. But the world stands; and we are now assured their alarm was groundless. Did the Spirit of God teach this belief? Or was it occasioned by a misconstruction of the words of Christ?

But admitting these objections are nothing, it is proper to ask, which of the numerous translations that have been produced, all differing in some respects, shall be considered as the one which has every word inspired? Shall it be our authorized version or some other one? Or if the translations are all allowed to be uninspired, which original manuscript shall we take? Which out of the several hundred various readings shall we adopt as the one which has every word inspired? The Samaritan? Or the common Hebrew text? With the emendations proposed by Kennicott and others or the text as it stood before the collations of modern critics?[9] Is the text of Erasmus, of Robert Stephens, or of Griesbach, the one which has every word inspired?[10]

The celebrated passage in 1st John 5:7, is rejected by Griesbach and many other eminent biblical critics because that out of one hundred and thirteen Greek manuscripts of this epistle which have been collated only one contains this verse. Other critics say it ought not to be rejected because in Tuscany or some other place it is probable that there are a great many more manuscripts which have not been collated. How do we know, then, that the Greek text, which we have, is the inspired one? Among the manuscripts already collected there are several hundred various readings; and if there are a great many more which have not yet been collated, perhaps when they are, we shall have in some respects a new Bible.

I grant the various readings or the differences in the several manuscripts are not very important, unless we suppose every word in the Bible has a meaning, which indeed seems a necessary conclusion, if every word be inspired. But perhaps when we have collated the other manuscripts which it is supposed are still in existence we may find some essential differences. And if we had the thousands which, it is supposed, have been destroyed we know not but differences still more material might be discovered. The Holy Spirit seems to have been strangely neglectful of the preservation of his words. If the very words of the Bible were of sufficient importance to be inspired, it is matter of sincere regret that we have not those precise words or that we cannot tell whether we obtain them or not.

[9] [Ed. By the authorized version Brownson probably means the Hebrew Masoretic text; the Samaritan (Hebrew) version of the Pentateuch was slightly different from the Masoretic (i.e., the standard Jewish) text, which had added vowel points and accents to the original unmarked Hebrew text. Benjamin Kennicott (1718-83), canon of Christ Church, Oxford, was a Hebraist and a biblical scholar who made a comparative critical study of the various Hebrew manuscripts of the Old Testament. The results of his work were published in *Vetus Testamentum Hebraicum cum variis lectionibus* (2 vols., 1776-80).]

[10] [Ed. Desiderius Erasmus (1469?-1536) was a clerical humanist who in 1516 prepared a celebrated edition of the Greek New Testament, which he then translated into classical Latin. Robert Stephens (c. 1500-70) published several editions of the Latin Bible from 1528 to 1546. On Stephens, see Hugh Pope, *English Versions of the Bible* (St. Louis: B. Herder Book Co, 1952), 116-17. Johann Jakob Griesbach (1745-1812) published from 1775 to 1777 an edition of the Greek New Testament from multiple surviving manuscripts; his edition laid the foundation for all subsequent critical work on the Greek text.]

These considerations involve so many difficulties that it seems wisdom to abandon the position that every word of the Bible is inspired. It is better to do it of our own accord than it is to hold on till we are compelled to relinquish our grasp. And notwithstanding I dread as little as any one can the sophistry of infidels; I think when they attack this position of ours, they have strong reasons to bring against us. Let this point be conceded. We do not contend that *every word* of the Bible is inspired. And this concession in my opinion does not injure the reputation of the Bible or in the least impair its utility.

No. 6. On Inspiration (March 21, 1829): 85-87

Any man capable of putting three ideas together must be convinced from the remarks I have already made that it is useless to contend that *every word* of the Bible was dictated by the infallible spirit of truth. Certainly the Bible which we have is not free from errors. But the least error is fatal to the position that every word is inspired, if indeed inspiration be what people generally imagine. But there are some who conclude the Holy Ghost only dictated the arguments and doctrines, while the words were chosen by the writers themselves. This hypothesis does not obviate the difficulties or reconcile the discrepancies, which are manifestly to be found in the sacred book. The instances we enumerated to disprove that every word was inspired, bear equally hard against the supposition that all the arguments and doctrines are given by inspiration.

It would not be difficult to produce examples of false reasonings or illegitimate deductions, of unsupported premises and conclusions without premises, but, lest some timorous soul might think my reverence for the book is less than it really is, I let them rest till called up by others who may have more leisure and inclination to find fault. It will be enough to exhibit one or two examples of discrepancy in doctrine.

The Jewish lawgiver informs us in the second precept of the Decalogue that God is a "jealous God, visiting the iniquities of the fathers upon the children to the third and fourth generations, of them that hate him" [Exod. 20:5; Deut. 5:9]. The term jealous can hardly be applied to God. It is generally used in a bad sense, to express an ignoble passion; and though it is sometimes used in a good sense, it is still a sense inappropriate to God. In its best sense, jealousy means a strong desire to retain something which we have, or to which we have a claim, joined with the fear of losing it. But how God can *fear* he shall lose what he desires to retain is not very easy to conceive.

But it seems contrary to all ideas of moral justice for God, because the fathers hate him, to punish this hatred in the persons of their descendants, even to the third and fourth generations. Some despotic governments, I know, have allowed bills of attainder, which had the effect to disfranchise or disinherit the children of him against whom they were passed; but our government through the enlightened philanthropy which characterized its founders prohibits all such bills; and I can hardly believe that God has not as clear ideas of justice as had the convention who framed our constitution.

But Ezekiel teaches us a doctrine very different from Moses. He assures us, in the name of the Lord, that we shall no longer use the proverb, "the fathers have eaten sour grapes, and the children's teeth are set on edge" [Ezek. 18:2]; that the soul that sinneth shall die, every one for his own son, not the father for the transgression of the son, nor the son for the father. Did the Holy Ghost dictate both these doctrines? If he did, one would think he had forgotten the law he gave to Moses before he gave the one to Ezekiel, or, that during that lapse of years, had improved in the science of legislation, and was now ambitious to atone for the errors of his first attempts.

The Jewish lawgiver recommends the law of retaliation, commands us to follow the principle, "an eye for an eye, tooth for a tooth, burn for a burn, hand for a hand" [Exod. 21:24-25], etc. That is, if a man put out one of my eyes, I am to put out one of his; if he knocks out one of my teeth, he must be served the same. This is not a very wholesome principle. It encourages revenge and is calculated to keep up an endless train of wrongs and outrages. Jesus corrects this law, commands us not to resist the injurious, and instead of doing by others as they do by us, we are to do by them as we *would* they should do by us; that instead of revenge we should forgive our enemies and do good unto them that injure us. These doctrines are in direct opposition to each other, and it seems not a little strange that God could be the author of both. I am not ignorant of the exposition usually given to these passages, but I detest them all; they have little other effect than to make darkness still darker. I should indeed feel more obliged to the Holy Ghost if he had used a little more precision in his statements; and I should be much more willing to give him the credit of dictating the book, if he had preserved a little more coherence in its several parts and presented it in a manner so lucid that we should be at no loss to comprehend his meaning.

It is unnecessary to pursue this kind of reasoning farther; and, perhaps, I ought to make some apology to Bible-worshiper for having carried it so far. But I am little accustomed to make truth pay homage to falsehood; and, as I have not yet learned to apologize for telling the truth, I think I shall not turn out of my way to commence the study now. I shall never deprecate the vengeance of those who advocate error. I shall only claim the privilege to smile when they rage and to pity them when they shrink from the approach of light.

The remarks already made evince that caution is necessary in proving a doctrine from the Bible. Some of its doctrines are manifestly incorrect, whether we determine according to our natural ideas of justice or by the suffrages of the later Bible writers themselves. It is important, or rather necessary, even to determine the question whether any part is inspired, and if so, what part this is? Before answering either of them, it will be proper to answer another, what is inspiration?

People generally suppose inspiration means an infallible aid from the Holy Ghost, which enables the subject to speak the truth and nothing but the truth, and to disclose facts worthy to be believed, which facts none of our senses are able by their constitutional power to discover. The mode or manner is various—dreams, visions, audible sounds, and inward suggestions are those commonly enumerated. As for dreams, the writers of the Bible very likely had them. We have them now and we have no reason to doubt that the Jews had dreams as well as we. But as dreams are often incoherent and not worthy of much credit, I do not think them the safest sources of knowledge. Some, perhaps, can show why the dreams of the ancient Jews are more worthy of credit than ours; but, until they do this, I must say with Jeremiah, "the prophet that hath a dream, let him tell a dream; and he that hath my word, let him speak my word faithfully. What is the chaff to the wheat?" [Jer. 23:8].

That they formerly had visions and saw strange sights none but incorrigible skeptics will presume to dispute. One tells us he was caught up to the third heaven (whether in the body or out, he could not tell) and saw things which it was not expedient for him to relate. Others saw things which they did relate. But whether they were in the body or out, asleep or awake, is more than I know and in some instances probably more than they knew themselves. Perhaps the testimony of such persons would have weight in a court of law, especially three thousand years after their death, though rejected with contempt by their contemporaries.

Audible sounds they might have heard. I have heard many. Sometimes they told the truth, and sometimes they did not. The only kind of inspiration which to me appears rational is inspiration by *suggestion*. The word inspiration is from *in* and *spiro*, to breathe, and signifies something breathed into or suggested to the mind. Hence the Holy Ghost is said to breathe into the mind or suggest to the mind the lessons he wishes it to communicate. The inspired person feels a certain impulse under the influence of which he speaks. If he feel the impulse of truth, what he says will be true; if the impulse of error, what he pronounces will be false.

Admitting then that we ought not to disbelieve that the writers or some of the writers of the Bible were inspired by the Holy Ghost, we must still inquire who or what is the Holy Ghost? Notwithstanding I have taken no small pains to become acquainted with this celebrated personage; notwithstanding I have read several genealogical and physiological accounts of him; I must acknowledge what I know will not much recommend me to my pious readers, that I know but very little about him. People have talked and written a great deal about him; whether correct or not, probably an *uninspired* man ought not to assume the province of determining. But as I am no believer in *Ghosts* nor Hobgoblins, I conclude that nothing more should be understood by the term as we find it in the Christian Scriptures than A HOLY SPIRIT. I know it is sometimes called *the* Holy Spirit, but this is only a mark of distinction by which we are to know the spirit of which the writer speaks is that holy spirit, ardor, energy, or disposition which governed or actuated Christ and his Apostles. I assume this position here, but shall prove it, to my own satisfaction at least, when I come to treat upon the third person of the "ever blessed Trinity."

The sacred writers were inspired then by a holy spirit and wrote what such a spirit or disposition induced them to believe to be correct. I do not call this inspiration supernatural, but extraordinary. It enabled these holy men to do and to say what they would never have thought and what none would ever have conceived under any other circumstances whatever. They wrote as they were moved upon by this holy spirit or governing power of their minds. This spirit prevented them from falling into any known or wilful errors, but could not preserve them from all errors, as may be seen from the instances already enumerated. The great mistake of the religious world is in attaching infallibility to this spirit. This has led them to belie their own reason, to deny the testimony of their sense, and to fall into "divers" extravagances in attempting to reconcile contradictions. Admit my views of inspiration and we can then easily account for the discrepancies which every honest man must admit there is in the Bible. They are nothing more than a matter of course. The writers were numerous; they lived in different ages and wrote in different languages and it would have been singular, indeed, if there could be found no incoherence in their views. But infidels have no right to triumph. Good men, and even wise men, may fall into mistakes; and shall we consider it strange that the sacred writers, though actuated by the best spirit in the universe, have, in discussing so many intricate subjects, committed a few trifling mistakes? Certainly not.

In answer then to the question is any part of the Bible inspired, I have no hesitation to say yes; and if asked what part, the answer is ready. The Bible is traditional, historical, moral and doctrinal. The book of Genesis is traditional; it needed no extraordinary inspiration to write that. The historical, including the laws of the Jews, as well as the history of their nation, required no inspiration different in *kind* than what is given to every man. The moral part could be learned from observation. The doctrinal part of the Old Testament is mostly superseded by the new; consequently, I consider as inspired only the doctrinal part of the Christian Scriptures or of the New Testament. I have nothing to do with the old, only as it serves to explain or develop the meaning of the new.

NO. 7. ON MIRACLES (April 4, 1829): 102-03[11]

Time has been when to reason was crime and to speak the truth was deemed treason against the sovereign of nature. Much of the spirit, which then prevailed, may yet remain, but the march of improvement has so far softened the rigors of our institutions that one may now venture to state his honest convictions without endangering his head how much soever he may expose himself to starvation or to the loss of all means of support.

The church has in all ages manifested an exceeding fondness for the marvelous, and indeed has rested the most important parts of her creed on the supposition that its first defenders performed certain wonderful feats or miracles. A miracle, according to the definition usually given, is something which takes place contrary to the laws of nature or something which is done in opposition to them. It is certain no being less wise than Omniscience can determine whether a thing, according to this definition, be a miracle or not. Nature is a broad term. It comprehends whatever is. It would not perhaps be difficult to demonstrate the absolute impossibility of miracles in this sense of the term, but it is unnecessary. But we ought to clearly perceive all the laws of nature and to know all the possible operations of

---

[11] [Ed. Brownson will again take up the issue of miracles during his Transcendentalist period. See, e.g., "Norton on the Evidences of Christianity," *Boston Quarterly Review* 2 (January, 1839): 86-113.]

which these laws are susceptible before we pronounce anything to take place contrary to the laws of nature.

All we know of nature is that little part which has come under our own observation and all we can affirm of the laws of nature is what our experience has determined to have been its order or mode of operation since our observations commenced. Should I be told a clergyman raised by a word a man from the dead, all I could say is that such things are contrary to *my* experience. Should my informant insist upon its being a fact, should he allege he saw it, and should he adduce sufficient evidence to convince me it is a fact, I should not say it was contrary to nature. I should pronounce it *natural* because it had been *seen* and experience attested its truth. But this act could not be called a miracle. The most that could be said of it would be that it was an extraordinary or an uncommon occurrence.

To pronounce such an event contrary to the laws of nature would require us to know positively there is no law by which it could be done, therefore must have been done in opposition to them all. Our knowledge is too limited for this. And, as all that we have, by which to determine what is the law of nature is our experience, the same rule which leads us to attribute the growth of a tree or the revolution of a world to the laws of nature, or which would call them natural occurrences, would require us to affirm the same of raising a man from the dead, if we had even seen such an event. Raising a man from the dead by a mere word would be no miracle.

But admitting it would be a miracle what would it prove? Supposing one should assert two and two are four and should raise a man from the dead, would that make his assertion more true? Certainly not. If one should assert two and two make five and should, to prove this assertion true, raise a man from the dead, should arrest the sun and chain the world in the midst of its course, would that prove that two and two are five? I think every schoolboy would, notwithstanding such tremendous display, still continue to say two and two are four. What then can a miracle prove?

There are various extraordinary occurrences related in the Bible; such as the sun's standing still, the dead's being raised by touching the bones of a prophet, the whale's swallowing Jonah, the devil's carrying Jesus Christ around, setting him upon a high mountain and upon the battlements of the temple, a talking serpent, a warning ass, transformations, bursting of tombs, rising from the graves, ascending to heaven in a chariot of fire, etc. Now, these things are said to have taken place. Doctors have written to prove the verity of the history recording them and it would be impious for us to withhold our assent; but what do they prove? Supposing I should assert that there is a God and should raise a man from the dead, what would I prove? Simply that I have raised a man from the dead; nothing more. My act, or this exertion of my power, could have, in the nature of things, no more connection with the moral truth or with my assertion that there is a God, than my being able to whip my boy proves that I should be justified in so doing. An ignorant, gaping multitude might admire the feats of a juggler and conclude he had made a league with the devil because he could do that which they were unable to perform, but that is no certain evidence their conclusion would be true.

Should I assert that mankind will rise from the dead or that myself were the Son of God, and to substantiate my assertions should perform signs and wonders, cast out demons, heal the sick and do that which nobody else could do, I should not prove my assertions. I should only prove myself an extraordinary person, capable of doing what the spectators of my strange acts would be incapable of performing. This would be all. There being no perceivable connection between the doctrines I assert and the work I perform, I could only prove, by my acts, that I had performed them. This reasoning is so plain and so conclusive that I am surprised that any should rely on the miracles which Christ performed as evidences of the doctrines he taught.

It will be admitted as nothing singular that persons beholding the wonderful works of the saints of old should be impressed with the conviction they were from God. Should I see one raise to life another who I knew was actually dead doubtless I should be so lost in wonder that I should believe almost anything the person should assert. It is not then denied but in the age in which they were performed these extraordinary performances were calculated to make the people believe on the persons who made them. There is nothing strange in this. In that age, these things, or this supposed evidence, addressed to the outward senses might have been useful, perhaps the best kind of evidence the people then were capable of appreciating. They doubtless had their use. It is remarkable that miracles, or what are so called are most abundant among ignorant people. The reason is probably because, incapable of investigation, they must have something to astonish.

To rely on miracles or extraordinary occurrences as conclusive evidence of moral or religious truth is by no means the mark of a philosophic mind, how much soever it may characterize the ignorant. They are only particular events and cannot prove general truths.

They no more prove anything but themselves that they have occurred than I should prove myself a god by cutting off one of my hands. We are unable to draw any inferences from such things. Were they regular and of frequent occurrence, we might perhaps have some rational opinions respecting the cause or power by which they are produced. To us they appear strange anomalies in the operations of nature and as such we must leave them.

One thing it may be well to notice, that the credit or importance attached to miracles is proportioned to their antiquity or distance. In reading the history of the Jews, one meets with signs and wonders on every page, particularly at the period the House of Israel departed from Egypt. But is it not a little singular that this people who was loaded with so many prodigies from heaven, who were led by a cloud by day and a pillar of fire by night, who saw the sea open to give them a passage and the water gush from the rock to quench their thirst, should have disregarded all and remained a stiff-necked and rebellious people? The only solution worthy to be given is these remarkable occurrences, which to us are rare as angels' visits, were then so common they passed as the ordinary events of the day.

The miracles recorded in the Bible were doubtless performed. I admit these acts were done. I do not dispute the Bible. I only allege that these miracles are no evidence to us of the truth of the doctrines taught in the Bible. This distinction is of importance, as it preserves the truth of the Bible and obviates the objections which infidels have urged against it. The events were performed. They were isolated facts. They do not, they cannot prove the truth of any abstract doctrine, whether moral or religious. These miracles then stand as they were recorded, but we should seek elsewhere for the evidence of the truth of Christianity. Christianity must be supported by facts of a different character or it will fall before the attacks of its sharp-sighted opposers.

No. 8. SCRIPTURE INTERPRETATION (April 18, 1829): 117-19

It is strange that paying so great attention to the Bible as all Christians do they should be so ignorant of the true method of Scripture interpretation. I did intend to give an enlarged view of this subject, but have been so long detained on some other particulars that I shall dismiss it with a few general observations.

To point out all the errors common to Scripture interpreters would require more time and room than I can allot to so ungrateful a task. It will be enough to exhibit the true method.

We are to take up the Bible as we do any other book. We are not to expect a particular meaning in every word. The style, though generally correct and precise, is still like the style of all writers—has its inaccuracies. The language, though generally expressive, is not devoid of looseness, and though generally clear, is not always without ambiguity. We are therefore to form our opinions according to its general tenor rather than according to any particular passage. We are also to bear in mind that the Bible was not all written by one individual nor indeed all written upon one subject.

The last remark will be found of much use. Were I wishing to explain the writings of Paul, I should show myself a novice if I undertook to explain them by the writings of Joshua, unless indeed both were treating upon the same subject. If one writer says all are wicked we are not to infer all mankind are wicked unless indeed the whole world is the subject treated. If we wish to prove all mankind will be happy hereafter, it will be no proof to bring a passage which declares all shall be happy unless the passage occurs in a discourse on future life. Should we wish to prove that a part will be eternally damned, a passage which declares the wicked shall be punished will have no bearing unless there be something in the passage itself or its context which necessarily ties it down to a future world.

2.[12] To understand the Bible we must also consider the point the writer is endeavoring to prove or the conclusion at which he aims to arrive. That conclusion is binding; the several points upon which he may incidentally touch may or may not be of authority, though generally to be disregarded unless expressly proved or stated elsewhere. Allusions to particular opinions which are known to have then existed even when those opinions are not contradicted are not to be taken as parts of Christianity if not expressly stated in some other place.

A fact, which is or ought to be well known, that the economical mode of argument, as it was called, was extremely popular in the Apostles' times will justify this rule. It was customary then, and is so in some degree even now, for the controversialist to concede to his opponent all for which he contended except the very point in dispute. To illustrate this: It was the opinion of the Jews that by the transgression of Adam all his posterity became subject to death. This point you will find generally conceded. Particularly in the fifth chapter of Paul to the Romans, or rather Jews who dwelt at Rome. In this chapter Paul has one object in view, viz. that all mankind should, through the grace of our Lord Jesus Christ, receive eternal life. "You Jews," he would say, "suppose that mankind became subject to death through Adam's transgression, or rather, through his disobedience, sin entered into the world and death by sin. Be it so. What then?

[12] [Ed. There is no number 1 in the original text.]

The grace of God shall stretch beyond even this. This grace cancels all the damage received from the transgression of Adam, let that damage be great or small."[13] Here it is perceived that Paul settles only one question for this was the only question before him at the time. The other subjects incidently alluded to or points conceded may nevertheless become subjects of controversy.

3. The sense of Scripture language is to be considered as *one* in opposition to a double, or two-fold sense, one literal and the other spiritual. This rule is often violated. It is not infrequently we hear the most absurd doctrines pleaded on the authority of a hidden or spiritual sense of a passage. I once heard a man undertake to prove there were only three dispensations from the parable of three measures of meal; and many have argued that there were but four gospels or memoirs of Christ because there are four seasons in a year, four cardinal points, four dispensations, etc. Something like the man who undertook to prove that there could be only three parts in music, base, tenor and treble because there were only three persons in the Trinity.

I say but very little of the prophets. Their language, as the language of prophets is and always must be, is obscure. But the rule I have adopted fixes their meaning to the subject on which they are treating. There may be types and shadows but I do not understand them and I have never seen any two who professed to understand them that agreed in their view of them. When I read of Solomon's temple, I read of a building which actually was erected. When I read the description of that temple, I suppose I read a true description of real things, and am not aware that there is a spiritual meaning in every stone used in its building, or every timber, plank, board and other materials used in its construction.

A roving imagination may fancy images in the clouds and persons of a certain temper may see beings in the fire and fancy their acquaintances' health or condition from the arrangement of burning coals, but a sound mind, a chastened understanding, will pay little regard to such ideal stuff. An ingenious mind, by the aid of his two-fold sense, may spin out many, very many fine theories from the Bible. John Bunyan[14] is an example. Any who can have patience to read his works may have the substance and manner of what is called

---

[13] [Ed. Brownson paraphrases Rom. 5:12-20.]

[14] [Ed. John Bunyan (1628-88), author of *Pilgrim's Progress* (1678), was an Independent Puritan pastor in England who viewed human life as a continuous warfare for the salvation of the soul. His plain style and his imaginative and literal use of the Scriptures contributed much to the language of religion in England and the United States.]

the "primitive Fathers." But such theories are like the spider's web—may hold weak animals but the strong will disregard it. When we read other books we understand them according to the most obvious sense of the words. We must observe the same rule with the Bible. When we have determined a passage to mean one thing, we are to understand it as restricted to that thing.

4. As a general rule for understanding the Scriptures, we are to regard who is the speaker? What is the occasion on which he speaks? To whom does he address himself? And what is the most obvious import of his discourse? If we ask these questions and study diligently to answer them, we shall not fall into any material errors. We are told we must make the Scriptures interpret themselves; that we must explain Scripture by Scripture. This remark is correct when understood in opposition to explaining by the analogy of faith,[15] or by one's creed. But many, in attempting to explain Scripture, are as inconsistent as the wag who said he could prove it right for a man to hang himself. For instance: Judas went and hanged himself, go thou and do likewise. Or as the man who contended that the Bible commanded all prophets to be hanged because Jesus had said on these *hang* the law and the prophets.

We are indeed to explain Scripture by Scripture. But we are not to explain what is written on one subject by one writer, by what is written on another subject by another writer. As if we would explain a line in Shakespeare by a quotation from Brown's Philosophy on the human mind;[16] or an obscure paragraph in some history by a line from an ode to the moon. If two writers treat the same subject they may throw light upon each other, or if the same writer speaks twice upon the same subject, both passages may be consulted with advantage.

The propriety of these rules may not readily appear to all my readers and some may think they amount to nothing. We shall have occasion to refer to them before we get through our essay, their value will be tested and their usefulness will be evinced. We are now prepared for resuming the Trinity which we shall proceed to discuss.

No. 9. THE TRINITY RESUMED (May 2, 1829): 134-35

Having disposed of our preliminary questions, we are now prepared to resume our discussion of the trinity. My readers will understand me. I am not now inquiring whether Christ be the eternal God, or whether he be a super-angelic, a super-human or simply a

---

[15] [Ed. The analogy of faith means that the human expressions found in the Bible are to be interpreted in the total context of revelation and faith.]

[16] [Ed. Thomas Brown (1778-1820) was a Scottish Common Sense philosopher who emphasized the intuitive nature of human knowledge of cause and effect.]

human being. Each of these questions will receive a due share of attention as our essay proceeds. I am now considering the position that God exists in three distinct persons, the same in substance and equal in power and glory.

By turning to No. 2 of this essay, the reader will perceive it was there shown, this doctrine is not only not taught by reason, but that it is opposed to our natural apprehension of things, very nearly if not quite involving an absolute contradiction. I have, I think, in my remarks on the use of reason, clearly shown that the Bible cannot authorize us to believe or require us to contend for a doctrine which is unreasonable. I might therefore conclude the discussion of the trinity by saying it is unreasonable, and there is no authority which can establish an unreasonable doctrine. But I shall not avail myself of this argument. The trinity is said to be a Bible doctrine, and it is therefore proper to examine how far this assertion be correct.

Some Trinitarians, more zealous than wise, attempt to prove their doctrine from the Jewish Scriptures. The Jews, who may be supposed to understand their own Scriptures as well as Christians, strenuously deny that any such sentiment is taught in their books, and urge the fact as one of their chief objections against the truth of Christianity. This consideration alone is sufficient to convince any sound discriminating mind that the sentiment is not found in the sacred books of the Jews.

The Jews, who had the prophets and the traditions of their elders, never dreamed the promised Messiah was the second person in the Godhead. They considered him a temporal prince. They looked forward to his advent as the approach of an eminent man who was to exalt their nation and magnify the throne of David. An impartial view of the prophets will warrant this conclusion. No person, but a slave to prejudice, can discover a single prediction in the Old Testament, which bears the least allusion to the fact for which Trinitarians contend, that the Messiah was one of the ineffable trinity.

This, though of itself conclusive, may not satisfy those who see chariots in the fire and horsemen fighting in the clouds. One or two criticisms shall be noticed. In Genesis it is said, in our translation, "In the beginning God created etc." But in the original, the word rendered God is in the plural number. Now say these critics, the Hebrew language has three numbers. The singular which expresses but one object, the dual which expresses two, and the plural which expresses more than two. As the word rendered God is in the plural and not in the dual, they say it cannot express less than three. This indeed would prove as many as three Gods, to say the least, were it not also a fact that the word rendered *created* is in the singular. Then as they render the word "In the beginning Gods, not less than three and but one created etc." I mention this that my readers may see what kind of evidence is brought to prove a doctrine which nobody can understand. Admitting all this, it does not prove the trinity. The most that can be said is that it proves a plurality in unity. But it does not prove this. The Hebrews often join a noun with a plural termination to a singular verb to express dignity. The plural number answering the purpose of an adjective to that effect. Hence too, for the same purpose they say, "Jehovah Elohim" Lord Gods, or the highest God.

The authority of this part of the book of Genesis is very precarious. It bears the marks of a philosophy, superannuated by the discoveries of modern science and must be ranked with the numerous fictions of the East, invented to account for the origin of the world and the introduction of evil. But let this pass. A Jew would smile at such criticisms upon his language, and the discerning will not fail to conclude the cause which needs them is at best a weak one.

There is one passage more I notice, Deut. 6:4. "The Lord our *God* is one Lord." The word rendered *God* in this verse is said to be in the plural number, and as it is used in connection with the term *one*, it is supposed to teach the idea of plurality in unity. But as this does not prove the trinity, I might dismiss it, were there not a strong argument to prove the Trinitarian criticism is incorrect. Jesus Christ was doubtless as good a biblical critic as modern divines and the apostles themselves I think were not much behind. Christ quotes this verse, Mark 12:29, but translates this supposed plural Hebrew noun, by a Greek one in the singular. Now it is somewhat unaccountable that Christ should have failed to notice this plurality in unity had it existed; and he or the apostles must be considered very remiss in their duty not to have used in their translation a plural noun; and even our translators, strenuous Trinitarians, failed in their duty for had it been in the plural they should have written Gods, instead of God.

My reader will perceive, admitting all for which the Trinitarians contend from these passages, they only prove a plurality in the Godhead. This would sound strange to a Jew who everybody knows has always strenuously asserted the strict unity of the Deity. But, to prove this plurality is exactly the number three, neither more nor less, the sharp-sighted Trinitarian critic reads somewhere in the Old Testament, no matter where, that same one, addressing the Deity, said; "Holy, holy, holy Lord God"; repeating the term "three times," it is evident the speaker recognized three persons in the Godhead.

For, if he did not, why did he repeat the term holy, just three times, neither less nor more? This argument may speak for itself.

I have now presented all which I am aware that Trinitarians ever urge from the Old Testament in favor of the three-fold God. What it proves I know not, except the paucity of materials, which the advocate of this notion has with which to construct his mighty fabric. I have already stated the Old Testament cannot with consistency be alleged as proof of a Christian doctrine. I repeat the sentiment that I may not be misunderstood. This part of the Bible may teach us Judaism; but Christians are not Jews. The two dispensations have no other connection with each other than that both were given to the same people, and that the first teachers of Christianity were not only Jews themselves but they preached to Jews, and appealed to authority which the Jews acknowledged to convince them Jesus of Nazareth was the promised Messiah.

Had this distinction, which evidently exists between the two, been always observed, the religious world would have avoided many of the errors into which they have fallen. The old dispensation was given to the Jews. It served indeed as a schoolmaster to prepare them for the Christian, but it was to vanish on the introduction of that more perfect system. Christianity came with the blaze of the noonday sun, whereas Judaism shone only as the twinkling of a star. Shall we reject the sun, the glory of the luminary of heaven, for the feeble glimmering of a midnight star? Surely not. The New alludes to the Old; so are as necessary to explain these allusions the Old is valuable any farther it is as a statute repealed. I therefore dismiss the arguments drawn from the Old Testament to establish the trinity and shall consider in my next number those which are drawn from the New.[17]

---

[17] [Ed. Brownson never continued this Essay.]

14.

A SERMON. WHY MEN FOLLOW VICE.

The Gospel Advocate and Impartial Investigator
7 (January 24, 1829): 17-20

*The ways of wisdom are ways of pleasantness, and all her paths are
peace.* Prov. 3:17.

1. Most people, I believe, are willing to acknowledge "the way of
the transgressor is hard" [Prov. 13:15]; and very few but are equally
willing to admit, "the ways of wisdom are ways of pleasantness and
that all her paths are peace." The pain and anxiety which most feel
in by far the greater part of their pursuits, one would think, were
sufficient to fasten the conviction that they are wandering in error;
and also to excite an inquiry if they cannot adopt some expedient
more favorable to happiness. I say one would think the pain and
anxiety sufficient, and I believe it actually is. No man can be unhappy without perceiving it; and few who regard what passes in their
own minds can be at a loss to determine its true cause.

2. It is thus we often hear persons apparently the most guilty the
loudest in their complaints against vice. You never hear persons of
intemperate habits in their moments of sobriety commending intemperance or approving their own course. Speak to an intemperate
man of the deleterious consequences of intemperance. Tell him with
the deepest pathos that its tendency is ruin and he will perhaps surprise you with his acute perception of its destructive nature and the
masterly manner with which he develops its hidden enormities. No
man can lecture more profoundly or more successfully on the beauty
and the utility of temperance; and no man can feel more acutely that
he has "put an enemy in his mouth to steal away his brain." But
instead of this conviction, this acute sensibility leading him to reform, it often only drains another bowl to drown itself.

3. Hence perhaps we are able to discover the fallacy of a very
current philosophy among many who make great pretensions to correct thinking; whose principle dogma is, convince a man what you
propose is really good, make his mind perceive that it is truly desirable, and you enlist all his powers to accomplish it. This is not always

nor even very often the fact. There can be no doubt the intemperate is more clearly convinced of the importance of temperance than the perfectly temperate man is. This is evinced by those frequent resolutions which he makes to reform but which seldom succeed. And this discloses another mistake in supposing the will to be the governing principle of human actions.

4. It can hardly be supposed that a man's will is averse to happiness when indeed we see a desire for happiness is the first and the strongest principle developed in our nature. Nor can we admit that men are entirely ignorant of the true source of that which they so ardently desire. Ignorant no doubt they are in many respects; but I shall not be told a man endowed with the ordinary share of understanding is so ignorant as to believe that sin or vice is more conducive to his happiness than virtue. Nor shall I find much dispute respecting what is virtue or what is vice. How happens it then with this desire, with this conviction and this knowledge, that man still continues to pursue the road which leads to his own destruction? That I am right in my supposition respecting the will may be easily ascertained from the seventh chapter of Paul to the Romans, who speaks as every enlightened man who regards the operations of his own mind must speak. See verse 15: "For that which I do I allow not, for what I would that do I not, but what I hate that I do." Let then the question recur, how happens it that men with the knowledge of the road which leads to happiness, with a strong desire to walk in it, do, notwithstanding this knowledge and this desire, continue in a course which they are sensible yields them no enjoyment.

5. I know it has been thought the cause lies in the will. But *will* can hardly be said to exist in opposition to the clear conviction of the understanding and the strong desire of the heart. Call will what you please, you can make it nothing more nor less than the determination of the mind. How the mind can determine against that which it perceives to be for its own good, and against that which it has a strong desire to possess, is to me a problem not easy to solve. Let it be understood, we think it sufficiently evident, if not from the remarks we have made, from everyone's experience, that a man may, nay often does, continue a practice which the clearest convictions of his own understanding disapprove; that he may reject that which he believes is for his best interest, and that too, when he desires, yea, when he is exerting all his powers to possess it. For we still believe every rational man believes religion to be for his highest interest. We also believe that every sober-minded man knows whether he possesses it or not; that he knows also that vice is the cause of the uneasiness he

feels and that he is fully convinced that religion would relieve him of his uneasiness. How then can his will determine against it?

6. Now I believe it does not thus determine. I contend that *will*, instead of being against or being averse to walking the paths of wisdom, is in favor of it; that will, instead of being opposed to God, as too many theologians dream, is often the only friend left him in the human heart. The Christian world have here fallen into a gross mistake. In their zeal against sin, in their declamations against human depravity, they have divested the heart of every principle which is commendable and have described the powers of the mind as well as of the body without a single exception as enlisted in the service of Satan, as determined to dethrone Jehovah; and as resolved to trample everything bearing a mark of holiness in the dust. But this is all mere declamation. The language of Paul, in the chapter to the Romans, to which we have already referred, should make them blush for this ignorance and want of attention to the oracles of Truth. Paul, assuming the character of the unbeliever, says the "good *I* would," that is, the good which *I*, the intellectual man, my reason or judgement or will, "would do, I do not, but the evil I, the inner or intellectual man, would not, that I do." "I find then," continues the apostle, "a law, that when I would do good, evil is present with me; for I delight in the law of God after the inward man. But I see another law in my members, warring against the law of my mind, and bringing me into captivity to the law of sin which is in my members" [Rom. 7:18-23]. Some I know suppose Paul was here speaking of a man after regeneration, but of this there is no proof, and his adding immediately, "O wretched man that I am! Who shall deliver me from the body of this death?" [Rom. 7:24] seems to imply that it was a person unacquainted with the salvation wrought in the soul of the believer by Christ. If the Christian is subject to death, or if a man who is "born again," is crying for deliverance in this manner, I would not give much for his Christianity nor for his new birth. But that Paul was speaking of the unbeliever is made still more clear from the following verse, "I thank God that I am delivered through Jesus Christ our Lord. Do I myself then as a slave, serve with the mind, the law of God, but with the flesh the law of sin? By no means" [Rom. 8:25].[1]

7. The difficulty is now before us. The ways of wisdom are ways of pleasantness; mankind see them, desire to walk in them. What is the reason they do not? I believe this question, difficult as it may

---

[1]   (See Kneeland's translation which makes the sense clear and plain.) [Ed. Brownson refers here to Abner Kneeland's *The New Testament* (Philadelphia: Abner Kneeland, 1823), a translation a number of Universalists used.]

seem, can be answered. If we mark clearly, we shall discover quite an army of appetites and passions which overwhelm the reason, judgement or will and carry it away captive. These appetites and passions fasten upon their objects and demand immediate gratification. They are so noisy and impetuous in their demands that the voice of reason is overpowered and put to silence. The person is like a feeble bark destitute of chart or rudder, abandoned to the mercy of the raging ocean, and every moment in danger of being engulfed or dashed against the rocks. But it may be asked, what are these appetites or passions, whence do they derive their power? And if they are able to take reason and judgement captive, how can we avoid the slavery of vice to which they subject us?

8. To enumerate these appetites and passions is not the business of the preacher, but of the metaphysician; and we shall not now encroach upon his prerogative. Every man may easily understand what I mean by them. When a man has an appetite for ardent spirits, he is apt to indulge it when reason bids him forbear. And when this appetite becomes strong and urgent he indulges it even when he wills or determines to abstain. Everyone is sensible that when he gets very angry, the passion of anger overpowers his reason and he often does that which he bitterly regrets when it subsides. So probably of all appetites or passions of which we are susceptible. But whence do they derive their power?

9. This question has led to many disputes and given rise to many theories by no means favorable to virtue. Some, fond of any excuse, blame poor nature at a most unmerciful rate and say that all is owing to the peculiarities of our organic structure. That is, we are so made, the workman who manufactured us mingled the various ingredients in such irregular proportions that our constitution is the cause of all the evils which flow from our wild and ungovernable appetites and passions. This may be true; but, though it would exonerate us from all blame, it is not a very comfortable thought; for all the irregularities of which we complain, arising from our very natures, must be inevitable, and as we can hardly hope to change our natures, we must expect always to endure whatever evils they bring in their train. And, if we should admit it to be true, we should only, perhaps, have to call the most vicious man the most virtuous. For he that is the most vicious is so only because he has the most unfavorable constitution, and having to struggle against the heaviest load, he has tried probably the hardest to be good and should be rewarded according to his exertion and not according to what he has actually accomplished. A man has done well, that is nothing. He had no difficulties to encoun-

ter; his constitutional bias was in his favor and led him naturally by its influence to the performance of his duty. The vicious man has done bad. True; but then, poor man! He tried to do better, but his constitution was so perverse, he could not. He must be judged by the hardness with which he tried to be good. I always suspect those philosophers who attribute their imperfections to the perverseness of nature or the unfavorableness of their constitutional organization. It is a short way of removing a difficulty and of exonerating one's self, but not very proper.

10. But some are so very grateful to their heavenly Father, as to give him the credit of giving our appetites and passions this undue strength. He, having determined to exhibit all his attributes, resolved, as the best means of doing it, that all should become sinners, that he might convince them that he was merciful by saving a few and make them *feel* he was powerful by damning all the rest. He, therefore, very wisely, as Piscator,[2] an eminent divine of the Calvinistic church well observes, "created man to this two-fold end, that he should sin necessarily that he might be damned justly." But, notwithstanding this idea has many benefits and is "full of sweet comfort" to the elect, I am inclined to think it is not very honorable to God, nor very consoling to the greater part of mankind. At least, if it excite a hope of a pleasing state of things after death, it is not calculated to do much towards reforming mankind and increasing their happiness while here. It does not become man to charge his faults and sufferings upon Deity. He ought to have the humility to charge them to his own account. But enough, I need not pursue either of these ideas. The first, if admitted, must be a source of aggravation and the second of continual murmuring. We see the pleasant paths of wisdom; we see them adorned with flowers and everything inviting. We earnestly desire to walk them, but these vexatious laws of our nature or the imperfections of our constitution prevent us. This is hard; and it is no better to say the decree of the Almighty keeps us back. Some we see walking them. O how should we like to walk ourselves! But alas! The decree of heaven has *blocked* the way and we must continue in sin that we may be "damned justly." Not much consolation from such information.

11. But whence do they derive their power? This is easy enough answered. But we shall admit there is some difference in the constitution of different persons. Different temperaments no doubt dis-

---

[2] [Ed. Johannes Piscator (Latin for Fischer, 1546-1625) was a Calvinist theologian and professor at Strasbourg who became a pronounced Arminian at the end of his teaching career.]

pose the constitution to one pursuit, and may give favor to one set of appetites and passions rather than to another. But it will be found that habit is the demon. Habit, improper habits are what give the appetites and passions the power to run away with our reason and bring us in bondage to the law of sin and death. Such is our constitution that when we become habituated to any pursuit or when our mind has become biased in favor of any particular object, no after conviction, no reason of the judgement, no determination of the will has power to correct the error, but we are driven by a force we cannot control into the vortex of ruin or are lost in inevitable destruction. A temperate man takes a glass, now and then; the practice becomes habitual; the glass is more frequently taken, and the man who determined to preserve his character for sobriety, insensibly and involuntarily ends in a drunkard. So of almost any vice we may name.

12. But perhaps I may be allowed to enlarge upon this. Few persons are aware of the power of habit. Most men are carried along the current of things without reflecting whither they are borne or whither they are likely to land. An improper bias, given to the mind by the levity or indiscretion of the parent or instructor gives rise to a course of action, which, becoming habitual, determines the future character of the individual. Perhaps almost unknown to ourselves, we may nourish with maternal fondness some principle thus incautiously implanted, which may one day overwhelm us with ruin and disgrace. How many have started in life with the fairest prospects to themselves and with the brightest expectations to their friends! Their hearts were open, generous and humane. They bid fair to honor themselves and be benefactors to those with whom they were connected. Society with the warmest affection received them into its bosom, reposed the fullest confidence in their prudence and integrity; while everything seemed to rivet the conviction that they were traveling the direct road to virtue, to happiness and to honorable distinction. But alas! They stopped suddenly in the midst of their course; their sun set at noon; oblivion snatched them from our sight.

13. But have we ability to resist the power of habit? It may not be impossible, but it is extremely difficult for persons to shake off the power of habit and return to virtue when they have long been fixed in a course of vicious aberration. "Can the Ethiopian change his skin or the leopard his spots? Then may ye also do good that are accustomed to do evil" [Jer. 13:23]. Though we may at first grant no great indulgence to appetite and passion; though for a while we keep the path of virtue in our sight to which we are determined to return after we have made a few excursions for pleasure, we have the mortifica-

tion to discover one compliance paves the way for another; the fault once committed is committed again with less reluctance; the indulgence is extended; the practice becomes confirmed; the habit fixed and appetite has acquired a power next to impossible to subdue. The downward progress is rapid. We rush on with fatal impetuosity; we leap the precipice of destruction; and when completely ruined, look up with pain to the height from which we have fallen and wish, but vainly wish, to return! And alas! Generally the remainder of life must be made up of regrets the most painful and of remorse the most poignant for our past folly and temerity. It is then the grey-headed victim of improper habit, with one foot in the grave, and his frame tottering with age and debility, with his mind shrinking from the past and trembling with apprehensions for the future, exclaims, in almost the hollow voice of the tomb, "shun my example; avoid my track, it is the road of infamy; its end is death!" Can we avoid it?

14. I cannot bring myself to answer this question in the negative. Severe indeed would be our condition if habit had the liberty to fasten her chains, inflict her torture, and we have no power to resist or to defend ourselves. I cannot believe that Deity has subjected us to a condition so servile. He has given too many proofs of his goodness to allow his creatures to adopt a conclusion so dishonorable to him or so despondent to ourselves. The power must be lodged in the hands of men; but as the individual is not wholly culpable for the formation of improper habits, it is evident they have not always in their individual character the power to shake them off. This power is no doubt in the possession of community; and if the whole body could be persuaded to exercise it, vice would be abolished and virtue established. Most moralists have committed a fatal error on this subject. They generally make the *individual* culpable for all his vices, and have accordingly required the individual to reform. This is not correct; the vices of the individual are generally the vices of the age in which he lives, or of the particular persons or circumstances with whom he associates or with which he is surrounded. Habits are generally derived from a variety of causes which are unperceived by the individual and become confirmed before one is aware of their destructive tendency. To avoid them is the true method, to break their chain is difficult if not impossible. Mankind have no natural desire to be vicious. Everyone loves virtue and were it not for the improper bias which perhaps at a very tender age is given his mind; were it not that his injudicious education or the peculiar circumstances of his youth or of his late years have thrown him into a channel so broad

and so deep that he cannot leave it, he would always walk in the ways of wisdom. What shall be done?

15. Much can and much must be done before society will observe the pleasant ways of wisdom to walk in them. "Train up a child in the way he should go and when he is old he will not depart from it" [Prov. 22:6], is a maxim founded in experience as well as in revelation, and one too, which has never been known to fail when judiciously followed. But it is one which often requires greater knowledge as well as prudence and caution on the part of parents than they are in general qualified to exercise. We must begin by raising the standard of education. We must go back, mark the course taken by our predecessors; we must study to discover their errors, and in the system we adopt, we must aim to avoid them. We must study to enlighten the great body of the community and must contrive some way or other to get the force of habit on the side of wisdom. Habit is as firm a friend as it is a bitter enemy. It is just as easy to have habit in our favor, as it is to have it against us. All that is requisite is that we start right. Mankind in the infancy of the world were themselves infants. They were then ignorant of the ways of wisdom, knew not good from evil, until bitter experience taught them. They would then have returned, but alas! Cherubim and flaming swords guarded the tree of life, and they were destined to wander over the earth and select the healing balm from the vast variety of trees and plants which were thickly sown over its face. Having no criterion by which to distinguish the good from the bad, the false from the genuine until the effect determined, they committed a multitude of errors, which have continued to be committed over and over again by their posterity ever since. We must begin as it were *de novo*. We must begin with a strict inquiry what there is in our present system of things which is incompatible with virtue; also what there is which is good. This is no trifling inquiry. We must trace back each to its origin, point out its effects; if good, unite in embracing it; if bad, throw it away. In this inquiry we must not be guided by theory, but by experience, which we must consider an infallible test. Brethren, the magnitude of this work may seem discouraging. But if we cannot perform the whole let us perform what we can; be cautious what we teach our children and be strictly on our guard lest they imbibe some pernicious habit which will forever debar them from the paths of wisdom and virtue.

15.

A SERMON. ON FAITH
AND ITS CONSEQUENCES

The Gospel Advocate and Impartial Investigator
7 (February 7, 1829): 33-36

*He that believeth and is baptized shall be saved, but he that believeth
not shall be damned.*   Mark 16:16.

Most religionists depend on faith and estimate the worth of a
man's character from the firmness with which he believes certain
notions, and from the zeal and perseverance with which he labors to
support and extend them. From time immemorial it has been deemed
absolutely essential to the holiness of one's life that he believes what
his spiritual guides tell him is the will of God, and that he embrace
with all the ardor of his soul certain propositions relative to the unknown being called God, and to an unknown world called heaven or
hell. One's faithfulness in all matters of trust, his rigid justice in giving everyone his dues, his tenderness to the feelings and consciences
of those with whom he is associated, his readiness to relieve the distressed, to soothe the afflicted soul, and bind up the broken heart,
his general benevolence which leads him to do good unto all men as
he has opportunity, together with high attainments, or great mental
endowments, avail nothing in the estimation of the pious, if he do
not also embrace, as the one thing needful, the creed which from its
popularity is denominated orthodox or sound doctrine.

This sentiment, supported by however respectable authority, has
had the most injurious effect on man individually, and on society
collectively. Supported by it, the priest has bound a "threefold cord"
around the hearts of those who looked to him for direction, which
has irresistibly drawn them to support his interest at the expense of
their own and other's good. By it, he has produced a servile and im-
becile disposition of mind, as deleterious to society generally as it is
degrading to the individual. Authorized by this sentiment, the professed man of God has vented his own wrath and hurled anathemas
of the Almighty against the peaceable, the moral and apparently the
most benevolent and humane members the community can boast;

has torn society asunder, spread ruin and moral desolation, and converted the otherwise happy world into a miniature picture of what he, following his gloomy imagination, painted as the eternal abode of the damned.

This sentiment, this idea that one's holiness depends on his faith and not on his works, has fostered spiritual pride, made him who fancied himself sound in doctrine feel himself superior to those who were so unfortunate as to believe differently though their conduct was in the highest degree useful to the world. It has elevated him in his own conceit and induced him, standing upon the pinnacle of his imagined dignity, to look down with contempt upon his superiors in virtue and exclaim, "Stand by, I am more righteous than you." It has given respectability to the knave and clothed the hypocrite with sanctity. It has furnished a mask for the villain and enabled the most abandoned, the most profligate and the most vile, to triumph over the wisest and best, and to have their names enrolled in the registers of heaven and themselves to be canonized as saints for the worship and imitation of mankind.

This sentiment and its necessary appendage that no one can hope for happiness in the world to come who is not orthodox in his creed is that which has kindled the flame of persecution, which has fired the zeal of the holy warriors and armed them with fury against those deemed heretical in their faith. It is that which enveloped the Middle Ages in thick darkness, relieved only by the fires which consumed the wretched victims of clerical rage. It is that which erected the Inquisition and confined thousands in its cells, which tore the husband from the arms of his wife, the son from the embrace of his father, the daughter from the affection of her mother, and burned them for the glory of God and the good of souls.

It is this sentiment, now advocated by almost everyone who pretends to religion, that severs the cords of fraternal affection, alienates the hearts of kindred, that destroys mutual confidence, and produces most of that bitterness, hostility, backbiting and defamation which now rage to such an alarming extent, and which are so deeply regretted by every benevolent soul.

From every quarter we hear the confused roar of religious discord and contention. Society weeps the injury she receives from this fundamental error. Virtue stands aghast, honesty calls in vain for admission, and humanity, or the disposition of heart which would lighten the load of common misery and irradiate our countenances with the smile of felicity, is compelled to shed her tears in secret and breathe her prayers to the winds. A merciless demon, who quaffs with joy the blood of heretics, who laughs at the widow's tears and mocks the orphan's just complaint, reigns as god and commands the homage of the deluded multitude.

"Believe or you will be damned," "*believe or you will be damned to all eternity*," is the watchword of the spiritual corps. "Believe or you will be damned," is the text, is the beginning, is the middle and end of every sermon, which orthodoxy, in frantic rage, thunders from her ten thousand desks, and "you are blasphemers of God," "enemies to all good and revilers of everything holy," are the honorable epithets you will receive from her charity, if you have the audacity to question the correctness of her assertion.

And what is worse, vain man, weak, presuming man, pretends all this is done by the command and for the glory of God! Impious wretch! Dost thou think thou art obeying the command or adding to the glory of God when thou art destroying the happiness of his children? And thinkest thou the God of heaven, the God of nature, Creator and upholder of an infinitude of worlds and of beings, regards thy opinion, brother of the worm and offspring of the clay? Of what weight is thy opinion, poor vain thing, in the great scale of Wisdom? And how much importance to Omniscience, thinkest thou, will be thy opinion, whose feeble knowledge scarce spreads an inch around? And thou wouldst murder thy brother, and damn his soul forever merely because he does not happen to believe as thou dost? This is obeying the command of God? This is adding to the glory of God? Go, groveling creature, lick dust with the serpent, but raise not thy eyes to the sun lest the impartiality of his rays which give light and warmth alike to the believer and to the unbeliever should reprove the contractedness of thy notions and the intolerance of thy feelings! Mark not the falling shower nor the universal supply which nature yields for all her children lest thy soul should breathe a purer air, and thy mind be compelled to acknowledge "the Lord is good unto all and his tender mercies are over all his works" [Ps. 145:9].

Alas! nature is discarded, the voice of reason is made dumb before implicit reliance, and ancient prejudice, recited by the priest, overpowers every consideration which might tend to enlighten the mind, enlarge its views and make it think more honorably of God and more benevolently of men. The Bible is quoted, and presumptuous man would feign make the voice of God bear witness to that which if true would make Deity worse than the imaginary king of hell, and creation but a proof of his wrath and malignity. God cannot reveal, he cannot say that which would destroy the happiness of his creatures. God never did and never can, if he be a being of goodness, command any man to destroy the happiness or the life of another; nor can he be glorified by the cruelty and intolerance of his children. But here comes in my text as a supposed refutation of what I advance: "He that believeth and is baptized shall be saved, but he that believeth not shall be damned" [Mark 16:16].

Grant this text means what popular sentiment contends: that it plainly declares that all who do not believe on the Lord Jesus in this life, shall be eternally damned in the world to come; grant this and look at the consequences, yes weep for the consequences. Go to the Indian, bowing before his Brahma; to the Thibetian, adoring his god Lama; threaten him with eternal woe, if he does not bow before your Lord Jesus, and believe what he has taught; go tell him this, and mark his sarcastic reply: "Who is this Jesus? Why you have some new god. His name, his character and his doctrine, are equally unknown to us; and this is his disposition to damn all who do not believe his doctrine whether they have ever seen him, heard him, or heard of him, or not?" Justify your sentiment, ye would-be saints, in the eyes of enlightened reason, or be silent.

Shall the heathen, who have followed the light vouchsafed for them by nature's God, be eternally damned because they have not believed what they never heard? And you would, ye wise ones of the earth, boast of the compassion of your Savior; you would call your God good and yet have us believe the heathen—the old, the young, the middle-aged, and infants—will be eternally damned because they have not performed an impossibility! You would convince us of the mercy and loving kindness of God by exhibiting for our amusement the picture of mothers with their infants, wives and their husbands burning in a lake of fire, writhing with anguish, begging for help, but in vain; while God mocks, angels laugh, and saints clap their hands with joy, and shout hallelujah? And *this* you would persuade us is justice? JUST! To burn the tender infant, to overwhelm the mother with keener anguish at the misery of the loved one of her bosom, and burn herself too, because forsooth she has not believed what she has never heard, nor never has had an opportunity of hearing! Gracious heaven! When will men think of thee as they ought!

You need not go to the heathen to find those that shall be damned, if this sentiment be true. Look on thy infant, fond mother. O, I know it is dear to thy heart. Thou has depicted on it its cheek all its father's greatness, and all its mother's loveliness. It smiles. I see thee hug it closer to thy bosom while all the mother burns within thee. That infant shall be torn from thy bosom, snatched from thy arms. It shall be plunged into a lake of fire and thou will see it! *Thou* wilt see its hands, its feet, its body swell with pain: those eyes, on which thou are now looking, thou will see start out with anguish: Those lips, thou art kissing them now, will call, *call*, CALL in vain for a mother's voice and the maternal kiss to soothe its pain and lull it to rest. Yes, *thou* wilt see this, and if thou dost not believe thou wilt, thou shalt burn there thyself.

This is not all: every man, every woman and every child are at some period or other in their lives, unbelievers; all unbelievers must be eternally damned: all without exception then must burn eternally in that lake of fire! Weep, O heaven! And clothe thyself in sackcloth, O earth! Death eternal, death universal, shall prey upon the human race. Jehovah has failed in his design; Christ has died in vain, saints have prayed with fruitless breath, and the whole race of man have lived and toiled for nought! Why this sad catastrophe? Because we have not done that which we could not do. We have not believed without hearing or having evidence to convince our understandings that what we hear is true.

I cannot look upon this painful result and persuade myself that those whose sentiments inevitably lead to it are aware of the fact. They feel vexed that their neighbors do not believe like themselves and actuated by this vexation, they suppose God has the same feeling, and having also the power, will damn these wretches to all eternity. But let them forget this vexation and look calmly at the subject; and ask themselves if they believe that the sun which shines over our heads and shoots his transcendent beams upon our earth is a ball of ice? Suppose some superior being should command them to believe the sun is a ball of ice and threaten them with an eternal hell if they did not, could they believe any more on that account? They could not. Suppose the same or some other being should command them to believe that light does not follow the appearance of the sun in the east and should threaten them with an eternal hell if they believed that it did, could they believe differently from what they do now? They could not. What then is faith?

Faith is the assent of the mind to the truth of some proposition. If the proposition be made in terms the mind can understand, accompanied with evidence enough to convince it the proposition is true, it believes and it cannot help believing. Under any other circumstances we do not believe. We may say we believe, but we do not, we cannot. There is then no merit in faith or in believing, nor demerit in disbelieving. To save a man then for believing is saving him for doing that which he cannot help or which he could not have avoided, and if one is damned for not believing, he is damned for not doing that which he could not do, a course of conduct I dare not ascribe to my Father and my God.

Hence the mistake of those who expect eternal felicity in the kingdom of heaven as the reward for their having believed. Faith is not the thing which merits eternal salvation, and are we able to believe that we shall be rewarded with eternal life for that in which there is no merit, or that we shall be eternally damned for not having that which is deserving nothing, which also has no merit? The religious world continues to cry, "*believe*!" "The devils believe and tremble" [James 2:19]. Are they any the better for that? The religious world are expecting eternal life as the reward for their believing. Scripture asserts, "eternal life is the gift of God" [Rom. 6:23]. Let them read and understand. God has *given* us eternal life, and this life is in his Son (see 1 John 5:11). Let those who call themselves his favorites, beware how they charge him with falsehood.

What then is the meaning of our text? Simply this: Christ commanded his disciples to go into all the earth and preach the glad tidings of the reign of God unto every creature; he or any one that should believe or have confidence in the declaration or doctrine proclaimed should be saved, or should be cured or freed from sin; but he that should not, would be condemned or remain in condemnation, for everyone that is not in Christ, or that has no confidence in his doctrine, is condemned. But there is no condemnation to them that are in Christ Jesus. Hence they are saved from their sins, from the bondage in which they were through death; hence they are free.

The text is plain. It states a simple fact, what would be the consequence of preaching the gospel; and that it is a fact, interrogate experience: go to the disbeliever of the gospel, and what is his situation. You may see him shrinking from the presence of a God he fears but cannot love. He is conscious he has done wrong, sensible he has wandered from his God and that his affections are alienated from his heavenly Father, and he therefore fancies that God hates him. He is wandering in the mazes of ignorance, wretched and despondent. He dare not look to God for he paints him in the gloomy imagination a being, powerful, armed with vengeance, delighting to hurl his forked lightnings at his offending children and determined to pursue with infinite wrath until he sinks them to the nethermost hell. The poor sinner is convinced of the folly of his course; he knows no sublunary arm on which he can lean and find support; he fears to look to his God, through dread that deeper misery awaits him there.

Wretched is the condition of him who does not know Jehovah as revealed by Christ, the common Father and the common Friend. He cannot enjoy himself with society for his vices have destroyed their confidence. He trembles at every thought of death for he knows not what "dreams may come" in that world which he must enter. He starts back from the grave, fears eternal woe, or the cold, unending sleep of non-entity may be his doom. Hence he lives in perpetual bondage through fear of death.

The believer is made free. "Inasmuch as the children were made partakers of flesh and blood, he [Jesus] took part of the same, that through death he might destroy him that hath the power of death, that is the devil, and deliver them who all their lifetime were subject to bondage through fear of death" [Heb. 2:14-15]. This Christ has done by bringing life and immortality to light, by assuring us, though we die we shall live again, and because our Savior lives we shall live also. The soul, the moment this is believed, is freed from the bondage under which it before groaned. It no longer looks upon death as a curse but as the gate through which it must pass to enter the kingdom of its God and the apartment of its felicity. The corroding power of conscience is destroyed, sin is ended; righteousness reigns in the soul and all is peace and full of delight. God is no longer feared as a tyrant, no longer avoided as an enemy, but loved as a Father, a Friend, a faithful Friend, and bountiful Benefactor. If affliction comes across the soul, if the world be unkind, he can draw pleasure from himself and consolation from the confidence he has in divine protection.

The Christian who has made himself acquainted with God, who has learned from Christ that God is his Savior, that God will redeem him from the corruption of this world to enjoy a heaven of bliss, is happy, has a *present* salvation of which the unbeliever is deprived. This is the salvation spoken of in our text, and is a salvation which comes by faith, is the consequence of faith, not its reward. It is great, it is glorious; the soul thus saved, only knows how great and how joyous! O, the Christian knows and he would not part from it for worlds. It calms our fears, calls into exercise the noblest and the best feelings of our nature, and prepares us for the highest degree of enjoyment of which we are susceptible in this mode of being.

But the unbeliever is condemned, not indeed because he does not believe but because his deeds are evil. He has not that confidence in God requisite to call forth the virtuous principles of his nature. Knowing not the goodness of God, he is destitute of one of the most powerful inducements to reformation. He therefore plods on in his wickedness, verifying the assertion that "the way of the transgressor is hard" [Prov. 13:15] that there is no peace to the wicked, but they are like the troubled sea when it cannot rest, whose waters cast up mire and dirt" [Isa. 57:20-21].[1] His condemnation is what he suffers *here*, not what he may suffer hereafter. If he is wicked, it is not because he does not believe, but because he does not perform acts of righteousness; and if he is unhappy, it is not a punishment for his disbelief, but because he is destitute of that consciousness of his own integrity and virtue, and of that confidence in God which are necessary to produce his happiness. Beware of unbelief, not because it is criminal, but because you will thus lose a powerful stimulant to virtue. Cultivate faith in the Lord Jesus, not because faith is meritorious, but because it will have a tendency to make you more virtuous. May God grant us all that confidence in truth which shall make us all happy and virtuous.

---

[1] [Ed. Brownson quotes as if the citations were consecutive.]

16.

AN ESSAY ON DIVINE GOODNESS

The Gospel Advocate and Impartial Investigator
7 (February 7, 1829): 38-39

Mankind are often timorous creatures. They are afraid to hear anything advanced contrary to their own preconceived notions. I must, however, ask my readers not to be startled at anything I may advance in the following essay for it is my design to elucidate and defend the goodness of God from all the objections which have been urged against it. But I shall commence by stating these objections in all their strength and in all the force I am able to give them. We pay a poor compliment to the truth when we misrepresent or ridicule her opponent. To reason fairly is to give to the arguments on each side all the strength and all the cogency of which they are susceptible. I shall urge the objections to the goodness of God, give all these objections all the color of truth to which they can pretend and also do my best to remove them.

It is not necessary for me to attempt to prove the existence of some superior Being or some mighty Energy which pervades the whole of nature and enables it to perform its various operations. For the existence of such Being or of such Energy is sufficiently evident to everyone who will make use of his senses and exert his own understanding. But what this being is as to his essence or substance of his existence we know not; we cannot ascertain, therefore it is useless to inquire. How this being exists we know not and his physical connection with the universe it is impossible for us to explain. We can affirm nothing of the secret power which is everywhere to work for we know nothing. All we can affirm is that we see various events transpire and various changes in the natural world constantly taking place; that the mind is variously affected with joy or sorrow, with love or hatred, with pleasure or pain, all which we believe are the result of some cause. All we can do is to analyze the various effects we discover in the world of matter, and the various emotions, passions, and affections of which we perceive the mind susceptible, and to trace all these to the immediate, to the remotest antecedent in our power, and there rest our inquiry and stay our investigation. We can state the phenomena which have presented themselves to our observation, but whence they originated or upon what external power they depend is more than we can from the exercise of those powers we find allotted us in a single instance ascertain.

Nature is. Nature is wonderful. Wonderful because we know not how it came or how it is supported. We see that something exists. We cast our eyes abroad, behold a world ordained with everything that can fascinate, and filled with everything pleasing to the senses and gratifying to desire, we look, lost in admiration, we ask "whence came this beautiful, this magnificent fabric?" Accustomed to attribute everything we see to some cause, which precedes its existence, we accordingly at once infer that the world owes its origin to some cause which has produced it.

But so great, so beautiful and so systematically arranged is the universe that we easily conclude the cause producing it must be powerful and intelligent. I believe this conclusion correct but I do not *know* it. The world is; this is all I know. I have never seen its beginning nor do I know it will ever have an end. We may believe what we think we have evidence to believe; but whether the world had a beginning or will have an end, or not, is more than *human* knowledge can tell.

I make these remarks not because I intend pursuing the difficult questions which they excite but merely to awaken the attention of my readers to their own powers, and also that they may learn their own weakness. Man should ascertain his own strength, should know his own weakness, that he may not remain inactive nor attempt to scan subjects which must forever baffle his power to grasp.

I said it was not necessary for me to attempt to prove the existence of an Overruling Power. It is not because my readers do not doubt his existence. If they did doubt his existence I should not attempt to prove it, because I do not feel myself adequate to the task. I believe in the existence of a God; but I do not believe it because I think *nature* sufficient to teach his existence, but because I believe he has revealed himself to the world in his word.

Many a sincere Christian believes he can prove from *nature* the existence of a God. He may, but I cannot. What is nature? Nature is whatever is. It is the universe, with all its furniture of worlds, with all its inhabitants, with all the force and laws by which the whole is governed. Nature can prove nothing separate from itself; and should it prove the existence of a God, that God would either be nature or a part of nature. This is the same as atheism. The Deity, according to the notions of all intelligent theists, is independent of the universe. He existed "Omnific and alone." Now nothing we can see teaches this. The universe cannot teach this, for it cannot travel out of itself, and travel out of itself it must to prove that a being existed before it and still exists independent of it.[1]

I believe there is a God; but I take my belief from Scripture. Or rather Scripture affirms his existence, and nature assures me the existence of such a being clearly accounts for the existence of the objects I admired. One difficulty is removed. I know how the universe came; revelation has told me, hence its importance. My views are enlarged. I do not indeed know the whole, but I have learned a part. I am told there is a God who made the world. How he came, indeed, is not told. But say he was; there never was a time when he was not. Something must have always been or nothing would now be. The supposition of the existence of a God removes one difficulty, answers one question: how did the world come? And if it proposes another which it does not answer, it is attended with less difficulty; for it is easier to suppose the eternal existence of such a being, than it is to suppose that what we every day see changing and varying its form, if not its qualities, has been from eternity.

I rest the existence of God on this. I see nothing in nature which appears able to originate the idea of a God in my mind. But since revelation has informed me there is a God, everything in nature bears testimony to its truth. Revelation originates the idea, nature *proves* it, but could not of itself have taught it.

Taking it for granted on the authority of revelation that God is, the most important question which can occur is, what is he? Or, what is his character? This question is important, and we design to answer it; not indeed what God is as to his essence or the substance of his existence but what is his character, or what his mode of dealing with his creatures, good or bad.

All Christians, and indeed all theists, however illegitimate their conclusions, answer with one voice, "God is good." This is the assertion of our text and no one who believes in a God feels any disposition to contradict it. But is he good? The existence of evil presents itself as a prominent objection to the goodness of our heavenly Father. I take it for granted that Deity is infinite in wisdom and in power. The Bible declares this to be a fact, and none who believe that will question the position. Evil seems an imperfection. Pain is not a proof of perfection; and the fact that there is so much misery in the world seems a strong proof that the world is imperfect. But why did

[1] [Ed. *The New York Gospel Herald* 1 (March 28, 1829): 110-11 objected to this argumentation and on the basis of it charged that Brownson was becoming a "secret agent in the cause of infidelity."]

a being possessed of infinite wisdom and of infinite power make an imperfect world, unless he designed that it should be a miserable one? If he designed it a miserable one he is not good, for no good Being designs misery or evil. But if the idea that this is an imperfect world be denied, and it be said that it is perfect, it is still worse; for then we must say, it is just such a world as Deity designed it; and, as it produces misery, we must say he designed it, consequently he is not good.

(March 21, 1829): 87-89

There is no doubt evil in the world. But, because there is evil, I am not disposed to deny there is also good in the world. I detest that sickly disposition, that pitiable state of the brain that wastes itself in groans and shrieks, which can see nothing but misery and do nothing but exclaim, "Ah me! How wretched is the world! All is vanity, undeserving a wish or a thought!" The world is valuable. It affords much pleasure, many hours of enjoyment, and doubtless might be made to afford many more. The mountain of human misery may rise before us to impede our path. We are not to stand trembling at its base, vainly expecting some miracle or some convulsion of nature to remove it. Our industry must surmount it or level it with the plain.

I have said there is evil in the world. No one who can see, hear or feel, can have any doubts of the fact. The only question which ought to occupy our attention is how can we remove it, or how can we preserve ourselves from its destructive ravages? But mankind are not satisfied with this simple question, nor with the labor it would require them to perform. They have asked, they are impatient to know, how evil came, and how God can be good in admitting it into his system, or in permitting it to remain after once admitted. Wisdom never asked these questions, but since they are asked, wisdom requires us to return the best answer in our power.

"God is good," it is said; how happens it then that there is evil in the world? There is much in the world which appears to us useless or worse than useless, productive of pain, severe in degree, and often long in duration. Can a God of infinite Goodness be the author of this?

"We make ourselves miserable," it is said. This assertion, with some qualification, is doubtless true. But what are we? Have we anything we have not received? Whence then the power to make ourselves miserable? From God? What then is the difference? God makes us miserable; he gives us the power to make ourselves miserable? Would the father who loved his child give him the means of destruction? And can it be a proof of goodness in God to give us the means of destroying ourselves? There is no difference whether God makes us miserable directly, or puts into our hands the power, and we, in the exercise of that power, make ourselves miserable. The chain has an additional link, but, in one case as well as in the other, has one end fastened on Deity and the other on man.

But man is not the only being that suffers. The earth is covered, the air and the water are filled with sentient beings. For as our knowledge extends, wherever there is sensation there is pain. The beast, the bird, the fish, the insect, suffer as well as man. Animal feeds on animal through the whole of nature. Man destroys everything. He tramples upon the insect world, and at every step crushes a multitude of little beings. He takes the life of larger beings for his food or his sport, and even of his brother to gratify his avarice, his ambition or his revenge. "The whole creation groaneth and travaileth in pain" [Rom. 8:22], is this all owing to man? Some maybe, but much he cannot prevent, if indeed he can any. Why was the world subject to this?

"The world is cursed for the transgression of man," say those who dream of nothing but maledictions from God, and whose consciences sting with remorse. But why? Man may have sinned, but why punish the harmless brute? Why doom every grade of being to wretchedness for man's transgression?

Misery may be called the punishment of transgression, but not in every case. Sin, no doubt, brings misery. It would not be sin if it did not. But does sin kindle the subterranean fires, bursting in volcanoes to sweep off thousands of all ages and sexes who are innocent? Does sin produce the earthquake, cause the ground to open, and swallow whole cities in sudden destruction? Is it sin which forbids the ocean to send forth its vapors, the rain to fall, and prevents the earth from yielding its accustomed supply? Does sin wing the pestilence, and carry indiscriminate death to the guilty and to the innocent?

Questions innumerable like these might be asked, but it is useless. Everybody knows there is evil in the world. How did it come? Why does a good God allow it to remain?

These are questions which occur to every thinking mind, questions which create our embarrassment, and often lead us to doubt the goodness of God. Look at the subject once more. Everybody must admit that a good Being will not voluntarily produce misery or evil. An Omnipotent Being cannot be compelled to produce it. If God be Omnipotent, and produce it, we have a right to infer he does it voluntarily, from choice. Can he then be good?

Two questions now occur. 1st, Is there evil? 2d, Did God produce it?

The first is already answered in the affirmative. What shall be said to the second? God does either directly or indirectly produce it. How then is he good?

Two considerations may set this subject in a different light.

1st. The evil which now exists may be the result of an organization, which, notwithstanding it produces this result will upon the whole be the cause of a superior degree of happiness sufficient to overbalance the pain which is now suffered.

2d. The present may be considered the infancy of the world, and the evil which we endure is necessarily connected with the imperfect development of its properties, but may serve, under the present constitution of things, to hasten the period of perfectibility.

1st. In all our reasonings we must, in spite of all our dissatisfaction, take things as they are. We cannot unravel creation, disorganize the universe, scatter the whole to its original chaos, and give directions for its reconstruction. Finite man, weak, erring man, need not presume to soar to the seat of Power Creative, and dictate to the Omniscient rules by which to arrange the universe. Deity has made it, or it is made, and all we have to do is to make the best of it. Our inquiry now is, has Deity given in the construction of this system of things, in the organization of matter, in the distribution of animal and intellectual functions, sufficient evidence to warrant the belief that he is benevolent, that he is good to the sentient world.

Evil is of two kinds, moral and physical, or such as flows from the misconduct of moral beings, and such as flows from those parts of nature over which moral beings are supposed to exert little or no control. This distinction may not be very accurate, but it is the one commonly made and is sufficiently accurate for our purpose.

Only moral evil comes under our first consideration. This class needs examination. Man is an active being, but he often acts wrong. This acting wrong brings misery. But the virtuous, or those who obey the laws of God and of man are miserable and often the most miserable. Universalists generally are tenacious of the position that the most virtuous are the most happy, and the most vicious are the most miserable. This position is doubtless correct when set in its proper light, which is not often done. The reasoning most fashionable on this subject would lead us to conclude, the virtuous man is *always* happy, while the vicious man, on the other hand, is always miserable. The last is true, but the first is false.

Nothing is more evident than that the virtuous do suffer. In all national calamities there is little distinction between them and the vicious. In the sack and massacres of cities, in the general operations of war, the innocent and the guilty are involved in the same fate. Scripture asserts, and experience fully proves, that when we see a man deeply distressed we are not thence to infer he is a great sinner. Witness the case of Job; no matter whether the history be true or fictitious. The principle it develops is often found in real life.

Mankind are fond of theories. When they get into their heads a favorite theory, they labor to make all facts bend to its support. The true method is to make theory bend to facts, not facts to theory. It is a fact, the virtuous are often miserable. It is a fact, that a man's apparent suffering affords little evidence of his moral character. Poor consolation indeed it would be to tell a man racked with pain, suffering under heavy afflictions, that all is a just punishment for his sins.

The true state of the case is this; vice, sin, or transgression, always brings misery to the one who is guilty. But the misery does not stop with the guilty. Its destructive force strikes the virtuous as well as the vicious. The crime generally brings misery upon the head of its author, and upon those, too, with whom he is connected, whether innocent or guilty.

(April 18, 1829): 119-20

The man who stabs his rival in the dark, or the one who procures the assassination of his enemy, suffers; [he] is no doubt deeply miserable in consequence of the act. It were well if the suffering ended here. The rival perhaps had his friends; these may weep his death. The enemy may have been a useful member of society; society suffers his loss.

The drunkard destroys his own happiness; destroys his constitution, ruins his health, dooms himself to drag out a loathed existence till he sinks into the grave unhonored and forgotten. But the wretched consequences of his intemperance stop not with himself. He destroys the happiness of a virtuous wife, reduces her and a family of innocent children to want, to beggary and disgrace.

Wars no doubt originate in wickedness. Their authors no doubt suffer; but wars involve the innocent as well as the guilty in their destructive consequences. Sin brings misery. The sinner must always be miserable. But the sin of one man may destroy the happiness of thousands, or had ten thousand been innocent, his sin might have embittered their peace. Moral evil is the result of the misconduct of moral beings. The evil is not confined to him that does the wrong. It extends farther, and generally to all with whom he is connected. Why was such a state of things allowed? Why was man made capable of thus destroying his own and the happiness of those with whom he is connected?

Before answering these questions we must look at man, ascertain what powers and faculties are allotted him, and what is the immediate cause of this destruction of felicity. "The proper study of mankind is man";[2] but we have been attempting to scan Jehovah, when we should have been studying ourselves. We are almost ignorant of the very rudiments of human nature and can affirm but little concerning the principles of human action. One thing however is certain; man is an active being and is capable of doing whatever he wills to do when no external cause prevents.

I am not about to lose myself in the intricate mazes of free will and necessity. I am not enquiring the guilt which may be attached to an individual, or the criminality of our actions in the sight of God. Such an enquiry belongs to another subject. I do not now ask whether man is good or bad in the sight of his Creator, but whether we have reasons sufficient to establish the position that God is good to his creatures. I do not follow the tract of the theologian, but would, if possible, discover one which the philosopher need not blush to pursue.

I said I was not about to lose myself in the intricate mazes of free will and necessity. I am not; and yet I cannot dismiss the subject without remark. Both the advocates of the one and of the other are wrong or are right, just according to the light in which we view their remarks. If we say man has ability to pursue a correct course or always to perform those actions which will bring happiness to himself and others regardless of the circumstances by which he is surrounded, we say wrong. If we say we are doomed by an irreversible law of Fate or predestination to suffer all the misery there is in the world without any ability to remove it, we say wrong. But if we say man is governed by the laws of nature, that is, the various objects with which he is surrounded act upon him, as well as he upon them, we say true. If we say man has the power to improve his condition, to lessen the evils he suffers and to enlarge his enjoyments, we say right.

The doctrine of free will, according to the views of most theologians, is only an imaginary notion, advocated for the purpose of making man guilty before God, to give God the right to punish, and it is upheld because we are fond of blaming those who do not act according to our wishes. In a theological sense, I consider it not only

[2] [Ed. From Pope's *Essay of Man*, 2:1.]

false, but highly pernicious. It becomes a fruitful source of hard feeling and recrimination, and seems to authorize the cruel and arbitrary punishments so often inflicted upon those who do not please us, or upon those who do not bow with servility to one or many ycleped lawgiver or magistrates. We have fostered the notion that man is accountable for his actions; that whenever he does wrong it is through depravity or malice, hence we learn to hate him and pour upon his head the whole of our overflowing vengeance. This is no trifling evil; it is one which stands at the threshold of improvement and forbids entrance.

The doctrine of Fate or predestination is no better. I never could approve of the *fatum* of the Stoics not only because it is generally impracticable but because it seems to tell man "be still, everything is fixed and it is useless to move." One may preach Fate and predestination to an army of ignorant soldiers on the eve of battle, or to a dying man, now no longer able to do anything for himself or for others, but beware how you preach it to him who is capable of exertion and who ought to be engaged in active life.

Say to one depressed by the numerous ills of life that his sufferings are unavoidable; that he must wait till the wheel of Fate revolves, before he can expect relief; tell him this, you augment his misery, destroy all exertion, and sink him in profound indolence to yawn out a wretched existence in the vain expectation that some god may interfere in his behalf and cause the sun of felicity to gild his habitation. Man is made an active being; and it would seem from what we can discover that he is constituted in some measure the artificer of his own fortune. We desire happiness. The immediate cause of our failure is not the stern decrees of Fate nor the maledictions of a malignant Deity. We act, but we act wrong; and this acting wrong is the immediate cause of our misery. Why do we act wrong? If we can discover any means by which we can exonerate Deity from being concerned in this, we may pronounce him good, at least not evil.

There have been various answers given to this question, some of them it will be well to note. "The irreversible laws of Fate or necessity," say one class. But the evil tendency of this answer has been already considered. If we admit it we remove no difficulty. If Deity is superior to Fate, why does he subject us to a monster so cruel and unfeeling? If he is not superior to Fate, then he is not God, or at least according to the notions of all theists. This answer, if admitted, either plunges us in atheism or charges our sufferings upon God. It is therefore rejected.

"The special Providence of God who has foreordained whatsoever comes to pass," say another class. This answer charges our sufferings directly upon God. For, if our acting wrong be the cause of our misery, then God, if he cause us to act wrong, is certainly the cause of our suffering. Where then is his goodness? A good being cannot produce evil, and if God does, he is not good. "But men," the advocates of this notion allege, "do wrong voluntarily. God ordained they should follow their own volitions and be miserable in consequence of following wrong ones." Very well. How came men voluntarily to do wrong? How came they by such dispositions? How came they to have such wills? If a wrong will be the cause of our going wrong, whence derived we this wrong will or what is its cause? Now this system supposes God ordains the means as well as the end. If he ordained one, he must the other on this plan. But had he not so ordered that we should have these bad wills, he might have been greatly disconcerted in his arrangement. The scheme supposes, indeed, the will is free, but it supposes also that God by his providence has molded it to the shape that he wishes.

"God foreordains whatsoever comes to pass." If this be true, then everything takes place according to his appointment. No matter how complicated the machine, no matter how many wheels within wheels, all are necessary and each one must be under his control. If all the results depend upon the motion of a particular wheel, it would be folly to say the maker constructed the whole machine, and yet had no share in the wheel which gives motion to all the rest. All the results according to the plan before us are made certain by the decree of the Almighty, and yet the least deviation or contrary motion of the will would disconcert the whole. The plan is therefore rejected because it makes God the efficient cause of our sufferings.

A third class attribute our acting wrong to the depravity of our wills. This is nearly allied to the one just dismissed. It supposes that our wills are independent; that God will do them no violence. Our wills are wrong, hence we act wrong. We may have another link to our chain, but we have removed no difficulty. How came our wills to be depraved? This answer is none at all. It, under the appearances of assigning a cause, assigns only an effect. It declares acting wrong to be the result of depravity. May I not ask, is not depravity the result of doing wrong? How then can it be the cause? The answer is unsatisfactory. We must have another.

(May 2, 1829): 135-36

A fourth answer to the question, why do men act wrong, attributes it to our ignorance. This answer is one which I have repeatedly urged. But it must be understood with many qualifications or it will mislead.

Love of theory is the greatest enemy to the discovery of truth. Men seem anxious to reduce all things to a few first principles that the cause of everything may be given in a word. This were well, if they knew everything. We know but little and much we do know depends for its existence on that which we do not, which we cannot know. Thousands of events are daily and even hourly occurring, which we are unable to trace to any antecedent or cause. The world is a system of perpetual change; and, though we admit general laws, by which the whole is governed, the number of particulars, which occur as exceptions, are often more numerous than those which follow the general rule. It is, therefore, in vain to expect any one thing can be the cause of that which everything conspires to produce.

Still we may from what we know form some rational conclusions respecting this so much agitated question. I may repeat here, the substance of what I have said in many other places. But it is necessary to a regular discussion, if indeed my rambling sentences can claim that appellation. This, however, is nothing more than what others do. If we told nothing but what we knew and told that but once, we should soon be condemned to uninterrupted silence.

If we may be allowed to figure to our minds the commencement of this world, we may readily suppose that it could be in the first stage of its existence nothing more than an infant just drawing its breath. It would be idle, at least reasoning from analogy, to suppose the infant was wiser or more knowing than the adult. Setting aside the fictions of poets and the dreams of those who are dissatisfied with the present about the golden days of antiquity, when all was peace and holiness, we may pronounce man, when first permitted to breathe upon this "terrestrial ball," an infant and like all infants destitute of knowledge. The tree of knowledge indeed grew within his reach; but as yet its fruit was untouched. The tree of life grew there too but it was unheeded. All the energies of intellect were unawakened, all that mental and moral vigor, which were to exert that mighty influence on the affairs of the world, which we see it has then slumbered in embryo. The seeds of all the passions—which were to germinate, spring up and produce the mighty harvest of every species of fruit— were indeed, planted in the infantile mind; but, as yet were uninfluenced by the vegetating power. Such was man.

His first sensation was want. He was uneasy; he sought to remove his uneasiness. Ignorant, not knowing aliment from poison, unacquainted with the constitution of things, unable to predict the

consequences of his actions, he acted simply from impulse, unguided
by the least ray of light he was equally liable to act wrong as right. He
was like the babe, put everything into his mouth which came in the
way of his hands. If he swallowed a poison he knew no antidote, but
was as likely to swallow another. He took a wrong step, he was lost in
the wilderness, saw no mark that was familiar, none which could
direct to the spot he wished to reach. To rest inactive he could not, to
proceed he must, but ignorant of the way, he would as soon pursue
the wrong as the right path. He proceeded, but instead of following
a straight-forward path, which would have conducted him to a hab-
itable spot, he traversed the wilds in circles and though wearied with
endless exertion, he found himself either returning to the same spot
or wandering still farther into the immeasurable gloom. Such was
undoubtedly the original condition of man, and such the immediate
cause of his first errors and the commission of those acts which involved him in wretchedness.

Admitting what I have here alleged, we may assume the reason
why we go wrong is because we are ignorant. But there is a fact which
stares this theory in the face and which may appear to some an insur-
mountable objection. The fact is, mankind do not, at least when
viewed as individuals, do not do as well as they know. It is not seldom we see a man doing that which he is sensible, in every moment
of reflection, is opposed to his best good. How can this fact be reconciled to the position that ignorance is the cause of our acting wrong?
The solution is easy. Man is a creature of habit. When men are accustomed to any practice, they acquire a habit which makes it often
extremely difficult to avoid it. This principle is one which should not
be overlooked. Man through ignorance went wrong, habit confirmed
him in a course of aberration. He also goes wrong through the influence of others when his own judgment if followed would direct right.
We act upon each other. Commencing wrong we established wrong
principles, gave wrong impressions to each other's mind, a wrong
bias to the minds of children; erected society upon a wrong basis,
hence through the influence of these considerations, we often continue to go wrong when we know better. Ignorance, however, is the
efficient, though habit and the influence of improperly organized
society is the immediate cause.

We have found the cause of moral evil, it is traced to the misconduct of moral beings. We have found the cause of the misconduct of
moral beings, it is ignorance, the imperfect constitution of our nature or rather to the want of experience or necessary knowledge when
we first began to act. But we have removed no difficulty though we

may have prepared the way. Why did a God infinitely good and wise place us here with so little knowledge, liable to all the pains and calamities which proceed from our ignorance? This is the question, and it is the same as to ask, why did God make us as he has? Now I have no right to ask this question and certainly shall not attempt to answer it. We may discover from what has been offered that man is made subject to vanity, is placed here ignorant, and compelled to learn his duty and his felicity in the severe school of experience. Whether God could have made him a different being or not is no concern of mine, since man is made as he is. The only proper inquiry is, has Deity so constructed him that he is capable by the means put into his hands to obtain more good than evil, more happiness than misery? If we can answer this question in the affirmative, we may pronounce our Creator good. If we must reply in the negative, Deity so far as our knowledge extends must be called evil.

Are we susceptible of happiness? Are we able to procure happiness enough to overbalance the evil we suffer? To the first we say yes; to the second I will not reply until further inquiry. We must take the world as it is, for all seems of a piece; and if we make an alteration in one part, without a corresponding one in every other, we disconcert the whole. We suppose, for indeed much of our reasoning on this subject must be hypothetical, that man is fitted to his condition, that Deity in making him gave him those powers and faculties, susceptibilities etc. which should fit him for that particular station he was designed to occupy. Man seems a progressive being, whether viewed in reference to the individual or to the species. Admitting this, we can devise no better plan on which he could have been created; we can propose no alteration in his constituent principles without making him worse.

The question why did Deity permit evil to enter his system is an improper one. We see evil flows as a necessary consequence from the present organization of things. The question why Deity organized nature as he has is improper. We are only to ask, is there more good than evil to be derived from it? This is the question and my next will attempt to answer it. Our love to God will never be strong nor permanent until we are fully convinced he is good; and our love to mankind will not be as it should until we have the most ardent love for the Creator.

(September 19, 1829): 294-95

This has been delayed on account of a press of other matter though perhaps not more interesting, at least from its character demanded a more immediate insertion.

The question now to be answered is an important one. Is there more good than evil in the world? The dreams of the optimist are fascinating; they serve to beguile many a weary hour of its tediousness. But they are dreams. So far as this world is concerned there is evil, evil absolute and often insupportable. Why it was introduced into this system man does not, cannot, know; how it exists, how it prevails he may know and by what means it can be removed or lessened, he ought to know, and must know, before he can be happy.

Is there more good than evil in the world? The question is not easily answered. Who can measure all the painful emotions ever felt? Who can measure the pleasurable ones? Till this is done we must remain ignorant of the true answer. Let the question be varied. Is a world so constituted that man *may* enjoy more happiness than he suffers of evil? This is in fact the important question. This looks back only for instruction, while it looks forward to a more blissful station and points out the way by which it may be obtained.

Evil has originated in our imperfection, it is preserved by the ignorance of mankind, and experience proves it may be destroyed by duly enlightening the mind. Knowledge will dissipate the clouds of sorrow, dispel the shades of misery and light the human race to the fountain of felicity. If this be true man may be more happy than he is miserable; and if this is made to appear, we may pronounce the Creator of the world good in creating it. This is as far as we can go. Nature will never prove the unbounded goodness of God. A survey of nature will prove he is rather good than evil and we must leave it to revelation to prove the extent of his goodness.

To ascertain whether knowledge will make our condition better than it is, let us look again at existing evils. The evils termed physical are few and are not of the most grievous kind. The noxious effluvia of swamps, of stagnant waters, cause diseases; decaying animal and vegetable substances poison the air, infect the lungs, produce sickness and pain. But these swamps may be drained. The hand of industry may remove the stagnant pool and art may guard against the diseases occasioned by the decaying substances mentioned.

We speak of sickness, of colds and fevers. But these are not always owing to changes of the atmosphere nor to the poisonous effluvia floating in the air. They often arise from undue exposures, from excessive labor, from unwholesome diet, and from mere mental agitation. In a well regulated state of society these exposures, these excessive exertions, might be avoided. Experience might determine the most wholesome food and by securing to active industry its just reward, there would be no necessity of eating that which is unwhole-

some. In a well regulated state of society the wants of all might be
satisfied with a moderate share of labor, the wants too, might be
much circumscribed. Hence that painful anxiety of mind, which often ruins the body as well as itself would not be felt; cheerfulness
would always be preserved and with it health.

Sickness is also occasioned by indulgence, by indolence which
destroys the activity of both mind and body and generates disease or
disposes the body to receive it. Intemperance in eating or in drinking
vitiate[s] the stomach, deranges the whole system and hastens disso-
lution. But these may be avoided. Not indeed by merely preaching
against them. We may declaim against vice eternally and be eternally
vicious. But by substituting an innocent gratification for a destructive indulgence. Give the mind some employment in which it can
take interest, or let the hands be engaged in some task which is honorable and useful. Let both mind and body be exercised and these
indulgences will become less and less frequent until they finally disappear.

There is one fruitful source of vice, of misery. It is the wrong
estimation we make of things. It is the misfortune of the world to
prize things in an inverse ratio to their real worth. The most useful
profession is deemed the least respectable and the most worthless,
the most honorable. The badge of labor, of useful labor, which should
be the badge of merit, of distinction, of honor is by the strange perversity of men's taste the badge of degradation. The bloated aristocrat
in his hall of laziness or of vicious indulgence who disdains any useful labor and would think himself degraded by being beneficial, this
bloated, worthless wretch looks with contempt upon the humble
mechanic or the industrious agriculturalist.

This makes those who are of the lower class, as it is improperly
and cruelly named, impatient of their situation, makes them loathe
their labor, anxious to be idle and useless that they may be respectable. This not only leads to crime in the poor classes, but leads to that
idleness and listlessness which are the chief causes of that indulgence,
that pride and those practices which degrade and destroy the more
wealthy and opulent. Having no employment or unable to employ
themselves in any useful occupation, they wear out their lives in im-
moderate eating, drinking, or some kind of intemperance, which
would have been avoided had they deemed it not only innocent but
honorable to cultivate a garden, a farm, to pursue a mechanical profession, or had they obtained a relish for knowledge and been prepared to feast the mind with its fruits. Proper instruction would cor-

rect many of these wrong habits of mind, would give more beneficial instructions. With these institutions we might become happy.

Whoever will look on life as he should will admit we have all the materials we need, we only require to be taught how to use them in order to be happy. We can then exonerate Deity from the charge of a want of goodness. The world is a blessing to us; if it be not it is our fault and not the fault of the one who made it. We may be happy, and doubtless the time will come when all will enjoy themselves.

We have only to take up revelation, where our reason stops, and add inspirations to experience. Life and immortality are brought to life through the gospel. We are taught we shall live again, become the inhabitants of another world where all our doubts shall be removed, where the darkness which now encumbers our vision shall be removed, and we enabled to see the goodness of God shine alike resplendent in what we have suffered and in what we have enjoyed.

To a future life I look for the evidences of the unbounded goodness of God. All may finally terminate in good and the remembrance of our pain may enhance our bliss. As we have discovered we may improve our condition, let us attempt it and wait patiently for the full revelation of that which can be but darkly seen in this world of existence. My Essay is closed.

17.

SUNDAY MEMORIAL

The Gospel Advocate and Impartial Investigator
7 (February 21, 1829): 56-59

The Rochester Observer, of the 6th, contains an article, over the signature of "Jay,"[1] animadverting on Mr. Johnson's Report published in our last,[2] and advancing sentiments which we had not expected to see owned even by the ultra-orthodoxy of the age. We published the Report with approbation. We considered it, and we have not changed our mind, an able production, clearly pointing out the danger and unconstitutionality of the prayer of the petitioners, and we hardly expected to hear anyone openly opposing it. But the orthodox seem regardless of reason, of justice, or of anything else, except to carry their own points. What are we to conclude is the spirit of that man who can pronounce Mr. Johnson's Report, "an ingenious plea for infidelity?" Yet "Jay" pronounces it such.

One would think from the language of certain papers and of certain divines that true religion is unable to support itself; and that to grant universal liberty of opinion is to encourage infidelity. How are we to understand this, that men are prone to believe falsehood rather than truth? That if truth and error are left free to exert their powers, that error will gain the victory? To us it has passed into a maxim that whenever a man asks other aid than argument or the exhibition of facts to support his sentiments that he is conscious they

---

[1] [Ed. "The Sabbath Memorial—Report of the Committee in Senate," *Rochester Observer* 3 (February 6, 1829), 23. Jay accepts the Report's premise of religious liberty, but asserts that the Memorials to Congress on Sunday mail do not seek to determine which religion should prevail in the country (as the Report implies). The Memorials ask Congress to protect the religion of all the American people who do not want Sunday desecrated. And, Jay maintained, government is bound by the will of the people and the people want to preserve Sunday as a day of rest.]

[2] [Ed. Colonel Richard M. Johnson (1780-1850), congressman (1807-19) and senator (1824-29) from Kentucky, was chairman of the United States Senate Post Office Committee. His committee recommended that Congress reject the recommendation of many petitioners to cease sending mail on Sundays. For Johnson's report, see *GAII* 7 (February 7, 1829): 45-48 and *Niles's Register* 35 (January 24, 1829): 352-53; and for the report and a minority senator's dissent, see

cannot be supported by argument or fact. The Report in question would lay no restraint on opinion. It would follow the letter and the spirit of the Constitution and leave every citizen of these United States free to adopt such religion as should appear to him worthy of credence. But this, according to "Jay," is "an ingenious plea for infidelity." Surely Paine, Hume, Volney nor Voltaire never offered so powerful an argument for infidelity as is contained in this short expression.[3] If the religion of Christ cannot exist without a law to protect it, without a legislative act prohibiting any conduct or belief contrary to its requirements, then we would say abandon it and let infidelity or something else, which would not abridge the natural rights of man, be embraced.

It is known to our readers that a memorial to Congress from various sections of the United States, signed by numerous petitioners, has been prepared, praying Congress to pass a law prohibiting the transportation of the mail on the first day of the week. As the conductor of a religious paper, we should have been silent on this petition had we not conceived the principle involved in it, one which, if sanctioned by government would be alike dangerous to religion, to ecclesiastical and to civil liberty. We might have mistaken the character of the memorial, but "Jay" has given it one even worse than we expected.

"The real difference between the Memorial and Report, is that the one assumes us to be a Christian people, the other that we have no religious character whatever." This remark is incorrect. The Report maintains the principle that government is a civil institution; that it can institute no inquiry into the religious opinions of its citizens, neither what they *are*, nor what they should be. Consequently our government, as such, has no religious character. It can have no religious character, unless it declare some system or other must be adopted by its members, which, if the Constitution mean anything, it has no power to do. It is not meant by this that the members of the several branches of our government have no religion. Their religion belongs to them as citizens, but it is not known in their official character. The inaccuracy of "Jay's" remark may be seen. The Report assumes our *government* to have no religious character; the Memorial

Niles's Register 38 (March 20, 1830): 73-77.]
    [3] [Ed. Constantine Volney (1757-1820), French philosopher and historian, was the author of *The Ruins or, a Survey of the Revolutions of Empires* (ET, 1792; Exeter, 1823), which promoted deism, tolerance, free inquiry, unalienable rights of human beings, and self-government. Brownson had read and quoted from the book periodically in his diary. Voltaire, pseudonym of François-Marie Arouet (1694-1778), was a celebrated French deist author.]

that our government is Christian and consequently under obligation to protect or support Christianity.

Jay remarks properly enough, "the main question suggested by the Report, is, Has our government a constitutional power to favor the prayer of the Memorial?" And that to settle this question we must consider, "first what is the power of our government in matters of religion, and then, what is the legitimate construction of the Memorial."

As it regards the power of government, Jay *says* he agrees with the Report. "All will unite in the doctrine so repeatedly asserted in the Report, viz. that the power of government is limited to the protection of its citizens in their religious rights—that it does not extend to the definition of doctrines, the arbitration of controversies, or the prescription of duties." "Let it be understood," he says again, "that upon the first point, viz. the power of government in matters of religion, there is a perfect agreement between the petitioners and the committee. They both deny its authority to frame a religion for the people. They both maintain its obligation to protect the religion which the people have framed for themselves."

Jay calculates too much upon our want of discernment if he thinks we can discover no discrepancy between the Report and the doctrine he has ascribed to it. The Report does *not* maintain that government is under obligation "to protect the *religion* which the people have framed for themselves," but, that it is under obligation to protect the religious *rights* of its citizens. Protecting religious *rights* is one thing, protecting a *religion* is another thing, very different in principle and in its results: as different as an established religion is from one unestablished. Jay either mistook the doctrine of the Report, or he has thought a little deviation from truth, might be advantageous to the cause he has espoused.

All that government has power to do is to protect the religious rights of the people, to prevent one man's injuring another because he adopts a different creed, to prevent anyone from suffering in his civil rights or immunities because he does not adopt the creed of the majority. It is a fundamental maxim of our government that every man has a right to worship God when and where his conscience dictates. One man is not accountable to another for his religious faith, nor indeed is he accountable to society. This is a matter between the individual and his Creator, cognizable by no tribunal but that of his God. This is one of those rights of which, under no form of government, and in no circumstances whatever, can man divest himself; and whatever government or whatever set of men would take it away or usurp dominion over it has proceeded thus far in the march of tyranny, has laid the foundation for the most odious and the most unlimited despotism.

The doctrine of Jay that the government is under "obligation to protect the religion which the people have framed for themselves" involves the grand principle of religious freedom, and if admitted by our government would lay the axe at the root of that tree of liberty, planted by our fathers and watered by their blood. It would fell that tree under whose branches for half a century we have reposed securely, and on whose fruit we have fed with gratitude to the great Father of all. The legitimate construction of the Memorial, according to Jay, is, that "it does not ask government to determine what religion we shall have, but to protect the one *which* we have." That is, we do not ask government to tell us what religion we shall have; no, *we* have decided that question already or we have decided what *ought* to be the religion of the United States, and we only ask government to give it a legal sanction. Is anyone prepared to say that government has the power to give the sanction of a law to a religious opinion? The petitioners come before Congress with the remark that Sunday is a sacred day, a day which must be kept holy unto the Lord; for this, they allege, is the law of God. Should Congress say it *must* be thus observed, we ask if Congress would not in this case recognize the observance of Sunday as a law of God? And if they did, how far would they be from determining in one instance at least what is the law of God? The petitioners say, "we believe the law of God forbids the transportation of the Mail on the first day of the week; we therefore wish you to prohibit its transportation." [If] Congress do it, do they not then assume the province of determining what is the law of God? Suppose these same petitioners should come before Congress, say they believe the preaching of certain sentiments are forbidden by the law of God, and therefore pray a law be passed prohibiting one from preaching them, could not Congress with as much propriety grant their prayer in the latter case as in the first? Should Congress grant their prayer in one case and not the other, would it not appear evident that they resolved themselves into a tribunal to determine which is the law of God? And should they grant both is Jay or any other man prepared to say government has not exceeded its constitutional limits?

But what kind of protection do the petitioners ask for their religion? Do they wish it protected from the cavils of infidels, from the attacks of heretics, or from its desecration by those who believe it? Government says to them, and always has said to them, "Citizens,

you are free to embrace what religion you please. No man has a right
to molest you in your religious opinions. All that is required of you is
that you do not molest others; that you preserve inviolate for others
those rights which they are required to preserve sacred to you. Do
some believe differently from you? You believe differently from them;
both your opinions are sacred to each of you in the eyes of government; but you must manage the affair yourselves. Government cannot protect one party more than the other. If it aid one, it injures the
other. Government, therefore, cannot interfere." Is not this protection enough? If infidels are free to cavil at the religion of Jay and his
party, Jay and his party are just as free to cavil back. If heretics declaim against the corruptions of the orthodox, the orthodox have the
same right to declaim against heretics, and we think it a poor compliment to truth to fear she will be beaten in fair combat with falsehood. Government does protect the religious rights of the people,
but it supposes each individual has the same right, whatever may be
his opinions. Is not this protection enough? What more can Jay and
his party ask? Perhaps we can ascertain.

"The petitioners assume it as a common conviction of the citizens of our country, that Christianity is true including the sacred
character of the first day of the week"; and this assumption Jay tells
us, "forms the real constitutional basis of the memorial." Granting
for the present this assumption is true, we still deny the constitutional character of the memorial. We have not the constitution before us but pledge our character for the correctness of our remark,
that Congress can at no time pass any law establishing any religion,
but every man shall be left free to worship God according to the
dictates of his own conscience. Now granting the whole American
people should be agreed in the belief of any system of religion, Congress cannot without violating the constitution pass any law making
that religion the religion of the people, nor can they pass any law
which has the effect to establish any part of that religion as necessary
to be observed.

We would now ask if the effect of the prayer of the petitioners if
granted would not require *all* the people of the United States to observe the first day of the week? And would it not be a violation of the
spirit of the law they wish Congress to pass, to labor or to attend to
any kind of secular business on that day? We would ask if the observance of the Sabbath is not a part of the religion of the petitioners? It
is then certainly, to their apprehension at least, a religious institution. Does not a law then requiring its sacred observance establish by
law so much of the religion of the petitioners? The Sabbath is a part

of their religion. The Sabbath is established by law. A part of their religion is then established by law. And why may not the whole be established by law as well as a part.

But if the people of the United States believe "that Christianity is true including the sacred character of the first day of the week," what need of a law to protect it? Who is there to desecrate it? Or who is injured? No man is disabled from holding any office because he is a Christian, and no one is forbidden to observe the first day of the week as holy or to keep it as sacred as he please. If some are so conscientious that they cannot perform what government requires done on that day, they are not compelled to do it; and when all become so conscientious that they will neither convey the mail nor open the post-offices on that day, the mail of course will stop without any law. Government compels no one to labor on the first day of the week. Those who do, do it voluntarily, and as long as this is the case no one has a right to complain. Perhaps, however, the secret of uneasiness may be found elsewhere. There is a plan on foot to prevent any except these conscientious Christians from holding any offices under our government; and unless the mail stops on Sunday and the post-offices are closed on that day, then these *conscientious* ones can neither be mail contractors nor post-masters. To stop the mail on the first day of the week becomes therefore a necessary step to the introduction of the grand project. Perhaps another reason why these measures are on foot, why those who call themselves the majority are praying for protection from the minority is that it is of no consequence that they are protected in the enjoyment of their own opinion for themselves while they are compelled to see their neighbors protected in different opinions. Some men have a singular way of interpreting liberty of conscience or liberty of opinion. They say government secures to all the liberty of opinion and is bound to protect them in their opinions. "Now," say these persons, "we believe, our conscience dictates the Sabbath day ought to be kept by every individual, holy unto the Lord, therefore government ought to command and compel every one to keep it holy; and if it does not pass any law to this effect, it exposes us to the pain of seeing that which we deem holy profaned." They forget that those who differ from them have consciences as well as themselves and that government is under as much obligation to one party as to the other.

> In matters of religion as in all other matters, our government is bound by the will of its constituents. It may not decide what are the laws of God, but it is bound, in its public measures to regard

the decisions of the nation. The petitioners have asserted and made the assertion the basis of their memorial, that the decision of the nation is in favor of the Christian Sabbath.

We object both to the doctrine and to the fact of this quotation. Government in matters of religion is bound by the Constitution. They can pass no law establishing any religion. No, not even if it be the *will* of every man, woman and child in the United States. If the will of the constituents can govern in this case what was the necessity of a constitution, particularly the article in question. Government can obey the will of their constituents in no case where that will is opposed to the Constitution. Suppose it should be ascertained that it was the will of all the citizens of the United States that the President should hold his office during life, or that the Presidency should be hereditary in the family of our present incumbent could Congress pass a law to that effect? They could not for their power is limited by the Constitution. Why then talk of the decision of the nation when that decision cannot be regarded by Congress without violating the Constitution. Should it be the will of its constituents government may establish a religion by law, if Jay's doctrine be true, notwithstanding the Constitution to the contrary. We are ambitious to see this sentiment stamped with the public abhorrence; for it strikes at the very root of our government and leaves us prey to every whim that may occupy the mind of the nation.

If it be said the will of the people must govern, we grant it, but the Constitution must be disregarded or altered before Congress can have the power to pass any law different from what is now constitutional. A thing which we pray may never come, at least, never to favor a particular set of divines for of all government ecclesiastical is the most liable to abuse.

But we deny the fact that the decision of the nation is in favor of the Christian Sabbath. A majority may think it ought to be observed but a large portion of that majority are opposed to having any law passed on the subject. But no matter if the majority wish it established by law, all that government can say is, "citizens those of you who wish to keep the first day of the week holy can do it." This is all that in justice any should ask. A Mahometan, should he wish to reside in this country, is as much under the protection of our laws as the Christian, and government has no more right to violate his Sabbath [which is Friday] than it has the Sabbath of the Christian. The Jew is as much protected by our government as the Christian, and he no more than the Christian can be deprived of his rights of conscience by the will of a majority. Religion is a thing that cannot be determined by a plurality of voices, it can neither be bought nor sold; it cannot be robbed or given away. The right to worship God is an unalienable right; and the right to adopt the mode when it does not infringe the rights of others is equally an unalienable right. And we hesitate not to brand him who would divest a fellow being of these rights because he has the majority with him, a misguided zealot, or a bigot who would not refuse, when occasion should offer, to kindle the fire of persecution and even light the faggots to consume the miserable being who should not adopt his creed.

The talk of regulating a man's conscience by the will of the majority is to revive the recollection of doctrines and times which every Christian should wish to forget. One man's conscience is as dear to him as another's; and no matter whether he be alone or have the world with him. There is no reason, no justice and no religion that can allow the consciences of the majority to govern those of the minority. Let Jay, then, cease talking about the majority and the decision of the nation. If the nation have decided we shall not publish our journal, Congress cannot sanction that decision because the Constitution declares the liberty of the press shall be preserved; and if the nation have decided we must all profess the doctrine advanced by Jay in the article we have examined Congress can pass no law upon it for the Constitution secures freedom of opinion. We conclude with the wish that Jay may profit by our remark and that every one of his party will recollect, if they are the majority, they need no law in their favor; for the minority seldom oppress the majority; and if they are the minority, our government protects them from every encroachment. Let them be satisfied.

18.

FREE ENQUIRERS

The Gospel Advocate and Impartial Investigator
7 (March 21, 1829): 89-90

Those who call themselves Orthodox may be sure of our respectful attention, long as we are able to write; but they will pardon us if we leave our examinations of the validity of their claims to pay our compliments to another class who are making some noise in our little world.

This class is composed of deists, skeptics, Free Enquirers, and materialists. By the by, a friend, more timorous than discerning, whispered in our ear the other day that somebody thought the editor of the Gospel Advocate had a strong claim to admission into this honorable corps. Be this as it may, our sentiments are neither the better nor the worse for any supposed coincidence between them and those advocated by the classes we have mentioned. We, however, wish our friends to look at our statements and if what we allege for facts be true, they must not censure us, for we cannot make truth bend to their wishes nor to our own. Each one must bend himself to the truth or else he will always find cause for dissatisfaction. But our readers need not be alarmed. For, before we conclude to dispense with the gospel, to abjure our Savior, and relinquish our hope in a future state of existence, we shall change the name of our paper, our friends shall have timely warning.

But it was the Free Enquirers we proposed to notice. How numerous this class may be we cannot say nor is it of much consequence. The organs of the party in this country are the Free Enquirer, lately published at New Harmony, but now transferred to New York; *The Correspondent* published also at New York, and one or two more publications, we believe, though we have no knowledge of any except these two.[1]

---

[1] [Ed. The *Free Enquirer* (from 1825 to 1828, published as the *New Harmony Gazette* in Indiana; from 1829 to 1835 as the *Free Enquirer* in New York City) was the organ of Fanny Wright, Robert Dale Owen and other radical free thinkers. The New York *Correspondent* (1827-29), edited by George Houston, an English immigrant printer, was another free thought organ which featured scientific and anti-clerical essays to promote the thought of Thomas Paine and other deists and rationalist thinkers. On Houston, see Sean Wilentz, 153-55, 163-64, 167.]

The Free Enquirer is edited by Miss Frances Wright, Robert Dale Owen, and R. L. Jennings.[2] Miss Wright is a lady of talents and of no small philosophical acquisition. Did we believe in the transmigration of souls, we might think old Epicurus had re-appeared in the person of Miss Wright, different from what he appeared in the garden, only in the acquisition of a few feminine graces and perhaps a few visionary notions common to both sexes. We mean this as no reproach for we consider Epicurus best deserving the name of philosopher of anyone antiquity can boast. We were agreeably surprised to find Dr. Good, in his Book of Nature, has not been ashamed to rescue the name of the philosopher from the reproach which has so long deceived the world.[3]

Miss Wright's avowed object is to improve the condition of the human race. This is a good object. We can wish her success in this; for anyone who can feel, knows there is need enough. We have seen two of her lectures on knowledge.[4] We approve them and indeed we have advanced the same principles both in our sermons and in our essays. There is nothing in the lectures which should alarm the honest enquirer after truth.

It will, however, be remarked, these lectures are only abstract principles. Perhaps we should differ in our deduction from these principles and in our application of them to the improvement of the human race. We believe, however, Miss Wright would in carrying her first principles out in detail leave man destitute of all religious notions and deprive him of the benefit of all written laws. Man must have religion. He has always had some kind, and to us there appears nothing better calculated to elevate his conceptions and ennoble his nature than the religion of Jesus. Written laws, and indeed all government would be unnecessary, if mankind were just; but whether all can be made so is very doubtful to us. Man is a bundle of appetites and passions, irregular and violent in their operations. Some government will be necessary until his nature is changed, which we think will require more power than the Free Enquirer can exert. And whether the change would make the man better is a matter of doubt. Some things are beautiful in theory, but are the reverse in practice. Miss

---

[2] [Ed. Wright and Owen identified in the Introduction. Robert L. Jennings was a Scot free thought rationalist and an avid follower of Thomas Paine.]

[3] [Ed. John Mason Good (1764-1827) wrote the popular *The Book of Nature* (Boston: Wells and Lilly, 1826).]

[4] [Ed. These lectures might be among those published in *On the Nature of Knowledge, and Kindred Inquiries. Being a Series of Lectures by Frances Wright* (London: Watts and Co., 1903).]

Wright has a *beau ideal*, perhaps good, but most probably like all ideal beings better suited to some other world than to this.

Her co-editors, Mr. Owen and Mr. Jennings, we presume, are of the same sentiments with herself. They are men of no mean abilities. Mr. Owen has been the principal acting editor of the Enquirer for some time past. We have read his productions with pleasure. He is a good natured man. Cares little about any man's God or creed; and, what we like him for, he always keeps his temper and manifests a truly catholic spirit. But we should think him blest or curst with too much philosophical indifference to work any extensive revolution. Men are successful in proportion to their zeal, not to their knowledge. Of Mr. Jennings we know little; some few of his articles we have seen, which elicit some talent.

The *Correspondent* is edited by George Houston and is very different in character from the Free Enquirer. The Enquirer may certainly claim the praise of liberality, but the *Correspondent*, in the rancor of sectarianism, may contest the palm with the most staunch, thorough-going orthodox publications of the day. Mr. Houston will pardon our freedom, but we think if he cannot exhibit as powerful arguments as religionists, he can match them in virulence. And if he does not believe the orthodox creed, he seems not much deficient in its spirit.

Fools and knaves, dupes and impostors, are the charitable epithets he heaps upon us poor creatures who are so old fashioned as to believe the Bible. Alas for the believer in the Bible! He can expect no mercy at the hands of the relentless editor. We have sometimes thought if the spirit which breathes in his paper should become predominant that we foolish creatures who cling to the religion of Jesus would be put to death merely that the land might be purged of the enemies to his beautiful theory. Though upon second thought we conclude it would be like the spirit of all sects when in power, treat kindly all who submit. Mr. Houston has suffered imprisonment for his sentiments. He, no doubt, feels acutely. We would make all allowances necessary. But we do think one precept from that book he despises would be comfortable to his feelings. It is the precept which requires us to forgive our enemies.

The sentiments of this paper are such as are held by modern deists, or, perhaps materialists; we have not read the paper attentively. The value of such sentiments have been pretty well tested. We are not very sure they will be useful to the world. We do not, however, deny the editors of these papers the right to circulate their sentiments. They have the same right we have to circulate ours. But still we do not perceive their peculiar worth.

Both these papers attack religion. If they hurled their blows at superstition only, it would be well. It may be the result of education, it may be folly; but we have found religion very comfortable to our feelings. When we were overwhelmed with adversity (and we have been), it was not a little consoling to reflect the world is under the control of a wise, powerful and good Being who will cause all things to work together for good, and that our light affliction here will work for us a far more exceeding weight of glory.

We are opposed to superstition, to bigotry, and to false systems of religion. But we have not yet become so *enlightened* as to be pleased with universal skepticism, or with the cold unfeeling dreams of the deist, or the colder speculations of the materialist. Creation loses its beauty, the world its charms, when we consider it the fortuitous production of chance or of blind necessity. And then, to think we live, toil a few days, sink into the grave and are no more, is not well calculated to prompt exertion, or keep up our spirits amid the numerous incidents of life.

But if these editors convince us (and we are willing to be convinced) that their course is calculated to regenerate the world and make man universally happy, they may then have our good wishes and our co-operation. They go too fast for us. We condemn them not, but would say, the progress of truth is always slow, and they, in our opinion, far outstrip her in the race.

19.

THE TIMES

The Gospel Advocate and Impartial Investigator
7 (April 4, 1829): 103-05

Under this head I propose making such remarks upon the present state of things, of the institutions which are or which ought to be adopted, as my observations and reflections have suggested. I shall pursue a rambling strain; and I advertise my readers that if they will profit by what I have to present them, they must note my remarks rather as individual sayings than as parts of a regular discussion.

I dislike that sickly disposition which takes affright at every incident or shrieks alarm at merely the rustling of a leaf. But a just apprehension founded on a full view of the dangerous movements of an ambitious faction, whether of a religious or political character, is salutary to the preservation of liberty or of the rights of every member of society.

The basis of virtue is intelligence; and the welfare of every state, of every body, civil or ecclesiastical, requires the active industry of all its members. Each member should also clearly perceive his importance to the whole and fully understand the part which in the general distribution is allotted him to perform. It therefore becomes important that the elementary principles, on which the permanence and utility of society are based, should be frequently exhibited that the old may refresh their memories and the young learn by what rules their conduct should be governed.

Liberty, equality and justice are three terms frequently used in civil and moral institutions though they are unknown in most religious theories. These terms are the synonyms of each other. Liberty is equality, and equality is justice. Neither can subsist in any state where there is not an equilibrium preserved between all the members of which that state is composed. The lenity of a sovereign or the indifference of a predominant party may leave the great body of the people in the exercise of their inherent rights; but whenever an individual or a party gain an artificial superiority over their brethren, liberty, equality or justice rests upon no solid or permanent foundation and is every moment in danger of being annihilated.

It is the boast of our government that the people are their own rulers. All men by our Constitution are declared equal. All have the same rights and immunities and are entitled to the same voice in deciding by what laws they will be governed. Our Constitution supposes there is an equilibrium between all who adopt it and that in administering the affairs of government, one man is of equal right with another. Whenever, then, one man acquires some additional weight in the eyes of government so that he overbalances another, the fundamental maxim of our Constitution is violated and liberty is endangered.

This equality is, however, only nominal. Probably it can never be reduced to practice for while there exists, as we know there does, a physical inequality, it will be hard to preserve a moral or political equality. Should we examine our government in detail, pursue it through all its ramifications, we might be forcibly impressed with the difference between the equality which it preserves and the one it declares everyone's birth right. Setting aside the great difference it makes between the two sexes, a difference that probably can plead nothing better than caprice, we may observe several classes of citizens which do in effect rule the others with as much absolute authority as ever was possessed by a despot.

An absolutely free government can exist only in theory. It never has been and I know not as it ever can be reduced to practice. Indeed all government is a usurpation of right, justified only by the necessity of imposing some restraint upon the passions of all, for the benefit of each.[1] The true art of all governments is doubtless to govern as little as possible, and it seems to have been the mistake of all, attempting to govern too much. All that government should aim at is to preserve as much equality among its subjects as possible. It deviates from its legitimate object whenever it gives to an individual, to a party, or to any body, larger or smaller, any additional weight or importance in the affairs of state.

All government receives its authority from opinion. Hence, nearly all which has existed, has endeavored to mold the opinions of the

---

[1] [Ed. Brownson's position here is analogous to the view of William Godwin (1756-1836) who argued for the necessary evil of government until human beings had progressed sufficiently in knowledge, virtue, and justice. See his *Enquiry Concerning Political Justice and Its Influence on Morals and Happiness*, ed. F.E.L. Priestly, 3 vols. (Toronto: University of Toronto Press, 1946), 2:2-3, 214-15. This critical edition was based upon the second revised edition of 1798, the text that Brownson read during the 1820s. In his autobiography, Brownson asserted that Godwin had an enormous influence upon him. See *Works* 5:50-56.]

people in favor of itself. It has, therefore, often imposed restrictions upon speech, upon the press, prohibiting the teaching or the circulating of opinions, which would tend to undermine its authority or to weaken the support it requires for its subsistence. It has labored to fortify itself by imparting power to individuals or to parties who are the most influential in the state; associating with itself the bigoted attachments or superstitious fears of its members; giving to a part the power to maintain the obedience of the rest.

All states in their first organization are more or less free, liberty generally predominates. The government is weak, but the people are powerful. A struggle commences, a grasping for power. The government extends its prerogative, joins with those whose interest it is to enlarge its power, addresses itself to the love of power which is common to its citizens, forms a party in its favor, enlists the most influential to support its claims by giving them leave to rule; and then after a struggle separates its interests from the people, and ends perhaps in tyranny or despotism. Every man loves power, every party whether religious or civil is fond of dominion. With parties as with individuals this becomes the ruling passion. Hence under a free government, this is the most dangerous enemy to be encountered and to resist its encroachment is nearly all government can or ought to do. But to do this requires the utmost vigilance and caution as it respects its own measures or the measures of any class of its citizens.

There are numerous methods of acquiring power, or for one to exercise more than his portion of authority. These methods are such as are afforded by superior wealth, abilities, education, and artful management of prevailing opinions etc. Against the acquisition of wealth, of individual wealth, government cannot, ought not to interfere; but against the acquisition of wealth to be held by particular bodies or corporations especially against such bodies or corporations as do not submit to the authority of the magistrate in disposing of the wealth they acquire, government can and ought to be on its guard and to raise its authority. Religious bodies and sectarian corporations in particular come under this class. But as I shall treat these more largely hereafter, I let them pass for the present.

Of superior abilities I say nothing. They are beyond the reach of government and would prove its destruction were it able to reduce them. The good which flows from them overbalances the evil they sometimes occasion. Of education much may be said and much may be done.

(May 2, 1829): 136-38

In writing the Essays under this head, I wish to forget the clerical character as well as that I am the partisan of a sect. My object is to point out some errors, which have been tolerated, and to develop the best means of procuring the welfare of the human race while inhabitants of the earth.

Though I disclaim as unworthy of him who is ambitious to obtain just sentiments and just feelings, all national partialities or antipathies, I still feel my bosom glow with warm emotion when the name of this country is mentioned. Not because it is *my* country, but because its government, I believe, is the best human wisdom has ever been able to devise and because I think the philanthropist may labor here with the best prospect of meliorating the condition of the human family.

The benevolent mind turns with joy from the despotic governments which have prevailed and which now prevail over the greater part of the world, the benevolent mind, sickened with these, may turn with joy to our more favored land, illumined by the morning sun of liberty. Here one may say the human race has survived its downward progress and has begun to rise in the seal of knowledge and independence. We gained a victory, not for ourselves, but for the world; we triumphed over arbitrary power and the trophies of that triumph may yet be erected in every clime and by every people.

We have declared ourselves free. We are now teaching the world [that] man is capable of self-government. We are a school in which nations are to learn the rights of man, and be taught the road to the acme of human greatness and felicity. Our republic stands like the beacon upon some lofty eminence to light the care-worn and depressed sons of despotic climes to home and to happiness. If we are wise, if we do not allow our light to become darkness, posterity shall bless our memories as benefactors of the human race, as the regenerators of the world.

Though our institutions may not yet bear the stamp of perfection, though men may be susceptible of greater liberty than our government allows, every philanthropist, no matter where he resides, should lend all his support to our institutions that we may never retrograde but keep onward in the march of improvement. If we fail, human happiness may slumber for a hundred centuries; if we succeed, the splendor of our example may enlighten the world. What then is our duty! How careful should we be in every step we take, in every measure we adopt!

I have said that the basis of our government is intelligence. Ignorance may sap the foundation of our liberty. But knowledge, salutary in its influence, will give permanence to our institutions and send the blessing of freedom, civil and mental, to the latest posterity. The patriot then will labor to enlighten his countrymen and the friend to man will do all in his power to render knowledge universal. I have said our government declares all men equal and proceeds upon the maxim that one man weighs as much as another. The destruction of this equality may prove dangerous. When one outweighs another, he may obtain more than his share and perhaps obtain the adoption of measures unequal in their bearing. Hence our caution is required to prevent the equality, which our government recognizes, from being destroyed.

It requires no stretch of thought to perceive that knowledge is power, that in our government the man who is well informed can rule the ignorant, and even deprive him in many instances of the exercise of his rights. What shall be done? Shall we deprecate knowledge and labor to bring all *down* to the same standard? No. We should level upward, bring the ignorant to the standard of the wise, and aim to elevate those who are now the lowest in the scale of intellectual acquisition to those who are the highest.

Our resort is to education. But education may be wrong as well as right. And though education undoubtedly is in this country nearer what it should be than in any other, yet even here, with a few exceptions, it is almost anything but what it ought to be. We have schools, no one can find the least fault with the number. We expend money, enough and more than enough, yet, the education we get is worth but little, little, I mean, compared with what it might be.

Our common schools, incomparably better than our high schools or colleges, amount to but little. What do they teach? The scholar to think? Do they point out to him the nature or reason of things? No. They put into his hand a book he does not understand and compel him through fear or flattery to wade through it and commit it perhaps, without exercising a single faculty of the mind, except the memory; and after wasting eight or ten years of his time, they send him into the world, learned indeed, but nearly as ignorant of everything, as he commenced, with the exception of a few words and sentences he may have committed to memory without once thinking of their import.

A child thus *educated,* may make no little show among those who have been deprived of any education, but is entirely ignorant of business, or destitute of all knowledge which is applicable to the purposes of life. And what is worse, the habits thus acquired, prevent the child from obtaining knowledge when he has left the authority of the pedagogue. The object of all education is, or should be, the acquisition of useful knowledge. Acquaintance with words is useful only as it introduces us to the *things* signified by them.

One learns to read that he may receive the pleasure of becoming acquainted with the ideas of authors; and derive profit from the knowledge they may afford him. But one may as well be ignorant of letters, as to read an author without understanding what he writes. One studies grammar that he may know how to speak and write his language correctly. But if one wastes three or four years in committing to memory the dreams and arbitrary distinctions of grammarians without becoming acquainted with the principles of language or knowing how to apply what he had learned, he has spent his time in vain. The same of every other branch. Nothing should be learned for itself but as it can be made subservient to the important purposes of our existence.

Our common school teachers are not to blame because they do not teach their pupils to think, for few of them know how to think themselves. The people are not to blame for procuring such teachers for they can procure but few others, and a small part only know that such teachers are not as good as any. I blame nobody. I only advert to an evil which, if we wish our children to become acquainted with things, we must set our wits at work to remove. Before I get through I shall suggest some hints to effect an object so desirable.

In looking at our common schools, one cannot fail to observe the great waste of time, compared with the little that is good for anything which the child acquires. Most of the children in this state for instance are at school the greater part of their time from the age of five to fifteen. Ten years, time enough to give any one education sufficient to qualify him for any station he may be required to fill in our country. And yet, more than one half are unable at the expiration of the time to understand the force of a simple argument, or to judge with the least accuracy upon any subject which requires the exercise of thought.

It is apparent that a material defect in our schools is that the teachers do not develop the intellectual powers of the pupil, do not discipline the mind, nor prepare it for relishing the beauty of knowledge. We are told such a child "won't learn," that the teacher cannot induce him "to get his lesson!" Now this is nonsense. Every child loves to learn. Anyone may mark the animation of a child when he obtains a new idea. But the subject requires another N[umber]. I must therefore request my readers to wait for it.

(September 5, 1829): 280-81

Having at length disposed of some matter from correspondents that demanded admission and having paid sufficient attention to the charges implicating our orthodoxy, preferred against us by our friends, who, it is probable, are less acquainted with the ground over which we have traveled than we are, and by those who perhaps read more than they think and believe more than they read, we return with pleasure to greet our readers once more under the Essayist.

We promised some farther remarks on the subject of education. No subject is by the writer of this deemed more important and none deserves a more serious attention from anyone who regards himself as one of the human family. The proper instruction of youth is matter of grave concern for on it depends the solution of the question, whether MIND shall go forward or whether it shall sink back into the feebleness of ignorance and false learning, which so long held the human race in worse than Egyptian bondage. Yet, this is an enquiry we cannot readily answer. It will perhaps be profitable to look farther at the defects of the present system, and it may be, the errors of others will teach us wisdom.

It has already been stated as one prominent objection to the present system of education that it does not teach the learner to think nor to reason. Hence, perhaps, the cause why there are so many *dull* scholars and why there are so many bright and active children who hate the school and loathe a book. A mistake runs through the whole system and is imbibed by almost every teacher and every parent that children have peculiar gifts, that unless they have a natural taste for the acquisition of certain branches they cannot learn them.

I would these persons, in some other respects, would believe more in nature and less in education; but in this instance their creed should be reversed.

"What man has done man may do" is a maxim that should be engraved over the door of every schoolhouse, and instead of a child being told he has no genius for such a branch, he should be taught mind is omnipotent. Children have no *natural* bias for one study more than another; and I have never seen any possessing the common mental faculties, but are capable of acquiring all the knowledge taught in any of our schools, and acquiring it in half the time and with half the expense usually employed. Children are fond of new things, fond of new ideas; and if our teachers would give them ideas instead of compelling them to commit to memory words and sen-

tences they do not understand, there would be little difficulty in fixing the attention of the most unpromising and least tractable.

Let us look at one of our common schools and point out the
curious method adopted by most of our teachers. To begin with the
teacher, he has learned (it is very doubtful whether he knows) to
read, that is to call his letters and words as he sees them, in some style
or other with a good deal [of] facility. If he happens to be *educated*
under one who had learned to pronounce correctly, we may, probably, find not much to condemn in his pronunciation of all words he
remembers to have heard his master pronounce; but if he has not a
pronouncing dictionary in his hand, it is best to stop our ears when
he comes to any others. So much for single words. In the enuncia-
tion of sentences, all rules of emphasis and cadence are murdered,
and if he reads for any length of time, you may yawn at his monotony or wish him whipped for his affectation. The sense or meaning of the author, that is a thing quite unknown and even unthought
of, if the piece be poetry, you wonder where is its harmony and are
strongly inclined to look over his shoulder to ascertain whether every
line begins with a capital.

Having examined him in reading, question him on orthography.
He may perhaps know letters are divided into vowels and conso-
nants, and perhaps a consonant cannot make a syllable of itself. Farther, it is very doubtful whether he can proceed. On etymology and
syntax, if he has a good memory he may tell you what the grammar
book says, but of the reason or propriety of one of the rules he re-
cites, it is very doubtful whether he has any idea at all. In arithmetic
we may find him able to answer most of the questions set down in
his book as far as the RULE OF THREE, and some may go further.
Thus far the writer was enabled to go when quite a boy the inspector
certified that he was qualified to teach a common school, and he was
deemed quite "good in figures." The higher branches of mathematics are not much taught in our common schools, though when they
are, it is little more than committing to memory what is found in the
textbook.

In geography a little may be known, but in most cases the teacher
refers to his book to ascertain whether the scholar has answered right
or not. He may have some acquaintance with history, at least, so far
as to remember that in "Adam's fall we sinned all," and about natural
history enough to say, the "cat doth play and often slay." He may
perhaps know enough about rhetoric to tell you Blair has written
lectures on the subject, and he may recollect that Duncan or Watts or

somebody has written a treatise on logic.[2] As to his general literature and refinement of taste nothing need be said for little of these is ever exhibited. He may have read Watts' psalms, the New England Primer, and some other books.[3] In the art of thinking, the extent is that he shall spend a winter easier in imparting his knowledge and "teaching the young idea how to shoot" than he can in driving through the storm and cold at some useful employment.

Such is the teacher. I would not be understood as meaning this is the character of all school teachers, but still it is an unexaggerated picture of a vast number, and I fear a large majority of the common school teachers in this state. Now how much are we to expect from this teacher? Let us examine his course of instruction.

The teacher comes into his school, sour, ready to eat up his scholars, or with an affected dignity makes them afraid to ask him a single question or to state a single difficulty. The child is presented with a book at the knee of the master with the question, while the knife, perhaps, points to the first letter in the alphabet, "what is that?" and thus to each letter till the whole alphabet is gone over. The little boy or girl is then sent to a hard seat where it must stay, motionless and noiseless, without anything to arouse or call forth the young mind for an hour and a half. Thus, day after day, the child is sent to school. If fatigued, if feeling the buoyancy of the age and the desire to be active common to that period, a laugh or a whisper is discovered, the stentorian lungs of the teacher are in requisition, perhaps his rod, the little urchin is half freighted out of his wits, learns little more than to hate the school and dread to hear the parent tell him to go.

Having got out of the ABCs he finds no more encouragement. Still it is the dry tedious task of learning mechanically, learning to spell words, the meaning of which he does not know nor can he guess the use. He is then put into a reading lesson and begins to read, no—man—may—put—off—the—law—of—God; without once thinking, or being required to think of the meaning of what he is reading. The same defect runs through the whole course of studies in the school. The teachers give few explanations, they encourage few

---

[2] [Ed. Brownson is probably referring to Hugh Blair (1718-1800) whose *Essays on Rhetoric* (London, 1784), William Duncan (1717-60) whose *Elements of Logic* (London, 1748), and Isaac Watts (1674-1748) whose many works, including his *Logic* (1725), were read by Universalists. On this see the Introduction.]

[3] [Ed. Isaac Watts's *The Psalms of David* (1719) and the *New England Primer* (c. 1690) tied religious and moral teaching to instruction in the alphabet and reading.]

questions for they are unable to answer them. Thus it is, time is squandered, money wasted, and children destroyed at school. But, I will not pursue the disgusting picture.

Children should be taught, wherever it is possible, by having the objects with which they are to become acquainted presented to them. Let them examine and the voice of the teacher give a description. Let reading be thought as an amusement, give the child a description which he is anxious to learn and he will soon master it. Study should be his pastime and instruction should be given in a manner not only plain but interesting. Give to the young mind ideas, keep the boy awake with novelty, be pleasant to him, and teach him as though you were telling him a story to please him. But I have not time to enlarge.

20.

REVEREND ABNER KNEELAND[1]

The Gospel Advocate and Impartial Investigator
7 (April 4, 1829): 106-07

It is with shame and bitter regret we have witnessed the cruel and unfeeling persecutions of this aged and faithful and talented defender of liberal sentiments. We have been silent, for we waited for older men to speak. They have spoken, but with one[2] solitary exception, it has been to show how well they can persevere in ingratitude. It has then come to this, that we boys, mere striplings in Israel, must show our manhood by insulting grey hairs and build up the cause of the Redeemer by hurling our anathemas at one who has nearly worn out his life in defending our common cause?

Three associations have withdrawn fellowship from Br. Kneeland, and several editors from whom we had hoped different things have approved of their conduct. What was the charge? None, or none that Universalists should not blush to own. Did they prefer any charge? None, or if they did, Br. Kneeland was tried and condemned unheard. This done too by persons who profess to be Universalists! It must have been an inconsiderate act, and we should hope that its authors will see its impropriety. We think publicly to withdraw fellowship from a preacher without even notifying him that he is accused of the accusation or giving him a chance to defend himself is as anti-Christian as it must be painful to the feelings of the one thus treated.

But why was this done? Because *somebody* thought that if Br. Kneeland was not publicly disowned, the orthodox would say, what? Why that Universalists fellowship a man whose faith is incorrect. The amount of it seems to be this: Br. Kneeland either preached or published something which was not generally understood and our timorous friends were afraid the orthodox would call it atheism, and that would prove ruinous to our cause. So it is men start at a shadow and shriek at the rustling of a leaf.

---

[1] [Ed. Kneeland identified in Introduction, p. 27 above.]
[2] One other editor has indeed not joined in the proscription.

We have no personal acquaintance with Br. Kneeland. We have read his writings, or some of them. From these we have received a favorable idea of his talents. And though we may not be as quick as some to detect heresy, we are free to confess, we have seen nothing in his publications offensive to our orthodoxy. For our self we are well aware how this controversy originated. In our opinion it was at first purely *personal*. But let that pass.

Many Universalists have, no doubt, entertained the idea that Br. Kneeland is skeptical. Let it be so; though we have no evidence to satisfy *us* that such is the fact, let it be that he is skeptical, that he does not believe as much as some of the rest of us; what shall we do? Excommunicate? Where is the blush to crimson [on] our countenances when we speak of excluding one on the account of his faith? Let us go and ask pardon of the orthodox for what we have written and published against them, for excommunicating believers in Universalism from their church, before we adopt their practice.

"But," says one, "would you fellowship an atheist." Yes, as a man, and would protect his reputation from unjust reproach. "But would you fellowship him as a preacher?" If I believed with him I would say so; if I did not, I could let my own opinion be known and should not fear what I believed to be false would gain the victory over what I deemed truth, if both were told. We are at a loss to understand excommunication among Universalists. We have no *hell* in which we can burn anathematized members; but we believe all are brethren; and we, for our self, know no better way to do with delinquent members than to treat them kindly and endeavor to heal their backslidings.

"But we shall suffer reproach from unworthy members." *Who* will suffer reproach? We are sick of this squeamishness. We want more independence of mind. If a man preaches atheism, any fool may know he does not preach Universalism. As for reproach from the orthodox, we expect, and we scorn it. Let us be careful and not fall into their errors. Let us not reproach everyone who may not believe quite as much as we, to make ourselves popular among the orthodox. We have spoken plainly. It is our custom. We mean no offence to anyone. Our object is to do justice to one whom we think to have been injured in the house of his friends.

21.

TO JAMES LUCKEY, ESQ.

The Gospel Advocate and Impartial Investigator
7 (April 18, 1829): 127-28

Dear Sir: After an absence of some years, I was gratified to meet and renew my good feelings to one whom I ever considered as a valued friend. I was happy to see you at your house, and though our sentiments on some points of theology were different, there was the same reciprocation of good feeling which I trust we had formerly indulged towards each other.

Our conversation, you recollect, was on the goodness of God and the final salvation of all men. I stated what I believed, that the goodness of God must be given up or the conclusion admitted that every individual He has created will be, finally, a gainer by his existence. You admitted and contended for the goodness of God as well as myself, but considered my conclusion not necessary because, that the goodness of God allowed evil to exist at present. That is to say, if God can be good and allow evil to exist today, why may he not be good and allow it to exist tomorrow? According to your request and to my promise, I now proceed to show wherein I think your reasoning incorrect, and also to give you some farther evidence of the correctness of my own.

There are, sir, some points in which we agree or at least, if not, I shall on my part concede. The point in dispute is easy to understand. It was started by an argument used in my sermon, which you was so good as to hear. I was laboring to prove the salvation of all men. I argued it from the goodness of God. God is a good Being; as such he cannot make his creatures miserable nor allow them to suffer if he has the power to make them happy. He has the power to make them happy, he therefore will. This was my conclusion to which you objected. It is not necessary to infer that all mankind will be happy because God is good. God *is* good, but he does suffer his creatures to be miserable. If my conclusion were true, mankind would be happy now. But as they are not all happy now, my conclusion, you say, is contrary to fact and therefore is incorrect. This is the argument on both sides. I admit the fact for which you contend, but also contend that if you urge it against my conclusion, it will destroy either the

power or goodness of God. The object of the controversy is to reconcile the goodness of God with the existence of evil. I say that his
goodness cannot be maintained unless we suppose its termination in
good. You say it need not thus terminate because God who is good
allows it to exist. You will now perceive where we differ. I assume the
position that the existence of evil is an objection to the goodness of
God unless we look to its termination. You assumed the position
that God is good, and that evil is no objection to his goodness because he is good. Yours, I admit, is a common and not an inconve-
nient kind of logic; but, to me not wholly correct.

Suppose, sir, we try this mode of reasoning. You admit that it is
wrong to murder or that murder is an evil. Suppose, then, a man
whom you had always considered a good man should be arraigned
for murder and it should be proved that he had murdered; would
you contend his conduct was right? Would you say the man had
done well and that his act of murder was no objection to his goodness because he was a *good* man? Would not the act prove him not a
good man? I submit to your own good sense to determine.

Apply this reasoning. You say God is good. If I prove that he
makes his children miserable or what is the same thing, gives them a
constitution which proves an eternal evil to them, should I not prove
your assertion false? If I prove this, should I not prove that God was
not good? So far as the principle is concerned the cases are parallel
and I leave you again to decide.

Allow me to enquire, what is goodness? Now we all know very
well what the term means when applied to man. We all know that a
good man will not bring evil or misery upon anyone if he can avoid
it. Yea, he will do more; he will make all happy to the extent of his
ability. This is goodness. Apply the term to God. If it mean something else when applied to him that something else is not goodness
and should be called by another name.

You and I both used the term when speaking of God. I believe it
a proper term and I use it in its proper sense, the one I have given it.
Now is God thus good? You say he is. I bring the evil which now
exists among his children as an objection. You deny it as an objection
because God is good. You will perceive you take the very point for
granted which you ought to prove, to wit, the goodness of God.

You may say I admit he is good. So I do, when you admit the evil
he tolerates in this system of things is introduced for an ulterior design or that it shall terminate in our advantage. You may deny that
God is the author of our misery; so do I, that he is directly the author. But he has given us a constitution and this constitution results

at present in our sufferings. I contend that this constitution will result in our felicity else God was not good in giving it. Now as I am
assured that God is good and as I cannot reconcile his goodness on
any other hypothesis, I conclude all will receive happiness enough
from this constitution which we have, taking the whole of our existence into consideration to overbalance the evil which it occasions. If
you say that evil will eternally continue, I contend you deny the goodness of God.

Having given this statement of the argument and this general
view of the ground I shall take, I wait your reply.

(May 30, 1829): 176-78

Dear sir — your reply to mine of April 18th has been duly received,[1] and I beg you will accept the assurance of the high estimation I have of that disposition, which can rise superior to petty religious prejudices and retain the man and the friend even while contending for different theological notions. I approve the candor of
your communication but, while I cheerfully reciprocate its friendly
spirit, I must tell you I think it far from meeting the nature of the
argument, far from proving my conclusions wrong, or yours correct.
The three positions you have assumed, if supported, might sustain
your notions of the final destination of man, but these positions must
be *proved* or they avail nothing.

The first which relates to the existence of evil was fully considered in my other letter and I can find nothing in yours which has the
least tendency to invalidate what I have stated. I admitted evil did
exist but concluded it must cease to exist or the goodness or power of
God must be given up. Now I consider this a proposition that no
man of common sense can doubt unless he believes that the eternal
existence or misery is a benefit.

How, sir, will you prove to me any being is good? By declaring
he is good and then if his conduct is destructive, declare that destruction is good because the being who is the author of it is good? Sir,
you cannot but perceive the fallacy of such reasoning and yet you
reason in the same manner. You tell me God is good. I bring the evil
which exists in the world as an objection to this goodness. I tell you
goodness is an definite term, it has a distinct meaning, that it is opposed to evil and that the being who does evil is not good. You say
the evil which exists is no objection to his goodness because he is
good. How do you prove this? If I should break your head, how

[1] [Ed. See James Luckey, "Rev. O. A. Brownson," *GAII* 7 (May 16, 1829): 152-54.]

correct would be the argument "the man who broke your head Mr. Luckey is not a bad man because he has done so serious an injury for he is a good man?"

Now Sir, you know there is evil in the world; you know that misery preys upon all ranks and conditions, that thousands are deeply wretched during nearly the whole of their existence in this world. Look at the disorder and confusion which reign in the moral world, the wars, the civil commotions, pregnant with fury and death, the domestic discord, the private and oft concealed griefs of thousands; look at these which pour over the world and destroy everything good or desirable. Go read your Bible and learn all these come from God, as nearly all religionists hold, and tell me in what the goodness of God consists? I am free to confess from the existing state of things that so far from pronouncing God good, that is, if he be the author and governor of the world as the Bible declares him, I should consider him the reverse.

You pretend to reason from facts, but you in reality reason against facts. You assume the position God is good and because he is good, the existence of evil can be no objection to his goodness and because evil exists now without destroying his goodness it may eternally exist. This conclusion, sir, is at war with common sense, with self-evident facts. God you say is good. To whom is he good? To that feeble infant now in a paroxysm of pain, gasping for its first breath and after a few hours of agony dies? May I be delivered from such goodness. He is good you say and is he so to those thousands who languish in dungeons, to those he now overwhelms with the ocean's fury, with the volcano's rage or engulfs in the ruins of the earthquake? You may say so, but an angel from heaven should receive the *lie direct* if he should assert it: That is if no ultimate advantage is to redound to these victims sufficient to overbalance the pain they have endured.

But you may ask does not the Bible declare God is good and do not these evils exist? Yes, I admit both. I admit these evils exist and that the Bible declares God is good. But, sir, I deny the possibility that the declaration that God is good can be true unless evil shall be so modified that man shall be a gainer by his existence.

You speak of "general good." Suppose sir there had been only one man created, what would have been for his general good? Happiness without any doubt. Does it alter the case by supposing there are two men? If you had been the only man created, you must admit your creation was no act of goodness unless it became the cause or occasion of more happiness than misery. May you not say the same of yourself if there be another created. Does my creation weaken your claims? Or have I not just as strong a claim as I should have had, if you had not been created? Consider each individual while discussing this question as a separate and distinct creation, and your "general good" or the good of the whole will resolve itself into the good of all the parts.

You say the misery we endure is a punishment which God inflicts upon us for our sins, but this will not help the matter, unless you allow the punishment must terminate in good. Why does a good God possessed of all power make a man capable of sinning, place him in a situation where he knows he will sin, and then inflict endless punishment? Reconcile this with infinite goodness, and I will break a man's head, and tell it is through kindness, or make one as miserable as I can, and tell him it is because I love him so much.

You ask, "if it be consistent with goodness to punish us now, who shall say it will not be consistent to punish us eternally or who shall say how long this punishment may be continued before it encroach upon goodness?"

The answer, sir, is easy. Your child disobeys you. You inflict a suitable chastisement, one which is beneficial and you have done a good act. But take a club big as you can wield with both hands and beat that little smiling girl of yours, as long as she can live, or as long as you can inflict the blows, do this sir and I leave the parent to decide its *goodness*. Apply this and the first member of your question is answered. The second is just as easily answered. Punishment ceases to be just and consequently good, the moment it produces a greater quantity of pain than it returns of pleasure.

You mention some examples of suffering and evil but as I do not perceive their bearing on the question I must pass them over. But sir I cannot forbear noticing one of your expressions, "I would" you say "had I the power, provided I should not be found fighting against God, destroy evil of every name and nature from the earth." Now this is one of the most singular confessions of a man in your situation I ever heard. Would you indeed destroy evil and suffering of every kind and is nothing but power wanting? What think you of God? Has he the power? Allow him then to have as good a disposition as you manifest and the world will be happy. But you seem to doubt if you should really undertake to destroy evil of every kind whether you should not be found fighting against God: Surely you must think very highly of your God to be afraid to combat evil lest you should be found fighting against him. Do you really think God is opposed to the destruction of evil? Your words imply it and your arguments seem to confirm it. Pray tell me in what your God's goodness consists?

You say it is consistent with God to punish eternally. This is your second position but you must prove your first, for if you fail in that you cannot support your second. I think you have failed in the first. For before you can prove it you must show that God is good to the being he makes miserable or that he may make one wretched and claim that one's love and gratitude. This you have not done, this you cannot do. I have neither time nor room in this letter to reply to the last position you have illustrated, but will consider what you have there advanced and give you my thoughts upon it soon. In the meantime I wish you to reply to what is here advanced and also continue the argument under your third head.

(June 13, 1829): 186-88

Dear Sir: I have received your second letter containing a reply to my last and also a continuation of your argument under the third position assumed in your first.[2] You will please accept my thanks for the favor and my assurance that I am pleased with the earnestness with which you vindicate your views though I may not admit the conclusions of your argument.

I redeem my promise by proceeding to give a partial review of your statement that "it is in perfect accordance with the mercy and goodness of God, connected as they are with his other attributes, that the wicked be punished with everlasting destruction from the presence of the Lord and the glory of his power." By this statement I understand you to mean that God can consistently with his mercy and goodness make the wicked endlessly miserable. I do not ask whether he will do it or not, but whether he can do it and retain his character for goodness? There are few subjects in theology more important than this and no questions under existing circumstances can be asked in reference to the Deity more deserving our serious attention.

I do not pretend to scan the Almighty. I pretend to know nothing more of him than he has revealed in his works and his word. But this question does not require us to explore the depths of the Divinity; it presents a plain subject easy to be understood and capable of being answered without "rushing into the skies." Is it consistent with goodness to make any creature endlessly miserable? Do we understand the nature of the question? God moved by his own will without the least compulsion creates a certain being, gives him all

---

[2] [Ed. See letter in *GAII* 7 (June 13, 1829): 190-92.]

the susceptibilities, powers and faculties which he does or can possess, places this being in such circumstances that he remains a sinner during his probationary state, and then makes him endlessly miserable. Can he do this and be good? Can he do this and prove himself just? Let us consider for one moment what is goodness. I have before defined the term, but I must do it again. Now language was not invented to express the attributes of God, but things with which we come in more immediate contact. Such things as have a tendency to prolong our existence and to produce or increase pleasurable emotions in our bosoms we term good. Such as have an opposite tendency, that is, destroy our existence or make us miserable we call bad or evil. This is what the terms good and evil when strictly defined mean among us. Now these terms must mean the same thing when applied to God or they are misapplied. Now if Mr. Luckey will say that God creates a being who, in consequence of that creation, is endlessly miserable, it is a self-evident position that God is not good to that individual. You may disguise the matter as you will, it resolves itself into this, God is not, he cannot in the nature of things be good to one who has to groan eternally in hell.

"If you say," you remark, "that God must save all or his goodness must be relinquished, I say he must damn all or his justice must be relinquished." How will you accommodate this matter? To my thinking, very much as Solomon proposed to adjust the dispute between the two harlots, viz. by dividing the child. Goodness declares all mankind should be happy, justice according to your notions says all ought to be damned, and Deity being obliged to pay as much attention to the voice of one as of the other attempts to compromise the affair by taking part to heaven and sending the rest to hell. This sir, is dividing the child in good earnest. Let humanity speak.

Now the case is, we often speak of the attributes of God in a manner calculated to produce the illusion that he is divided; we speak of justice and mercy as if they were distinct beings, of goodness and love as though they were separate entities, but the fact is there are no such things as justice and mercy and goodness, etc. in existence, or at least we can form no idea of any abstract existences to be called by these names, yet because it is the custom of speakers and writers to use the abstract for the concrete we are apt to imagine there are some such beings.

There are just and merciful agents. We say justice is an attribute of the Deity; it were better to say God is just. We say "justice of God." But what is it? Simply God acting in a certain manner towards his creatures. We use the expression "mercy of God," what do we mean? Simply God relieving the sufferers of their pain. Of his "goodness," his making his creatures happy. God is good; whatever he does is goodness. Justice is only a particular display of goodness, or if you please justice is the foundation of all goodness; I care not which way you turn the matter. God is good, is just, is merciful; whatever he does is just, is good, is merciful; none of these propositions contradict the other, but are all acts of the same individual, of the same indivisible agent, who does not, cannot change, but may labor for the good of different classes of individuals, and as he labors for one or another class, he is said to be just or merciful.

Now it is all useless saying God's justice requires one thing and his mercy requires another thing right in opposition. I wish our metaphysical divines would either study metaphysics thoroughly or else let them entirely alone. There is no difficulty in ascertaining the origin of the illusion under which your mind, as well as the minds of others, labor. By some means or other a vague notion has been imbibed that a something called justice demands the eternal punishment of the wicked, and a something else called mercy is anxious for the salvation of all. Now there is no such thing that a wise man, when he considers the subject, can believe. The notion is borrowed from earthly courts and we have vainly imagined heaven adopts the same principles as do the governments of earth.

We speak about bringing a man to justice, and this too long after the crime committed may have been repented of, and the man become a peaceful and perhaps virtuous citizen. Never was language more misapplied. We may rest assured that if we borrow our notions of the criminal jurisprudence of heaven from the criminal code of earth, we shall charge the Almighty with a practice that ever has disgraced every earthly tribunal.

You say that God labors for the "general good." Here you have borrowed your theology from the imperfection of men. No doubt a sovereign must content himself with promoting the general good of his kingdom. Why? Because it is better some few of his subjects should be miserable than it would be to have all happy? You will hardly assign this reason. The reason is plain. The sovereign is an imperfect being and he cannot make all happy. His subjects have a variety of dispositions, follow various employments, and he cannot always check the evil of the one or always ensure the success of the other. Hence if he make them generally happy, we say he does well, not because there can be nothing better, but for the reason he has done all his limited powers would allow him to do. Now sir, if you choose to bring Deity down to the level of an earthy sovereign, I may admit he does very well considering his power, but I might some-times regret he was unable to make all his subjects happy. Then there would be no tears throughout his domain, then we should hear no widow complain, no fatherless child cry for the father executed for his crime, for then I may say no crime would have been committed.

But you may say it is essential to all good governments, that is, it is for the general good that offenders be punished. Why? Because it is a beautiful or an entertaining spectacle to see one "hang by the neck until he is dead," or because it is very exhilarating to the be-nevolent soul to see some poor son of misfortune confined in the gloomy cell. I risk nothing by an appeal to your own feelings in this case. It is perhaps proper that offenders in an earthly government should be punished because governments have not yet become able to give to all the power and disposition to do right. But if the govern-ment were able to prevent the crime I hardly think it can be just for that government to punish an offender. For certainly it is better to prevent than to punish crime.

Now sir, will you say God cannot punish crime? Or will you say that it is a proof of his goodness that he permits us to run on in sin until we have ruined ourselves, that he may gratify himself by send-ing us to hell to roast eternally? Or will you to relieve your embar-rassment call it a "mystery" and silence the voice of reason by ex-claiming, "God moves in a mysterious way!" The subject is perfectly plain. Everybody knows it is better to prevent a man from doing wrong than it is to punish him after he has done it, for punishment but increases the amount of misery.

You speak about David, say he "gave thanks that the first-born of Egypt were smitten," etc. All this may be very well. But you will recollect the Scriptures call David a "man of blood," and he might have another title which I will leave you to give. I will only add I am not particularly anxious to learn morality or to take my ideas of jus-tice from one who was a notorious violator of both the sixth and the seventh precept of the Decalogue. The other instances you enumer-ated may be dismissed, for they took place so long ago that the cir-cumstances necessary to enable us to form a correct judgement about them are forgotten.

You attempt to prove punishment is not disciplinary, but it is unnecessary for I deny all *punishment* and consequently do not con-tend it is disciplinary. Now do not misunderstand me. I believe: "The universal cause acts not partial, but by general laws."

He has made us, given us all the powers he designed should be-long to our rank in the scale of being. Now according to the manner in which these powers are developed, we are happy or miserable. This I believe is the principle of his government. He works no miracles to prevent the natural consequences of our actions. Now if it can be shown that we shall continue to sin to all eternity we shall be miserable, or if we are eternally among sinners, we shall be eternally unhappy.

I have no evidence that God will ever change and I do not believe his government will ever be in the least changed, but all the results of that government may not yet be developed and that which now seems imperfect may be but the first principles, which when carried out in detail, will present us all the perfection, beauty and felicity we can wish. But so far as I know anything about the subject, I believe Deity has placed our fortune in our own hands and it depends on our own exertions, whether we are happy or miserable. So it is here and so I believe it will be hereafter.

Now I say man has the means of making himself happy, that is, God has placed the means within his reach. God will not exercise these means for us; we must exercise them for ourselves and the only question with me is will all men exercise them? If you sir will grant me two things, I will ask you to do no more. First that God has placed these means within the reach of all, and second that he will never take them away. The first is a sentiment of your church and I think you will not deny it. The second is true, if God be unchangeably good, which I think you will admit to be a fact. My conclusion is that all men have and always will have within their reach the means of making themselves happy. Will they exercise these means? Scripture must decide. My next shall adduce the proof from the sacred volume.

Your last letter shall be dully noticed. Our readers may compare your reply to number one of mine, and draw their own inferences. You have availed yourself of an argument which precludes all reply from me. I mean your ignorance of certain things and your distrust of your own abilities, your diffidence in your own reason; and, as much you have produced appears to have been written under the conviction reason is a useless thing, it is unnecessary to reason against it. Your scriptural arguments will be considered in my next.

(July 25, 1829): 234-36

Dear Sir. Owing to the multiplicity of my engagements I have delayed answering your last longer than I intended.[3] I avail myself of the first leisure I have to atone for my neglect. In my last I intimated

---

[3] [Ed. Third letter evidently not published in *GAII.*]

302   The Early Works of Orestes A. Brownson: Volume I

that my next would exhibit the direct scriptural proofs of the salvation of all men, but in my interview with you at my house, you thought I did not treat your letters with sufficient attention. I am sorry sir, I have given you any reason to complain. You shall have no cause to reiterate that complaint. For I will now attend to what you have offered.

I am pleased to find you saying in your last that you "wish to be open to conviction, and to treat this subject with that dignity the concerns of eternity demand." This is well. Unless a man is willing to be convinced, logic is spent in vain upon him. Your favorite poet will tell you,

> A man convinced against his will,
> Is of the same opinion still.[4]

I know little about the "concerns of eternity" consequently may unwittingly transgress the "dignity" they demand, but I hope I shall always observe that dignity which a love of truth always inspires.

I told you that in the question before us it was necessary to consider each individual a distinct and separate creation. I gave my reasons. You have very easily disposed of the position. You had only to say, "with a moment's reflection, you will not wonder if I should manifest more surprise at this assertion of yours than you did at my disposition to destroy evil, for it is certainly most absurd." Sir, I admire the facility of your logic, you reason with unequaled dispatch, but if it were seasoned with a little proof it would be more acceptable to my taste.

"It strikes me forcibly," you say, "that we should take things as they are." Very well, we find evil as one of the things which are. Evil is not a characteristic of good, and the being which produces it knowingly is bad. God according to your views is the Author of "the things which are," consequently of evil; now if you do not look to its termination, how will you maintain the absolute goodness of God? You may say he is good, and if your mode of argument be correct it will be argument enough.

You say "it remains with me to show that God's administration will be changed." I beg your pardon, as that is a position I have never assumed, and as I maintain the reverse, I think it would be ungenerous to compel me to prove it. For that would require me to prove your side of the question as well as my own. Remember "we must

---

[4] [Ed. Quote is similar to Samuel Butler's (1612-80) "He that complies against his will, is of his own opinion still," in *Hudibras,* part 3 (1680), canto 3, 1.547-48.]

take things as they are." You say the government of God will not be changed. Now it is very evident, man here is a progressive being and that God gives him the means of salvation. I have the right therefore to infer man will always have the means of salvation within his reach, at least, it remains with you to show they will ever be taken away.

You say I "infer God's administration will be changed." I am sorry sir to insinuate your memory failed you in this instance. I happen never to have made such a statement, on your account sir I regret I neglected it. You say my "whole creed depends on my notions of right and wrong" or of "what would be right and wrong in an infinite God." And will you tell me on *whose* notions of right and wrong your creed depends? Surely sir, I know not what alternative you can have; you must take either your own notions or the notions of another, and will you blame me because I prefer my own.

You seem to think it very unsafe and very absurd to rely on conclusions which our "corrupt natures and ignorant minds may tell us is right or wrong." I regret sir, we have nothing better to rely on. If you know of anything which can draw conclusions but "our corrupt natures and ignorant minds" I would thank you for some information. But you say what is "right or wrong in a God." Now I have been so foolish as to suppose *right* is right the world over. I affix to this term a definite idea. When one tells me God will do *right*, I understand the expression. When one tells me God *will* do so, I say I do not know whether he will or not but I say he *will* if he does *right*, so of wrong.

You also seem afraid of such conclusion because your ignorance of the "government of God" is so great you cannot tell "what is right or wrong in reference to that government." Great as your "ignorance" is, will you not tell us it is right for God to punish the wicked eternally? Or do you not pretend to determine whether it is right or wrong for him thus to punish?

You also say "facts make you afraid to trust your hopes of salvation on *this* (?) hypothesis!" Very well I hope you will rest upon the rock of ages, though you may think your *ignorance* too great to look for it. Your next *fear* arises from a shadow for the position before which you tremble is a creation of your own fancy. I disown it.

The poetry you have quoted is very fine, but the author of it understood making rhymes better than ethics or theology. You "protest against reasoning from our notions of right and wrong against the government of God." I suppose sir, you would have us reason without any notions of right and wrong? No doubt were we to do this your notions of theology would be as *reasonable* as any other. But you add "God can and does govern, with reference to the 'general good' of all his creatures." I thank you for this statement. Allow this to be true and I have no disposition to reason against the government of God, nor even against yourself. It cannot be for your "general good" to be made endlessly miserable, nor for the "general good" of any other creature. "God governs with reference to the general good of *all* his creatures," all then must receive more happiness than misery from their creation. This, sir, is all for which I have contended. Sir, be on your guard; you may become a Universalist before you are aware of it.

You seem to think "we should not place too high an estimation upon ourselves as *individuals* when weighed in the balance of the whole." Very good advice; but what is the whole but an aggregate of individuals? And if the interest of the individuals be disregarded, how much attention is paid to the interest of the whole. I do not suppose that an individual is all in all. But I do suppose that God in the multiplicity of his affairs will not become so confused as to neglect any individual. He pays the same attention to every individual as he would had that individual been the only one created. As very well expressed by Pope in the following lines which you have furnished me though applied as if in refutation of yourself.

> Who sees with *equal* eye as God of all,
> A *hero* perish or a *sparrow* fall;
> Atoms or systems into ruin hurled,
> And now a *bubble* burst and now a world.[5]

With regard to what you say of "Ananias and Sapphira,"[6] I wish you to inform me where was the *justice* in killing them if they received no benefit from being killed? You ask me "with what propriety do the Scriptures call the punishment of the wicked the *curse* of the divine law." Not recollecting the passages of Scripture to which you refer, I reserve my answer until you produce them. You wish to know "if that can be a *curse* which is the only *effectual* thing that Almighty Wisdom can devise to *prepare* the finally impenitent for happiness?" I should think not. If my creed be true you say "the sinner will enjoy a much more effectual means of salvation in hell than ever he did on earth." Suppose he does, have you any objections? I think you ought rather rejoice at the prospect that he who was incorrigible here, will be reformed hereafter. Certainly I discover

---

[5] [Ed. Pope's *An Essay on Man*, Epistle 1, Lines 87-90.]
[6] [Ed. On Ananias and Sapphira, see Acts 5:1-14.]

nothing in this which should pain a good Christian, do you? But this is merely gratuitous. I have never said anything about sinners being reformed in hell, and certainly did not know it was a part of my creed till you thus informed me.

But you seem troubled to ascertain how, if punishment terminate in good, it can be called a "*curse*." Now suppose you should drop that term and admit man never was *cursed* what would be the harm? A command I think was once given to this effect. "Bless and curse not" [Rom. 12:14]. Let us obey the command. You think the "plan of redemption" more fully illustrates the glory of God than creation. It may be so, though I know not what that has to do with this controversy. "But according to my hypothesis it is reserved for hellfire to eclipse the whole." This is something new to me. And you are confident that "when the celestial beings bring forth the headstone and some are crying grace, grace, unto it, others will cry, fire, fire?" This sir, will remind us of a Methodist Camp Meeting scene, and do you think a recollection of one of those scenes will be unpleasant to you in another world?

"But seriously, I appeal to every unprejudiced mind with what kind of propriety, hell-fire or any punishment which is necessarily inflicted on the wicked can be called a *curse*, so long as it is not only necessary, but absolutely essential to their eternal happiness?" Seriously then, "I would also appeal to every unprejudiced mind with what kind of propriety" a God of love, who "governs with reference to the 'general good' of *all* his creatures" can be supposed to "curse" any of those for whose "general good" he governs!

You say you "have never seen an answer to the declaration our Lord made to Judas that would weigh one straw in the scale of *common sense*." Alas for the credit of the Methodist commentator, "the greatest Divine" as you once told me, "in the world," the really erudite Dr. Adam Clarke.[7] He has given a long dissertation on this subject and had he always been as judicious and as correct he might have justified your eulogium. But this passage will avail you nothing. Dare you say the sinner who repents of his sins, will not be saved? Presuming you will not deny what you profess to believe and what may be so easily proved, it is enough to say Judas repented and threw from him the wages of iniquity. To the particular passage you have quoted, "It had been good for that man had he never been born"

---

[7] [Ed. Adam Clarke (1762?-1832) was a Methodist preacher and theologian who authored numerous theological and pious works. One of his most widely used works was an eight volume commentary on the entire Bible (1810-26) that combined critical and scientific with popular and pious reflections.]

[Mark 14:20], I reply it was a *proverbial* expression, common to the Jews in our Savior's time and means nothing more than that the person of whom it is spoken will be exposed to some great and severe evil. This is abundantly proved by your own commentator, Dr. A. Clarke, and consequently need not be labored by me.

If this does not satisfy you, answer me the following queries. Judas was indeed one that was lost, but Jesus came to seek and to save that which was lost, will he find Judas? Christ said to his disciples, Judas being one, hereafter "ye shall sit upon twelve thrones judging the twelve tribes of Israel" [Matt. 19:28; Luke 22:30]. Will Jesus perform his promise? If he does, will Judas remain eternally in hell? I shall dismiss your letter with only a slight remark; you have said much about "hell" and hell-fire. I do not wonder at this. It is the principal ingredient in your creed and makes the principal theme for all the declamation for which your preachers stand preeminent. Do not misunderstand me. I look upon the Methodists as I do upon all other denominations who embrace the notion of endless misery as being sometimes pretty good people, but defending a most shameful creed. You will remember in your future letters that I am not a "hell-fire" preacher, and therefore it will be unnecessary to attribute the notion to me.

I wish you to take my views from my own writings. I am not accountable for the sins of others, nor are their virtues to be attributed to me. I shall hereafter proceed with my direct proof of the doctrine of universal salvation and notice your objections as you present them. You will have the goodness to review your last letter and point out wherever I may have done you injustice.

22.

CHURCH AND STATE

The Gospel Advocate and Impartial Investigator
7 (May 2, 1829): 139-40

At this time when the agitation of the public mind on the subject named in the caption of this article menaces some mighty convulsion, the patriot and the friend to equal rights should stand firm and watchful, ready to repel every invasion on the rich inheritance left us by our fathers. The writer of this disclaims the character of an alarmist. He is not ambitious to be thought one of that number whose idle fears brood over imagined dangers, and conjure up monsters or giants at every step, armed for the destruction of our rights. No, he has confidence in the virtue, in the intelligence and the firm and determined adherence to liberty which characterizes the great body of the citizens of these United States. He would disclaim his country and banish himself to some desolate region if he thought the lessons of antiquity were forgotten, or if the memory of our struggle for independence were not embalmed in almost every heart.

The citizens of our country are attached to liberty; they almost idolize their government and there are but few comparatively speaking of our whole population that would not sacrifice their lives to preserve the freedom of our institutions. But paradoxical as it may seem there appears to us serious cause for alarm. Men are creatures of circumstance. Parties are the same. A party starting on the best principles and having the best object to accomplish may, nay often do, in the pursuit of their favorite object involve the most serious and even the most injurious consequences in their exertions.

We will not indulge in invective, nor will we waste our time in blaming those who now threaten us with the destruction of all for which we wish to live. The motives of men, the secret springs of their actions, are not exposed to our view and we shall not assume the prerogative of the Almighty to look into their hearts. Their actions, their measures, are open to inspection and we shall exercise our right to animadvert when we think them wrong.

It is said religionists are endeavoring to *unite* church and state. I do not believe this to be the wish of those who manifest the most unfriendly disposition to our government. The Presbyterians are accused of wishing to unite church and state. I do not believe the accusation to be correct. They would reject with scorn any interference of the government with their religious affairs, except to give them money if the government pleased. No, their ambition, if they have any, is of a higher kind. They want no *union* but they might not refuse to *control* the state, to make the state subservient to their own views.

I see no plan on foot, which to me appears designed to effect a union between church and state, but the measures which have alarmed me seem calculated to keep the church separate from the state, to raise up an ecclesiastical government which shall control the civil. The Presbyterian clergy, and I fear others as well as they, have a number of projects, for what purpose they were started I know not and care not. They were ostensibly started for the purpose of evangelizing the world. Thousands gave their support and thousands still give their support from this conviction. The object is ostensibly good. Men engaged to accomplish it with the best motives and by exercising the best feelings of the heart. But there is not the less danger on that account. We have not less dread from the mistakes of conscience than from the violence of depravity. A man, conscious of rectitude of intention, fully convinced the object of his wishes is good, will hear no reason, yield to no argument or persuasion which might show him the danger of his course.

But where is the danger? Men love power; parties are actuated by the same passion. Our religious people have engaged in mighty plans. They have enlisted a great army who are all engrossed in the benevolent enterprise. Difficulties occur, obstacles to the completion of their designs are presented, they therefore will naturally labor to acquire power. To become able to control the civil government, to make that bow to their dictation will throw an immense disposable force into their hands, and enable them if that be their wish to establish their creed or to gratify their ambition by the exercise of power if that be their object. The natural progress leads to this result and though thousands may be engaged who never dream of such a conclusion, yet their strong desire to do good by giving influence to their party directly leads to it or will if circumstances are favorable. This is their reasoning. "Our object is most glorious. It is to advance the cause of the Redeemer, and to benefit mankind. We have the good of mankind at heart, but alas! we have not the power to do the good we wish, we must therefore increase our power." Thus selfishness seems excluded and the conviction that they are increasing their influence for the benefit of the world sanctifies, in their own view, all their measures.

But there is a danger. Men ambitious of personal aggrandizement, and such men are never wanting, will join this party, mold its ruling passion to their own interest, and by making a skillful use of time and circumstance, they will not only defeat the good intended but effect much injury. Here is the danger. The orthodox seem now ripe for some ambitious clerico-demagogue to execute his plans. By concealing his designs, adopting the watch-word, and making free use of the cant phrases of the party, and paying hypocritically the necessary homage to popular institutions, he may accomplish his nefarious projects ere many apprehend danger. This is what I fear.

Did the great body of our citizens believe there were any serious plan adopted to render the church independent of the state, to raise up an ecclesiastical hierarchy to overwhelm our civil institutions, they would rise in their majesty and consign it to nonentity. But the majority believe the thing is impracticable and hence those who are suspected of the design defend themselves upon the apparent impossibility of its being accomplished. Our danger is in our security. Were we awake, were we watchful on this subject, there could be no danger. But we slumber; and those who would enslave us are constantly administering soporifics that they may be left to act unobserved.

I have been called to this subject by a letter which I have just read from Dr. Ezra Stiles Ely to a Mr. Montgomery in Virginia, in which the Dr. disclaims all intention or wish to give his creed a legal establishment, and also disclaims the same not only on his part, but on the part of the Presbyterian clergy generally.[1] It little avails one accused of stealing to declare he is no thief or for one accused of injustice to say he is honest. Dr. Ely, however honest or upright may be his intentions, however firm his attachment may be to our civil institutions, has lost the confidence of the public; and however much he may be esteemed by his party, his name will never until he performs some extraordinary lustration be free from reproach. As a man I know him not, as an individual I attach to him no consequence, as the mouthpiece of a party he should be severely rebuked; and his projects should be treated with indignation. To spare him is treason to liberty. In his language is concentrated the violence of sectarism, the rancor of exclusive orthodoxy, and the impudence of benighted bigotry. He brands as *Deists* and *rejecters of Christianity* those who advocate equal right, carries the reproach to the government, which

---

[1] [Ed. Not able to locate the letter to Montgomery.]

he thinks will favor *Deism* sooner than any class of Christians. I shall
bestow on him some attention and promise my readers that the suspected union of church and state or as I should term it, the usurpation of the church over the state, with what facts I can collect on the
subject, shall be laid before them and fully discussed. The times require watchfulness and we dare not join with those who cry "peace,
peace," when there is no peace. The public mind must be fully aroused
or we fear the gloom of monkism will spread over the land.

(July 25, 1829): 240-41

Some time since we published an article, under the above head,
and promised to remark still further upon the subject, as we should
find leisure. We have been prevented from continuing our remarks
for the want of room, but we will assure our readers and our orthodox friends generally that we have not and probably shall not abandon the subject.

We have already stated that we did not think a *union* of church
and state, the particular object of clerical ambition, that they aimed
at a higher object, designing to make the state *bow* to the church and
statesmen obey the dictation of priests. The Presbyterian would revolt at the idea of being a Presbyterian if the law compelled him to be
one; and should this government ever make the requisition, he would
exhibit all the turbulence of John Knox,[2] and for aught we know, the
unconquerable rebellion of his Cameronean ancestors. But the Presbyterian, while free to embrace what religion he pleases for himself,
has never shown himself unwilling to *force* his religion upon others.
He doubtless would have no objection that government should give
him the means to render contemptible all who do not choose to
adopt his faith.

The measures which have been adopted are of a dangerous character. Measures, which if not soon overthrown, will one day doom
our much loved country to experience the sad reverses which have
blackened the history of all others. Of all crafts priestcraft is the most
subtle in its designs, the most successful in its measures, and the
most dreadful in its influence.

The history of the past should warn the present. Saul, the first
and best of the Kings of Israel, was opposed, was branded with reproach, lost his kingdom and his life merely because he did not choose
to be a tool of the priests of his nation. David, a king unprincipled
and pusillanimous, an adulterer and a murderer, was raised to his

---

[2] [Ed. John Knox (1513-72) was Protestant reformer in Scotland who had a
great influence on the establishment of Presbyterianism there.]

throne and supported on it, pronounced a man after God's own heart, for no other known virtue than devotion to the priest. The whole history of the kingdoms of Israel and Judah clearly demonstrate the danger of an overgrown and ambitious priesthood. They oppressed the people, plotted with the enemies of the nations, and were seldom unable to have the nation conquered by some petty neighbor. They screened themselves from indignation by saying God was angry because they went after idols and therefore *sold* them into the power of their enemies to be punished. There is no doubt they were *sold*, and just as little that the priests took care to secure the *price*.

The Christian Church started without any patronage of state. At first, weak, it depended on divine protection and the force of persuasion. But not contented with this, they soon organized themselves into a separate government, formed a sort of republic, governed by their bishops. Organizing their body more artfully, cementing it more firmly, and concentrating its power, they were at length enabled to place at their head the Emperor of Rome, and to have their religion established as the religion of the Empire. Under Constantine the church triumphed, but the triumph of the church was the downfall of the empire. The emperors turned bishops, invaded with impunity the few rights left the people, and neglected the welfare of their subjects to settle the question either by the arguments of reason or the sword whether Christ was of the *same* or a *like* substance with the Father?[3] With bishops for their ministers and ecclesiastics for counselors they hastened the Dark Ages which hung with horrid night over the world.

What are we doing now? Our clergy are at work. They have a government *separate* from the state. They have disciplined or are disciplining their followers, amassing vast funds, which they hold independent of the state; they are preparing a powerful army, under skillful leaders, and for what? Yes for what?

We think one government enough for one people. "No man can serve two masters" [Matt. 6:24]. No man can serve the priest and be true to the civil government, at least, to a civil government like ours. The clergy, who have organized the government to which we allude and which must be termed an ecclesiastical government, have few feelings in common with the spirit of republicanism. Look at the

---

[3] [Ed. Brownson refers here to the fourth century doctrinal battle in the Christian East over whether Christ was of the same (i.e., homo) or like (homoi) substance with the Father. Some, like Brownson, have reduced the issue to the insignificance of a difference in Greek vowels.]

plan of this government. It consists first of individual churches, governed by certain individuals termed elders. These elders with the church which they govern are accountable to the Presbytery, which is composed of ministers and ruling elders from the individual churches. This Presbytery is accountable for its measures to the Synod, which is composed of delegates from the several Presbyteries. The Synod in its turn to the General Assembly, which is composed, if we mistake not, of delegates from all the Synods in the U[nited] States.

From this rapid sketch it may easily be seen the Presbyterians have a very well organized government, a government which exerts a more powerful control over the true believer or is deemed more binding by him than our national and state governments. Ask the conscientious Presbyterian which of the two governments he ought to obey in case they should happen to clash, and he will readily say, the "ecclesiastical," for he is bound to obey God rather than man. Should then this ecclesiastical government have views different from those entertained by our civil government, it may easily be told on which side will be found the adherents or the members of the ecclesiastical establishment.

Now it should be borne in mind the "General Assembly" is in fact the supreme government of the Presbyterian Church. From it there is no appeal and it is difficult to conceive even that the people can overrule its measures, unless they rise en masse and say "we will not hear the clergymen of which it is composed preach." But then the clergy need only threaten the rebels with excommunication and with the fire of hell to recall them to obedience. This "Assembly" consists of individuals from all parts of the country; they can meet in secret conclave, adopt such measures as they choose. By private circulars they can fix the duty of every clergyman of their denomination, and they will never want for means to excommunicate and destroy anyone who has the boldness to disobey or to refuse to support their measures.

If a church rebels that can be excommunicated, so of a Presbytery or of a Synod. When we consider the terror there is in excommunication from the church of God to every sincere Presbyterian, we may form some idea of the control this assembly has over the church. We ought also to take into our account the habitual deference to the clergy, reverence for their persons and conviction of their importance, in saving the soul, which inspire the breast of every true believer and faithful member, then we may without much difficulty perceive it no hard matter for this Assembly to bring nearly the whole body of their church into their measures; and when the measures are to aggrandize the church we shall find none to dissent among the whole body.

No one will deny such a government as this, though professing obedience to the powers that be, is not dangerous, only when their leaders will adopt no dangerous measures or have power to effect. We may see then on what a brittle thread is suspended our liberty. Give this church the exquisite kind of leaders and sufficient power and they may dictate every measure of government, blast the reputation of every political man who refuses to bow to them. We propose to show in our future numbers that the leaders of the church mentioned have the disposition and are fast acquiring the power to control our civil government.

(August 8, 1829): 251-53

In our last we gave a promise that in our future numbers we would show the leaders of the orthodox party have the disposition and are fast acquiring the power to control our civil government. We are duly sensible of the high character the clergy sustain; we know full well the measure of their revenge upon the audacious spirits who presume to question the sincerity of their professions, and we would not prefer the charge we have without sufficient evidence to support it. We are hostile to no one. We should despise our self if we could descend to the meanness of fixing the odium of the measure upon any class, for the sinister purpose of gaining credit for our particular tenets. We have foresworn the spirit of sectarism, and we despise it as much, and would oppose it as quick, in a Universalist as in a Calvinist. This we think may easily be supported from the course we have pursued and from the liberal censures we have received from many who possess the name though not the spirit of Universalism.

We respect no man merely for his profession, or indeed if any, it should be the hitherto humble but always important professions of the agriculturalist and of the mechanic. On the pursuits of these depend the very existence of society; and if we must have a privileged class, these shall have our vote to be its members. The clergy have indeed long made one of the privileged class, but it has long been the misfortune of the world to value things in an inverse ratio to their real worth. A clergyman should be respected as a man, but not as a clergyman, and he should be valued according to his real utility to the world. To us it is a matter of indifference how the world be benefited if the benefit be actually conferred, whether it be in preaching, in singing or in praying. The clergy have an interest in common with the rest of mankind. When they do not imagine they have a *separate* interest, we shall never be found opposing them; when they do, we shall deem it our duty to admonish them and bid the people "beware!"

If we turn to the history of the clergy and learn what has been their character in times past, we may also learn that to *suspect* the clergy as ambitious of obtaining an undue proportion of power is no crime and to find it really so would not contradict their established character.

With the history of the priesthood we have made our self somewhat familiar. This indeed was our duty since the world will have it, we are a priest our self, though we think not a very worthy member of the ancient and honorable fraternity. But our familiarity with their history has not increased our respect for the institution nor for its members; and certainly we have seen no cogent reason why we should wish to be under the immediate control of the clergy. We pass over the many gross impositions they have palmed upon us, the pious frauds they have committed and the thousand silly stories they have made us believe. The people in these respects have little reason to blame any but themselves; they should never have resigned their own understandings.

If we may credit anything in history we may pronounce the *accumulation of* POWER, the leading object of the clergy in all ages and in all countries of the world. We will not pretend to say the accumulation of power has been always for the purpose of their own aggrandizement, we should hope to find the majority actuated by nobler motives, but whether so or not, they have always converted the power when acquired to exalt the dignity and to secure the independence of their own order. They may have deemed that they needed power to be useful and that the greater their influence, the more beneficial they might be to the world. This indeed might be true and might have been a laudable ambition had they always been infallible and not subject to the same imperfections as the rest of mankind. But if one is killed, we do not know that it helps the matter to have lost his life from a benevolent or from a murderous intention in the one who killed him. Though this consideration may lessen the guilt it does not remove the injury; and though we may not *blame* the clergy, we have suffered and it is little matter of importance to the sufferers, to be told it was done by persons desiring to benefit them or by those wishing only to benefit themselves.

There can be no doubt many of the clerical profession have been honest men, but even the honest have not been much less injurious than the dishonest. They have given a sanctity to the institution, which has preserved it and thus prevented the abolition of the order and with it its numerous train of evils. But honest or dishonest, benevolent or malevolent, they always seem anxious to have their hand in everything which is doing, they have claimed the honor of every important discovery, of the introduction of every useful measure; and when they were unable to support the claim, or when it was notorious the measure or discovery was independent of them, they have branded it impious and persecuted the author. We might mention a Galileo, a Tycho Brahe and a host of others who have spread a halo of glory around the human race, men to whose bold and persevering efforts, the present philosopher is so deeply indebted; but they felt the weight of clerical wrath and Galileo was incarcerated for teaching, and obliged to recant, to renounce as false a doctrine which every schoolboy is now instructed to believe true.

We said the priesthood have always aimed at the accumulation of power. They have; and they have never given sleep to their eyes nor slumber to their eye-lid when they had it not or until they had set some machine to work to procure it. Masters of the human heart, they have laughed when the people talked of liberty; and when the people by positive laws abolished their powers they recovered it by enforcing the law of superstition. An empire has never been enslaved but the priests have upheld the masters, produced for the tyrants aid sacred texts and pious expositions. They have contributed their share in fomenting most wars whether foreign or civil. They seldom refuse their prayers or deny the benefit of their holy rites to the king or to the officer who hearkens to their lessons, nor have they ever been sparing in their anathemas to the one who contemns God by refusing to consult them.

They preach the divine right of kings, advocate legitimacy and maintain the inviolability of the throne whenever they can thus secure a splendid establishment for themselves; and they proclaim the sovereignty of the people and justify innovation when they have anything to hope for themselves by a change. They cry down education, or seem to encourage it, just as it is deemed necessary to maintain, or to increase their influence over the human mind. Their policy has always been the same, though the measures adopted vary as circumstances require. In an age of ignorance and wonder, they performed miracles, maintained their power by confounding the reason and rendering the judgement useless. When the people became too enlightened to pay implicit confidence to all their marvelous works and marvelous stories, they anathematized knowledge and extolled ignorance as the mother of devotion. They stamped a celestial curse upon the exercise of the mental powers and offered heaven to those who would believe without reason.

When the keys of knowledge were finally wrested from them by the hands of the profane laity, when science began to blaze forth in powerful contrast to the rays of darkness shed by them, and when they could no longer lull the active mind asleep, they became learned, seemed to advocate knowledge. They placed themselves at the head of all the seminaries of learning, became tutors in the families of the opulent, and penetrating into courts they became the instructors of kings and princes. Thus they managed to control what they could not prevent nor destroy, and to turn into the channel of their own ambition the stream which might have watered the whole earth.

Nor did they encourage knowledge though they fostered education. They called the mind from the contemplation of nature, from acquiring a knowledge of things, to ponder over their venerated lore; and they wasted on the obscurity of a long since fulfilled prediction, or in acquiring a dead language of dead people who left in their history neither greatness to imitate nor wisdom to admire, the time and the powers which under more favorable circumstances would have made us acquainted with the means of improving our condition of relishing the beauties of nature and of adoring the beneficent Father of all. They taught words without ideas, made their pupils learned without knowledge and substituted praise for science in the room of science itself, and self-conceit in the place of love of true wisdom.

Wherever the priesthood has been predominant the people have been enslaven; the mind has been deprived of its vigor, bound in the shackles of a senseless superstition, it has been incapable of exertion. Vice has been encouraged. Donations to the church for the benefit of the clergy has supplied the place of virtue, and atoned for a life of crime. Zeal in defending the absurdities and immoralities of the predominant religion has been deemed sufficient to open the gates of heaven and give a claim to the joys of the blest. Proffering peace they have given us the sword; professing to beat the sword into the ploughshare and the spear into the pruning hook, they have converted the implements of husbandry into the instruments of war; promising a heaven hereafter they have given us a hell on earth; and claiming to be the ambassadors of God and the messengers of love, they have stirred up the demon discord, alienated the affections of kindred, invaded the sacred apartments of domestic life, destroyed conjugal, filial and fraternal affection; trampled upon the rights of conscience and cursed, in the name of God, all who have not pronounced them a blessing to the human race and given them tithes of all they possess.

Arrogant in their pretensions, claiming exemption from the common frailties of humanity, and familiar intercourse with the invisible God, they have demanded implicit obedience and heaped the whole mountain of their vengeance upon the inquisitive spirit who presumed to enquire the warrant of their authority or the propriety of their conduct. Long as they could, they smothered the desire for knowledge and that Christendom is now enlightened they say is owing to them; though the most careless reader of history must know they persecuted with a relentless spirit the philosophers and reformers to whom we are indebted for modern improvements. Such has been the character of the clergy and such the evils they have heaped upon the human family; such their general features, wherever found or whatever name they bear, Pagans, Jews or Christians, Mussulmans or Brahmans, followers of Zoroaster or worshiper of the Lama, and if there be any difference if one class be worse than another, the palm of the greatest *evil is fairly due the Christian.*

Such is their character. We are at loss to reconcile the discrepancies we find between their professions and their practice. With the best profession on earth or to be found even in heaven, their practice has even disgraced his majesty of hell by being charged to him. Had they come to us as men and acknowledged themselves of like passions with the rest of us, having the same imperfections and liable to the same errors, we could have passed over their inconsistencies, by supposing they had mistaken the best means to make the world virtuous; but when they come as chosen servants of God we are confounded. To call them honest but ignorant, would be to accuse Jehovah of having made an unwise choice, and to pronounce them knowing but dishonest, seems not much better, and yet we know of no other alternative.

Such having uniformly been the character of the clergy, such having been their constant aim and practice, and such the abuses they have tolerated, that we ask, did we wrong to suspect? Did we wrong to bid our readers watch! But we have more than suspicion, we have more than *cause* for suspicion, we have evidence to our mind clear and satisfactory. The orthodox clergy have engaged in a vast enterprise; a mighty project is conceived and all the energies of the order are in requisition to bring it forth. Whatever it may turn out to be, we have seen enough to convince us it was unholy in its conception and if executed will be ungodly in its influence.

Our readers will perceive this portrait is designed to show what power the clergy have heretofore aimed at and the evils they have inflicted. They will from this view admit it is *possible* for the clergy now to aim at similar power, and if they obtain it, what surety have we that they will not bring similar evils in their train? We have not yet dismissed this subject. Facts are to be laid before our readers and facts which will make them enquire, "where is the spirit which achieved our independence?" shall be laid before them.

(August 22, 1829): 265-68

But few facts are required to establish what has been asserted respecting the disposition of the clergy. If they are suspected of aiming at the supreme control of all matters, whether of church or state, a slight view of their profession will render it impossible to separate this disposition from their own views and feelings in reference to their duty.

The clerical office is different in kind from all others. The clergyman does not receive his appointment from man; he bows to no human tribunal; he acknowledges no human laws as equal to those he is entrusted to enforce; pleading the appointment of the Almighty as the warrant of his authority, he holds, as he imagines, the laws of God, laws which all earth and all heaven are bound to obey. He stands commissioned from the court of heaven, a court to which all earthly courts must bow. Placed thus high above all human authority, all civil governments must be the ministers of his will; and all kings, rulers and magistrates, must be his waiting boys.

The clergyman fancies himself the ambassador of God; clothed with divine authority, he comes wrapped in the dignity of heaven; he claims all the submission due to the majesty of his master, and all the attention and deference due to the sacredness and the high importance of his mission. He comes not to negotiate peace between contending rivals, but, as the minister of the lawful sovereign who has regained his throne to proclaim terms to defeated rebels; not to persuade, but to command them to ground the weapons of their rebellion and to return to their duty; to submit themselves to their rightful sovereign against whom they had rebelled.

He considers all men in a state of rebellion and that they must support the church of God before they can be treated as lawful subjects. His message is, "Children of men! hear the words of the Almighty King. You have rebelled against your sovereign, you have leagued with his enemies, you have attempted to wrest from his hand the scepter of command, you have labored to dethrone him, and you have trampled his laws under your feet. In this state of rebellion you are entitled to no mercy, are deserving no compassion. But the King, your legitimate sovereign, is no tyrant. He has declared your death, but he will spare you if you will submit; if you accept the offers he makes, you are reprieved, you are pardoned. Throw down your arms; trust yourself to his mercy; support the church which he has planted as a rallying point for all who will return to their duty, and all shall be well; flock to this standard, the standard of the rightful Lord and of the true God, and your rebellion shall be forgotten, your sins blotted out."

From this message, which every clergyman feels himself commissioned to deliver, it is evident that to support the church is the duty of all, as the only sure test of their obedience to God. From this we learn that the church is deemed superior to the state, and certainly its officers superior to the officers of civil government. All are bound to obey God, rulers as well as people; to obey God, we must support the church; and as the clergy are the officers of the church, as they are the ministers of God, the interpreters of his will, the ones he makes use of in his intercourse with the human family, therefore, by a slight change of terms, the whole comes to this conclusion, to obey God is to support the church; to obey, or to support the church, is to consult the will of the clergy, and to yield implicitly obedience to their commands.

Such is the dignity and high authority with which the clergyman fancies himself clothed that it is impossible he should deem it proper for him to sanction the measures adopted by a rebel government, and in his estimation every government is rebellious that does not support what he believes the cause of God. With these feelings, can he deem it wrong to advise those rebel governors or rulers of their duty? Or *compel* them to perform it when they will not be persuaded? Certainly not. He is appointed God's vicegerent on earth; it is his duty to be faithful to his master and he would feel self-condemned should he neglect to make governments as well as people obey the will of heaven.

And why should it be considered strange that clergymen should have the disposition with which they are charged, when the very warrant they plead, when the charter of their order imperiously requires them to exercise it? It would be strange, indeed, if the confidants of the Almighty, persons acquainted even with his *secret* will—individuals whom he has called and qualified with the effusion of his spirit to lead men to heaven, and to be the instruments of their eternal salvation it would be strange, indeed, that they should have no desire to direct us in our duty here, and instruct us in what relates to this world as well as what relates to another; and it might seem strange we should distrust those who enjoy the confidence of the Omniscient God, or that we should obey them less in reference to time than to eternity.

The message of the clergyman has been stated; let it be more particularly examined. According to all his preaching, the first duty of the people is to "seek the kingdom of God." This, by a liberal translation, is the "church militant." The people must take little thought for this world, they must fix their thoughts on eternity, remember this is not their abiding place, that there is in eternity a blest city and that it should be their principal object to enquire by what means they can receive in that happy place a mansion of felicity for themselves. Towards this object as the magnet of the soul it is said every desire should point; and to gain it, no sacrifice should be deemed too great—no, not the loss of a right eye, a right hand, or even of life itself.

As the means to gain this, everybody knows, the church must be supported. This being the temple of God, whatever gift made to it, whatever obedience is paid to its mandates, God accepts as if done to himself, and will amply reward us for it in the eternal world. It is therefore we are commanded to support the church. It is the visible glory of God; by supporting it we glorify God. Hence it is, we are to give to the church and to give as we shall wish we had given when we come to die. Hence the frequency with which the clergy dwell on this theme; and hence, too, the liberality which the pious and the devout and the sinner about to die, anxious to atone for a misspent life, manifest in their donations. For the whole of man's duty may be summed up in a word, "support the church."

But this duty is binding on men in their collective as well as in their individual capacity; on rulers as well as upon the ruled; upon all in authority, as well as upon those who must obey; and all authority is from God, and as all rulers hold their power as a trust from him, they are bound to exercise it according to his will, to use all for his glory. Now, as the clergy are the appointed interpreters of the divine will, and as they claim to be sole directors in all matters relating to his glory, the whole resolves itself into this conclusion, "All rulers are bound to obey what the clergy tell them is the will of God, and to do what *they* declare will be for his glory."

Hence it is easy to perceive that the profession of the clergy naturally generates the disposition with which they are charged; and it requires no peculiar intellectual acuteness to discover that when a clergyman has a selfish or ambitious spirit, he may hide under the duties of his profession the worst and the most dangerous designs. It has already been shown that the clergy have never been wanting in the disposition to make the sanctity of their profession subservient to individual aggrandizement; and it seems proper they should exhibit strong proofs of a reformation before they can make the judicious believe they will not conduct in the same manner again. If honest in his profession, the priest must have the disposition with which he is charged; he cannot think it wrong for him to control civil government for he is above it, and the glory of God requires him to do it; if dishonest, nothing better can be expected, and none who have any discernment will consider themselves more safe.

Such are the clergy, such their profession; let their conduct now pass in review. The last 25 years have been a busy time with the priesthood, years of great activity, of great mental agitation, years replete with danger, and it is hoped they will not prove barren of instruction. Every engine seems to have been put in motion; every machine which clerical ingenuity could construct has been put in operation; and every method which could reinstate the clergy in their lost possessions, and re-establish an odious hierarchy, degrading to the name of religion, and disgraceful to the people who will bear it has been adopted and with no small success.

It will be unnecessary to run over all their arts and machinations. As one proof of their wishes, and strongly presumptive of their designs, our readers are referred to a CIRCULAR[4] which the orthodox handed round among those of their own stamp. It is three or four years since it found its way into the public journals and we are satisfied its authenticity is beyond a doubt and its genuineness no subject of dispute. The orthodox are charged with it and they have never, to our knowledge, denied it. A few extracts will show its spirit and its object.

After touching lightly upon the apparent union which then existed among several denominations of Christians, upon the *brotherly love*, upon the awakened zeal and extended religious impressions occasioned by Theological Seminaries, Bible, Missionary, and Tract Societies, and the probable blessings which were to flow from the establishment of the *National* Tract Society at New York under the united care and superintendence of the most distinguished clergy of various denominations, it proceeds:

"From this view of sentiment and feeling, students of different persuasions can meet and read the same religious authors, in the same Institutions, under the same Professors for the acquisition of Theological knowledge. Thus, while errors and corruptions are detected

---

[4] [Ed. Not able to identify the circular.]

and exposed, will correct and orthodox religious sentiments be promulgated and defended by learned Students employed in the same holy and divine calling, for one common purpose. It is by these means, we see so many of our first men becoming converts, more and more to the Christian faith, and devoted to the interests of Bible, Missionary, and Tract Societies. At the seat of the General Government, we see Congress electing Chaplains in rotation to offer up prayers for the success of their deliberations. While we witness such concert among the higher orders of society, as to religious worship, with a favorable disposition to the distribution of Religious Tracts, properly composed, we have a good right to conclude it will *issue in a wise National Creed*, and that the most pious and enlightened men in our country will see the impropriety of sending out Missionaries and Divines to preach the Word of Life with discordant and conflicting views."

"This pious unanimity and zeal will be apt to produce its own temporal reward. See the want of it in the late war, when the influence of many disaffected Clergymen was powerfully and successfully exerted to paralyze the energy and operations of government. They were not then allowed to feel and enjoy the benefits which their religious labors might confer on their country. Since, their station has become more respected; the most respectable layman feels himself honored to join the Presbyterian and Baptist, the Episcopalian and Methodist, assembled together to deliberate on the best means which their joint councils may suggest for the extension of religious knowledge. The Clerical robe is becoming less the theme of scoffers, and more and more a proud and honorable badge to him, who, for his Theological attainments is entitled to it."

"By enlisting moral and religious, and consequently numerical force, in the cause of Religion, all the opposition of infidelity will be borne down and overpowered. Until those collisions and conflicts of opinion, growing out of the same Christian belief, shall be annihilated or greatly abated, our country, in times of distress and danger may be divided and distracted by religious feuds and quarrels. The business of Government ought, as much as possible, and may be practicable, to produce unanimity and concord, both in our civil and religious institutions."

"As sure as the force of circumstances produces order and system in the world, and as sure as there is a tendency and gravitation in natural and physical bodies towards each other, so sure, in the moral and religious world, will the lesser bodies or sects be attracted to the largest. Among refractory and apostate spirits, opposition may be expected, *but it will be made to yield to the power and influence of evangelical truth."*

"A reference to the state of Christianity in England, furnishes an ample solution to this position. A great majority of the people there are reconciled to the established order, and unite in giving their support to the State. I do not say this because I am an Episcopalian, for I am not; but to enforce the necessity of unanimity in the prevailing religion of the State; or, of making it *National in its form, tendency, and operation*; since that may be considered orthodox, which has the most adherents, who are made so by birth, education, or accident; as each sect pretends, from Scripture, to derive proof to its system. It is the force of circumstances we have been speaking of, which has produced the established religion of England, the choice of its people, and which is necessary to its peace, the security of the Government, and the strength of the nation."

"What a beneficial influence would it have on public sentiment and feeling, if the index of its character should be distinguished by a more *national costume*, which would be solemn and imposing, and such as would secure to the sacerdotal character that reverence which is due to it. The emblems of worship, properly prepared and arranged, and approved of by a majority of the nation, might be made to correspond with it in other respects. Will it be believed, that thus qualified, any of the leading sects of this country would repel the *sanction of the government* if offered to them? Are the professors of worship in England to be, and would those in this country, preferring a different mode, be consigned to perdition for differing from each other?"

"From what has been said we may rationally conclude, that a zealous co-operation among the most respectable religious sects in our country, is tending to a consolidation, in the principles, doctrines, and forms of worship, so desirable to every true Christian, and which may eventually bring about a Conventional arrangement as to a settled form. These anticipations may be further realized, in securing from Congress an appropriation of a portion of the public lands, to a limited, and yet sufficient number of the Clergy, and for a well defined course of Education. This is prospective, and those who are fastidious about it, may gradually sacrifice their prejudices and scruples, which will be likely to be dissipated by the light of religious knowledge, on the altar of harmony and concord."

(September 5, 1829): 284-87

But few remarks are here required to place the extracts made in our last in their true light. The authors of the circular seem confident the various measures which they mention, and which the orthodox clergy advocated with characteristic zeal at that time, and which they cherish with all of maternal fondness at this time — the authors seem confident these measures will result "in a wise national creed." This seems to have been at the date of the circular the object of their wishes, and we shall soon proceed to show their disposition has not changed.

By forming this combination, or by bringing about this consolidation of the principal religious denominations, and thus enlisting "numerical force" on their side, "all the opposition from infidelity will be borne down and overpowered." Now this term "infidelity" is a word of vague import, very different in its meaning at Rome than at Constantinople. It means, however, in religious parlance, whatever opposes the orthodox, or predominant religion in the country in which it is used. It is the chief weapon of the orthodox, the principal argument used by the clergy to silence those who are doubtful about the propriety of their measures. It is thrown as a mark and the person to whom it is applied is designated to destruction, or as deserving the abhorrence of those who love the clergy. Still, to an enlightened mind, the application of the term is a badge of honor; as in fact the word infidel denotes a person who prefers honesty to hypocrisy, and liberty and mental freedom with the few to slavery with the many. The clergy would overpower all infidels, stop their voices, and prevent them from enjoying those rights for which our fathers fought, bled and died.

This topic must not be so soon dismissed. There is a large class of our population, aye, and the very bone and marrow if you please of our population, who study rather the ordinary concerns of life than theology; who, having the interest of their country at heart, have not found leisure to attend to all the nice distinctions, invisible to all but theological eyes, in which religion is made to consist. These persons, marking the contending factions of religionists, the general uncertainty of all their speculations, adopt a moral practice for themselves; or, at least, treat the great topics of dispute among zealots with indifference, and sometimes, perhaps, with silent contempt. These men, heretofore, have been our public spirited citizens; they have been our warm hearted patriots; the defenders of our country, the framers of our constitution; our magistrates, representatives, and presidents. Under this description is ranked a Franklin, a Jefferson, a Madison, and by far the larger number who are conspicuous in our history, a large share of those whose virtues have rendered our republic illustrious, who have pointed out to her the path of glory.

But these persons, by the orthodox, would be accounted infidels because they professed but little and practiced much. These persons, by the religionists, are held up as mournful proof of the depravity of human nature, as men with superb talents, but destitute of grace; and who, with all their excellencies, with all their virtues, with all the utility of their lives, are now probably suffering the gnawings of that worm which never dies. Instead of teaching the youth to imitate their virtues and their usefulness, the clergy tell them to avoid their practices, and to look with horror upon their want of zeal for the church.

But these persons are persons of this description, who have filled the public offices in the gift of a free people with so much dignity, with so much usefulness and glory to their country, are to be "borne down and overpowered," compelled to become sectarians before they can hold any public office, hypocrites before they can be trusted with the public good. Such a course would soon stamp our republican government with infamy; would, to the no small joy of all crowned heads, overthrow our free institutions, and rear a detested monarchy on the ruins of liberty. It were indecent to express our abhorrence of this plan, or the indignation it must excite in every enlightened, in every patriotic bosom. But such, fellow citizens, is the avowed object of our idolized priests, to effect which they declare themselves at work. We would invoke the shades of the martyrs of our revolution to frown indignant upon such measures, and upon the shameless avowal of them. We may not be endangered, but alas, we may feel too secure. There is something rotten, there is something wrong, when a class of men, so numerous and so powerful as the orthodox clergy, dare avow such sentiments, or when they can even embrace them.

The clergy seem anxious to be distinguished by a "national costume," which, "*solemn and imposing*," will secure the "sacerdotal character" its dignity. Not willing to trust to the naked beauty of religion, and rest their dignity on the utility of their lives, on the benevolence of their characters, they are ambitious of a *dress* which shall extort unmerited respect, and give them undue influence which they despair of obtaining by the simplicity of their doctrines, or from the beneficence of their practice.

"These anticipations," they think, "will be realized in securing an appropriation of a portion of public lands, to a limited and yet a sufficient number of clergy, and to a well defined course of education." There is no difficulty in comprehending this sentence. If the clergy were always equally intelligible, the world would not be disgraced by religious contentions, nor the church deformed with incomprehensible dogmas. Congress has the care of large tracts of public lands, some very valuable, and almost indescribably excellent. These lands would make a fine patrimony for the church.

Reader, how do you think the clergy expect to grasp these lands? Such men as Col. Johnson would not be too ready to bestow such valuable presents upon a class of men who have abused him and all other patriots, who have disturbed the ashes of the dead and branded with reproach those who gained our independence. But think ye of no feasible plan? Let none be members of Congress but those who are devoted to the clergy, none but those who depend on the orthodox for their votes; let none but these have charge of our public lands and how long would it require to obtain a law appropriating a part or all of these lands to the service of the church? If the orthodox could govern the polls, these men would fear no public censure, they would be supported in their unhallowed measures.

Have not the orthodox a plan adopted; have they not avowed it their intention to support no man for office, unless he is sound in the faith? Whether so or not, what we have alleged shows very clearly the orthodox are determined to receive some state patronage; that they are laboring to gain for themselves an establishment that will interfere with the rights of our citizens; that they are laboring to accomplish an object which menaces with death every spark of genuine liberty. True, we are told the people of these United States are too well enlightened to ever submit to this. It may be so. We pray God the result may prove it so. But of one thing we feel confident, that if we remain inactive, boasting how well we are enlightened, we may regret that we had not deemed ourselves more ignorant.

The disposition which we charged to the clergy appears from what has been said evidently theirs. But we have more facts to offer; language which speaks, or should speak, in a voice of thunder to every freeman. We shall present our readers with the part of a famous sermon of Doct. E. S. Ely, of Philadelphia, preached on the anniversary of our independence, deemed an appropriate discourse for our nation's jubilee.[5] The extracts we shall make have been already before our readers, but they should be repeated till every one gets them by heart; till every manly principle of his bosom burns with honest indignation at the unhallowed spirit which dictated them. They form a link in our chain of evidences and ought not to be left out. Had the author of the sermon a conscience and did he believe in the awful day of judgment about which he preaches, he would tremble lest this sermon should rise up against him and condemn him to that hell to

---

[5] [Ed. On the sermon, see the Introduction, p. 22 above.]

which he so liberally dooms the infidel and the heretical. But God is merciful and we rejoice to think that even Ezra Stiles Ely will yet become holy and happy.

It is only necessary to remark, Dr. Ely is one of the leading members of the Presbyterian church, being standing clerk of their general assembly, and the one often pitched upon to write and publish their reports. No censure has been passed upon him for this publication by the church to which he belongs, though that church has not been sparing in its denunciations upon those who have condemned his sentiments. From the high standing of the man and the general approbation of his party, together with many other circumstances not necessary to mention now, we consider the sermon official, as authorized, at least, bearing the implied sanction of the whole Presbyterian order in the United States. We would not be uncharitable nor would we degrade charity to mere blindness and credulity; but here follow the extracts, they may speak for themselves.

"Let it be distinctly stated and fearlessly maintained in the first place, that every member of this Christian nation, from the highest to the lowest, ought to serve the Lord with fear, and yield his sincere homage to the Son of God. Every ruler *should* be an avowed, and a sincere friend of Christianity. He should know and believe the doctrines of our holy religion, and act in conformity with its precepts. This he *ought to* do; because as a man he is required to serve the Lord; and as a public ruler, he is called upon by divine authority 'to kiss the Son.'"

"Our rulers, like any other members of the community, who are under law to God as rational being, and under law to Christ, since they have the light of divine revelation, ought to search the Scriptures, assent to the truth, profess faith in Christ, keep the Sabbath holy to God, pray in private, and in the domestic circle, attend on the public ministry of the word, be baptized, and celebrate the Lord's Supper. None of our rulers have the consent of their Maker that they should be pagans, Socinians, Mussulmans, deists, the opponents of Christianity."

"In other words, our Presidents, Secretaries of the Government, Senators, and other Representatives in Congress, Governors of States, Judges, State Legislators, Justices of the Peace, and city Magistrates, are just as much bound as any other persons in the United States, to be *orthodox* in their faith, and virtuous, and religious in their whole deportment. They may no more lawfully be bad husbands, wicked parents, men of *heretical opinions*, or men of dissolute lives, than the obscure individual who would be sent to Bridewell[6] for his blasphemy and debauchery."

"God, my hearers, requires a Christian faith, a *Christian profession,* and a Christian practice of all our public men; and we as Christian citizens ought, by the publication of our opinions to require the same."

"Secondly — Since it is the duty of all our rulers to serve the Lord and kiss the Son of God, it must be most manifestly the duty of all our Christian fellow-citizens to honor the Lord Jesus Christ and promote Christianity by electing and supporting as public officers the friends of our blessed Savior. If all the truly religious men of our nation would be punctual and persevering in their endeavors to have good men chosen to fill all our national and state offices of honor, power and trust, their weight would be soon felt by politicians; and those who care little for the religion of the Bible, would for their own interest, consult the reasonable wishes of the great mass of Christians throughout our land."

"I propose, fellow-citizens, a new sort of union, or, if you please, *a Christian party in politics,* which I am exceedingly desirous all good men in our country should join; not by *subscribing a constitution* and the formation of a new society, but by adopting, avowing, and determining to act upon truly religious principles in all civil matters."

"If three or four of the most numerous denominations of Christians in the United States, the Presbyterians, the Baptists, the Methodists and Congregationalists for instance, should act upon this principle, our country would never be dishonored with an *avowed Infidel* in her national cabinet or capitol. The *Presbyterians* alone could bring *half a million of electors* into the field, in opposition to any known advocate of deism, Socinianism, or any other species of avowed hostility to the truth of Christianity. If to the denominations above named we add the members of the Protestant Episcopal Church in our country, the electors of these five classes of true Christians, united in the sole requisition of *apparent* friendship to Christianity in every candidate for office whom they will support, *could govern every public election* in our country, without infringing in the least upon the charter of our civil liberties."

"It will be objected that my plan of a truly Christian party in politics will make hypocrites. We are not answerable for their hypocrisy if it does."

---

[6] [Ed. A prison in London, near the so-called St. Bride's well.]

"It will be objected, moreover, that my scheme of voting on political elections according to certain fixed religious principles, will create jealousies among the different denominations of Christians. But why should it? Our rulers which we have elected are of some, or of no religious sect. If they are of no religious denomination, they belong to the party of Infidels. If they are of any of the denominations of true Christians, it is better, in the judgment of all true Christians, that they should be of that one company than in the company of Infidels."

"I am free to avow, that other things being equal, I would prefer for my chief magistrate, and judge, and ruler, a sound Presbyterian; and every candid religionist will make the same declaration concerning his own persuasion; but I would prefer a religious and moral man, of any one of the truly Christian sects, to any man destitute of religious principle and morality."

"Let us all be Christian politicians, and govern ourselves by supreme love to our blessed Master, whether we unite in prayers or in the election of our civil rulers. Let us be as conscientiously religious at the polls as in the pulpit, or house of worship."

"Let us never support by our votes any immoral man, or any known contemner of any of the fundamental doctrines of Christ for any office; and least of all for the Presidency of these United States. Let us elect men who dare to acknowledge the Lord Jesus Christ for their Lord in their public documents. Which of our Presidents have ever done this? It would pick no infidel's pocket, and break no Jew's neck if our President should be so singular as to let it be known that he is a *Christian* by his Messages, and an advocate for the Deity of Christ by his personal preference of a Christian temple to a Socinian conventicle. It would be no violation of our national constitution, if our members of Congress should quit reading of newspapers and writing letters on the Lord's day, at least during public worship, in the Hall of Representatives."

"We are a Christian nation; we have a right to demand that all our rulers in their conduct shall conform to Christian morality; and if they do not, it is the duty and privilege of Christian freemen to make a new and a better election."

(September 19, 1829): 298-99

The sentiments contained in the extracts from Dr. Ely, inserted in our last, have obtained no small notoriety. When compared with the object stated in the "Circular," we have noticed, little doubt is left as to the real object of the Orthodox. Their intentions become obvious and their plans are exhibited in bold relief. They proposed an amalgamation of the principal religious denominations from which it is hoped will result a "wise national creed." And to maintain this creed, they express themselves desirous of procuring "a portion of the public lands" for the benefit of the clergy. That is in plain English, our orthodox friends wish to fix the support of the clergy upon a solid basis to obtain for them sufficient state patronage to have them paid from the national treasury.

Our government, instead of being a civil institution must become the pillar of the church and employ its influence and resources in the maintenance of ecclesiastical discipline. The government, indeed, is not required to say what religion it will support, but it is to bow to the most numerous and the most influential party. This is evident from the whole tenor of the orthodox logic. They complained of the committee in Senate, because they did not grant the prayer of the petitioners respecting the Sabbath Mail. They blamed the committees, on the ground that the petitioners had the majority of the Republic on their side. Hence on their ground, when the majority of the people ask government to aid their religion, government must do it.

We ask not, say the people, government to decide what religion we shall have, but to protect the religion which we have. Protect the religion of the minority? No. But the religion which the majority have said they will have. Hence it is plain to what class of the clergy, the public funds must be appropriated: not to all, but to a limited, yet sufficient number of the orthodox, and that sect may be considered orthodox who have the greatest numerical force. On this ground, the authors of the "Circular" would have religion established and by so doing "all opposition from *infidelity* would be borne down and overpowered."

No doubt such an object may seem very desirable for some, but to those who may chance to be of the minority, it may not seem worthy of all praise. But how is it to be accomplished? Our Government, say those religionists, is bound to obey the will of its constitution for that is the will of the majority. Governments like ours can be molded with perfect ease when the people are rightly instructed and are properly marshaled to the work. The majority of the people may say "we will have such a religion," no one can prohibit them. They may say they will have a certain sum paid to the preachers of that religion, and the national treasury must pay it; the people are sovereigns. Only one thing is wanting, that is to have those who manage the government prepare to adopt the measures. Now for Dr. Ely's plan.

"I propose fellow citizens a new party in politics — a Christian party." What is this for? Reader canst thou not perceive? Know then the orthodox want the government to aid them, to patronize their plans and to give them the public lands. Infidels would not do this. It is therefore necessary to have none but *Christians* elected to any office, yea more, none but orthodox Christians, who are ready to aid the orthodox clergy in the support of their party. We will have a Christian party in politics, we will elect none but of a certain faith, and those we elect must understand we elect them for the promotion of our religion. They must know their duty is to aid our plans as a sort of compromise for their election.

Such is the plan. Americans, when you submit to this, when you ask a religious *profession* of your representatives, your legislators, judges and other officers, you may expect Salem witchcraft to return and the period of hanging Quakers and banishing Baptists will again come round. You may think this day is far distant. Be it so. But God in mercy avert it from our children and grant the Beast, which preyed upon our ancestors, may not live to devour our children.

While on this subject, the memory of the past rises, crowded with mournful images, pictures appalling to less sensitive hearts than ours strike the vision; a warning voice from other days comes on each breeze. Sad as the funeral dirge sighing through the cypress grove, it bids us "beware." The hallowed name of religion may become the password to death and the zeal, which the profession of piety consecrates, may be fed with unholy fires and burn to the lowest hell. Cold is the heart that does not love the great Author of nature, unfeeling and unrefined is the sensibility that does not receive its highest bliss at the altar of the Most High; but colder still and more dead to feeling the one which can even contemplate, without "trembling alive all o'er," the return of priestly ignorance and clerical misrule. The clergy have reigned. They have, seated upon the thrones of the Caesars, made their power felt far beyond the farthest limits of the Roman name. And then "darkness was visible" relieved only by the fires which lit the victims to their tomb. Is that period to return? Is that gloom to be spread over our sun lighted land? It may be so.

But why declaim? Why call up the melancholy picture of other times? Why weep over the woes endured by generations gone? Whoever knew priestcraft softened with tears or mellowed by visions of sorrow? Priestcraft! offspring of hell! relentless as death, all devouring as the grave, with an imagined warrant from God stalks forth with the spirit of the devil and spares neither age, sex nor condition; neither vice nor virtue, nor aught good or bad, dear to the heart or indifferent, that may grapple with its plans of universal dominion. If defeated, it sits like Marius[7] on the ruins of Carthage, smiling in scorn, writhing its lips with revenge and planning new scenes of murder and devastation. If successful, it breathes with the withering siroc and fattens on the sighs, tears and woes of its enslaved victims. A heartless monster! hoping to reach heaven by filling up mountains of wretchedness, or if doomed to hell, anxious to involve a universe in its ruin. But enough. It was in honor of this monster Dr. Ely preached his sermon, and it is for this, their God, the orthodox clergy are laboring, and at his shrine they pay their morning and evening devotions. Deluded wretches, let them worship on, but God forbid any more should be seduced to join in their unholy worship!

We need look no further. Dr. Ely has exhibited the plan. He has told us for whom we must vote and he has declared it his anxious desire to form a party, which shall obey the directions he has given. That party is forming; his principles are being reduced to practice, and who can tell the results? Do they lack power? Our future numbers will consider this enquiry.[8] Sabbath schools must pass in review and we shall glance at the Mammoth Bible Society,[9] and other mis-named benevolent institutions and ask, how large are their funds? How fast are they increasing? Who has the control of these funds? And what warrant have we that these funds will be judiciously managed and properly expended? Reader, turn not idly from this subject, man may "steal the livery of the Court of Heaven to serve the Devil in."[10]

[7] [Ed. Marius Gaius (157-86 B.C.) was a Roman general and consul.]
[8] [Ed. There was no future number on this issue.]
[9] [Ed. Not able to identify the Mammoth Bible Society.]
[10] [Ed. Robert Pollok (1798-1827), *The Course of Time* (1827), Book 8, 616.]

23.

VINDICATION OF UNIVERSALISM

The Gospel Advocate and Impartial Investigator
7 (May 2, 1829): 140-41

I would call the attention of that class of my readers who fear I am deistical, to the following extract from an article published in the *Religious Inquirer*,[1] a paper which ranks high among the first publications of our order. The reader will find the line drawn between the Deist and the Universalist with sufficient accuracy. The observations made are liberal and do justice to the writer's heart as well as his head. It is unnecessary to say the editor of the Gospel Advocate can and does respond to the sentiment which it clearly states. It is enough to say he is not conscious of ever having published a single sentence when fairly interpreted which would contradict what is there asserted.

I have always written as I speak, freely and fearlessly. It is to me of no consequence, at least little subject of care, whether my sentiments approach deism, or Calvinism, or Arminianism, or any other *ism,* if they are supported by facts. To awaken enquiry is more my design than to dogmatize; hence I labor to encourage investigation and pursue that course, which to me appears most likely to arouse the mind, and call forth its dormant energies. I have never felt the least fear that when the mind is free and active that it will prefer falsehood to truth. Therefore I have not felt as many do in reference to what I have written. Man must learn to decide for himself and to confide only in his own convictions. All that writers or preachers should do is to present the materials for a correct decision and then leave every man to decide for himself; he will do well enough.

With regard to the Bible, I make one remark and hope my readers will remember it: I have ever laid it down in all my writings that so far as the character of God is concerned, so far as it respects worship to him, together with our destination after death, the Bible is our only guide, and is, so far as we do or can know, both safe and competent. With regard to this world, our relations with each other,

---

[1] [Ed. The *Religious Inquirer* (Hartford, 1827-30). Brownson reprinted the article on the agreements and disagreements between Universalism and Deism in *GAII* 7 (May 2, 1829): 141-42.]

our duties as individuals and as members of society, I follow the Bible where it agrees with facts or where it gives directions, but rest chiefly on what is collected from the light of nature, the apparent constitution of things, the lessons of experience, etc. This may be deism. But it is different from what those who bear that name profess. I hold the Bible infallible where the light of nature fails. When I contemplate the heavens, I wish a telescope to enlarge, to extend my vision; but when I am examining my books, or the objects in my room, I feel no want of such assistance. When I wish to become acquainted with the affairs of the invisible world I take the Bible and follow it implicitly; when I look at the things of the earth, I am satisfied with my natural eyes. The Bible is my spiritual telescope, with which I survey the world of spirits, and regions after death. But when used in surveying the affairs of men it sometimes distorts the object and encourages the suspicion that its design was to view heaven and not earth. I therefore use my natural eyes wherever they can be of use and take the Bible only when they fail.

My writings relate chiefly to the affairs of this world, consequently little use is made of the Bible. When I treat Bible subjects, I use the Bible; when I philosophize I invoke philosophy. Charity they say begins at home, to which I would add, wisdom also begins at home. Therefore we should first learn ourselves, become acquainted with the earth, and then we may carry our researches into the heavens to the full extent of our abilities. Such is the character of my creed; believe it, those who are convinced it is true; reject it, those who can produce a better or show it false.

24.

REVIEW OF AMICUS

The Gospel Advocate and Impartial Investigator
7 (May 30, 1829): 169-72

I insert in this number another communication from Amicus,[1] and as he had not given notice of an intended continuation, it cannot be deemed improper to present a brief review. Amicus has said some very good things; much he has said he might have learned from my own writings, and, though not wholly, yet very nearly expressed in the same terms.

I agree with him in most of the abstract principles he stated in his first communication, though some of them are shaded in a manner I think calculated to produce wrong impressions. In stating the manner in which we acquire our knowledge he is correct. In speaking of the "seductive wiles" of falsehood, he has attributed more art, as well as more beauty to that haggard wretch than I believe her to possess. Truth in my opinion is by far the lovelier of the two, and I believe there is scarcely a fool living but would choose truth rather than falsehood were he to see them both.

As it respects our fallibility and the shortness of our life, what Amicus advances may be true, but does not deserve the importance he seems to believe. Man is capable of perceiving truth and of distinguishing it from falsehood. Not indeed all truth, I will admit; and hence the first step we should take is to learn where the line, which divides things we can know from things we cannot, should be drawn. The one class of things we may study without much danger of error; of the other, all we can learn, with the powers we now possess, will be conjecture.

Much is said about the "fallibility of our nature" and the little dependence to be placed upon the deductions of human reason. This is the mere cant of the priest. If no dependence is to be placed on our own ability to determine what is true, how shall we be assured the Bible is not a cheat; if we are never to trust our own powers, how are

---

[1] [Ed. The first letter from Amicus was "Mr. Editor," *GAII* 7 (May 16, 1829): 154-56. The letter Brownson refers to here is published in *GAII* 7 (May 30, 1829): 174-76.]

we to know that what the priest tells is not false? The case is, the argument is often alleged as a reason why we should not dispute the assertions of our religionists, but it is in reality an equally strong argument why we should not believe them. If a man tells me I ought not to disbelieve a thing because I am a fallible being, and because I may be deceived, I reply I ought then not to believe. I am a fallible being, I may believe what is not true.

His remarks on the shortness of life are doubtless true; but if he intends to enforce the argument he has suggested, he will perpetuate all the ignorance and all the miseries under which we groan. Happily however for the world people are beginning to treat such arguments as they deserve. If the farmer should reason as Amicus would have me reason, he would say each spring, "I will not plough my ground, nor scatter any seed into the earth, for I may die before it will ripen." Amicus would tell us, what everybody knows, that if in our enquiries after knowledge "we begin back in embryo, we may die before we can grasp the whole of knowledge." Very true. But what shall we do? Take everything as we find it and make no exertions? By no means. Learn what we can, and leave our successors to perfect our enquiries. But Amicus says if he draws from "nature alone," now if he can point out any other sources of knowledge than nature, he will confer on me a favor, which I fear, I shall never have the pleasure of acknowledging. Perhaps he will think the uncertainty of life is so great that it will be best not to attempt it.

I think I do not misunderstand his argument. He doubtless considers we must take the experience of our predecessors and also the Bible. I admit both, for both are indeed the same. The Bible is the experience of individuals who lived in former days and is to us a historic record, supported as are all other historic records. With regard to what has been transmitted us from other times, we are to ascertain what is true or we are to ascertain what others have established as truth, and this must form so much of our stock of knowledge, we may then be said to be so far in advance. But as every man who knows anything must know antiquity as well as our immediate predecessors have transmitted us error as well as truth. To adopt, as the foundation of the temple we would raise, what has thus been furnished us without discriminating the durable from the perishable materials would be building upon a mixed foundation, liable at every moment to give way and destroy or render useless all our labors. We must begin back and though the labor of others will lessen and facilitate our own we must still traverse the whole ground, find the true path of enquiry, walk it far as we can, and leave to those who come after us to progress farther.

What he alleges respecting the possibility of my having sometimes mistaken falsehood for the truth is very possible.

That I should err is nothing unaccountable and Amicus need not have labored so hard to make me think it very probable. I, like the rest of my species, am liable to err, and also, as I believe, all are capable of ascertaining some things for a certainty. What Amicus alleges as a reason why I have erred is unworthy his own sagacity and the freedom of enquiry which even he would allow.

He thinks it strange that all who lived before me have been mistaken, that all the wise, the pious, the acute and the reverend, should have discovered no truth, and that the editor of the Gospel Advocate alone should be the happy man, to be blessed with the possession of truth. Now I am strongly inclined to reply to such reasoning, fudge! What does it amount to? I remark on this, I have never insinuated that all who lived before me have been entirely wrong. Most of the sentiments I have advanced, if not all of them, have been advanced for ages. I have availed myself of what others have written, and I believe I hold some sentiments which all denominations of whatever name or character also hold; I have aimed to discover those sentiments in which all mankind either do or must agree as soon as they have examined them.

I treat either as false or unnecessary most of those notions which divide mankind. For I have discovered that all things which are susceptible of demonstration require only to be perceived by the mind, together with the evidence by which they are supported, to have all agree to their truth. Who doubts a theorem in mathematics when he understands it? Who that has seen the sun doubts its circular form? Now to avoid contention, experience has discovered this grand truth, *we are to contend for nothing which is not susceptible of proof or of being established by evidence.*

I have also remarked those things about which mankind differ are destitute of sufficient, or what is the same thing, of evidence enough within our reach to establish them. And still farther, these things which rest upon doubtful authority are of no great consequence to the peace and welfare of mankind here, however valuable they may be to us hereafter. Now I am not the first who has made this discovery. My own observations have convinced me it is true. I have therefore stepped forth for the purpose, not of convincing others, but, to induce them to mark their own experience, and to convince themselves, or to ascertain the correctness of my position from *their* observations. This may be "presumption," it may be "audacity," but the same might be said of everyone who has come forward as a reformer. It might have been alleged of Luther, it might have been alleged of Jesus, it might have been alleged of Moses, and it may be alleged of anyone who shall at some future day come forward to expunge the errors which the sagacity of the present day may overlook; and very likely 30,000 years hence some philosopher like myself may be found pleading for reform and another like Amicus may accuse him of presumption, of audacity etc. But what of all this? Shall we be discouraged from doing what we can or ridiculed for proclaiming what of truth we are confident we have discovered? Such things deter not me.

Amicus says I have proscribed the doctrine of "imputed righteousness." I am not aware of having written anything against it; I may, but I do not recollect. I however do not believe the doctrine. To me it is one of the most absurd as well as the most deleterious sentiments that ever priestcraft taught or ignorance believed. To me it is a libel on common sense, a "caricature" of Christianity, and an affront to all sound morality. In the sermon to which Amicus alludes there is not a single word said about "imputed righteousness," and the seeming contradiction with which he has made himself so merry is easily reconciled by any mind sufficiently capacious to reconcile two facts, one growing out the abuse of a theory and the other out of its right use.

The two facts, which appeared incomprehensible to Amicus, stated in the sermon, are, first, the notion that men are virtuous because they adopt a certain creed or that they must be orthodox to be accounted holy has been the cause of incalculable misery to the world — let the history of the church determine whether this assertion be correct or not. The other fact is that a rational belief in the doctrine of Christ is favorable to virtue—let the Christian answer whether this be correct or not. What all this has to do with imputed righteousness I know not. Amicus has undertaken to prove the doctrine, but he has so explained it that no theologian who prays to be saved "for Christ's sake" will own it.

If I am able to understand his reasoning, he does not mean that faith is justification, but that as a righteous being, God could not justify us for our works, he must, therefore, keep us eternally condemned unless he can find a substitute for good works. That is to say God could not pronounce the sinner just *de facto*, nor by any existing law, so he introduces faith *post facto*, and declares that he who will believe shall be accounted just or righteous, notwithstanding so far as the fact is concerned, he is unjust, still a sinner.

I know not by what rules the court of heaven is governed but I believe every wise man would despise an earthly court, guilty of such trifling, not to use a harsher term.

I believe no such doctrine. I do not believe Deity allows of any fictions of law. Earthly courts indeed do. The English government declares the "King cannot do wrong," though he may be the biggest scoundrel that was ever ranked as one of the biped race. Amicus would make the court of heaven do the same. Here is a murderer. God cannot at once pronounce him a good man; that would be false, but God can say to him "murderer, believe I died on the cross in Judea, and that you will be damned to all eternity if you don't believe it, and I will pronounce you a just man." I dislike such trifling. God will pronounce no man just until he is just and he will receive none until he is personally holy, "for without holiness shall no man see the Lord" [Heb. 12:14].

The true doctrine, I believe is this, Christ's life, preaching, suffering, death and resurrection are calculated, when believed, to produce righteousness in us; and when we become personally righteous, then and not till then we are *ipso facto* justified. There are no fictions, no accounting things which are not, as though they were, except as God's superintendence of all things, and his prescience enable him to predict the thing when it has not actually transpired, and he knowing that all men through the influence of the means adopted will become just, he may sometimes pronounce him so when such is not the fact. But everything of this kind is spoken in reference to the end which God knows to be certain, and not in reference to what at the particular point of time may be the actual character of the individual.

The passages of Scripture, quoted by Amicus from the writings of Paul, may easily be reconciled to what I have stated by bearing in mind that Paul often become "all things to all men that he might gain some" [1 Cor. 9:22]. That is, Paul always in his reasoning regards only the particular point which he is at any particular time endeavoring to prove. The extracts from his writings, introduced by Amicus, have relation not to what we call good works, but to the works enjoined by the Jewish ceremonial law. The letters were addressed to Judaizing Christians, who contended that believers in Christ should observe the Jewish rites and ceremonies. Paul reproves them; and declares "Christ is the end of the law to every one that believeth" [Rom. 10:4]. End of what law? End of the law of good works? Of the law which enjoins personal holiness? No. But of the law which enjoined the offering of a lamb or a he goat as an atonement for sin. Paul contends that the "hand writing of ordinances is blotted out" [Col. 2:14], and that we are to walk in "newness of life, after the spirit and not after the flesh" [Rom. 8:4]. That is, the various things which the law of Moses enjoined, which could not make the comers thereunto perfect, are no longer to be insisted on, as to be true followers of Christ, we are to "walk after the spirit" [Rom. 8:1]. Or in the language of Christ "be ye therefore perfect as your Father in heaven is perfect" [Matt. 5:24], or in the words of John "he that doeth righteousness is righteous, even as he is righteous" [1 John 3:7], and "know that every one that doeth righteousness is born of him" [1 John 2:29].

Now all this is perfectly plain. Understand Paul as speaking of the works of the Jewish law, which works were only a "show of good things and of will worship," bear in mind that these works were discarded by the gospel as unable to atone for sin, as the Jews believed, and that instead of performing these we must have faith in Christ, or fidelity in his doctrine, that is, faithfulness in the practice of moral goodness, and Amicus' doctrine of "imputed righteousness" "falls over the precipice of forgetfulness."

It is true, the Scriptures say that a man "is justified by faith" [Rom. 3:28] but this does not mean that a man is justified *for* believing, but the man is justified *in* believing. That is, faith works by love and purifies the heart. Faith becomes the moving cause of our justification, not because it possesses any merit of itself, but inasmuch as it is a means and some say the only means of producing moral goodness. So Christ is said to be "our righteousness" [1 Cor. 1:30]; but this is to be understood only as Christ's righteousness has the effect to produce righteousness in us.

It is not necessary to dwell longer on this. The remarks I have made exhibit the only rational ground on which the apparently conflicting passages of Scripture can be reconciled. If Amicus complains that I have not noticed every passage he has quoted, I will answer him, the general remarks made will serve to explain them. I have given the rule, let Amicus and my readers generally test its correctness and applicability. The language of James who is as good authority as Paul or any of the twelve will best express my feelings on this subject. "What doth it profit, my brethren, for a man to say he hath faith, and have not works? Can faith save him? If a brother or sister be naked, and destitute of daily food, and one of you say unto them, 'depart in peace, be ye warmed and filled'; notwithstanding ye give them not those things which are needful to the body; what doth it profit? Even so faith if it have not works, is dead being alone. Thou hast faith and I have works: show me thy faith without thy works, and I will show thee my faith by my works. Thou believest there is one God; thou doest well: the devils also believe and tremble. But wilt thou know, O vain man! That faith without works is dead? Was not Abraham, our father, justified by works, when he offered up Isaac his son upon the altar? Ye see then how that by works a man is justified, and not by faith only." (See James 2:14-24 inclusive.)

Now if the language of James means anything and to me it is certainly very full of meaning, and withal perfectly intelligible, and as authoritative as any part of the Bible—I say if the language of James means anything it must mean that faith of itself is of no use, like the body when its spirit has fled, that faith is useful only as it prompts good works and that instead of a man's being justified because he has faith right or wrong as Amicus would insinuate, none can be justified until they have good works or are personally holy.

I have now replied to all that I consider worthy of notice in these articles; I have given my views on the subject suggested by the remarks of Amicus; I have given some of the reasons why I adopt them. Amicus has given the reason for his; all is now before our readers, who must determine for themselves. I shall cheerfully insert whatever communications Amicus may choose to favor me with, if written in a style and with ability equal to those I have noticed. My columns are open to all well written articles, coming from whatever sect they may, from orthodox or heterodox, believer, or skeptic. The only restriction is, they must be compressed within due bounds, and couched in temperate language, and breathe that tone of dignity and good feeling which every man of sense must wish to cultivate.

(July 11, 1829): 216-18

In my last I inserted a third letter from Amicus,[2] apparently designed as a reply to my review of his other two. As I said before, his communications contain some very good things. I think very well of the abilities of my correspondent; and I wish every man had a little more of one virtue of which he possesses a good share — candor. I must however tell him, the size of my paper requires him to take "leisure to be brief" and give us *multum in parvo*.[3] I shall be glad to hear from him often, I care not how closely my sentiments or my writings are scrutinized.

With his first paragraph I have no particular fault to find. I am unable to find any essential difference between the conclusions to

---

[2] [Ed. The third letter is found in *GAII* 7 (June 27, 1829): 202-05.]

[3] [Ed. Latin for "much in a little space."]

which he has arrived and the statements against which he reasons. The fact on the subject there agitated, I apprehend to be this. Man is a finite being; he must therefore be limited in his mental powers; but he also has some powers, but their extent is not yet learned. Let man go to work, learn what he can do, and then it may easily be determined whether I have supposed him to have more power than he has.

The second paragraph of this article deserves notice because it has apparently, in the estimation of Amicus, caught me in something like false reasoning. In my review I state man loves truth; that even the fool would prefer truth to falsehood were he to see both together. I also say that man is capable of ascertaining truth and of distinguishing it from falsehood. Amicus is at a loss to determine if these statements be true, "how it happens that error has so many votaries at her shrine?" There is no difficulty in this. To have power to discover truth or to be made capable of obtaining such a power is one thing; to exercise that power is another thing very essentially different. Now I believe man is capable of distinguishing truth from falsehood, that is, in most of the subjects which can be submitted to human observation, and the reason why we have so much error in these things is that we do not use the ability given us or if we do it is wasted on subjects which we can never fathom. I would have man draw the line between the world of reality and the world of conjecture, and have him study the former diligently if he cannot learn the whole let him at least learn something. The latter may be delivered over to poets, priests, prophets and misanthropes, to be peopled with just such beings as they may choose to create.

The point which Amicus seems anxious to establish is one which nobody, in his senses, can or will presume to deny. It is simply that man has much weakness as well as some strength. Everybody knows this. His objections to me seem to have arisen from the fact that I alter the collocation of a few words in his statement. For while he in a loud voice says, man has MUCH weakness and barely whispers he has also *some* strength; I in a uniform tone say "man has much strength and also some weakness." Both our positions are right. Amicus seems anxious to make all feel their weakness, while I wish to have all feel their strength as well as their weakness. Mankind have heard nothing for ages but their fallibility, their utter inability to judge of truth. It is time to speak a different language that they may rise from the pitiable condition into which such lessons, injudiciously pronounced, have plunged them, to a just self-respect and to a just confidence in their own powers.

The third paragraph is very well. It varies little from what I believe to be correct. Amicus in this paragraph grants all the liberty for which I ask. The fourth paragraph however deserves more notice, not because it is more important, but as it touches upon some points of reasoning, which I have adopted which may need more explanation than I have hitherto afforded.

Amicus says I "seem to scruple their being any other source of knowledge than nature." I do. But did I understand the term *nature* in the sense he does, I should not. Nature, in the sentence of mine to which he alludes, stands for the universe, with all its laws, dependencies and connections, not as we may suppose nature was some thousand centuries ago, but as it has been and as it is now. I suppose man to be in a state of nature now as much as ever he was that the savage is no more in the state of nature than he whom we call civilized. Hence there is no going backward or forward we are to take things as they are.

I cannot help smiling at the fear Amicus has of going back. I know not whence comes this fear. It cannot be from his aversion to labor, his letters amply refute such a notion. Now all I wish of him or of any other one is to look carefully at the various religious notions which now prevail, and fully, that is so far as can be, test their correctness and to embrace and defend all that he convinces himself is true. But I am averse to taking up opinions as we find them and yielding or pretending to yield them assent without examining their claims upon our credence. If Amicus would recommend this course he and I differ and probably ever shall.

But Amicus thinks I have involved myself in difficulty—I mean to look out for that. I say *nature* is the only source of knowledge. But I profess to believe in the existence of God, and that too, when I say nature is unable to teach us his existence. How shall this be reconciled? Ans. The existence of God is a matter of faith and not of knowledge. We believe he exists but we do not know it, at least I do not, whatever may be the case with others.

But there is another point which Amicus has indirectly stated. He enumerates a number of events which are said to have taken place, mentions several individuals of whom he says he has heard, as Washington and Bonaparte, etc. and asks if he has no "knowledge concerning them." I supposed that Amicus was too much of a metaphysician to ask such a question. "But is not *information* knowledge?" This depends on what is meant by information and also the particular sense in which the term knowledge is understood. When I have the testimony of a man, I believe to be worthy of credit, I receive his testimony. If one, whom I have every reason I can have to believe honest and competent to judge, that is, has a discriminating mind, relates an event which he might know and which he had no interest to misrepresent, I rely on his relation with *nearly* the same confidence I should had the event come under my own observation.

But we may as well look at the point at once. By this indirect course Amicus would design to show the Bible or revelation is knowledge. This I shall deny. The truth of the Bible is a matter of belief or unbelief and there are perhaps as many who disbelieve it as who believe it. Amicus may know it to be true, at least I do not know he does not, but I know I do not, though I may believe it given by inspiration. So far as the Bible rests on demonstration or appeals to the operations of nature which come or may come under our observation, it may be called a source of knowledge. But thus far it is not to be distinguished from nature for it is in fact the same. When it quits this world and tells us of another, treats of things we cannot see, and of things unconnected by any known tie with earth, though it may be true, we must say it is only a matter of faith, it may or it may not be so, we can only *believe*.

On the source of knowledge, much may be said. I conceive the only inlets of knowledge are our senses; certainly the only objects these can receive are the objects of nature. We may imagine a thousand things, we may believe a thousand things out of the course of nature, but such things are matters of faith and not of knowledge. The speculative parts of a religious creed, viz. the existence of God, our accountability to him, and our final destination, or a future state of existence, together with the truth of revelation are all matters of faith and not of knowledge. I will not say, the inspired persons who have given us the Bible did not know; but as we can never possibly determine whether they did or could know, their record becomes to us simply a matter of faith; and all we can know is whether they actually told the things they are said to have told or not. This is a matter of testimony and if Amicus will have it that what he terms information is a matter of knowledge, he may, and my position will still remain true, "nature is the only source of knowledge"; though indeed, revelation may afford evidence for faith.

Amicus says I "ridicule such rules of government as his speculations would form," and he attempts to show mine are equally ridiculous. I stated, God will pronounce no man just until he is just. The process of justification, according to my views, is very simple. No obscurity, no happy uncertainty of law nor ambiguity of legal phraseology about it. It is simply for a man to *be* just and God will justify him. But, Amicus says, on my principles, a "man may escape punishment." And pray, does not the sinner escape punishment when Christ is punished *for* him as the doctrine of imputed righteousness supposes? Say I am a sinner. I deserve a certain amount of punishment. Christ endures that for me. Do I suffer? Christ has paid the debt, I am therefore permitted to go free. But one thing now is wanting, my personal character is unholy. What shall be done? Why, Jesus Christ's character is holy. God says let that holy character be attributed to me. Amicus would say I am now holy in virtue of this imputed righteousness of Christ. But when we reflect that holiness is of a personal character, it will be perceived that my own character has undergone no real change. And should God pronounce me holy, just, or justified, merely because Christ was holy, he would pronounce me thus when in fact I was the reverse. I cannot believe God will ever do this. This is accounting things which are not as though they were.

But Amicus says, on my notions the sinner may escape, though "he have transgressed every moral obligation." How? Why, "he may come into the court, acknowledge he has done the act of which he is accused," but may justify himself by saying, "I am not now transgressing. I am now just. To punish me for what is just is wrong. Or, to punish me now would be punishing the just, would be punishing the righteous, and as I am now at peace, violating no law, I ought to be acquitted."

If Amicus will grant me one thing, I will say the plea of the sinner is sound, and should be received as satisfactory. Only let it be a *real fact* that he has reformed and is just, when he makes this plea, and I will contend he should be released. Earthly courts can never have this knowledge; they must therefore take such measures as will protect society from his violence. The welfare of the many is paramount to the welfare of one. Wisdom must select the best means to promote the greatest happiness for the greatest number. This is the rule with society. If punishment be necessary, it must be inflicted, though in a well regulated country I believe it unnecessary and cruel. But this can never be said of God. He knows whether the person is reformed or not, whether he is just or not, and as all he requires is that we be just, when we are so, we shall be justified. Say one has sinned. What then? If you admit punishment, say he will be punished enough to reform him. Say he is now reformed, what more? Nothing. God forgives the wrong he has done, blots out the memory of that wrong, and he is now accepted as just, justified, holy and righteous. What has the work of Christ to do in this? 1st. He assures us God will thus forgive and accept those who reform. 2nd. This assurance, together with other things he taught, with his example, and his death and resurrection which confirmed the whole has tendency to produce this reform. Christ thus brings us to repentance or produces righteousness in us, thus he is said to be "our righteousness."

But Amicus fruitful in objections and filled with a laudable zeal to defend himself, attacks through the medium of this argument of mine, my favorite tenet the final salvation of all men. He says, "all do not become righteous anterior to the termination of this mundane existence; the means of holiness extend not beyond this life. How then can all become just? I would thank Amicus to bestow a little attention upon the middle term of his syllogism, for as it now stands, it is most shamefully neglected. How does he know "the means of holiness do not extend beyond this life?" When he proves this, I will notice his question. I believe the reverse and my reasons are here: God is holy, will he be displeased to see his children like himself? Will he ever place his own offspring beyond the reach of holiness? [Will] an infinitely good God place those he has made, those he has commanded to be righteous, in a situation where they must eternally remain unrighteous? Will he who delights in goodness ever prevent his own offspring from growing better?

I know no reason why mankind, if they retain their moral and intellectual nature in another world may not improve there as well as here, and if they have the means and do not use them, that is another thing to which we will attend when laboring to prove all *will* be saved. But there is no other name than the name of Jesus given *under heaven*, whereby men must be saved. Very well. *Under heaven*, that is, on the earth during life, though there may be other names in eternity. But who dare say Jesus may not be as efficient to save us after death as before? *Name* of Jesus means doctrine of Jesus, and there is no other doctrine by which any can be saved for it is the doctrine of life and immortality. But who can say this has no efficiency after death. God will have all men to be saved. His will must be done. If all do not become righteous here they must hereafter; and I dare not limit the Almighty, I dare not say he has but one set of means for our salvation and that he can use this set only in one place.

The remainder of this article is answered in my other review of Amicus. He has said nothing new here and I have now neither time nor inclination to add anything to what I have there presented my readers; and I have another reason, the doctrine of *imputed righteous-*

ness makes part of my essay on Christianity[4] and will there be amply discussed when I get through a few discussions I have on hand so that I can progress with it. Most if not all that is written about the law and justification by the law, or by faith, relates to the early controversies, either between the Christians and Jews or the followers of Paul and the Judaizing Christians. Let Amicus follow out this thought and the rules I before gave him, and I think he will agree with me that a man must become just to be so pronounced by his heavenly Father and with the Apostle that "without holiness shall no man see the Lord" [Heb. 12:14].

I hope to hear from Amicus often. But he must not think himself neglected, if I do not reply to everything he may write. If he would compress his thoughts within a smaller compass and not amplify quite so much, his style would possess more real beauties and be read with more interest. He sometimes travels too far for a word when he might get a better one nearer by, better because more familiar to his readers. With these remarks we dismiss the article under review, hoping Amicus, whoever he may be, will not in the expectation of having Christ's righteousness imputed to him, neglect to procure any of his own.

(August 22, 1829): 265

In the present number of our paper, will be found a fourth communication from Amicus.[5] It contains not many good things, nor many bad things. Its subject matter is trifling and the words in which it is expressed are indifferently enough thrown together. It would have been published and passed by without notice had not the writer suspecting his opponent was about to leave the field assumed a degree of courage very unbecoming a young priest in disguise.

We never assumed a warlike aspect. The remarks of ours, which seem to have given new life to Amicus, were founded upon the fact that we had many subjects to treat and that we did not choose to waste many words with a writer, who could have little success in making proselytes, and who could not be refuted until he advanced some position tangible to the mind. Our columns were open to his productions for, although he was generally vague and not infrequently erroneous, his articles contained many good things and as we consid-

---

[4] [Ed. Brownson never did take up the issue of imputed righteousness in his "Essay on Christianity." His rejection of the doctrine, however, is clear in his earlier "Review of Amicus," *GAII* 7 (May 30, 1829): 169-72 (pp. 335-41 above) and his "Sermon on the New Birth," *GAII* 6 (August 16, 1828): 257-62 (pp.137-49 above).]

[5] [Ed. The fourth letter is in *GAII* 7 (August 22, 1829): 268-70.]

ered him a young writer and partly opposed to us we were willing to encourage him what we could.

But he now manifests a disposition to brand us recreant, declares we are no true knight, etc. We have little of the spirit or the language of the chivalric ages, and if we had, it has not yet appeared that we should receive any peculiar honor or lasting fame from an encounter with Amicus. We profess little acquaintance with the arms of the tournament, and though we would never refuse a courteous challenge from a good knight and true, we shall not regard with particular attention him who evidently has only one spur to his heels. Amicus should know it is no part of a true knight to exult over his fallen opponent; and certainly, it seems very awkward in him to reserve the exhibition of his prowess, until his opponent, waiting in vain for the attack, retires in disgust from the lists. Let our Sir Knight Incognito reflect, it may be time to grant quarters when his opponent shall ask, and soon enough to boast of victory when to the poignard of mercy he yields himself vanquished.

The remainder of his article does not merit a reply. The conclusions he has drawn from our reasoning are unwarranted and, if warranted, avail him nothing until he shows faith may not be exercised in another world as well as in this. If he does not believe the means of holiness are confined to this life, and he intimates he does not, he must admit the gospel can be efficacious after death as well as before, unless indeed, he supposes there are other means than those in the gospel by which we can be made holy. But this he denies. There is no other name he contends by which men can be saved, and he has proved himself priest, in sentiment at least, by his pious warning to us not to expect happiness from any other than the "Dear Redeemer." Let him solve the difficulty for himself.

He has his hobby, imputed righteousness; perhaps he may become righteous if some other being's righteousness be imputed to him. We wish to have some righteousness of our own. We consider the gospel designed not to make another's righteousness answer instead of ours, but to make us righteous; and we think it will eventually make all righteous. If Amicus considers us wrong, let his objections come in a tangible shape and if we do not meet him "boldly and bravely" then let him brand us recreant. Come forth Sir Knight, prove your courage, let us know with what skill you can "break a lance or wield a sword."

25.

MY CREED

Gospel Advocate and Impartial Investigator
7 (June 27, 1829): 199-201

Almost every man has a creed. There are few who do not worship their creed with more devotion than they do their God, and labor a thousand times harder to support it than they do to support truth. Now I do not like to be singular and I know not why I may not have a creed as well as other folks. But if *I* publish my creed, consistency may require me to defend it and when I have once enlisted self-love in its defense, I may become blind to the truth and may choose rather to abide my first decision than to admit I have once decided wrong. But a creed I must and will have, and my readers shall know what it is.

My creed shall consist of FIVE points,[1] and shall embrace all the essentials of true religion; and furthermore I wish to premise, that my creed was not adopted merely today, but has been cordially embraced and of its correctness I have had no doubts, for at least nine months, though I may not have lived agreeably to its injunctions. But we are all frail creatures and it is very difficult to find no discrepancy between a man's faith and his practice. Moreover I would allege in behalf of my creed that it is plain, easy to be understood, and withal involves no mystery. The pious may, however, from this circumstance be led to doubt its *divine* origin and infidels may like it so well that I shall be shut out of the church. But I will state it, though I must still further allege that I believe it to be based on eternal truth and that it is calculated, if obeyed, to harmonize the world and enable the vast family of man to live forever beneath the smiles of fraternal affection. But for the creed.

Art. I. I BELIEVE every individual of the human family should be HONEST.

---

[1] [Ed. An allusion to the five points of Calvinism defined by the Synod of Dort (1618-1619): i.e., total depravity, unconditional election, limited atonement, irresistible grace, and perseverance of the saints. Brownson's creed is an attack upon Dortian theology. See *Works*, 5:43.]

Art. II. I BELIEVE that everyone should be BENEVOLENT and KIND to all.

Art. III. I BELIEVE that everyone should use his best endeavors to procure FOOD, CLOTHING and SHELTER for himself, and labor to enable all others to procure the same to the extent of his ability.

Art. IV. I BELIEVE everyone should cultivate his *mental powers,* that he may open to himself a new source of enjoyment, and also be enabled to aid his brethren in their attempts to improve the condition of the human race and to increase the sum of human happiness.

Art. V. I BELIEVE that if all mankind act on these principles they serve God all they can serve him that he who has this faith and conforms the nearest to what it enjoins is the most acceptable unto God.

This O ye! who accuse me of infidelity is my creed; read it, obey it and never again tell me I am a disbeliever. Do you ask for evidences of its correctness? Find them where you can, in the Bible, in the Koran, in the volume of the universe, in our individual capacities, in our social relations or wherever else you can. The best evidence I can offer is that if anyone will believe, and obey, he will want no evidence. That is to say, if anyone will do the works here required, he will find so much pleasure in the performance that he will ever after wish to continue to do the same. I would quote Scripture, but people say I do not believe it; how they should know I do not is more than I can divine. They have never derived that knowledge from myself for I have never had it to give. But there is one passage so much in point I will quote, "The ways of wisdom are ways of pleasantness and all her paths are peace" [Prov. 3:17]. But here is another still better, "Righteousness keepeth him that is upright in the way" [Prov. 13:6]. "There shall no evil happen to the just" [Prov. 12:21]. "The lips of truth shall be established forever" [Prov. 12:19], and, "The just man walketh in his integrity and his children are blessed after him" [Prov. 20:7]. And again, "Thou shall love thy neighbor as thyself" [Matt. 19:19], and "whatsoever ye would that men should do unto you, do ye even the same unto them, for this is the law and the prophets" [Matt. 7:12]. Moreover I must be permitted to quote still further, "But if any provide not for his own, and especially for those of his own house, he hath denied the faith and is worse than an infidel" [1 Tim. 5:8]. "Do good unto all men as you have opportunity" [Gal. 6:10]. "But whoso hath this world's goods and seeth his brother have need and shutteth up his bowels of compassion from him, how dwelleth the love of God in him?" [1 John 3:17]. "Prove all things hold fast that which is good" [1 Thess. 5:21]. "Apply thy heart unto instruction and thine ears unto the words of knowledge" [Prov. 23:12]. "To do justice and judgement is more acceptable unto the Lord than sacrifice" [Prov. 21:3]. "To love God and his neighbor as himself is more than all whole burnt offerings" [Mark 12:33]. "Pure religion and undefiled before God and the Father is this to visit the fatherless and the widows in their affliction and to keep our self unspotted from the world" [James 1:27]. "And this commandment have we from him, that he who loveth God love his brother also" [1 John 4:12].

These among many other passages of the same import I might adduce to show my creed is scriptural, but presuming each one reads the Bible for himself I leave it to him to find evidence in the book itself. I forbear to expatiate on the moral beauty of my creed or to dwell upon what I consider will be its salutary tendency; and, though not skilled in the language of cursing, I will yet say that to expect happiness without obedience to this creed is vain. I shall not tell people they shall go to hell if they do not believe it, but I will leave them, if they do not obey its injunctions, to say, whether they have not a hell in their own bosoms.

I have now stated my creed, yet I am not so vain as to suppose all will embrace it. The orthodox will reject it because it is not mysterious and the priests generally because it will require them to pay as much attention to the flock as they have hitherto paid to the fleece. The heterodox will dislike it because it will require them to treat the orthodox as kindly as they do themselves, and what perhaps is still worse, it will not allow them to be illiberal against illiberality. And infidels of all descriptions will reject it because I have proved it by Scripture. All hypocrites will condemn it because it strips off their mask and compels them to be useful in order to be respected. The selfish will anathematize because it requires them to regard the welfare of others. And the indolent will be outrageous upon it because it requires them to be active. Hence I conclude there will be only *few* who will hear it with gladness. As it is likely to meet opposition from every quarter, I shall flatter myself that it is true.

If anyone complains it is defective, I will tell him if he performs all it enjoins, I will engage St. Peter shall open the gates of heaven to admit him to the mansions of the blest. But I will just whisper in the ear of my reader, I conceive this creed to be the END towards which all should labor, that I do *not say* it is unnecessary to believe anything else, but that nothing else is useful any farther than it tends to this end. Now my reader, if you by believing that Jonah [was] swallowed

[by] the whale or the story about the witch of Endor, with various others of the same character, I say dear reader, that if believing these marvelous stories will make thee a better man—and a better man, whoever thou art, I know thou dost need to be—then I have not the least objection even shouldst thou believe the moon is made of "green cheese." Now ye doctors of divinity hurl your anathemas. Let everyone be HONEST.

26.

A SERMON. ON TRUSTING IN PROVIDENCE

The Gospel Advocate and Impartial Investigator
7 (July 25, 1829): 227-31

Although the fig tree shall not blossom, neither shall fruit be in the vines; the labor of the olive shall fail, and the fields shall yield no meat; the flocks shall be cut off from the fold, and there shall be no herd in the stall: Yet I will rejoice in the Lord, I will joy in the God of my salvation. Hab. 3:17, 18.

No injunction is more frequently enforced, no duty, whether moral or religious, whether natural or positive, is more frequently recommended with every variety or argument than is our supposed obligation to trust in God and to commit all our interests to the disposal of the Most High. From time immemorial has this been enjoined as our most imperious duty, and everyone who has been able to procure a surplice or a black coat and ascend the steps of a pulpit deems it his prerogative to exclaim continually "put your trust in God"; and everyone who has been the subject of "special grace," who has had his sins washed away by the outpourings of enthusiasm, assumes to himself the right to warn sinners to repent, to harp constantly upon the great duty of trusting in God and to exhort us to be resigned to the Divine will even though that will should consign us to eternal night.

But notwithstanding the hoary age of this doctrine and the character of those who have labored to explain and to enforce its obligation, it is little understood and perhaps there is no duty the nature and reasonableness of which is not more clearly perceived and more duly appreciated. It may not then be unprofitable for us to spend a few moments at this time in examining into the *character* of this injunction, its *reasonableness*, and also to *enforce* it so far as found to be proper, and to draw from it such inferences as may prepare us to go forward with renewed ardor in the great work of meliorating the condition of mankind.

1. There are few subjects which have not a negative as well as an affirmative side. Trusting in God is *not* sitting inactive and vainly imagining the Deity will provide for our wants without any exer-

tions of our own. This is presuming on Providence and expecting that which everything in nature assures us we shall not receive. All nature is in motion. Throughout the whole one part seems to act for another; and throughout the whole of this vast machine called the universe we see a concatenation of causes and effects, or of certain means adapted to the accomplishment of certain ends. To expect any of these ends will be accomplished without the appointed means being used is to expect that which we have never yet seen verified and something which we have no warrant to believe we ever shall.

That God governs the world is admitted by the philosopher as well as by the Christian, but that he governs it by a special agency or by any immediate control need not and when properly understood will not enter the creed of either. It is indeed often asserted, but will never be believed by him who has any just conceptions of the great system of things with which we are connected.

There is too much imperfection, too much evil everywhere prevalent, to allow us to pronounce everything the work of an all powerful, wise and benevolent God. Say Jehovah is a being of absolute, of unbounded perfection, and reconcile, if you can, this idea with the assertion that he governs every event, and that his immediate agency produces everything which is in the existing state of affairs. Let your eyes run over society; mark the evils which prey upon the human race, man devouring man; brother supplanting brother; nations warring against nations, pestilence winging its noxious flight, scattering death in its progress; famine sweeping off its thousands, carrying destruction to every department of life; poverty, stern unyielding poverty, binding millions in its grasp, and making them mere footstools for the more prosperous; take this view and tell me is this what we might naturally expect from a Being whose nature is love and whose power is infinite?

God no doubt governs the world. But he governs by those laws he inscribed on matter when he gave it birth, and by those he impressed on organized life on the morning of its creation. These laws all nature does and must obey. I ask not their wisdom nor their utility; but without some knowledge of them, hopes of happiness are vain.

Man cannot be rich without the use of means, learned without application to study nor knowing without investigation. Just as absurd to expect that God will make one happy when he neglects the means which the order of the Divine government requires him to exercise. The laws of God stamp indolence as the severest curse ever endured by man; these laws have determined man shall be an active being, and that his felicity shall be purchased by the sweat of his brow. Neither Providence nor grace promise us aught that is good for trusting in God while our duty is unperformed, or while we neglect those measures we should adopt.

2. But trusting in God, as it should be understood, is to exert ourselves and to repose the fullest confidence in Providence that when we have performed our duty, our labor shall not be in vain; that though we see not the desired reward, though we obtain not the desired good, we are to rely on Providence that it will soon or late be received.

There is in man no small disposition to fret at the circumstances in which he is placed, and to be impatient of the least cross or disappointment he is compelled to experience. He cannot, and if he can, he ought not reconcile himself to suffering without endeavoring to remove it, but if he trusts in God, feels the confidence, which constitutes the duty we are illustrating, that all things will eventually work together for good, he will cease to complain of much which would otherwise excite constant murmuring.

To trust in God requires us to believe God is good. Without the conviction that he is good, we cannot trust him. Nor can men put their trust in a being they believe to be bad. Paint the character of God as I have often seen it represented, and by those too who imagined they loved him; paint him as he often is painted, the tyrant and not the Father of nature, seated in the distant heavens, looking down with scorn upon the multitude below, mocking the miseries of his people, and commanding the angels of his vengeance to kindle the fires of hell, where the victims of his hate shall writhe with the bitter pangs of remorse, their bodies swell and burst with the perpetually increasing heat of Almighty fury! Paint him on Sinai convulsed, surrounded by the smoke and flames of the enraged mountain, hurling the winged bolts of wrath at man, at weak defenseless man, sporting with untold torture, drinking pleasure from the dying groans of creatures himself has made, his eye resting with delight on a ruined and devastated world! Paint him thus, and say ye who have hearts to feel, and more than all minds to think can ye love him? Swells the heart with the warm, the blissful emotion of love as you contemplated the picture! Does his character inspire you with confidence! Feel you a desire to fly to his arms and trust your all to him?

Deluded man may say he trusts, but his heart turns rebel to his words, and give him liberty and it will overflow with indignation at the thought. Nor will man willingly place himself within the power of one he hates; and the very constitution of his nature compels him to hate a being like the one we have described. To trust in God, to put confidence in the Most High, we must believe him good and to trust all to his wise disposal, we must view him as the universal parent, unbounded in his love and overflowing with kindness to all.

When we view Jehovah as the parent of the universe, when we contemplate him as that Being whose nature is love, on whose countenance eternally plays the smile of benignity, who speaks but to bless, and issues no command but to beatify sentient existence, mercy beaming from his presence and all the virtues, all the excellencies and all the perfections surrounding his throne and giving permanence to his reign and felicity to his subjects; when we thus view his character, we see so much loveliness, so much worth we fly at once to his arms, we lean on his bosom, we trust ourselves, our all to this wise and parental care.

But to trust in God we must believe him not only good, but we must believe he *loves us.* Vain were the attempt to put our trust in a being we believed regarded not our interests. Though his bounteous hand were seen pouring down blessings upon others, though for them he should distribute the choicest of heaven's treasures and permit the glories of the celestial regions to beam in full effulgence upon their habitation, and though he should commission the angels of love, of peace and pleasure, to smooth their path and to carpet it with flowers—all were useless, would be unable to inspire the least confidence in the bosom of the forlorn individual who believed himself forsaken or unbeloved by the Great Father of all. "Others," he would say, "others receive, let others trust. But for me, for me what hope? Deity disregards me. Heaven speaks, but not for me. I hear a voice, but it comes not to the heart; it wakes within me, lone and dejected, no confiding emotion. The sun displays his beams; the showers distill their genial influence; the germ springs forth, the green blade appears; the air becomes fragrant with unfolding blossoms; nature changes her verdant robes, puts on her golden crown and her luxuriant harvest gladdens the hearts of thousands. But what is all this to me? Jehovah does not love, he does not regard me. What is there to remove the solitude I feel within? What to chase away the dark, desponding thoughts, which sting through the brain? What can inspire *me* with confidence in God? Or lead me to recline on his bosom for protection?"

Such would be one's reflections were he called upon to put his trust in that God who, as he believes, does not regard him. But change the case, let a man believe that God loves *him,* and has a regard for *his* welfare, that the laws of nature and of Providence are designed as much for him as for any other, then he will feel himself safe, will see a being he can deem worthy of confidence, and he will give his heart to God and trust all to him. But unless it be allowed Jehovah is good unto all, that his tender mercies are over all his works, that he regards the interests of all he has made, can any particular individual without a *special revelation* to that effect, believe assuredly he is loved by heaven? Or without this conviction can he have the assurance required? While I admit Deity disregards some, how am I to be assured I am not one whom he disregards?

Trusting in God then implies a conviction of his goodness and not only of his goodness in the abstract, but of his tender regard for our individual interests. I have already told you what I mean by putting our trust in God. It is after we have performed our duty, after we have done all we can do, to rest convinced there is one Being, who overlooks creation, who has by his wisdom so ordered it that our labors shall never be in vain; that, when we do all that human ingenuity can accomplish, though all around may be darkness through which the eye cannot pierce, though calamity upon calamity may have driven us from the sunshine of prosperity into the shades of wretchedness, though the fig-tree should not blossom, the vines yield no fruit; though the olive should fail and no meat be in the fields, the flocks desert the folds, and no herd be in the stall, we are to rejoice in the Lord, to joy in the God of our salvation. We are to recognize in all this a wisdom at work; a superintending Providence exerting its control to make these discouraging circumstances, these untoward events but the harbingers of a brighter day, the introduction to some good hitherto unknown.

The reasonableness of this confidence is obvious. I will not refer you to books, nor will I attempt to prove it by the *dicta* of other ages, I ask not for precedents, I care not for authority, however respectable, I refer you to the heart. My appeal is to the native undisguised feelings of the human heart, and by their decision will I abide. I would not damp the courage of a fellow being, by dwelling on his weakness, nor repress the ardent aspirations of hope by pointing to the evanescent nature of all sublunary good. But the world is a scene of perpetual change; life is exposed to a thousand cares and anxieties, to a thousand contingencies which we can neither foresee nor prevent when we do; sorrow will steal in upon the heart and the firmest will at times bend beneath the pressure of grief.

There are moments, there are days, yea months and not infrequently years, in almost everyone's life, when the world has lost its power to charm; when the spirits sink; when the heart becomes vacant; when a tedious and an undefined feeling of lassitude, disgust and depression, usurps the whole man and renders the mind painfully sensative to the minutest incident that strikes across it. It is then we look eagerly for some arm on which to lean. The arm of flesh is a broken reed. The world can present nothing which the heart does not reject, or deem unable to support its sinking hopes. Where shall we go? Where find the arm which can uphold?

Often does a dark cloud hang over our prospects and hide from our sight all future good; a thick impervious gloom gathers round the heart; where is the sunbeam to dispel that cloud? Where the light to dissipate that gathering gloom? Look, ye who sigh at your condition, ye who weep over your misfortunes and despair of felicity yet to come, look to God, to that Great Being whose power is everywhere felt, whose wisdom is everywhere displayed, and whose goodness is unto all; fly to him, lean on his Almighty arm, light will burst from his throne, the clouds will disperse and the cheerful sun of hope will shine upon the heart.

The thought that nature is but the will of an all-wise, powerful and benevolent Being, gives new force to the mind, inspires it with invincible courage, gives it additional elasticity, which throws off the burthen of wretchedness it had borne, enables it to rise superior to adversity and to hide the present by drawing upon the exhaustless stores of the future. There are those who say there is no God, those who suppose the world obedient to no hand but stern necessity; I have had such thoughts, but they shot through the heart with pangs too severe to describe and they seemed to poison the soul and to dry up all the sources of its felicity. But when those thoughts departed and I felt myself once more in the embrace of the Godhead, encircled by the arms of Divine affection, no argument was wanting to convince me that man disbelieving in God must be unhappy, and he who can put no trust in the Most High must be miserable indeed.

Man labors neither long nor successfully when he has no confidence that his labors will be rewarded. When he believes he can accomplish nothing he will not accomplish half he might had he believed he could and would be successful. Let an army front an opposing one, feeble and disheartened by the conviction it cannot conquer, and you may vouch for its defeat. Its attack will want spirit and it will fail to prosecute any advantage it may gain. It is the same in every department of life in everything about which we can be employed. Whatever has a tendency to inspire man with firmness, to give him confidence of succeeding in his exertions will not only give him more internal enjoyment, but by the mental force it gives, will enable him to accomplish more than would otherwise have been in his power.

Let an army rush to battle under the full conviction their cause is espoused by heaven, and that God will crown their arms with victory; they fight with redoubled force and persevere with the most undaunted resolution. Let every man be engaged in those employments which, he believes, God will prosper, let man trust in God, and he will go forward with cheerfulness and exert a power in his labor of which he was before unconscious. With this confidence he rises a more noble being, a higher dignity clothes his countenance; a loftier fire shoots from his eyes; his whole soul becomes enlarged; his thoughts more sublime, and he half imitates the perfections of that God in whom he trusts. Danger is despised; troubles and difficulties give way and adversity itself becomes but the means of his elevation.

This confidence in God is called a duty and he who has it not is branded a criminal. It may be so. I call it not a duty and certainly he who has it not is sufficiently wretched without being upbraided as guilty. It is not mine to say who is guilty before God. The secret recesses of the heart are closed to my observation and the criterion by which man is to be declared guilty before his God is unknown to me. But whoever learns the character of the great Parent of all, as revealed in his works and in his word, *will* feel the confidence required. Whoever contemplates the stupendous display of his loving-kindness, made by the gospel which brings life and immortality to light, to cheer the hearts and dissipate the fears of a long benighted and disconsolate world, will feel the goodness of God, and will not hesitate to trust in his Providence and rejoice in the Lord, yea joy in the God of his salvation.

I need not labor to *enforce* the lessons of my subject, but when I view the loneliness of Zion, mark the desolations of the church of God, I cannot resist the opportunity to draw from it arguments to soothe the anxious mind and to inspire the benevolent heart with courage to persevere in the cause of humanity.

Long has the philanthropist mourned over the folly and credulity of mankind, long has the tear glistened in his eyes as he surveyed the widespread ruin of the human race, the spiritual famine and moral pestilence by which they have been consumed, their hopes blasted and themselves doomed to drag out a cheerless existence, unknown to the health of virtue, unsupplied with the bread of life. On every hand we have seen a universal commotion, and from every quarter we have heard a continual buzz, all striving amid the confused din of business to lessen their uneasiness and to increase their enjoyments, and still from every quarter through every age and in every country is reiterated the question, "who will show us any good?"

Prophets and priests have pretended to give us directions, have seemed confident that if we followed their prescriptions, our maladies should be healed and our souls supplied with bread, with wholesome food. We have listened attentively to their doctrines, we have followed with undeviating accuracy their directions, the evil has not disappeared, the pestilence yet rages and the famine has not abated its fury. The church was established; the spires of Zion rose sublime to the skies. Her lofty walls, her splendid palaces, the rich decoration of her temples seemed to promise a retreat that would shelter us from the storms of the world and present whatever could charm the eye.

But the glory of Zion has departed! The church has been stripped of its beauty and become the sport of everyone who passes by. That splendid city, founded by the Savior of the world has been deserted, and those institutions which should have been the nursery of virtue and the asylum of the oppressed, which should have healed the broken hearted, comforted the mourner, lightened the heavy laden of their burthen and enabled the weary to find rest to their souls, those institutions, planted as it was said, by the Deity and were the peculiar objects of his care, institutions which were to send peace on earth and good-will to man, have long since been laid in the dust. The temples of pure religion have been demolished and their lofty columns overgrown with moss.

The empire of Christ, which promised so much felicity to the world, has been over-run by the ruthless invader, its glory has fled before the ravaging Goth, and its peace has vanished in the triumph of barbarous sectaries. A thousand petty communities have been established and humanity has wept over the bitter wars which they have constantly waged against each other. Religion has been sacrificed to the demon of discord and felicity on earth to a dream of a phantom world.

Many have indeed arisen to humanize the savage hordes, to soothe their animosity, to mollify their rage, to dissipate the clouds which hang over our moral heavens, and to pour in light upon our dark habitation. But they have often fallen a prey to the zeal of those for whose benefit they labored. A deaf ear has been turned to their lessons, their names branded with reproach and their souls anathematized and sentenced to eternal woe.

And even now, when the human race seem to have survived their downward progress and are beginning to rise in the scale of moral and intellectual worth, the prospects of Zion are deeply shaded with gloom, and it requires no ordinary share of moral courage to stem the current of popular clamor and of sectarian invective. Even now the benevolent heart is often pained to see how few arc the friends of truth! How few can be collected to hear those sentiments which ennoble man and do honor to his Creator! While the temples of discord, of folly, of superstition and of ancient fraud are crowded almost to excess, the number of those who bow at the shrine of just knowledge is few and of that number many are timid and half discouraged.

But my brethren, however much we may deplore this state of things, a just confidence in God, bids us not be depressed, by no means to abate the least in our benevolent exertions. Know, the world is governed by a steady, unerring hand. No lawless tyrant sways the scepter of universal empire; no arbitrary misrule reigns in the heavens. A certain ORDER is established. The primordial laws of nature retain their primitive force. These laws fix to every act its due reward. Obey these and man is happy. The reward may often be delayed but it shall come. The labors of virtue shall not be in vain. He who comes forth to enlighten the world, may rely on the Sovereign of the universe to give effect to his exertions. He may read his success in every law of nature. Knowledge shall prevail over ignorance, honesty over craft, and sincerity over hypocrisy. Sooner shall nature fail, sooner shall the sun withhold his influence and the planets fly from their orbits than that virtue shall not be rewarded and philanthropy not receive her recompense.

The time may be long ere the millions of our race will awake from the stupidity into which the folly of other ages has thrown them. Long may we have to plead with man to be wise. But if we kindle the fire of intellect, the breath of the Almighty shall fan it to a flame, and its illuminations shall irradiate the world. Though we may not see the full harvest of what we sow, posterity shall; nations yet unborn shall reap the fruit of our labors. We may look down the stream of time and see generations hereafter to be influenced by the opinions we form and by the institutions we establish. Every new truth we discover and every just opinion we inculcate will be attended by an ever accumulating degree of felicity for those who shall come after us. Away then with despair. Farewell to dejection and to gloomy forebodings. Let us feel the importance of the work we have commenced. Let us rest assured God reigns and that his Providence will protect us, and then we may ever say, "Although the fig tree shall not blossom, neither shall there be fruit in the vines; the labor of the olive shall fail, and the fields shall yield no meats; the flocks shall be cut off from the fold, and there shall be no herd in the stalls: Yet we will rejoice in the Lord, we will joy in the God of our Salvation."

27.

MR. REESE'S LETTER

The Gospel Advocate and Impartial Investigator
7 (July 25, 1829): 236-40

Towards the writer of the letter in today's Advocate, signed W. I. Reese,[1] we profess no other sentiments than those of friendship and ardent desire for his prosperity and usefulness in the cause of truth and humanity. We respect his talents, his virtues and his indefatigable industry. We rejoice to hear his labors in the place of his residence are eminently blessed to the spread of that doctrine and to the building up of that cause which we hold dear and which we believe is calculated to promote the best interests of the human race.

It is true we think Mr. Reese has a little too much of the *leaven* of orthodoxy, that his mental vision in some respects is enveloped by a misty atmosphere, and that he is too tender or has too much sensibility on some speculative points of polemical theology. Our readers may discover some warmth of feeling in the letter he has addressed us. They may, perhaps, discover some expressions and some charges, which persons not skilled in sectarian controversy, might deem rather inconsistent with the "meekness of the gospel and the candor true philosophy always inspires," and some things which are not dissimilar to *personal* abuse. But they must not be too hard upon one who not having argument, truth nor reason on his side chooses to let off his battery at the *person* of his opponent rather than to be beaten or to fail of gaining his cause. Everything of this kind, we hope, our readers will attribute to our friend's abhorrence of every species of infidelity and to his laudable zeal for the gospel of Christ.

His letter has made us look ridiculous enough but we shall not mind the garb so far as it is personal. We will simply tell him, it will not be necessary for him to write Mr. Doubleday[2] to correct the matter of the Advocate. The editor is responsible for what appears in our paper and if anyone is dissatisfied with what it contains, he is to be

---

[1] [Ed. William I. Reese's (d. 1834) letter was in *GAII* 7 (July 27, 1829): 231-34.]

[2] [Ed. On Ulysses Freeman Doubleday, publisher of GAII, see *Who Was Who in America: Historical Volume 1607-1896*, revised (Chicago: Marquis Who's Who, 1967), 223.]

blamed and not Mr. Doubleday. We can but smile at the insinuation we are "betraying" the cause of Christ, and while we are conscious of our honesty (*honesty* being the first article in our creed) we shall not trouble our self at friend Reese's charge of *dishonesty*; and we strongly suspect that if we had been *less* honest we should have been less censured.

The letter labors with some art, with some zeal and less plausibility to fasten upon us the charge of atheism. This charge is supported in the following manner: First, we reduce the standard of *inspiration* too low or we admit only a *natural* inspiration. Second. If our standard of inspiration is correct, we do not admit enough of the Bible to be inspired. Third. We deny *nature* is able to teach the existence of God, that being taught only by *revelation*. Therefore we must be an atheist; for if nature does not teach his existence and there be only a *natural* inspiration, then certainly we have no evidence of the existence of God, and if we believe, we must be very credulous, a charge he thinks we should not be willing to admit. And so we think.

This statement, we believe, contains the full force of Mr. Reese's objections. If we remove this he must withdraw his charge, as we doubt not he will be ready to do. Since we received his letter we have reviewed all our articles to which exceptions are taken, and find them all to be parts of unfinished discussions.[3] Perhaps had our friends waited a little longer their uneasiness would have been removed. And, for the life of us, we cannot perceive why our friends should have been alarmed. We have uniformly encouraged free enquiry, we have insisted upon our readers examining for themselves and that they should abide the convictions of their own minds. Now had they believed that "error is harmless when reason is free to combat it," they would not have cried even if we had advanced some erroneous notions.

We have an objection, a strong objection to Mr. R.'s mode of argument. It is crushing us with the might of authority, silencing our voice by the *dicta* of other times. He calls not in question the correctness of our statements, he presumes not to accuse us of misstating a single *fact;* it is only our opinions are supposed by him to be contradictory to each other, and to a certain notion which somebody has believed. It is not enough to tell us such a sentiment contradicts the Bible, or disproves the existence of God; but is that sentiment true?

[3] [Ed. Reese objected primarily to Brownson's "An Essay on Christianity," and quoted particularly from essays no. 1 (pp. 201-05 above), no. 2 (pp. 205-11 above), and no. 6 (pp. 222-26 above). He took issue with Brownson's view of the knowledge of God and the inspiration of Scripture.]

Is it based on fact? If it be it is enough: no matter what it contradicts. He who cannot say so, he who will deny fact, or labor to explain it away is more in love with his own opinions than he is with truth.

Mr. Reese, unintentionally we presume, has taken a very ungenerous ground with us. There is no way except a man's own declaration by which you can ascertain what is his belief; now this we are denied. For, though we should "assert a thousand times we believe in God," it seems we are not to be credited. It is a matter of wonder, Mr. Reese should believe us to be an atheist upon so slight evidence as our own declaration. We have asserted time after time that we believed in the existence of God, and we never have, to our knowledge, used a single expression which implies anything different. Candor would take us at our profession and charitably conclude if our premises involved a denial of the existence of God, we were not aware of the consequences.

But our premises, it is supposed, lead to atheism. What are these premises? Nature does not teach the existence of God. Revelation teaches his existence. Inspiration is an extraordinary impulse which enabled the sacred writers to do and to say what none others ever did or ever could have done under other circumstances. Only the doctrinal parts of the New Testament are inspired, because the Old is most superseded by the New. Therefore we do not believe in the existence of God. Now this to us is no reason at all, and unless a man be *inspired* he can perceive no connection between the premises and the conclusion. For our self we should think there was as much probability of discovering the philosopher's stone as of finding any.

But we will bear with our friend. He shall have "line upon line, and precept upon precept." The premises shall be examined in detail. First of inspiration. The question now is, not what is inspiration, but what have we laid it down to be. "A suggestion to the mind of a person, made by a holy spirit in not a supernatural, but an extraordinary manner. The person inspired feels a certain impulse which enables him to do and to say what he never could have done under any other circumstances."[4]

This is the view we have given in our essays on inspiration. By "holy spirit" we understand holy power, or energy in general, but more particularly the power, energy or spirit, by which Christ and his apostles performed their miracles. The sacred writers it is commonly supposed were inspired by the Holy Ghost. By the "Holy

---

[4] [Ed. Quote from "Essay on Christianity," *GAII* 7 (March 21, 1829): 87.]

Ghost" Mr. Reese understands the "holy doctrine of Christ."⁵ And, we understand by it, that holy energy which God gave in an extraordinary manner to his Son and to the apostles. By *this* we supposed them to be inspired. Mr. Reese must suppose they were inspired by the "holy doctrine of Christ." Our readers may determine which exalts inspiration the most.

But we do not "call inspiration supernatural, but extraordinary." True: and because not knowing the full extent of nature we were diffident about pronouncing a thing *above* nature. Second. Because, though the power which governed the mind of the inspired might be supernatural, we believed the knowledge was communicated through the medium of the natural organs. That is, the men who "spoke as they were moved" were natural men, men like others, subject to the same frailties, liable to the same errors as others, only as they were preserved by this extraordinary influence. Now as we did not profess to understand exactly the process, we used the term *extraordinary*, as being a more indefinite term than supernatural and consequently admitting a greater latitude of meaning. Third. Because the word extraordinary may mean as much as the other term, or at least we have been in the habit of using it in the same sense which many do the word supernatural. The Christian world for three or four hundred years quarreled about a single diphthong; we do not intend to follow that example.⁶ Mr. R. may use the term supernatural if he pleases. We have never said we believed it improper. We have only said we preferred another term. The one we preferred means *out of the ordinary mode*; and in the place we used it, means that the sacred writers did not receive their knowledge as other men do. But, in an extraordinary manner, by the influence of *a* (or *the*) holy spirit, which suggested to their minds what to say. Mr. Reese says this is *natural*; it may be so. Let him prove it is natural. We know nothing in nature like it. We have never seen anyone inspired in this manner. If Mr. Reese has he may bring forward the facts; we will listen.

2nd. The second objection is that we do not admit *enough* of the Bible is inspired. Mr. Reese says, in a letter, published in the 2nd No.

⁵ (see his controversy with A, Gospel Adv. vol. 5.) [Ed. Reese's controversy with A was occasioned by Reese's "Exposition of Matthew 12:31-32," *GAII* 5 (February 4, 1827): 57-59. The exchange of views on this passage took place from March to September in 1827. See *GAII* 5 (March 31, 1827): 95-100; (April 7, 1827): 105-07; (April 21, 1827): 119-21; (July 14, 1827): 219-22; (July 21, 1827): 225-27; (August 4, 1827): 241-43; (September 29, 1827): 307.]

⁶ [Ed. See footnote # 3, p. 311.]

of the Evangelical Magazine,[7] a letter designed as *cautionary* to our self, that he "knows of no Universalist who believes every word of the Bible to be inspired." Mr. R. professes to be a Universalist, consequently he does not believe the whole to be inspired; now we may both be wrong. But that is nothing to the present discussion. The only difference between Mr. Reese and our self on this point is that we do not believe quite so many words are inspired in a book, which he admits is not all inspired, as he does. If Mr. R. can say the Bible contains ten uninspired words and still be a believer in the book, shall we be denied that appellation because we think it very probable it contains a dozen words which were not inspired? Mr. R. admits a part of the Bible is inspired. So do we. He exercises his judgement as to which part that is, may not we do the same?

But Mr. R. says we "must admit the prophetical writings." We have said nothing about these. We said in our Essay, "as the doctrinal parts of the Old Testament are mostly superceded by the new, we *consider* as inspired only the doctrinal parts of the New Testament."[8] What were our reasons? Because the Old was false? By no means. But because the Old had been mostly superseded by the New. The Old is like a law repealed. It is no longer in force. The Christian Scriptures are an improved edition of the Jewish; and to us it seems no mark of wisdom to cling to that which is confessedly imperfect when that which is perfect is come. The Old doubtless contains truth, many notices of the revelation of God, but the New Testament must be consulted to find which the parts are, for the Old has no authority except sanctioned by the New. This is what we have uniformly taught on this subject.

But the prophets. We confess our inability to understand a prophet's language. Their words no doubt have meaning, very important meaning, but we know not what it is. But as most divines admit the event must determine the prophecy, and not the prophecy the event, we shall leave all prophecies to the events to be ascertained by them whether true or false. It is said the principal use of prophecy is after the event, that we recognize in its fulfillment the wisdom of the Being who predicted. The passages from the prophets, cited by Mr. Reese, doubtless mean what he says, but it required the inspira-

[7] [Ed. In a letter to the editor, Reese, without mentioning Brownson by name, argued with those who asserted that nature could not originate the *idea* of God and who held that the only parts of Scripture that were inspired were the doctrinal parts of the New Testament. See his letter in the Utica *Evangelical Magazine* 3 (April 25, 1829): 11-12.]

[8] [Ed. Quote from "Essay on Christianity," *GAII* 7 (March 21, 1829): 87.]

tion of the New Testament to discover it. Our dull sense would never have dreamed of any such similitude had not a voice from heaven thus proclaimed; and unless that voice is again heard we dare not flatter ourselves we shall be able to understand the enigmas of the prophets. Mr. R. may understand them. It is well; we would that we did, but we do not. Perhaps we are not *spiritually* discerned.

But, let this pass. Mr. R.'s principal objection arises from the supposed fact: to admit no more than we do is inspired prevents us from maintaining the existence of a God. But this objection is slight. Were the Bible destroyed, the evidence of the existence of a God would remain, and that too without admitting nature can teach his existence. Had we asserted that none of the Bible was inspired, Mr. R. could not have proved us an atheist, even from our own premises. This will soon appear.

3rd. Mr. R. alleges that we assert *nature* cannot teach the idea of God. We do: that is to us, to our mind, though we do not deny that it may to others. But Mr. R. has also quoted some passages from our Essays which seem to assert that nature *can* teach the existence of *God*. We need not repeat the passages. One set of passages assert nature cannot teach the existence of *God*, the other that nature does teach the existence of "some Mysterious Power, some Mighty Energy which pervades the whole, and enables the universe to present its various and ever-varying phenomena." But is there not a contradiction here? None. By the term God we understand a Being separate from nature, intelligent, independent, who originated nature and exerts a voluntary control over it. By the power or energy, which expressions we use, we mean nothing more than the great active principle we everywhere see exerted. This power is indeed God, but nature could not teach us that fact, nature cannot teach his personality and his voluntary control over the universe. This distinction is important. We may have produced some ambiguity by not having always regarded it. This mighty Power or Energy is taught by nature and every atheist may admit it. But, the other ideas, which we believe are essential to the term GOD, as all theists understand the term, we teach are learned not from nature, but from revelation.

But we say, "man wherever beheld no matter in what age or what country, recognizes an Overruling Power on whom he is dependent, and to whom he believes himself to owe allegiance." True, and we mean man in every age and in every country of the world believes in the existence of God. We believe this, not in the sense which nature may be said to teach a sort of philosophical God, but in the sense in which revelation teaches his existence. But we admit "only the doctrinal parts of the New Testament are inspired." True. But the above assertion teaches the belief of a God [who] was in the world before the New Testament was written. True, and we believe also before the old was written. How shall we reconcile this? Very simply.

We have nowhere taught we are dependent on *inspiration* for our ideas of God, but on revelation. The theological notions of the Bible, whether you speak of the New or of the Old, are older than the book in which they are written; and we would not be supposed such a consummate fool as to say man in every age believed in God, and yet the idea of a God was never in the world till the time of Jesus Christ. Now in our vocabulary the Bible and revelation are not synonymous terms. We consider revelation a communication made from God to man, and made in the early ages of the world. Being made before the dispersion of mankind, it was easily carried with them as they wandered from each other, and thus became spread over the earth. The sacred books of all nations exhibit some traces of it, though the most pure and authentic accounts of it are found in the Jewish and Christian Scriptures. The doctrinal parts of the New Testament teach what this revelation was. Here our friend Reese will learn the revelation which teaches us the existence of God. But as this revelation became corrupted by all nations, so that it was nearly useless, about two thousand years ago, God sent his own Son and his disciples to separate what was true from what was false and to tell us plainly what is truth. This is found in the New Testament. Hence this is the book which we consider as inspired or as authoritative. The Old contains much truth; the sacred books of the Hindoos and of the ancient Persians also contain much truth; but the Christian Scriptures teach us to separate what is true from what is false in those books.

Our reasons for admitting this early revelation, are: 1. The early notices we find of a Being denominated God. These notices could not have been learned from nature alone. 2. If we say the idea of God is not derived from a contemplation of nature, we must say it is either a self-evident proposition or else it is taught by revelation. If we say nature teaches it we supersede the necessity of revelation, but for revelation Mr. Reese contends as well as we. If we say it is a self-evident proposition, we must say that it cannot be doubted. For no one can doubt a self-evident proposition. But this is doubted as Mr. R. will admit for he supposes we are of the number who doubt. This therefore cannot be admitted. We must then say it was taught by revelation, and none later than the one we have supposed will meet the exigencies of the case.

3. Because the identity of all religions point to a common origin, even in those particulars which all competent judges admit are not taught by nature. 4. Because all divines, whether ancient or modern, with whom we are acquainted admit and not only admit but contend for this early revelation. And, 5. because deny us this, and we shall renounce our faith in Christianity or in its being a divine institution. Every moral precept and every doctrinal sentiment found in the New Testament is older than the Christian era by hundreds of years and many of them older than the oldest book in the Old Testament itself. Now deny these sentiments were taught by an early revelation, you deny the Christian doctrines were taught by revelation. All admit the Christian doctrines are amply sufficient. If these were all learned without inspiration, what, let us ask, was the necessity of any revelation at all?

Our views on this subject are now given. We think they are easily reconciled. We have taught, first, nature cannot originate the idea of God in our minds. 2. Revelation assures us there is a God. 3. This revelation was made in the infancy of the world by our heavenly Father to his children. 4. Only the doctrinal parts of the New Testament are inspired, consequently the only safe authority for determining what the original revelation taught. 5. Inspiration is a certain impulse given to the mind, by a holy spirit, power or energy, or the holy spirit by which Christ performed his miracles. This holy spirit breathes into or suggests to the minds of the inspired, what to say, and the inspired persons spoke what the "governing power of their minds," or the particular frame or "*disposition*" of their minds determined. These five positions harmonize with each other. And we are ready to defend any of them or all of them. But this we are not yet called upon to do. We mean to be always ready to give a reason of the hope that is in us to everyone that shall ask.

We trust what we have said will convince our readers that we may be a firm believer in the gospel of Christ notwithstanding Mr. R's formidable objections. We suppose our readers to have some mind for themselves. We have not descended into every minutiae as though we were dissecting mosquito bills. We have given general principles, which we intend to carry out in detail as we progress with our paper. We claim no exemption from the common frailties of our race, nor do we ask any extraordinary indulgence. We have professed the Christian religion, and we advocate it as we understand it. If we understand it wrong then show us our error, and not at first brand us infidel or atheist. For our self we despise these cant appellations and were none but our self concerned we should be ashamed to attempt to show them misapplied.

We are aware of the feelings of Universalists. We know very well they have a sensitiveness peculiar to those who consider themselves the minority. We know they tremble at almost every sentiment which is advanced lest the orthodox gain some advantage over them. Hence they often treat with extreme illiberality the most deserving, because the most honest and independent, of their preachers. They do this not because they dislike the sentiments advanced but because they fear somebody else will. We often meet with this and we just as often despise it. We were born free, we have maintained our freedom, and when we cannot, we will pray we may no longer live.

Mr. R. says he does not "*blame* us for our sentiments." We are very glad he does not. It might be mortifying indeed to be blamed by him. He is no doubt sincere in this, but if he has ever thought as far, he would doubtless with Dean Swift, tell us to keep our opinion to our self. Duly [grateful] for this liberality in friend Reese, we must assure him it never once occurred to us when writing the articles in question or when forming our sentiments to enquire whether we should become obnoxious to his blame or praise. He will pardon us for this oversight.

Mr. R. says we were once "an avowed atheist." This is something new to us, but he doubtless knows, and if he can make our readers believe we were once an atheist it will help him very much to make them believe we are one now. He is welcome to all he can gain by this. We will tell him we were once a Presbyterian and that we consider worse than atheism. But we are not now and we feel not ashamed to acknowledge our self wiser today than we were yesterday. He says too we "renounced our belief in the Scriptures a few months before we became the editor of the Advocate." Mr. R. however is not anxious to prove we are not a believer in Christianity. He then did not state this for that purpose. O no. It was only to make the public believe we are dishonest. Suppose it was so, what then? Is that a certain argument we do not believe now? Our religious faith is between us and our God, and we have formed it too, after long and painful research, and while clothed with the mantle of our own conscious integrity, we shall not start at such feeble missiles from him. Yet we think the venom of the shaft exceeds the vigor of the bow.

28.

EQUALITY

The Gospel Advocate and Impartial Investigator
7 (September 5, 1829): 282-83

The man who is capable of looking on human society with the eye of a philosopher, who can compare causes and effects, trace the secret springs of actions, and determine the influence of prevailing institutions, will readily perceive the cause of the crime and misery now prevalent is chiefly owing to the inequality which exists among us and which almost every institution tends to perpetuate and increase.

Perhaps it is not possible to bring all to the same standard while individual enterprise is allowed, and allowed it must be unless we would destroy society; it is hardly to be expected that all will be of the same size, that all will be equally successful. But it were a mournful truth, a depressive thought, to say nothing can be done, that we cannot lessen the distance between the parts or classes as they now exist. It were thinking meanly of man, meanly of his social powers, to say he is susceptible of no better state of society than the present. It were indeed paying little attention to past experience, as well as turning blindly from what may be seen in almost every exertion of which we are capable.

There is no natural difference between the members of society. The child of the poor is not, when born, more ignorant or more helpless that the child of the rich. In acquiring knowledge, the children of the opulent and powerful are not more apt, nor do they learn with greater ease or distinguish with greater accuracy than those of an opposite description. The ornament of science has often been the child of poverty, and the lower classes of society have yielded as great geniuses as the world can boast. There is not then, in the physical or intellectual powers of mankind, any reason why one class should be oppressed, why one should be called the higher and the other the lower. Nor, indeed, is there anything in their moral natures which should continue the inequality which now exists. The reason why we should despair of a reform, if despair we must, is found somewhere else.

The reason is not abstruse; it is on the surface, and the stupefied may understand and the blind almost see it. No matter how society became thus divided. It is divided, and we may see what perpetuates this division.

We have a privileged class which sprung up during ignorant ages. Time has confirmed their power and long habit has made us conclude we cannot live without them. We have the clergy, a non-productive class, who, in this country, consume annually twenty millions of dollars. These are employed to do what every man could do a great deal better for himself. They watch the interests of religion. But religion is a thing between the individual and his God; and it is much better for the individual to go directly to the throne of grace and pray for himself than it is to hire a priest to do it for him. For whatever we would have well done, we should do ourselves and not employ a hireling. But this class obtain a livelihood from their calling; consequently they will do all they can to flatter themselves and those who support them; their order is necessary.

Another class, an unproductive class, in many respects a privileged class, live upon the earnings of others, and trample upon those who support them, the lawyers. These men are but a moth to us. They professionally pretend to aid individuals in obtaining justice; but by the uncertainty they introduce into the laws, by the ambiguous manner in which laws themselves are framed, the aid becomes doubtful, for it is no sign a man has the right because he succeeds, or that he is wrong because he failed. Laws are always an evil, the less we have of them the better.[1] We send men to our legislature, we pay them high wages; they frame or enact at every session a large number of laws, drawn up with that peculiar ambiguity that, without a seven years study, the most talented cannot hope to understand them. Instead of taking common sense and natural justice for our guide, we attempt to shape our actions according to these unintelligible laws, get into a dispute and spend our whole fortune to pay the law to help us out.

Now if this class were all employed in cultivating the earth and the legislators were compelled to *fast* till they had transacted their business, or until they learned old laws should be just before they made new ones, that old duties should be defined before additional ones are imposed, we might hope for something valuable. The best law is a high moral feeling and the best lawyer is he who can best

---

[1] [Ed. Brownson articulates a principle dear to William Godwin. See his *Political Justice*, 2:397-413.]

draw forth the moral and intellectual faculties of the youth. Law never made a man honest, but it has made many a man bankrupt not only in wealth but in integrity and in respectability. Let laws be simplified, be reduced in number and always founded on natural justice; let legislators follow the plough and lawyers obtain their fee by pursuing the employment of the agriculturalist or the mechanic, and we should soon see crime diminishing and equality prevailing. But the lawyer will oppose this innovation.

Perhaps the inequality which reigns between the rich and the poor is the most destructive to peace and virtue. One man has a capital, he may employ it in agriculture; he finds the poor, sets them to work; if their number be great and nobody else to employ them, he reduces their wages so low that though they may live they can never hope to be otherwise than poor. These laborers have families and thus the number which must depend on the rich for employment and on the wages he may please to give for a support is constantly increasing, and the wages will diminish in proportion to the number of the laborers. Hence it is the laboring class of community are soon reduced to the lowest state of wretchedness.

A man has some hundred thousand dollars. He erects a large manufacturing establishment. The market is empty. The tariff or something else excludes foreign competition; demand is high; he employs a large number of laborers, men, women and children; gives decent wages and still finds it profitable. Others have also a capital; other establishments are erected; the market is soon supplied; thence follows a reduction of wages. The laborer must work more hours, produce more to obtain the same support. But this greater production gluts the market, a surplus is produced, and this reduces the wages still lower; and, it will be found, the more the laborer produces the poorer he grows. This seems a hard case, that plenty should increase poverty, a surplus should produce want. Yet so it is. The inequality which exists tends to perpetuate and increase itself.

But, there is a greater evil not yet mentioned. While one class labors and the other enjoys, the laboring class will always be considered the lowest. A new scale of worth will be introduced, the reverse of what it should be. A man will be respected in proportion to his idleness. Hence, the laborer learns to loathe his labor, he is impatient of his employment, he is anxious to be rich that he may be idle and be respected. Now spring the temptations to crime. The struggle to be rich commences; all ties are forgotten; all principles of honor and morality are abandoned. Fair means or foul, the intention is to be rich. Some perhaps are stimulated by want to relieve themselves, others anxious to place themselves on a level with those who consider themselves above them. Crime becomes frequent, jails and gibbets are in requisition, etc.

This theme need not be pursued. The remarks made elicit the inequality which exists, they show the evil which flows from it, and also that it is for the apparent interest of the higher classes to promote it. Something ought to be done. Political doctors manage this subject very poorly and religious doctors still worse. Religious teachers tell the poor to be content, for if poor here, they shall be rich hereafter. Political teachers devise means to increase the surplus produce, blindly imagining abundance will remove the evil when in fact we already produce more than enough. We may prohibit the manufactures of other nations and this may afford temporary relief, but it is only an opiate that may calm but cannot remove the disease.

Equality must be introduced. Every man should produce for himself or everyone should be engaged in some branch of productive industry. This would secure to each one a competence. In those branches which the individual cannot master, the principle of cooperation may be introduced. But there should be no such thing as a laboring class and [a] consuming class, one separate from the other. Secure to every man the products of his own labor and the evil will disappear. These are only a few hints thrown out, on which we intend to enlarge as we have leisure, particularly to point out how the proposed plan may be carried into effect.[2]

---

[2] [Ed. Brownson periodically returned to the issues facing the laboring class, but the most famous of his addresses on this issue was "The Laboring Classes," *Brownson's Quarterly Review* 3 (July, 1840): 358-95.]

29.

THE MISSION OF CHRIST

The Gospel Advocate and Impartial Investigation
7 (September 19, 1829): 295-97

The following article is occasioned by some remarks of a correspondent. The editor has said less on the doctrinal parts of the gospel than his readers might desire, less than he intended; for it was his design to have thrown in all he had to say on that subject under the general head of "Essay on Christianity." That design is not relinquished, but will assume a different medium than a periodical to gain publicity. Hereafter, we shall treat the several detached parts of the gospel as occasion may require.

The man who despises his own reflections, who cramps his mind by blind obedience to the *dicta* of others, is as unfit to write for the instruction of others as he is destitute of any rational sentiments of his own. Opinions should be *formed*, not *borrowed*; and as it may be presumed that what every man is required to believe is within his reach, everyone should not only exercise his powers, but he should learn to place the chief dependence on himself and trust to his mental energies for the acquisition of truth.

Religion, if true, is a thing in which all are equally interested. It ought to be equally adapted to the capacity of each individual. Whatever requires a mental power not common to all or whatever requires a degree of research and laborious investigation, which every man may not pursue consistently with his duty to himself and to society, or that which must make the many dependent on the few, making it the duty of a certain privileged class to explain, and the great body to yield therefore a blind assent is no part of a rational religion, and by those who reflect it must be forever rejected.

Religion is supposed to include faith or belief. Faith is the result of evidence or of that which the mind deems such. Every man is required to believe, the evidences should therefore extend to all and be equally within the comprehension of each individual. Man is a creature of numerous wants; he must labor to satisfy these; he must support himself and those who are dependent upon him. This must necessarily include a large portion of his time and prevent him from turning over all the legends of antiquity and of sifting the truth from the falsehood. True religion cannot require him to become acquainted with those evidences which it must occupy his whole life to learn. This would be charging Providence with a want of care in adjusting the balance of our duties. Nor can it be any better to hire a certain class to think and examine for us. This class may think more of their own interest than of truth, and a good living may seem the most agreeable fact to examine. Hence the great body of the people would be as liable to be deceived and to believe wrong as right.

The mission of Christ, according to the above reasoning, must be plain within the capacity of all, so plain that he who runs may read, and the way-faring man, though a fool, may understand; it must be understood by all it was designed to bless and the evidences of its truth should be such as the most stupid can comprehend and the most skeptical acknowledge convincing. In this mission we must discover an object to be obtained and we must see the means adequate to the end proposed.

The first thing to ascertain is what is this object, what is the end proposed by the mission of Christ? A difficult question to answer, not from its own nature, but from the obscurity in which ignorance or fraud has involved it. There is no need of running over a refutation of false opinions. No man who understands the nature of moral justice will admit God transferred our sins to Christ and cursed his son for that of which he was not guilty, nor will anyone who thinks be more ready to admit the righteousness of Christ will answer for us in the sight of God while we remain unrighteous ourselves. The very notion begins with a falsehood; it proceeds with cruelty and ends as it begun in a lie. God being always gracious, needed no sacrifice to appease his anger, or to dispose him to be merciful, and as the murder of an innocent person can never be very satisfactory to justice, all ideas of a vicarious atonement or of expiatory sufferings must be excluded from the mission of Christ.[1]

The object may be soon stated: the world was sinful, man was disobedient, ignorant, alienated from God, in a word, unrighteous. Though he was in this situation, God still loved him and in this situation God commended his love to them that "Christ died for the ungodly" [Rom. 5:6]. The mission was not to reconcile God; for God loved us. But did we love God? No; we needed a change; and as

[1] [Ed. Brownson clearly reverses this opinion in the early 1840s. See, e.g., his "The Mission of Jesus," *The Christian World* 1 (January 7, 14, 21, 28, 1843), (February 4, 11, 25, 1843), and (April 15, 1843).]

we were unrighteous, the object of Christ's mission was to make us righteous. "Thou shalt call his name Jesus, for he shall save his people from their sin" [Matt. 1:21]. "Him hath God raised up to bless every one of you by turning you *away* from your iniquities" [Acts 3:26].

We consider the object of Christ in his mission was simply to reform mankind, not by any supernatural means, but by a simple operation, differing in degree, but not in kind, from the labors of every reformer. I am perfectly aware that most Christians will think I degrade the works of the Savior; that the mission of Christ represented as being so grand and so august, is thus dwindled down to comparatively nothing. Right or wrong, this is all that Universalists and Unitarians allow, when their language is properly simplified, and all that can be supported from the gospel, when stripped of the pomp of custom, metaphor, which, to us, tends to destroy the simplicity of the Christian scheme.

It should be borne in mind that Jesus of Nazareth was one of those benevolent individuals who are far in advance of the age in which they appear. The true nature of his mission was but imperfectly understood by his immediate disciples and the succeeding age who incorporated or more in accordance with general belief began to incorporate with his precepts the pompous absurdities of prevailing systems of religion and philosophy, soon lost sight of their teacher, and retained nothing more of the Jewish reformer than the name. His pretended disciples soon raised him from a man to an angel, from that to a demi-god, and at length to a god. Thus deified, he must have a work equal in magnitude to his supposed majesty. Hence patching up or rather filling up the mountains of Jewish and Gentile fables, they imagined he came to do what there never was to be done. Throwing aside everything of this character, passing over the fables, wonders and prodigies, which ignorance and superstition ascribed to him, taking the outlines of his character as drawn by the four evangelists, we may pretty satisfactorily ascertain what he enjoined and what was the object he proposed to himself.

The Jews had a vague conception of some personage which should arise to deliver their nation and to raise it to the height of human glory. They called him "Messiah," that is, the *anointed* or a person commissioned, or, if you please, consecrated to a certain work. Whether Jesus of Nazareth was the person they expected is nothing neither one way or the other. The fact seems that he either assumed the character or the appellation Messiah was attributed to him, whether for the purpose of attracting the attention of the Jews does not readily appear.

The orientals, particularly the Magi, had by their astrological calculations and representations inculcated a belief that a great personage, the Son, the Angel of Light, should appear to destroy the works of Akriman (the Devil),[2] to *regenerate* the world, and to introduce the reign of Light, or the reign of good. This notion became incorporated with the Jewish and from the union of the two with some beautiful unintelligibilities from the Platonic school has been formed the absurd system of religion, known in the world for the last fifteen hundred years as the Christian, in which scarcely a particle of Christianity can be found.

The careful enquirer will perceive, and the philosopher, perhaps, be amused to examine, the struggle of the Jewish and Persian prophets; but the Persian has triumphed, and the Ebionites, the Nazarines, the primitive followers, the most orthodox are finally placed on the list of heretics and consigned over to damnation.[3] The Gnostics[4] have perished in name, but their system, with a loss of a few of its ears, and by the acquisition of a little Jewish phraseology and a little pagan idolatry has prevailed and forms the basis of the religion most admired by Christendom.

Abating from the doctrine of Christ what is borrowed from these sources, with a spirit of philosophical discernment, we may perceive Christ simply as a reformer, laboring to reform the abuses of his countrymen, to root out their prejudices, to *humanize* their minds, destroy their bigotry and intolerance, and to give them more enlarged views of God and of man. This will appear the object of his mission. To accomplish this, he labored with a zeal and perseverance worthy our imitation. But the doctrines he taught, the freedom of his strictures, and sometimes the severity of his censures, drew down upon his head the rage of the rich, the proud, the bigoted and the powerful. Unarmed, he could not stand the shock; he lost his life.

This object is still further enlarged when we take into view his doctrine; but even then his mission will be confined to mankind. Its object was to produce righteousness, to reform the world, to make

[2] [Ed. Akriman or Ahriman was the principle of evil in Zoroastrianism in Persia.]

[3] [Ed. Ebionites were a sect of Jewish Christians that flourished in the early centuries of the Christian era, emphasized the binding character of the Mosaic Law, and developed a strict ascetic mode of life. The Nazarines were also a sect of Jewish Christians which existed in early Christianity and which continued to obey many of the Jewish Laws.]

[4] [Ed. The Gnostics were a complex group of Christians in early Christianity who, among other things, emphasized the special interior knowledge (i.e., gnosis) they had received from God.]

the numerous family of man holy and happy. Was this a small object? Was this unworthy the Nazarine reformer? To us it appears the most noble, the most magnificent, and the most desirable object which man can conceive. For this the philanthropist may labor with the warmest zeal and for this he may well lay down his life.

But is this all we are to expect from the gospel? In one view, it is *more* than we can expect; in another view it is but an item. The gospel has *not* reformed the whole world; and if the only salvation spoken of in the Bible was a salvation limited to this life, universal salvation were indeed a dream. But there is another view of this subject: The *doctrine* Christ taught has relation to another world as well as this. This doctrine raises our hopes and will give us eternal life. But Christ did not make this doctrine; he only taught it; his death did not make it true; it only served as a seal to its truth. This doctrine he received from God; it is the doctrine of life and immortality, brought to *light* through the gospel, not made true by it. The gospel is nothing but its promulgation and the doctrine must have been true before its promulgation or else when proclaimed it must have been false. It is in this *doctrine*, not in the person of Jesus, we have hope of immortality. But as this was testified by the death and resurrection of Christ, it is therefore said, we have "hope in his death."—[*To be continued.*][5]

---

[5] [Ed. The article was never continued in the *GAII.*]

30.

A SERMON. MANKIND AUTHOURS [SIC] OF THEIR OWN MISERY[1]

The Gospel Advocate and Impartial Investigator
7 (October 3, 1829): 307-10

The foolishness of man perverteth his way and his heart fretteth against the Lord.   Prov. 19:3.

There is nothing more common than for men when in affliction to murmur against Providence and to charge their sufferings to the Almighty. Suffering, pain, anxiety or distress of some kind or other has been the common lot; and that the miseries the human race are compelled to endure are many and heavy to be borne no man of feeling can dispute. So general is the conviction that this is a world of sorrow that not a few have supposed it a vast Purgatory in which we are punished for sins committed by our souls in some other mode of existence. However this may be a careful history of the past and close observation of the present will establish the position of our text that "the foolishness of man perverteth his way and his heart fretteth against the Lord."

There are few studies more profitable than those which have for their object acquaintance with the cause of our sufferings and the means by which they are to be removed. Placed as we are here, surrounded by so much that is painful, exposed on every hand to a thousand dangers, ignorant of our best interests, and of the means by which it can be promoted, we are not to be surprised at the universal

---

[1] Delivered before the Black River Association of Universalists at Rutland, Jefferson Co. N. Y. June, 1829. Note. The following sermon, perhaps exhibits the outlines of that peculiar system, for which the author has received the censure of his brethren more clearly than any other he has published. It has been delivered in several places and has been equally praised and censured. Though hastily written and very imperfect as a composition, we yield to the pressing request of both friends and enemies to insert it in the Advocate. Whatever may be its character for *piety*, we are conscious its *morality* cannot be censured, and if it should be supposed deficient in directions to ensure heaven hereafter, no man of common sense can doubt the efficacy of its principles, if obeyed, in making mankind happy on earth. O.A.B.

enquiry, "whence came the deep, and often aggravated wretchedness to which life is subject?" Nor indeed are we to consider it strange that when we find all our fond built hopes destroyed, all our bright, and brightening prospects suddenly blasted by some unforeseen event; when we have toiled, exposed to the burning rays of a noon day sun, and amid the chill damps of evening, all is rendered vain by some contingency which we could neither foresee nor present; it is not strange that in these moments, when the heart is pained and the soul full of bitterness, men should murmur at their lot and think Providence less kind than he might be.

Though this murmuring is often charged upon us as a crime, I am far from blaming man for sometimes feeling his lot is hard and that he has little for which he should be thankful. It is easy for those who have never suffered, whose hopes have never proved deceitful, and whose hearts have never been involved in the ten thousand "ills which flesh is heir to," it is easy for such as these to rail against him who is not wholly resigned, who cannot see the hand of kindness in what he endures. But a superficial view of life, and a superficial view is nearly all that most men can take, will in some measure justify complaints and render him not criminal who cannot feel wholly resigned to what he suffers.

I would always recommend resignation to those evils which are proved to be unavoidable, but resignation, to the extent most religionists carry it, cannot be too earnestly deprecated. Had I the toothache, and were I unable to remove it by any skill of the dentist, I might, perhaps try to be resigned. But were I suffering the rage of penury, instead of being resigned, instead of thanking God for my wretchedness, I should endeavor to remove it by my industry in some useful calling.

There is nothing more injurious to society or detrimental to the welfare of individuals than the doctrine which teaches everything is from God, that it is our duty to submit to be resigned. Without calling in question in this place the truth of the position everything comes from God, we may remark the injunction is in the first place generally impracticable. Lacerated by want, despoiled by the injustice of a fellow being, racked with pain and disease, it is scarcely in the power of him who deserves the name of man, to be resigned. We may *say* we are, our tongues may pronounce the watch-word of the party and swear fealty to the doctrine, but the heart does, and will rebel. Who, when stretched upon a bed of sickness, when drawing near to the grave, when filled with the awful forebodings of what may be, life eternal or sleep without end, does not wish his pain removed and his existence prolonged?

> For, who to dumb forgetfulness a prey,
> This pleasing, anxious being ere resigned,
> Left the warm precincts of the cheerful day,
> Nor cast one longing, ling'ring look behind?[2]

Men can endure, they often endure much with firmness, without uttering the least complaint, but none love pain, none can feel contented to dwell in the midst of wretchedness.

The injunction is not only impracticable but every attempt to obey it is attended with consequences deeply pernicious. Go tell man, miserable man, that it is his duty to be resigned whatever be his lot; tell him that to complain is to rebel against heaven and you paralyze all the energies of his mind instead of arousing his soul, arming him against the ills he endures, stimulating him to remove them by some powerful effort; you lull him to apathy and perpetuate what you ought to destroy. Man should be an active being. He is not placed here to endure evil without murmur or exertion. His fortune is placed in his own hands; and if he will exert himself he may make life comfortable; if not perfectly happy he may approximate a better condition.

Whoever will look at the common notions on this subject may without any deep philosophical research readily divine their origin. They are but the tools of the priest and of the despot, invented to aid them in their attempts to domineer over men, to rob them of their possessions by teaching them subjection. All power was said to be of God; to resist them was to rebel against God. Hence the tyrant sat secure on his throne of oppression and blood. If the people suffered they were told it was the will of God they should suffer, and as they expected his blessing they must submit and if they would be certain of his favor they must be perfectly resigned.

I dislike such notions. They lead to imbecility of mind and to feebleness of exertion. I would rather magnify the evils we suffer, would paint them in the most vivid colors, that I might wake every energy of the mind, create a universal enquiry, and prompt everyone to the highest degree of action. I dislike doctrines of submission. I have found my highest felicity in being active, the same I believe is true of all. The constitution of everyone is for action, and would I could persuade all that indolence is a curse they cannot too scrupu-

---

[2] [Ed. Thomas Gray (1716-71), "Elegy Written in a Country Churchyard," stanza 22.]

lously deprecate, and that to try to submit to every untoward event is the surest means to perpetuate the misery we ought to remove.

But though I condemn the common doctrine of submission and resignation, I am far from justifying complaints against heaven, far indeed from saying our sufferings come from God and that we have reason to complain of the dispensations of his Providence. It is not to God we are to ascribe our misfortunes. "The foolishness of man perverteth his way and his heart fretteth against the Lord." To make this apparent let us look at life, ask of experience and be instructed by facts. Perhaps we shall perceive the evils of which we complain may be traced to some imperfection in ourselves, to the imperfectly organized society in which we live, and to the ignorance and pernicious habits which belong to us as individuals.

Look into private life, do you hear one complain of poverty, bemoan his hard lot and exclaim against the partiality of God who has made such inequality among his children? Look at this poor man, whose family is suffering all the rage of the most abject want. How came he poor? Can you not trace the cause to his misspent hours? To his intemperance? To his imprudence? Or to the rapacity of others? What has the Lord to do with this? Does he make one man an idler, another industrious? One economical, another profligate? You need not look so far. The cause is nearer home.

Mark that man. He is honest, upright and industrious. He is prosperous. He is respected. He fills places of trust, of honor and emolument. His children are trained to paths of usefulness and respectability. His houses and lands increase. He lives in the midst of plenty. Look again. Pass by his fields, the enclosures are broken down, the fences are removed, weeds infest the ground; briars and thorns grow unmolested, where once flourished what sustained life. Mark his house, its shattered condition; enter the once abode of felicity, look at that sorrowing female, half famished, brooding over her blasted hopes and the ruin of all that was to her lovely or desirable; look at her half naked and half starved children, calling in vain for a father's care. Has God done this? Has he reduced that family? Made that wife wretched? And those children worse than fatherless? Pass by to the tavern or the grocery, there sits the wretch carousing with the vilest, there the author of their misfortunes. His bloated face, his broken constitution and squalid aspect, reveal the cause. "He put an enemy in his mouth to steal away his brain."[1] His intemperance, his neglect of his affairs have wrought the change and sunk him so low.

---

[1] [Ed. Shakespeare, *Othello*, II, 3, 293.]

No need of ascribing it to God. No need of saying heaven made his wife and children wretched, twas caused by the foolishness of man.

Was that a man of wealth? Is his family now in want? Is the wife compelled to pine in secret, to feel the keen anguish which only woman can feel? Are his children doomed to grow up companions for the vilest? To become the inmates of a prison or the victims of a gallows? Look at the gambling table; there you may find the divinity that entails his curse; there you may see the curse of his ruin. In the haunts of dissipation he frequents you may find the god who sports with human happiness, who blasted this man's character and fortunes, and dearer than all, the peace and character of his family and caused the vast amount of sorrow.

I need not enlarge, I might exhibit examples of injustice, of fraud etc. but it is not necessary. The principle is the same wherever found. Our external condition depends chiefly upon ourselves. Not indeed wholly upon our individual exertions, but always either upon them or upon those of the society with which we are connected. Our own foolishness perverteth our way. We need not therefore arraign heaven with our misfortunes. Does God make the drunkard, the gambler, the debauchee, the knave and the murderer? No, breathe not the thought; it is man's indiscretion, man's own folly.

Extend your views from individuals, from private families to states and empires, and you may recognize the same principle. Do you weep over the ruins of nations which have been? Does your heart sink within you as you ask whither has fled the glory of states and empires so renowned in ancient story? Do you ask where is the industry, activity and wealth of Egypt, the commerce of Tyre, the refinement of Greece, the haughty greatness of Rome, once mistress of the world? Do you hear the night-bird flap his shaggy wings over the fallen colonnades and moss grown temples of Tadmour, the dismal owl call to this fellow, and do you see the beast of prey prowl where stood Babylon, Balbeck and other cities which so proudly shone in oriental climes? Do you wander among the ruins of art and look in vain for a thriving and happy population? Do you sit in solitude where once arose the joyous din of gladdened courts? What see you in all this? The hand of God? Or do you not rather recognize it as the work of man?

If you will be at the pains to look closely at the rise and fall of nations,[4] you will find that their prosperity and their decline may

---

[4] [Ed. Brownson's earliest diary indicates his preoccupation with the transitoriness of all things human, and especially with the rise and fall of nations. See, in particular, his "Meditations on the Fall of Empires," in "A Notebook of Reflections, 1822-1825," 45-54, in the Archives of the University of Notre Dame.]

alike be attributed to human agency. When a nation obeys the simple laws of nature, maintains strict justice in its internal and external affairs, when it allows free scope to individual enterprise and encourages industry and integrity in its citizens it prospers. But when vice is allowed to creep into its councils, when the courts become corrupt, the administration of justice entrusted to unskillful or to dishonest hands, when a thirst for dominion takes possession of its government, when inequality is produced among the citizens, when oppression on one hand and slavery on the other or one part enslaved by luxury and effeminacy and the other by poverty and want, the nation falls. The virtues which raised it are no more; the bands which cemented it are broken, it falls, crumbles to pieces and is lost in barbarism and wretchedness. Not by a malediction from God nor by any unfriendliness of Providence, of sternness of fate, but by the natural operation of those principles by which all things are governed.

Will you tell me the Bible reads a different story, that the word of God declares it is Jehovah who setteth up kings and pulleth them down, that it is he who causes the nation to rise or to fall? Thus I know the Bible teaches but it is in a refined or metaphysical sense entirely different from the one in which I am now treating the subject. The Bible declares God is good, and who does not know goodness cannot be the author of evil when it has the power to prevent?

If you will look into the mind at that internal anguish we feel, at the fire which consumes the brain and dries up all the sources of joy, you may test the same principle and find all is by "the foolishness of man."

Must we attribute our mental agonies to God? Or not rather to ourselves? Let us look closely, perhaps we have fostered some bad principle, nourished with more than maternal fondness some favorite notion, which has corrupted the heart; we may have performed some act which now returns with remorse, poisons the soul and darts the keenest pangs through all the inner man. Perhaps if we retrospect our lives with impartiality, we shall be convinced, the cause of our uneasiness is not seated in the distant heavens, nor lodged in the bosom of the divinity, but in our own bosoms, in our "foolishness which perverteth our way." Let us then cease to fret against the Lord, and let us too, cease preaching submission and resignation, let us, instead of weeping over our miseries, "by taking arms end them."

We are not to suppose God will for our sakes reverse the laws which he established on the morn of creation for the government of the world. The laws are lasting as the existence of Jehovah, and as unchangeable in their operation as his own immutability. It is for us

to find out those which lead to our felicity and to obey them. Instead
of sitting down with the dupes of priests and supinely waiting for
some divinity to interfere in our behalf, instead of wasting our time
and strength in praying some invisible being to suspend the laws of
nature, we should learn ourselves, learn our own strength, and rely
on our own powers. Call this want of reverence, call it blasphemy,
call it defiance of heaven, call it what you please, it is a truth attested
by all past experience, and proclaimed by heaven and earth, *that man
will never be universally happy, in this world, until he is convinced he
must rely on himself, and depend on his own exertions for his prosperity.*

I know what your teachers tell you; I know *they* labor to destroy
all self-confidence; I know they would make you despise yourselves,
believe you are nothing, can do nothing; I know too, they do this
under pretense of honoring God, but little thanks will God give them
for such honor, and little do they care for the honor of God if they
can be well fed and clothed themselves. They might be right in reference to another world. They design their instructions for a world
unknown to me. I shall not say they are wrong. If they design their
instructions for that world, it is well. Let them go and preach to its
inhabitants, we do not want them here. It will be time enough to
attend to the concerns of another world when we learn what those
concerns are and when we become interested in them. At present we
belong to the earth, to which I aim to adapt my instructions, and I
think it would be well if all would do the same.

But, to honor God! Who shall honor Jehovah? Has he entrusted
the keeping of his honor to us, to such weak creatures as we are? If he
has, he has had little regard for his honor for it is most certainly in
poor hands. But how shall we honor God? Shall the farmer honor
him by falling upon his knees and pouring forth a prayer, while the
weeds infest his garden and his fields lie waste, overgrown with thistles
and thorns? Shall he honor God by neglecting to cultivate the earth,
to raise sustenance for himself and family? By living in poverty, in
abject want, and ascribing all he suffers to the Providence of God?
Priests may say so. Fools may believe so. I cannot. If we neglect the means
of happiness, we must charge ourselves with the misery which follows.

I hate the common doctrine on this head. The priest, with all the
gloom of the graveyard, comes forward mid sighs, tears, and groans,
deploring the misery which prevails. He teaches all is owing to sin,
but sin he says we cannot remove, though we deserve endless damnation if we do not. We must pray to God, we must not presume to do
ought in our own strength. My brethren, the biggest knaves in the
world are often praying knaves. I would be grateful to my God for

the existence he has given me, for the world in which he has placed me, for the means of happiness which he has put within my reach, and for the hopes he has vouchsafed me, but I cannot importune him to bless me in my laziness or to make me happy in my foolishness.

Look at this doctrine, you are a farmer. Beware, plough not your ground, scatter no seeds in the furrowed earth, but go to prayer, pray the Lord to bless you in your "basket and in your store," and to give you your daily bread, how much grain, think ye, you would raise? Let the mechanic forsake his shop, the merchant his goods, everyone his employment, all go to the misnamed house of God, how long would they find bread and wine enough to celebrate the Lord's supper? Let us be devotional, but let us show our devotion by our industry, honesty and faithfulness in our several callings.

Would mankind be happy, let the idler forsake his idleness, the trifler his trifles, the drunkard his cups, the gambler his tables and his dissolute companions, the dissipated the haunts of dissipation, the fool his folly, the knave his injustice, the infidel his faithlessness, the evil his wickedness, the learned his pedantry, and let all engage in the acquisition of useful knowledge and in some branch of productive industry; evil shall then disappear, misery cease, universal righteousness prevail, and earth reflect the image of the paradise of God.

My brethren, I have now presented you my thoughts. God is good, no evil comes from him. Man is imperfect, ignorant, foolish and wicked, hence the origin of misery. God is right but man is wrong. Man is then the being to be corrected; he is the author of his own sufferings, let him reform and he may be happy. Let him continue inactive or depending on some invisible power to reform him and his misery may remain. Awake then, O man! Learn to depend on thyself, as thou hast caused thine own misery look to thyself for its removal and exert thyself without delay, and God will bless thy exertions.

31.

A GOSPEL CREED

Gospel Advocate and Impartial Investigator
7 (October 3, 1829): 310-11

Sometime since I published "my creed,"[1] and so far as I can learn, contrary to all my expectations, everybody liked it, only some thought it did not go far enough. That creed I considered necessary for everyone to believe; the one I am now about to present my readers is a matter of opinion on which everyone may exercise his own judgement, believe or reject, and still, for ought I know, be a good man. I do not consider myself any better merely because I believe it, nor do I believe anyone any the worse because he does not believe; though it is my opinion that its tendency will be the production of good feeling and an increase of enjoyment. My reasons for writing it are to gratify a class of readers who are anxious to know what a man believes and also to remove a complaint made to me by a valuable brother in the ministry, viz. that I do not let what I aim at be known.

I. The Gospel, according to my view of it, recognizes the existence of ONE God and of only one, who is the prime mover of all things, whose will has established the laws of nature, whose moral character is impartial justice, based upon universal goodness and infinite mercy.

II. This God exhibits in the government of the world wisdom to admire and goodness to adore; that all which is necessary for us to know of his power and Godhead is in stamped on his works and may be read in his word.

III. A particular display of divine love and mercy is recorded in the writings of the New Testament display made by Jesus of Nazareth, the greatest and best reformer ever vouchsafed us by heaven.

IV. The object of Jesus (or of God in raising him up) was to reform the world. Not to appease the anger of God, not to make an expiatory sacrifice to render God propitious, but to lead men to repentance or reformation.

---

[1] [Ed. Reference is to "My Creed," *GAII* 7 (June 27, 1829): 199-201 (pp. 349-52 above).]

V. The means used to effect this reformation are the example, the precepts, the sufferings, the doctrine and the death of Jesus Christ. These operate in a natural way, same as a good example to follow and a correct faith tends to purify the heart and lead to the practice of virtue. They operate not irresistibly but persuasively, do not compel us to be good but entice us to virtue.

VI. That no man will be sentenced to endless misery and that no one shall be doomed to endure more misery than naturally grows out of his physical and moral condition is a doctrine of the gospel. Yet this misery all must endure, and their only hope of relief is in the improvement of their condition, which improvement it is the duty and interest of all to effect. Deity forgives us past offences, gives us motives to reformation and exhorts us to reform, but Deity does not reform for us, we must effect this ourselves. The means are given us and if we do not use them the fault is ours.

VII. That all will finally become holy seems highly probable. Though some consider this point positively settled, yet as one class of these consider a part will never become holy and the other are positive that all will, I deem it a matter not positively decided; I should consider the salvation of all men as an inferential doctrine rather than as one positively taught. I infer it from the goodness of God and the perfection towards which all his works tend, which makes it almost certain that in their progressive operations the period will come when man will cease his folly and learn to pursue virtue as his chief good. It is also inferred from the fact that the goodness of God has made happiness possible to all, giving all the means of procuring it, and it would be absurd to say God will ever take them away, if they always remain we shall some time or other learn to use them.

VIII. Endless misery is no gospel doctrine, annihilation is no part of philosophy, and to suppose a total unconsciousness of being to last through eternity is not reconcilable with the resurrection of all as taught by all the New Testament writers. Hence my opinion is that all mankind will by some process or other, not known to me, pass from this state of being to another analogous to it. As man is a progressive being here, as his happiness is generally in proportion to his knowledge and active virtue, so I conclude it will be hereafter. And though my heaven has not so much immediate felicity as the Universalist supposes neither has it the misery of the orthodox hell.

I do not like the notion of teaching men they may sin all their lives and be equally happy at death with the most virtuous. I do not say this because I think it would be any loss to the virtuous, nor because I am unwilling the wicked should fare so well, God forbid that I should ever envy anyone the small pittance of happiness he may obtain. But the order of the divine government seems to be on different principles, and moreover such a sentiment does not seem to place the rewards of virtue in a light sufficiently clear to arrest the attention of the thoughtless and the careless. The rewards of virtue are permanent and lasting, and to have a good moral effect man ought to be taught the road to happiness lies only through the practice of moral goodness. As I am unable to perceive anything in death which can work a moral change any farther than a change of some physical properties may change the directions of the passions, I conclude our happiness in another world will be proportioned to our moral goodness, and I know no better criterion by which to determine that moral goodness on entering that world than by measuring the degree of improvement with which we left this.

We call a vicious man miserable. It is so in this world and I conclude it will be, so long as he retains his vicious character, whether in this world or in the next. This makes the restraint of vice clear and powerful. It comes "home to men's bosoms and business," and deters us by every consideration which can influence the mind. Heaven and hell are not considered local dwellings but mere states of the mind, both are felt in a certain degree here, and both for aught I know may be felt hereafter.

These notions make the other world one with which we can have some sympathy. If you will tell me of another world, tell me something tangible to the mind, something which I can feel. The vague report of a song eternal sounding upon golden harps, may be very pleasing to those who love music. But an idle song may loose its charms and it is a thousand times more pleasing to my mind to contemplate the future world as a scene of active virtue, where all the kind and benevolent feelings of the heart may be exercised, where we may do good to each other and employ our leisure and our new faculties in examining the works of our Creator. But enough for the present. This article contains matter for much future speculation. My readers will pardon me for troubling them with my notions about an invisible world. I do not often trouble them thus, and they must view this weakness, if such they will call it, with an indulgent eye.

I have now presented my speculative creed and I know enough of human nature to know it will be read with interest, and enough of sectarism to know it will be most grievously censured. It will suit neither orthodox nor heterodox, for by pursuing a middle course adopting the excellences of all, none will find their own peculiarities flattering, none of their dear propensities retained, I deprecate no censure. For the gratification of some I have given my opinion, all may make as much of it as they can, believe it or not is the same to me.

32.

TO THE UNIVERSALISTS

The Free Enquirer 2 (November 28, 1829): 38

Brethren. Four years last September, O. A. Brownson received from your general convention at Hartland Vt. a letter of fellowship as a preacher in your denomination; and the June following he was set apart to the work of the ministry by solemn ordination at Jaffrey N. H. Since that period he has labored with unremitting assiduity in the acquisition of correct knowledge and in the promulgation of truth, in such manner and in such portions as his judgment assured him would best accelerate human improvement. With what acceptance, it needs not now to enquire; suffice it to say, he has had his friends and his enemies; more of the former than the latter, he confidently hopes.

From the Universalists he has received many favors, many proofs of fraternal affection, which are remembered, and will be, long as human kindness has power to move his heart. His late visit among his Universalist friends in the eastern states has given him matter for grateful recollection. He was hailed as a brother and treated with all the kindness and esteem he could wish (and with more than he deserved). He will study to be hereafter not unworthy the continuance of the same treatment.

The recent expression of their confidence has endeared them to his heart; and it is with a momentary pang he says to his Universalist brethren that his connection with them by any other ties than those of common humanity and fellow being must hereafter cease, and that his fellowship with the Christian ministry is ended. Not by any vote of censure or act of excommunication, but by his own choice; feeling himself unable longer in justice to himself or to the public to attempt a discharge of those duties necessarily involved in those relations in which he has hitherto stood to the Christian public. He therefore wishes to be absolved from his obligations to obey the creed of any church and he will no longer consider himself bound by any laws but those of justice and his country.

In thus taking leave of the denomination to which he has been attached and of the Christian ministry of which he has been a member, he would say he has been guided by no motives of hostility to any sect or party nor to any individual of the human family. His own bosom has nought of anger or bitterness towards a single fellow being. Towards the human race he has no other feelings than joy for their prosperity and grief for their errors and sufferings; and he has no other determination in reference to them than to devote his time and talents, and if necessary, his reputation and even his existence for what he deems their best good.

And now in declaring himself no longer a sectarian, nor member of any sect or party less than that of the human race, he would say his sectarian feelings and prejudices and jealousies are buried; and he wishes hereafter to appear in the simple light of a human being, a friend to man. If in the progress of his sectarian warfare, he may have offended a single fellow being, or wantonly sported with one single honest prejudice, he sincerely asks, what he has already extended in his heart to the world, forgiveness.

The reasons for this change and for the determination will be found detailed hereafter as time may be found and room may offer, in the columns of the Free Enquirer; that is, so far as the public have an interest in knowing them.

One word more that the writer be not misunderstood; dropping the third person and speaking in the first. I do not renounce my former religious belief, nor do I denounce the denomination to which I was attached. I but say, I am no longer to appear the advocate of any sect nor of any religious faith. I am too ignorant to preach Universalism or any other religious sentiment; and I *will* be too honest to preach that which I do not know. I become an enquirer after truth in the field of knowledge. Bidding adieu to the regions where the religionist must ramble, casting aside the speculations with which he must amuse himself, I wish to be simply an observer of nature for my creed, and a benefactor of my brethren for my religion.

33.

TO THE EDITORS OF THE FREE ENQUIRER

The Free Enquirer 2 (January 2, 1830): 79

I have now commenced my labors in the good cause of human improvement. I now feel myself fairly rid of my sectarian prejudices and can say to myself "I am slave to no sect." Now this is a very simple expression, and, one would think, an indication of a very natural condition; but I will assure you it affords more pleasure to one who has all his life been engaged in a sectarian warfare to be able to say it in truth of himself than you can easily imagine.

There is something in "mental independence" peculiarly fascinating. I do not pretend to explain why, but such is the fact. Common sense has more charms for the mind than the most beautiful theories or rather dreams of religionists. If we could only persuade mankind to follow common sense; I mean, if we could only convince them it is no harm to follow its dictates, and remove the fears they have that God will hate them if they dare be as he made them, RATIONAL, they would soon become reasonable and happy.

My youth was spent in studying religious matters, but even then I disliked the restraints the clergy imposed upon the young mind. Yet I dared not encourage a thought to stray beyond the prescribed bounds. Still it would often be a subject of wonder to me why a Deity who did all things and could make all things just to suit him should allow to youth aspirations after knowledge which they were forbidden to indulge should give them an invincible curiosity and forbid them to gratify it. But the clergyman told me, all was for trial; and, though I thought it for vexation, I let it pass.

As I advanced towards manhood I labored incessantly to bring my mind to the standard of the church. This was no easy matter; for profane thoughts would continually obtrude themselves, unsanctified doubts would arise, and I would often find myself on the point of giving up my "hope" and bidding farewell to the church and its spiritual food forever. But I finally succeeded in settling down in the full conviction of the truth of universal salvation. Then I felt to rejoice, because I thought I should be at liberty to use my reason and indulge charitable feelings to the world.

But man seems fated to be disappointed. I still found I had my bounds beyond which I must not think, or if I did, I must not express my thoughts. And to allow it possible that other denominations might be as good as my own or have as good members was a stretch of charity which even my Universalist brethren were not always willing to allow. It took away the main argument by which they enforced the necessity of believing their creed.

It will never do for any religions sect to allow that people may be as good in other sects as in their own. For if it be so, why such a change? Why trouble the world about a change from which no practical benefit can result? But many pretended that Universalism made the believer a happier man than could be the believer in endless misery. All I can say is I have believed them both; neither made me happy. The happiness that either promises seemed too remote to afford much satisfaction. If the believer in endless misery sometimes trembles to think it possible some of his friends may be damned as well as his enemies, the believer in Universalism is but little comforted by thinking that his enemies as well as his friends will be saved. So far as my observations extend, very little solid happiness is received from the belief of any creed, however rigorous or however lenient; and the chief difference of character which I have found among professors of different creeds is: that persons of mild and benevolent dispositions embraced mild and benevolent creeds, and the reverse with those of opposite dispositions. As a general remark, I have found Universalists more benevolent and more forbearing than any other denomination; but this I consider not the effect of their doctrine, but the reason why they embrace it.

But even a member of this sect will find that, though he has a wider range, he still has his enclosures. Not so much because they fear the individual may be lost, as that his wanderings may give the orthodox or other sects occasion to cast some expressions upon the one to which he belongs. The Universalists, in many instances, censure me for leaving them not because they believe me less honest nor because they believe my welfare or the welfare of mankind endangered; but because it may prove injurious to them as a denomination or sect. Were it not for this, they would receive me as a brother, and have as much good feeling toward me as ever. This is the case with all sects; and it is one reason why persecution has been practiced.

All these feelings are now with me no more. I look upon mankind as brethren and feel desirous of ascertaining the means by which their happiness can be promoted; and I care not which sect supplies me with the best information. I am willing to learn from them all. I perceive not the necessity of blinding my eyes to the merit of one sect for the sake of exalting the worth of another; nor indeed of being a persecutor to appease the wrath of him who persecutes me. My sect is now the world, my party is everywhere, my creed truth wherever I can find it, and under whatever name it may come, prized equally high if among the orthodox of the day, or if with the reputed heterodox or if with neither. And this liberty to embrace truth wherever found is the mental independence I prize so highly.

INDEX OF BIBLICAL REFERENCES

12:31......................................182
12:33......................................350
14:20......................................306
16:15......................................220
16:16..............................244, 247

Luke 6:29...............................111
10:27 182
20:35-37...............................93
22:30......................................306

John 3:2..................................146
3:3 137
3:16...92
4:19...............................12n. 33
6:37-40...................................92
12:32......................................160
12:33.......................................92
17:3...............................164, 184
18:2..159
21:22-23................................220

Acts 3:21................................160
3:26..378
11:26.......................................87
20:35.......................................42

Rom. 3:8.......................110, 186
3:28...340
5:6..377
5:12-20........................231n. 12
5:21..186
6:1..186
6:23..249
7..165
7:15......................... 237, 238
7:18-23..................................238
7:24..238
8:1..340
8:4..340
8:20..163
8:22..256
8:25..238
10:2...76
10:4..339
12:14......................................305

1 Cor. 1:30..............................340
8:6.....................................91n. 1

9:22..339
15:22, 42-55............93, 128, 198

Gal. 3:8..............................198n. 4
6:10..350

Eph. 1:9-10..............................158

Col. 2:14..................................340

1 Thess. 5:21...........................351

1 Tim. 2:4.......................158, 198
2:6 198
5:8...350

Titus 2:11.................................150

Heb. 2:9..................................198
2:14-15..................................250
12..195
12:14.............................339, 347
13:8..205

James 1:13................................219
1:17..219
1:27..350
2:14-24..........................340-41
2:17...91
2:19..249

2 Pet. 3:9..................153, 158, 198

1 John 2:29...............................340
3:7...................................81, 340
3:17..350
4...................................12n. 33
4:8, 16....................................152
4:12..350
4:14..159
4:19.................................110, 181
5:7..221
5:11..249

INDEX OF NAMES AND SUBJECTS

happiness, 39
 desire for, 157, 180-81
 and errors of antiquity, 48
 and external conditions, 41
 means of, 301
 and religion, 124, 136
Hawaiian Islands. *See* Sandwich
 Islands
Healy, John, 8, 17n
Healy, Sally. *See* Brownson, Sally
heart, 167-68, 238
heathens, misrepresentations of,
 176-77
heaven, 391
hell, 199, 291, 304-05, 390
 as state of mind, 391
Henry IV (king of France), 141
Henry VIII (king of England), 78
Hercules, 52
Hindoos, 176-79, 202
Hindostan, missionaries in, 175-79
Hindu. *See* Hindoos
History of the Work of Redemption, A
 (Edwards), 4
Holy Ghost. *See* Holy Spirit
Holy Spirit, 138-39, 140, 225, 365-
 66
 alleged cause of regeneration,
  138-39, 143
 experience of, 18
 influence on religion, 87
 and revivals, 145-46
holiness, 155, 245, 346
Hopkins, Samuel, 19, 71, 71n,
 107n, 182n. 4
Houston, George, 276n, 278
humanity
 depravity of, 162-64, 239-40
 original condition of, 151-52
 as progressive, 303
 as religious, 87, 204
 as social, 204
 See also freedom
Hume, David, 269
Hunting. *See* Huntington, James
Huntington, James, 3-4
Huntington, Joseph, 5

I

ignorance
 and clergy, 315
 depravity, cause of, 164-65, 261-
  64
 and miracles, 228
 and religion, 54
 suffering, cause of, 185-86
India. *See* Hindostan
inequality, 372, 374
infallibility, and Bible, 202, 214,
 334
infants, 103, 184
infidelity, 142, 192
 and Brownson, 23, 26-27, 350
 and Sunday mails, 268
 opposition of and to, 322, 324,
  328
 See also atheism; deism; skepticism; unbelief
inspiration
 defined, 365-66
 extent of, 366-67
 extraordinary, not supernatural,
  225
 and revelation, 25, 218-26, 369
 See also Bible; revelation
interpretation, of Bible, 121, 229-32
inquiry, 11, 28
Inquisition, 52, 129, 245
Isaac, 61

J

Jefferson, Thomas, 324
Jenkins, Robert L., 277, 277n. 2,
 278
Jesus
 and Jews, 378
 name of, 346
 as reformer, 338, 389
 See also Christ
Jews
 and Sunday laws, 274
 and Messiah, 378
 priests of, 49, 50
 and resurrection, 88
 religious zeal of, 76-77

salvation
and action, 81
and faith, 249-50
and grace, 161
means of, 303
social and moral, 24-25
salvation, universal, 150-60
and Bible, 11, 159-60
and goodness of God, 292-306
as probable, 390
Samuel (biblical prophet), 76-77
sanctity, and virtue, 133
Sandwich Islands, missionaries in, 174-75
Sapphira, 304
Saul (king of Israel), 77, 310
schools, common, 285-87
science, 70
and religion 47, 69, 171
Scripture. *See* Bible
sectarianism, 88, 131-36
Seneca, 95
sense, spiritual, 207
Servetus, Michael, 78
sexes, differences of, 281
Shakespeare, William, 236n
Sharp, James (archbishop of St. Andrew's), 141
Shorter Catechism, 3
sin
bondage to, 241
as infinite offence, 193-94
and misery, 387-88
and punishment, 296
as selfishness, 107
See also evil; vice, causes of
skepticism, 291
and Brownson, 2, 167, 276, 279
See also atheism; deism; infidelity; unbelief
Skinner, Dolphus, 28,
slavery, 65, 75, 75n, 316
Smith, Joseph, 1
Smith, Reuben, 5, 6n. 17, 7, 7n. 20, 19n
Smith, Stephen, R., 13n. 35, 15n. 42
socialists, 17, 22-23

societies, religious, 82, 129
opposition to, 21
and power, 308-09, 321
societies, utopian, 23
society, 44, 242
Socinianism, 328
Solomon, 164, 298
sovereignty, of people, 315
Spirit, Holy. *See* Holy Spirit
state. *See* church; government
Stephen (martyr), 77
Stephens, Robert, 221, 221n. 9
Stoics, 260
submission, doctrine of, 382-84
suffering
causes of, 8, 183-85, 381-88
in creation, 256
expiatory, 377
of infants and innocent, 184, 258-59
Sunday, and limits of Congress, 271
Swift, Jonathan, 371

T

teachers, false, 127-28
teaching, methods of, 287
Theodosius (Roman Emperor), 78
theologians, defects of, 106-08
theology, popular, 18
Thibetian, 247
Thor, 52
Tibetan. *See* Thibetian
tradition, and primitive revelation, 87
translations, biblical, 220-21
Treatise on Atonement, A (Ballou), 5n. 15, 25
Trinity, 25, 205-11, 232-35
Trumpet and Universalist Magazine, 26n. 66, 29n. 75
trust, in Providence, 353-62
truth
over authority, 55
and moral health, 164-67
progress of, 44-75
and protection of, 115-16
Turner, Edward, 4n. 13